Lecture Notes in Computer Science   8664

Commenced Publication in 1973
Founding and Former Series Editors:
Gerhard Goos, Juris Hartmanis, and Jan van Leeuwen

More information about this series at http://www.springer.com/series/7407

Călin Caşcaval · Pablo Montesinos (Eds.)

Languages and Compilers for Parallel Computing

26th International Workshop, LCPC 2013
San Jose, CA, USA, September 25–27, 2013
Revised Selected Papers

 Springer

Editors
Călin Caşcaval
Pablo Montesinos
Silicon Valley
Qualcomm Research
San Jose, CA
USA

ISSN 0302-9743   ISSN 1611-3349   (electronic)
ISBN 978-3-319-09966-8   ISBN 978-3-319-09967-5   (eBook)
DOI 10.1007/978-3-319-09967-5

Library of Congress Control Number: 2014949396

LNCS Sublibrary: SL1 – Theoretical Computer Science and General Issues

Springer Cham Heidelberg New York Dordrecht London

Printed on acid-free paper

Springer is part of Springer Science+Business Media (www.springer.com)

Message from the Chairs

The 26th Workshop on Languages and Compilers for Parallel Computing was held in September 2013 in San Jose, California, USA. More than 50 researchers from around the world gathered together to present their latest results and exchange ideas on topics ranging from parallel programming models, compiler analysis techniques, parallel data structures and parallel execution models, to GPGPU and other heterogeneous execution models, code generation for power efficiency on mobile platforms, and debugging and fault tolerance for parallel systems.

The Program Committee, with the help of external reviewers, selected 20 papers out of 44 submissions for presentation at the workshop. Each paper had at least three reviews and was extensively discussed in the committee meeting.

We were honored to have two outstanding keynote addresses at LCPC 2013. Prof. Katherine Yelick, from University of California Berkeley and Lawrence Berkeley National Laboratory, presented "Avoiding, Hiding and Managing Communication". She discussed how new systems are constrained in terms of both power density and energy, and require new programming models as well as algorithmic work to reduce the amount of communication. She demonstrated how PGAS languages reduce the communication costs through overlap, caching and aggregation. As communication hierarchies are becoming more complex (memory systems and interconnect), new language and compiler techniques need to be developed. She also discussed work done in her team on new parallel algorithms that use structure to reduce the amount of communication, and discussed the challenges to automate such methods through compiler transformations and auto-tuning.

David Sehr from Google presented our second keynote. He discussed compilation technologies for executing native code in the browser. Browsers are currently available on all platforms, and thus provide a common environment to deploy applications. However, there are both performance and security considerations when executing arbitrary code off the web into a complex engine such as the browser. David presented Google's design of Native Client (NaCL) and discussed the compiler challenges to produce efficient code capable of running games at native speed. He concluded the keynote with a live demonstration of the system.

In addition to the paper presentations, we were fortunate to have six invited speakers who provided insights into new technologies and challenging research directions. We would like to thank the speakers: Benedict Gaster (Qualcomm), Rastislav Bodik (UC Berkeley), Jaejin Lee (Seoul National University, Korea), Samuel P. Midkiff (Purdue University), Lawrence Rauchwerger (Texas A&M University), and George Almasi (IBM Research).

The success of the LCPC 2013 workshop would not have been possible without help from many people. We thank the Program Committee members for their time and effort in reviewing papers. We thank Nancy May and Pamela Millart from Qualcomm for their help with the local organization. We thank the Qualcomm admin staff for providing support hosting the workshop. The LCPC Steering Committee, David Padua, Lawrence Rauchwerger, Alex Nicolau, and Rudi Eigenmann, provided continuous support and encouragement.

We also thank Intel Corp. for their generous support.

And finally, we would like to thank all the authors who submitted to LCPC 2013. They made the workshop enjoyable.

September 2013   Călin Caşcaval
                                                          Pablo Montesinos

Organization

Workshop Chairs

Călin Caşcaval	Qualcomm Research, USA
Pablo Montesinos	Qualcomm Research, USA

Program Committee

James Brodman	Intel Corporation, USA
Călin Caşcaval	Qualcomm Research, USA
Hironori Kasahara	Waseda University, Japan
Keiji Kimura	Waseda University, Japan
Pablo Montesinos	Qualcomm Research, USA
Sanjay Rajophadhye	Colorado State University, USA
Michelle Strout	Colorado State University, USA
Peng Tu	Intel Corporation, USA

Steering Committee

David Padua	University of Illinois at Urbana-Champaign, USA
Lawrence Rauchwerger	Texas A&M University, USA
Alex Nicolau	University of California, Irvine, USA
Rudolf Eigenmann	Purdue University, USA

Referees

Farhana Aleen	Fredrik Berg Kjolstad	Tomoaki Tsumura
Carmen Badea	Masayoshi Mase	Yasutaka Wada
Umeda Dan	Makoto Nakayama	Cheng Wang
Alexandre Duchateau	Catherine Olschanowsky	Youfeng Wu
Akihiro Hayashi	Hideki Saito	Koichiro Yamashita
Sunpyo Hong	Jun Shirako	Akimasa Yoshida
Guillaume Iooss	Mamoru Shimaoka	Tomofumi Yuki
Kazuhisa Ishizaka	Albert Sidelnik	Yun Zou
Chi-Keung Luk	Xinmin Tian	Xing Zhou

Supporting Institution

Intel Corporation, Santa Clara, CA, USA

Invited Talks

The Good, the Bad, and the Ugly: Heterogeneous Programming Models for Performance and Power in a Thermally Constrained World

Benedict Gaster

Qualcomm

Abstract. Heterogeneous computing is being realized in modern SoCs, because power and performance are key to delivering multimedia experiences in mobiles devices that are limited by physical thermal limits. Programming these devices is challenging - lack of shared virtual address spaces, different ISAs, different performance capabilities, are just some of the factors that complicate any programming model.

Heterogeneous programming can be pretty ugly in places and is not easy for the first time developer, however, it has also been proven on multiple devices, ranging from tiny mobile devices that fit a pocket, to supercomputers, providing its users access to huge possibilities. In this talk I will reflect on the good, the bad, and the ugly of design and feature capabilities of OpenCL 2.0 and it new formalized foundations for shared memory model programming and support for data- and irregular- parallel workloads. With a particular focus on OpenCL 2.0's low-level features for high-level programming abstractions we will discuss capabilities of Qualcomm's task based programming model, MARE, and how it might be integrated into a heterogenous platform supporting OpenCL.

Bio

Benedict R. Gaster is an architect working at Qualcomm on next-generation heterogeneous processors. Benedict has contributed extensively to the OpenCL's design. Benedict has a Ph.D in computer science for his work on type systems for extensible records and variants.

Why Parallel Web Browsers?

Rastislav Bodik

UC Berkeley

Abstract. The quality of web browsers is reaching the point where HTML5 apps begin to compete with native apps (see for example the Firefox OS or the sencha.com Facebook app written entirely in HTML5). Thanks to the portability of HTML5 apps, the adoption of the HTML5 would erode the domination of closed mobile app platforms. To secure adoption of HTML5 on mobile devices, mobile browsers may still need to improve, though — in responsiveness, energy efficiency, programmability, as well as usability.

Our research group has been working on browser technologies since 2007. We were the first to parallelize key browser components such as the lexer, parser, CSS selectors and the layout engine. This talk will describe our recent results and ongoing work. Our work divides into (i) technologies for performance improvements, via code synthesis and parallelization; and (ii) new techniques for programmability. From the performance category, I will demo our browser-based GPU framework for real-time visualization of large data. In the programmability category, I will show how we can equip the browser with programming by demonstration, which allows users to automate tasks, extract and visualize web data, and layout documents without knowledge of CSS/HTML.

Bio

Ras Bodik is a Professor of Computer Science at UC Berkeley. He works on various flavors of program synthesis, from programming by demonstration to compilers for declarative languages. His group has applied synthesis to high-performance computing, web browser construction, algorithm design, document layout, and biology. Their web browser project investigates how to run client application stacks on low-power devices. He also designed a course on programming languages in which students design learn small languages by constructing a small modern web browser.

SnuCL: A Unified Framework of OpenCL

Jaejin Lee

Seoul National University, Korea

Abstract. OpenCL is a programming model for heterogeneous parallel computing systems. OpenCL provides a common abstraction layer across different processor architectures, such as CPUs, GPUs, DSPs, FPGAs, and Xeon Phi processors. OpenCL ICD (installable client driver) enables OpenCL platforms from different vendors for different processors to coexist under a single operating system instance. Applications choose a platform and dispatch OpenCL API calls to the platform with ICD. However, current OpenCL has two major limitations. First, to use different processors from different vendors in a single application, programmers need to explicitly specify a specific OpenCL platform for each processor. Moreover, OpenCL objects (buffers, events, etc.) cannot be shared across different platforms. Second, OpenCL is restricted to a system running a single operating system instance. To target a cluster running multiple operating system instances, programmers must use an OpenCL framework together with a communication library, such as MPI. This talk introduces how to overcome the limitations of current OpenCL with SnuCL. SnuCL is an OpenCL framework that provides the programmer with an illusion of a single OpenCL platform image. It naturally extends the original OpenCL semantics to a cluster system running multiple operating system instances. Programmers do not need to explicitly specify a specific platform in SnuCL, and OpenCL objects can be shared across different platforms. SnuCL is open-source software developed at Seoul National University, Korea.

Bio

Jaejin Lee is the director of the Center for Manycore Programming and a professor in the Department of Computer Science and Engineering at Seoul National University (SNU), Korea. He received a PhD degree in Computer Science from the University of Illinois at Urbana-Champaign (UIUC) in 1999. He also received an MS degree in Computer Science from Stanford University in 1995 and a BS degree in Physics from SNU in 1991. After obtaining the PhD degree, he spent a half year at the UIUC as a visiting lecturer. He was an assistant professor in the Department of Computer Science and Engineering at Michigan State University until 2002 before joining SNU. His primary research focus in these days is on heterogeneous parallel programming models, and building efficient heterogeneous supercomputers.

Characterizing and Detecting Smartphone Energy Bugs

Samuel P. Midkiff

Purdue University

Abstract. Modern power constrained devices such as mobile phones require programmers to explicitly manage whether components (including the processor and display) are turned on or off. User defined defaults often give a period of time that a component (e.g., the processor or display) will be on, but after that time expires the device will shut down unless the program being executed actively and explicitly prevents it. Other components, such as the GPS unit, the GSM or wireless transmitters and receivers, and so forth may shut down at any time, even during a call or while establishing a network connection. The operating systems for these devices provide wake locks that allow library and application programmers to force a component to stay active until the wait lock is released. This talk will describe strategies for automatically detecting these bugs. We will finish with a short discussion of how this issue relates to parallelism and compiler infrastructure issues.

Bio

Samuel Midkiff is a Professor of Electrical and Computer Engineering at Purdue University, where he has been since 2002. He received his PhD degree from the University of Illinois at Urbana-Champaign in 1992 and worked at the IBM TJ Watson Research Center from 1991 until 2002. He has had the pleasure of working on the Parafrase, PTran, Ninja and Cetus compiler infrastructures. His research is currently focused on energy bugs in mobile devices, using semantic information in compiling and issues related to debugging parallel programs and web hubs.

KLA: A New Algorithmic Paradigm for Parallel Graph Computations

Lawrence Rauchwerger

Texas A&M University

Abstract. This paper proposes a new algorithmic paradigm for parallel graph computations, k-Level Asynchronous (KLA), that bridges the level-synchronous and asynchronous paradigms for processing graphs.

The KLA paradigm allows vertex-centric fine-grained expression of parallel graph algorithms, while enabling the level of asynchrony to be parametrically varied from none (level synchronous) to full (asynchronous). This enables improved efficiency by expeditiously using an appropriate combination of expensive global synchronizations, as in level-synchronous algorithms, and possibly more, but less expensive local synchronizations (and potentially redundant work), as in asynchronous algorithms.

To enable the expression of a wide variety of graph algorithms in the KLA paradigm, we classify algorithms into three categories based on the penalty paid for asynchrony (e.g., cost of correcting a wrong guess), which theoretically depends on the resilience (for correctness) of the algorithm to message ordering. We propose how to best apply the KLA paradigm for each category of algorithms and use it to implement several important classes of graph algorithms including breadth-first search type computations (e.g., single-source shortest paths), PageRank, k-core and pointer jumping.

Results of an implementation of KLA using the STAPL Graph Library show good scalability to more than 16,000 cores for a variety of important graph algorithms. Compared to traditional approaches, KLA improves performance of certain graph algorithms on real-world graphs by 6x or more.

Parallel Programming for the Cloud

George Almasi

IBM Research

Abstract. Love it or hate it, cloud computing is here to stay. It is the chief enabler of the race to bottom in cost of computing resources. Non-technology companies are relying on it to replace their IT infrastructure; many technology companies are betting their livelihoods on it; government[s] spy on it; in short, most everybody has a stake in cloud computing.

This talk focuses on the languages used for setting up and running a large cloud infrastructure compute farm. The cloud software infrastructure is a large parallel distributed computation similar to an HPC compute farm. The programming language approach taken is however fundamentally different. I will discuss how the words "performance", "scalability" and "consistency" apply to a motley collection of 100K+ lines of Python, Ruby and shell scripts, and how the best programming practices in these languages are used to deal with issues familiar to "real" parallel programmers: threads, locks, mutual exclusion, producer/consumer paradigms, fault tolerance etc., meanwhile allowing the cloud architect to keep his/her sanity while deploying and maintaining such a system.

Keynotes

Avoiding, Hiding and Managing Communication

Katherine Yelick

EECS Department, University of California, Berkeley, CA, USA
Lawrence Berkeley National Laboratory, Berkeley, CA, USA

Abstract. Future computing system designs will be constrained by power density and total system energy, and will require new programming models and implementation strategies. Data movement in the memory system and interconnect will dominate running time and energy costs, making communication cost reduction the primary optimization criteria for compilers and programmers. Communication cost can be divided into latency costs, which are per communication event, and bandwidth costs, which grow with total communication volume. The trends show growing gaps for both of these relative to computation, with the additional problem that communication congestion can conspire to worsen both in practice.

In this talk I will discuss prior work an open problems in optimizing communication, starting with PGAS languages. This involves reducing the communication cost, through overlap, and the frequency through caching and aggregation. Much of the compile-time work in this area was done in the Titanium language, where strong typing and data abstraction aid in program analysis, while UPC compilers tend to use more dynamic optimizations. There are still many open questions on the design of languages and compilers, especially as the communication hierarchies become deeper and more complex.

Bandwidth reduction often requires more substantial algorithmic transformations, although some techniques, such as loop tiling, are well known. These can be applied as hand-optimizations, through code generation strategies in autotuned libraries, or as fully automatic compiler transformations. Less obvious techniques for communication avoidance have arisen in the so-called "2.5D" parallel algorithms, which I will describe more generally as ".5D" algorithms. These ideas are applicable to many domains, from scientific computations to database operations. In addition to having provable optimality properties, these algorithms also perform well on large-scale parallel machines. I will end by describing some recent work that lays the foundation for automating transformations to produce communication optimal code for arbitrary loop nests.

Bio

Katherine Yelick is the Associate Laboratory Director for Computing Sciences at Lawrence Berkeley National Laboratory and a Professor of Electrical Engineering and Computer Sciences at the University of California at Berkeley. She co-invented the UPC and Titanium languages as well as techniques for self-tuning sparse matrix kernels. She earned her Ph.D. in EECS from MIT and has been a professor at UC Berkeley since 1991 with a joint appointment at LBNL since 1996. She has received multiple research and teaching awards, is an ACM Fellow and serves on numerous advising committee, including the California Council on Science and Technology and the National Academies Computer Science and Telecommunications Board.

Bringing Native Code to the Web

David Sehr

Google, Mountain View, CA, USA

Abstract. In this talk we discuss some of the security concerns we've faced when compiling for web applications and how compilers are used to build systems.

Bio

David Sehr is the lead of the Native Client project at Google. David co-founded this effort, which uses software fault isolation to run untrusted native code securely in a web browser or other environment. He has been at Google since 2007. Prior to that he was a Senior Principal Engineer in the compiler team at Intel Corporation. He received his Ph.D. from the University of Illinois at Urbana-Champaign in 1992.

Contents

Programming Models

Hierarchical Computation in the SPMD Programming Model   3
   Amir Kamil and Katherine Yelick

Porting Applications with OpenMP Using Similarity Analysis   20
   Wei Ding, Oscar Hernandez, Tony Curtis, and Barbara Chapman

Tasks

Task-Aware Optimization of Dynamic Fractional Permissions.   39
   Christoph M. Angerer

Near Optimal Work-Stealing Tree Scheduler for Highly Irregular
Data-Parallel Workloads.   55
   Aleksandar Prokopec and Martin Odersky

OpenCL Task Partitioning in the Presence of GPU Contention   87
   Dominik Grewe, Zheng Wang, and Michael F.P. O'Boyle

Heterogeneous Computing

Compiling a High-Level Directive-Based Programming Model for GPGPUs. . . .   105
   Xiaonan Tian, Rengan Xu, Yonghong Yan, Zhifeng Yun,
   Sunita Chandrasekaran, and Barbara Chapman

Separate Compilation in a Language-Integrated Heterogeneous Environment. . .   121
   Mike Murphy, Jaydeep Marathe, Girish Bharambe, Sean Lee,
   and Vinod Grover

Parametric GPU Code Generation for Affine Loop Programs   136
   Athanasios Konstantinidis, Paul H.J. Kelly, J. Ramanujam,
   and P. Sadayappan

Power

OSCAR Compiler Controlled Multicore Power Reduction
on Android Platform   155
   Hideo Yamamoto, Tomohiro Hirano, Kohei Muto, Hiroki Mikami,
   Takashi Goto, Dominic Hillenbrand, Moriyuki Takamura,
   Keiji Kimura, and Hironori Kasahara

Folklore Confirmed: Compiling for Speed = Compiling for Energy   169
  Tomofumi Yuki and Sanjay Rajopadhye

Debugging

Effectively Recognize Ad hoc Synchronizations with Static Analysis.   187
  Le Yin

AntSM: Efficient Debugging for Shared Memory Parallel Programs   202
  Jae-Woo Lee and Samuel P. Midkiff

DRIFT: Decoupled CompileR-Based Instruction-Level Fault-Tolerance   217
  Konstantina Mitropoulou, Vasileios Porpodas, and Marcelo Cintra

Algorithms

Optimizing the LU Factorization for Energy Efficiency on a Many-Core
Architecture   237
  Elkin Garcia, Jaime Arteaga, Robert Pavel, and Guang R. Gao

An Input-Adaptive Algorithm for High Performance Sparse Fast
Fourier Transform   252
  Shuo Chen and Xiaoming Li

Caches

Aligned Scheduling: Cache-Efficient Instruction Scheduling
for VLIW Processors.   275
  Vasileios Porpodas and Marcelo Cintra

Compile Time Modeling of Off-Chip Memory Bandwidth for Parallel Loops . . .   292
  Munara Tolubaeva, Yonghong Yan, and Barbara Chapman

Compiler Optimizations for Non-contiguous Remote Data Movement   307
  Timo Schneider, Robert Gerstenberger, and Torsten Hoefler

Transactional Memory

Combining Lock Inference with Lock-Based Software Transactional Memory . . .   325
  Stefan Kempf, Ronald Veldema, and Michael Philippsen

Speculative Execution of Parallel Programs with Precise Exception Semantics
on GPUs   342
  *Akihiro Hayashi, Max Grossman, Jisheng Zhao, Jun Shirako,
  and Vivek Sarkar*

Author Index   357

Programming Models

Hierarchical Computation in the SPMD Programming Model

Amir Kamil[(✉)] and Katherine Yelick

Computer Science Division, University of California, Berkeley, USA
{kamil,yelick}@cs.berkeley.edu

Abstract. Large-scale parallel machines are programmed mainly with the single program, multiple data (SPMD) model of parallelism. While this model has advantages of scalability and simplicity, it does not fit well with divide-and-conquer parallelism or hierarchical machines that mix shared and distributed memory. In this paper, we define the recursive single program, multiple data model (RSPMD) that extends SPMD with a hierarchical team mechanism to support hierarchical algorithms and machines. We implement this model in the Titanium language and describe how to eliminate a class of deadlocks by ensuring alignment of collective operations. We present application case studies evaluating the RSPMD model, showing that it enables divide-and-conquer algorithms such as sorting to be elegantly expressed and that team collective operations increase performance of conjugate gradient by up to a factor of two. The model also facilitates optimizations for hierarchical machines, improving scalability of particle in cell by 8x and performance of sorting and a stencil code by up to 40 % and 14 %, respectively.

1 Introduction

The single program, multiple data (SPMD) model of parallelism, in which a program is launched with a fixed number of threads that execute throughout the program, is the dominant programming model for large-scale distributed-memory machines. The model encourages "parallel thinking" throughout the program execution, exposing the actual degree of available parallelism, naturally leads to good locality, and can be implemented by simple, low-overhead runtime systems. Both message-passing models like MPI [19] and a number of partitioned global address space (PGAS) languages like UPC [6], Titanium [23], and Co-Array Fortran [20] use the SPMD model by default. Previous work on Titanium also shows that the simplicity of the SPMD model can be used to avoid certain classes of deadlocks, statically detect data races, and perform a set of optimizations specific to the parallel setting [15,16].

While SPMD has proven to be a valuable programming model, the restrictiveness of the flat SPMD model does have drawbacks. Algorithms that divide tasks among threads or that recursively subdivide do not fit well into a model with a fixed number of threads executing the same code. SPMD programming languages also tend to have a relatively flat machine model, with no distinction between

© Springer International Publishing Switzerland 2014
C. Caşcaval and P. Montesinos (Eds.): LCPC 2013, LNCS 8664, pp. 3–19, 2014.
DOI: 10.1007/978-3-319-09967-5_1

threads that are located nearby on a large-scale machine and threads that are further apart. This lack of awareness of the underlying machine hierarchy makes it difficult to reason about the communication costs between threads. While some SPMD languages do address these issues with teams or virtual topologies, they do not do so in a structured manner that provides flexibility and performance but prevents deadlocks.

In this paper, we address the shortcomings above by defining the recursive single program, multiple data (RSPMD) model. This model extends SPMD with user-defined hierarchical teams, which are subsets of threads that cooperatively execute pieces of code. We introduce new language and library features for hierarchical teams and describe how to ensure textual alignment of collectives, eliminating many forms of deadlock involving teams. Our implementation is in the context of the Titanium programming language, and we evaluate the language additions on four applications. We demonstrate that hierarchical teams enable the expression of divide-and-conquer algorithms with a fixed number of threads, that team collectives provide better performance than hand-written communication code, and that hierarchical teams allow optimizations for the communication characteristics of modern, hierarchical parallel machines.

2   Background

The single program, multiple data (SPMD) model of parallelism consists of a set of parallel threads that run the same program. Unlike in dynamic task parallelism, the set of threads is fixed throughout the entire program execution. The threads can be executing at different points of the program, though *collective operations* such as barriers can synchronize the threads at a particular point in the program.

As an example of SPMD code, consider the following written in the Titanium language[1]:

```
public static void main(String[] args) {
  System.out.println("Hello from thread" + Ti.thisProc());
  Ti.barrier();
  if (Ti.thisProc() == 0)
    System.out.println("Done.");
}
```

A fixed number of threads, specified by the user on program start, all enter main. They first print out a message with their thread IDs, or *ranks*, which can appear to the user in any order since the print statement is not synchronized. Then the threads execute a *barrier*, which prevents them from proceeding until all threads have reached it. Finally, thread 0 prints out another message that appears to the user after all previous messages due to the barrier synchronization.

Prior work has shown the benefit of assuming textual alignment of collectives [15]. Collectives are *textually aligned* if all threads execute the same textual

---

[1] Throughout this paper, we highlight team operations in a bold, green color and collective operations in bold purple.

sequence of collective operations, and all threads agree on control-flow decisions that affect execution of collectives. Discussions with parallel application experts indicate that most applications do not contain unaligned collectives, and most of those that do can be modified to do without them. Our own survey of eight NAS Parallel Benchmarks [2] using MPI demonstrated that all of them only use textually aligned collectives. Prior work has also demonstrated how to enforce textual collective alignment using dynamic checks [17].

The work in this paper is in the context of the Titanium language, an explicitly parallel dialect of Java. Titanium uses the SPMD execution model and the partitioned global address space (PGAS) memory model; the latter allows a thread to directly access memory on any other thread, even if they do not physically share memory. Titanium's memory model is actually hierarchical, exposing three levels of memory hierarchy in the type system and compiler by distinguishing between thread-local, node-local, and global data.

2.1   The RSPMD Model

While Titanium does have a memory hierarchy, like most other SPMD languages, it does not have a concept of execution hierarchy. Some languages such as UPC are moving towards an execution model based on *teams*, in which the set of program threads can be divided into smaller subsets (teams) that cooperatively run pieces of code. MPI has communicators that allow teams of threads to perform collective operations. Similarly, the GASNet [5] runtime layer used in Titanium now has experimental support for teams and team collectives. Teams in MPI, UPC, and GASNet are non-hierarchical groupings of threads and do not place restrictions on the underlying thread structure of a team. A thread can be a part of multiple teams concurrently, making it easy to deadlock a program through improper use of teams. Even correct use of multiple teams can be difficult for programmers to understand and compilers to analyze, as they must reason about the order of team operations on each thread. Finally, teams in MPI, GASNet, and UPC do not have a hierarchical structure, so they cannot easily reflect the hierarchical organization of algorithms and machines.

Instead of the flat teams of MPI, GASNet, and UPC, we introduce the *recursive single program, multiple data (RSPMD)* programming model that uses hierarchies of teams. In this model, threads start out as part of a single, global team. This team can then be divided into multiple subteams, each of which can be recursively subdivided. Multiple, distinct hierarchies can be used in different parts of a program. Hierarchies can be created to match the underlying machine hierarchy, as in the Titanium memory model, or to match an algorithmic hierarchy, as in divide-and-conquer algorithms. At each point in the program, a thread is active in only a single team, and any collective operation that it invokes operates over that team. In Sect. 3, we take care to define RSPMD language extensions that enforce this restriction and prevent misuse of teams that would result in deadlock.

2.2 Related Work

While many current languages besides the SPMD languages mentioned above are locality-aware, only a handful of them incorporate hierarchical programming constructs beyond two levels of hierarchy.

In the Fortress language [1], memory is divided into an arbitrary hierarchy of *regions*. Data structures can be spread across multiple regions, and tasks can be placed in particular regions by the programmer. Hierarchically tiled arrays (HTAs) [3] allow data structures to be hierarchically decomposed to match a target machine's layout, which are then operated over in a data parallel manner. Other languages such as Chapel [7] and the hierarchical place trees (HPT) [21] extension of X10 also have the concept of hierarchical locales. While these languages may be built on SPMD runtimes, they do not present the SPMD model of execution to the programmer.

Nested data parallelism allows hierarchical algorithms to be expressed in the context of data parallelism. The model has been implemented in NESL [4] and in Haskell [13]. However, irregular algorithms can be difficult to express in the data parallel model, and nested data parallel implementations have focused on vector and shared-memory machines rather than hierarchical machines. They also require more complicated compilers than SPMD languages.

The Sequoia project [9] incorporates machine hierarchy in its language model. A Sequoia program consists of a hierarchy of tasks that get mapped to the computational units in a hierarchical machine. The *team parallel* model defined by Hardwick [11] is a data-parallel analogue of Sequoia, where threads are arranged into a hierarchy of teams, each of which is operated over in a data-parallel manner. Unlike RSPMD, this model does not allow the expression of explicit parallelism. In both Sequoia and Hardwick's model, communication is restricted to between parent and child tasks or teams, making the models unsuitable for many applications written in SPMD and PGAS languages.

The hierarchical single program, multiple data (HSPMD) model is in some sense the inverse of the RSPMD model. In RSPMD, an initial, fixed set of threads is recursively subdivided into smaller teams of cooperating threads. In HSPMD, on the other hand, there is only a single thread initially, and each thread can spawn a new set of cooperating threads. The Phalanx programming model uses a version of HSPMD [10].

3 RSPMD Language Extensions

In this section, we define language extensions for Titanium to implement the RSPMD model. In designing the new additions to the Titanium language, we had a few goals in mind for the extensions to satisfy: safety, flexibility, composability, and performance.

1. **Safety.** Team implementations in other SPMD languages and frameworks do not generally impose any restrictions on their use. This can lead to circular dependencies in team operations, resulting in deadlock. For example, a set

of threads may attempt to perform a collective operation on one team, while other threads attempt to perform a collective operation on a different team; if the two teams overlap, then this situation results in deadlock. The Titanium team extensions should prevent such dependencies, as well as ensure that team collectives are textually aligned on all threads in the relevant team, as is done for existing global collectives.

2. **Flexibility.** Many applications make use of different thread groupings at different points in the program, such as a matrix-vector multiplication that requires both row and column teams. The team mechanism should be flexible enough to support such cases while still providing safety guarantees.

3. **Composability.** Existing code running in the context of a particular team should behave as if the entire world consisted of just the threads in that team, with thread ranks as specified by the team. This is to facilitate composition of different tasks, so that a subset of threads can be assigned to each of them. At the same time, the team mechanism should make it possible to interact with threads outside of an assigned team if necessary.

4. **Performance.** Team operations should not adversely affect application performance. This requires that team usage operations, which may be invoked many times throughout an application run, be as lightweight as possible, even at the expense of team creation operations that are called much less frequently.

3.1   Team Representation

To represent a team hierarchy, we introduce a new `Team` object, which represents a group of threads and contains references to parent and child teams, resulting in a hierarchy of teams. Like MPI or GASNet groups, `Team` objects specify team structures separately from their usage; this is useful when a program uses multiple different team structures or repeatedly uses the same structure, as in Sect. 4.2, and also allows team data structures to be manipulated as first-class objects.

Knowledge of the physical layout of threads in a program allows a programmer to minimize communication costs, so a new function `Ti.defaultTeam()` returns a special team that corresponds to the mapping of threads to the machine hierarchy, grouping together threads that share memory. The invocation `Ti.currentTeam()` returns the current team in which the calling thread is participating.

Figure 1(a) shows the team hierarchy created by the following code, when there are a total of twelve threads:

```
Team t = new Team ();
t.splitTeam(3);
int [][] ids = new int [][] {{0, 2, 1}, {3}};
for (int i = 0; i < t.numChildren(); i++)
    t.child(i).splitTeamRelative(ids);
```

Each box in the diagram corresponds to a node in the team tree, and the entries in each box refer to member threads by their global ranks.

The code above first creates a team consisting of all the threads and then calls the **splitTeam** method to divide it into three equally-sized subteams of four threads each. It then divides each of those subteams into two uneven, smaller teams. The **splitTeamRelative** call divides a team into subteams using IDs relative to the parent team. In this case, each child u of team t is split into two smaller teams, with threads 0, 2, and 1 of u assigned to the first subteam and thread 3 of u assigned to the second. This behavior allows the same code to be used to divide each of the three children of t, which would not be the case if **splitTeamRelative** used global IDs.

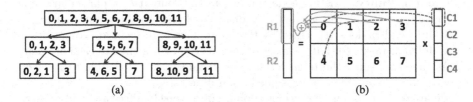

(a)   (b)

Fig. 1. Examples of (a) a team hierarchy and (b) blocked matrix-vector multiplication.

The `Team` class provides a few other ways of generating subteams, though we omit them for brevity. In addition, it includes numerous methods to query team properties; for example, the class provides a `myChildTeam` method for determining which child team contains the calling thread. Similarly, the `teamRank` method returns the rank of a team in its parent, which can be used to write code that is conditional on a team's rank.

3.2   New Language Constructs

In designing new language constructs that make use of teams, we identified two common usage patterns for grouping threads: sets of threads that perform different tasks and sets of threads that perform the same operation on different pieces of data. We introduce a new construct for each of these two patterns.

Task Decomposition. In task parallel programming, it is common for different components of an algorithm to be assigned to different threads. For example, a climate simulation may assign a subset of all the threads to model the atmosphere, another subset to model the oceans, and so on. Each of these components can in turn be decomposed into separate parts, such as one piece that performs a Fourier transform and another that executes a stencil. Such a decomposition does not directly depend on the structure of the underlying machine, though threads can be assigned based on machine hierarchy.

Task decomposition can be expressed through the following *partition* statement that divides the current team of threads into subteams:

```
partition(T) { B_0 B_1 ... B_{n-1} }
```

A `Team` object (corresponding to the current team at the top level) is required as an argument. The first child team executes block B_0, the second block B_1, and so on. It is an error if there are fewer child teams than partition branches, or if the given team arguments on each thread in the current team do not have the same description of child teams. If the provided team has more than n subteams, the remaining subteams do not participate in the partition construct. Once a thread exits a partition, it rejoins its previous team.

As a concrete example, consider a climate application that uses the team structure in Fig. 1(a) to separately model the ocean, the land, and the atmosphere. The following code would be used to divide the program:

```
partition(t) {
  { model_ocean(); }
  { model_land(); }
  { model_atmosphere(); }
}
```

Threads 0 to 3 would then execute `model_ocean()`, threads 4 to 7 would run `model_land()`, and threads 8 through 11 would model the atmosphere.

Since partition is a syntactic construct, task structure can be inferred directly from program structure. This simplifies program analysis and improves understandability of the code.

Data Decomposition. In addition to a hierarchy of distinct tasks, a programmer may wish to divide threads into teams according to algorithmic or locality considerations, but where each team executes the same code on different sets of data. Such a data decomposition can be either machine dependent or required by an algorithm, and both the height and width of the hierarchy may differ according to the machine or algorithm.

Consider a parallel matrix-vector multiplication as in Fig. 1(b), where the matrix is divided in both dimensions among 8 threads, with four thread columns and two rows. To compute the output vector, threads 0 to 3 must cooperate in a reduction to compute the first half of the vector, while threads 4 to 7 must cooperate to compute the second half. Both sets of threads perform the same operation but on different pieces of data.

A new *teamsplit* statement with the following syntax allows such a data-driven decomposition to be created:

```
teamsplit(T) B
```

The parameter T must be a `Team` object (corresponding to the current team at the top level), and as with partition, all threads must agree on the set of subteams. The construct causes each thread to execute block B with its current team set to the thread's subteam specified in T, so that thread ranks and collective operations in B are with respect to that subteam. As mentioned above, each subteam also has a rank, which can be used to determine the set of data that the subteam is to operate on.

As an example, the following code executes reductions across the rows of a matrix:

```
teamsplit(t) {
  Reduce.add(data[t.myChildTeam().rank()], myData);
}
```

The reduction executes over the current team inside the teamsplit on each thread, which is its associated child team of t. As a result, data from threads 0 to 3 are reduced to produce a result for team 0, and data from threads 4 to 7 are combined into a result for team 1.

It may be apparent that the partition statement can be implemented in terms of teamsplit, with teams executing code based on their ranks. While this is true, we decided that separate constructs for task and data decomposition would result in cleaner and more readable code than a single construct combined with branching.

Common Features. Both the partition and teamsplit constructs are dynamically scoped, changing the team in which a thread is executing within that scope. This implies that at any point in time, a thread is executing in the context of exactly one team (which may be a subteam of another team and have child teams of its own). Given a particular team hierarchy, entering a teamsplit or partition statement moves one level down in the hierarchy, and exiting a statement moves one level up. Statements can be nested to make use of multi-level hierarchies, and recursion can be used to operate on hierarchies that do not have a pre-determined depth. Consider the following code, for example:

```
public void descendAndWork(Team t) {
  if (t.numChildren() != 0)
    teamsplit(t) { descendAndWork(t.myChildTeam()); }
  else
    work();
}
```

This code descends to the bottom of an arbitrary team hierarchy before performing work. A concrete example that uses this paradigm is the merge sort in Sect. 4.2.

In order to meet the composability design goal, the thread IDs returned by Ti.thisProc() are now relative to the team in which a thread is executing, and the number of threads returned by Ti.numProcs() is equal to the size of the current team. Thus, a thread ID is always between 0 and Ti.currentTeam().size()-1, inclusive. A new function Ti.globalNumProcs() returns the number of threads in the entire program, and Ti.globalThisProc() returns a thread's global rank.

Collective communication and synchronization now operate over the current team. Both the partition and the teamsplit construct are also considered collective operations, so they must be textually aligned in the program. The combination of the requirement that all threads must agree on the set of subteams when entering a partition or teamsplit construct, dynamic scoping of the constructs, and textual collective alignment ensures that no circular dependencies exist between different collective operations. In the next section, we describe how textual collective alignment is enforced.

3.3   Alignment of Collectives

With the introduction of hierarchical teams, alignment of collectives must be checked dynamically at runtime. The full details of dynamic alignment checking are described elsewhere [14,17,18], but we will summarize the main ideas here.

Enforcement of collective alignment is divided into two phases, a local tracking phase and a collective checking phase. In the tracking phase, each thread records the control flow decisions that it makes that may affect execution of a collective. The Titanium compiler already statically computes which conditionals may do so; such conditionals are a small subset of all conditionals in a program, so the cost of tracking is low. Memory usage and communication costs can be minimized by computing a running hash of all such control flow decisions.

The checking phase occurs when a thread reaches a collective operation. Prior to entering the collective, it waits for a broadcast of the alignment hash from thread 0 in its current team. Once it receives thread 0's hash, it compares it to its own and generates an error if the two hashes do not match. Otherwise it proceeds with the collective operation. If no thread generates an error, then all agree on the hash, implying that they also agree on all control flow decisions that affect the collective operation, guaranteeing textual alignment.

Dynamic alignment checking avoids deadlock by requiring that every collective operation be preceded by an alignment check. This check itself executes a collective broadcast over a thread's current team, but this collective is the same on all the threads in the team, so it will never deadlock as long as a check is also performed when changing team contexts.

Previous work has demonstrated that the cost of dynamic alignment tracking and checking is negligible in actual programs [17]. In addition, an optional debugging mode for alignment checking is provided, in which the control flow history is compared between two threads whose hashes mismatch, and the earliest mismatch is reported. This mode also does not measurably degrade performance. Thus, not only is deadlock avoided with low overhead, but a meaningful error is generated that directs the programmer to the source of the error. This may be far from the point of detection, so alignment checking can facilitate debugging.

4   Application Case Studies

We now present case studies of four applications we used to guide the design of the RSPMD language extensions and evaluate their effectiveness: conjugate gradient, parallel sort, particle in cell, and stencil.

4.1 Test Platforms

We tested application performance on two machines, a Cray XE6 and an IBM iDataPlex, both located at the National Energy Research Scientific Computing Center (NERSC) at the Lawrence Berkeley National Laboratory (Berkeley Lab). The Cray XE6, called *Hopper*, consists of two twelve-core AMD MagnyCours 2.1 GHz processors per node, each of which consists of two six-core dies. Each die is referred to as a *non-uniform memory access (NUMA) node*, since each die has fast access to its own memory banks but slower access to the other banks. The IBM iDataPlex system, known as *Carver*, is a cluster of eight-core, 2.67 GHz Intel Nehalem processors connected by a 4X QDR InfiniBand network. Memory considerations limited us to 32 nodes for most benchmarks and prevented larger problem sizes from being run on the IBM machine.

In most of the benchmark applications, we focused on optimizing distributed performance. As a result, we used performance on a single shared-memory node or NUMA node as the baseline for our experiments. Optimizing execution solely on shared-memory multicores is beyond the scope of this paper.

4.2 Algorithmic Hierarchy

We began by examining two algorithms that are difficult to express in the flat SPMD model: conjugate gradient and merge sort.

Conjugate Gradient. The conjugate gradient (CG) application is one of the NAS parallel benchmarks [2]. It iteratively determines the minimum eigenvalue of a sparse, symmetric, positive-definite matrix. The matrix is divided in both dimensions, and each thread receives a contiguous block of the matrix, with threads placed in row-major order. The application performs numerous sparse matrix-vector multiplications, as described previously in Sect. 3.2. In addition to the reductions mentioned there, in each iteration of the algorithm, the elements of the source vector must be distributed to the threads that own a portion of the corresponding matrix column. Thus, team collective operations are required over both rows and columns of threads.

Prior to our language extensions, Titanium only supported collectives over all threads in a program. Thus, the original Titanium implementation of CG [8] required hand-written reductions over subsets of threads. These reductions required extensive development effort to implement, test, and optimize.

The team implementation of CG, on the other hand, makes use of both row and column teams. The existing CG code already computes the row and column number of each thread; we use them to divide the threads into row teams with a call to **splitTeamAll**(), which takes in the child team number and rank for the calling thread as arguments. We then use **makeTransposeTeam**(), which swaps the child team number and rank for each thread, to create column teams from row teams.

```
rowTeam = new Team();
rowTeam.splitTeamAll(rowPos, colPos);
columnTeam = rowTeam.makeTransposeTeam();
```

We use all-to-one reductions across each row team to send the result of that row team to a single thread in the team. We then use a broadcast to send data from that thread to all threads in the same column. Each reduction or broadcast requires only a single library call, as shown below.

```
teamsplit(rowTeam) { // Reduce row results to one thread.
  Reduce.add(allResults, myResults, rowTarget);
}
... // Perform required copies across columns.
teamsplit(columnTeam) { // Broadcast from column source.
  myOut.vbroadcast(columnSource);
}
```

The CG application demonstrates the importance of teams for collective operations among subsets of threads. It also illustrates the need for multiple team hierarchies and for separating team creation from usage, as the cost of creating teams is amortized over all iterations of the algorithm.

Figure 2(a) compares the performance of the team-based version of CG to the original hand-rolled implementation on a Cray XE6 and an IBM iDataPlex. We show strong scaling (fixed problem size) results for the Class B problem size. (Both axes in the figures use logarithmic scale, so ideal scaling would appear as a line on the graphs.) As expected, the replacement of hand-written all-to-all reductions with optimized GASNet all-to-one reductions and broadcasts improves performance over the original version. We achieve speedups over the original code of 1.6x for Class B at 128 threads on the XE6. On the IBM iDataPlex, Class B only scales until 64 threads, at which point the team version is 2.1x as fast as the original code.

We also ran experiments using the Class D problem size, though the graph is omitted for brevity. On the XE6, the team-based version achieves a speedup of 1.5x over the original code at 1024 threads. On the IBM machine, Class D achieves a speedup of 1.6x at 256 threads, at which point the original version stops scaling, and 2.7x at 512 threads.

Shared-Memory Merge Sort. Merge sort is a canonical example of a divide-and-conquer algorithm. An initial set of keys is recursively divided in half, until some threshold is reached. The subsets are sorted individually and then recursively merged with each other until all keys are in a single sorted set. This algorithm can be parallelized on a shared-memory machine by forking a new thread each time a set of keys is divided in two. However, since the SPMD model does not allow new threads to be created, merge sort is difficult to express in the flat SPMD model.

In the RSPMD model, however, merge sort is easily expressible by starting with a team of all threads and then recursively dividing both the set of keys and the team until only a single thread remains. Then each thread sequentially sorts its keys, and the sorted subsets are merged in parallel by assigning each merge operation to one thread from the subsets that are to be merged.

In order to express merge sort in this way, a team hierarchy is constructed that consists of a binary tree, in which each node contains half the threads of its parent. The following code constructs such a hierarchy, using the **splitTeam** library method to divide a team in half.

```
static void divideTeam(Team t) {
  if (t.size() > 1) {
    t.splitTeam(2);
    divideTeam(t.child(0));
    divideTeam(t.child(1));
  }
}
```

Then each thread walks down to the bottom of the team hierarchy, sequentially sorts its keys, and then walks back up the hierarchy to perform the merges. In each internal team node, a single thread merges the results of its two child nodes before execution proceeds to the next level in the hierarchy. The following code performs the entire algorithm. (The sequential sort and merge functions are omitted for brevity.)

```
static void sortAndMerge(Team t) {
  if (Ti.numProcs() == 1)
    allRes[myProc] = SeqSort.sort(myData);
  else {
    teamsplit(t) { sortAndMerge(Ti.currentTeam()); }
    Ti.barrier(); // ensure prior work complete
    if (Ti.thisProc() == 0)
      allRes[myProc] = merge(myRes(), otherRes(), newRes())
  }
}
```

As illustrated in the code above, the shared-memory sorting algorithm is very simple to implement using the new team constructs. The entire implementation is only about 90 lines of code (not including test code and the sequential quicksort from the Java standard library) and took just two hours to write and test. This sort is used as part of the larger distributed sort implementation below, so we will defer performance results until then.

4.3 Machine Hierarchy

We now turn our attention to optimizing algorithms for hierarchical machines. We examined three algorithms: distributed sort, stencil, and particle in cell.

Distributed Sort. The first algorithm we examined for hierarchical optimizations was distributed sorting, specifically the sample sort algorithm [12] on 32-bit integers. This algorithm consists of two phases: an initial phase that computes pivots based on a sample of all the keys and then redistributes the keys among all threads according to the pivots, and a second phase that sorts keys locally.

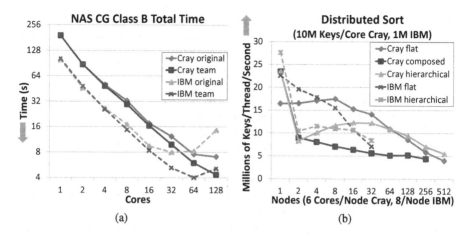

Fig. 2. (a) Strong scaling performance of conjugate gradient; (b) distributed sort performance, with a constant number of keys per thread

We explored three different versions of sample sort. The first is a *flat* version that is purely distributed, ignoring the hierarchical structure of the machine. This version uses sample sort across all threads and sequential sorting on each individual thread. In this version, key redistribution requires $n(n-1)$ messages where n is the total number of threads. The second is a *composed* version that uses sample sort across nodes rather than threads, but then uses shared-memory merge sort on each node. Here, key redistribution requires $m(m-1)$ messages, where m is the number of nodes. However, the composed version uses only a single thread per node for sampling and redistribution, so that it is equivalent to composing a communication library such as MPI with a shared-memory library such as Pthreads. The final version is *hierarchical*; it improves on the composed version by using all available parallelism in the sample and redistribution phase. The RSPMD model enable this version to be expressed, since it exposes hierarchy in the context of a single model.

The composed version, though it does not take full advantage of the hierarchy exposed by RSPMD, does illustrate its composability features. The following is the code required to implement the composed version, where `sampleSort` is the sampling and redistribution code from the flat sample sort:

```
Team team = Ti.defaultTeam();
Team oTeam = team.makeTransposeTeam();
partition(oTeam) { { sampleSort(); } }
teamsplit(team) { keys = SMPSort.parallelSort(keys); }
```

The RSPMD team constructs make this algorithm trivial to implement, requiring only a few lines of code and 5 min of development time. The code calls **Ti.defaultTeam**() to obtain a team in which threads are divided according to which threads share memory. It then uses the **makeTransposeTeam**() library call to construct a transpose team in which each subteam contains one thread from each node. The **partition** construct is then used to perform the sampling and redistribution on one of those subteams, after which the node teams execute the shared-memory sort. The team hierarchies in `sampleSort()` and in the shared-memory sort compose cleanly, without any modifications required.

Figure 2(b) compares the number of keys sorted per thread per second in the different versions of distributed sort. On both machines, the hierarchical version scales better than the flat version, resulting in a speedup of 1.4x for the hierarchical version over the flat version on 512 NUMA nodes (3072 cores) of the XE6 and 1.2x on 32 nodes (256 cores) of the IBM iDataPlex. Since sorting in general is not a linear time algorithm, the decrease in efficiency shown in Fig. 2(b) at higher numbers of threads is not unexpected.

As can be seen in Fig. 2(b), the composed version performs significantly worse than the flat and hierarchical versions on the Cray machine. Since the composed version is equivalent to composing distributed and shared-memory libraries, this demonstrates the importance of exposing hierarchy within a single model to obtain optimal performance.

Stencil. As another example of comparing the composition of distributed and shared-memory code to a true hierarchical version, we examined a stencil benchmark. A *stencil* is a nearest-neighbor computation over a structured n-dimensional grid and consists of multiple iterations in which the value of each grid point is updated as a function of its previous value and those of its neighboring points. In this benchmark, we execute a seven-point stencil over a three-dimensional grid. Since we are primarily concerned with optimizing distributed communication, we use a naïve, untuned shared-memory version of stencil as part of our experiments.

We compared two implementations of distributed stencil. As with distributed sort, the composed version uses a single Titanium thread per node to perform communication and multiple threads per node to perform computation in the external library. We also wrote a hierarchical version that uses multiple threads

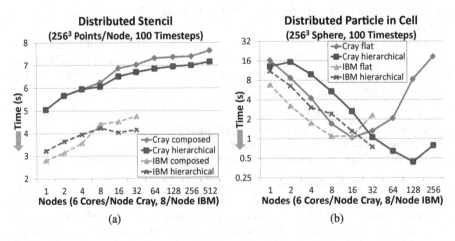

Fig. 3. (a) Weak scaling performance of stencil; (b) strong scaling performance of particle in cell.

for both communication and computation. Figure 3(a) shows weak scaling (constant problem size per thread) performance of the stencil variants. On both machines, the hierarchical version outperforms the composed variant at higher node counts, improving performance by up to 7 % on the Cray machine and 14 % on the iDataPlex.

Particle in Cell. The final benchmark we examined was *particle in cell*, which models the communication pattern in one phase of a heart simulation written in Titanium [22]. In this phase, a set of particles interact with an underlying three-dimensional fluid grid. We model this interaction by updating each fluid cell with a value from each of the particles that the cell contains. Both particles and the fluid grid are divided among the threads; however, a thread's particles are not generally located in its portion of the fluid, requiring communication to perform updates.

We compared two versions of particle in cell. The *flat* version divides the fluid grid and particles between each thread, which separately process their fluid cells and particles, performing any required communication directly between different threads. In the *hierarchical* version, the fluid and particles are divided among nodes, and the threads in a node cooperatively process the node's fluid cells and particles. In this version, communication is aggregated between nodes.

Figure 3(b) compares the performance of the two versions of particle in cell on a 256^3 fluid grid with particles on the surface of a sphere. The flat algorithm does not scale beyond 16 nodes on the Cray machine and 8 nodes on the IBM machine, while the hierarchical algorithm scales up to 128 and 32 nodes, respectively. On the other hand, the flat algorithm performs about twice as fast as the hierarchical version up to the former's scaling limits. This is largely due to the fact that the Titanium and GASNet runtimes are not optimized for shared memory. As a result, though the hierarchical algorithm does scale more, it requires four times as many processors to improve running time beyond the best performance of the flat algorithm.

5 Conclusion

In this paper, we presented RSPMD, an extension of SPMD that enables hierarchical programming in an explicitly parallel model. We designed RSPMD extensions to the Titanium language, combining a team data structure and dynamically scoped usage constructs to prevent erroneous usage of teams. We also described how to enforce textual alignment of team collectives at runtime, further avoiding errors in using team collectives.

We implemented four benchmarks using the RSPMD model: conjugate gradient, sorting, stencil, and particle in cell. We demonstrated that hierarchical teams enable divide-and-conquer algorithms such as sorting to be implemented elegantly, and that team collectives provide better performance and expressiveness than hand-written alternatives in conjugate gradient. We also demonstrated that hierarchical teams enable optimizations for hierarchical machines to be written in the context of a single programming model, enabling increased performance in sorting and better scaling in particle in cell. We further showed that our hierarchical model beats the standard mechanism of combining a distributed library with a shared-memory library in both sorting and stencil. These results demonstrate that the RSPMD model provides significant expressiveness and performance advantages over the flat SPMD model.

References

1. Allen, E., et al.: The Fortress language specification, Version 0.866. Sun Microsystem Inc. (2006)
2. Bailey, D., et al.: The NAS parallel benchmarks. Int. J. Supercomput. Appl. 5(3), 63–73 (1991)
3. Bikshandi, G., et al.: Programming for parallelism and locality with hierarchically tiled arrays. In: PPoPP '06: Proceedings of the Eleventh ACM SIGPLAN Symposium on Principles and Practice of Parallel Programming (2006)
4. Blelloch, G.E.: NESL: a nested data-parallel language (3.1). Technical report CMU-CS-95-170, Carnegie Mellon University (1995)
5. Bonachea, D.: GASNet specification, v1.1. Technical report UCB/CSD-02-1207, University of California, Berkeley (2002)
6. Carlson, W., et al.: Introduction to UPC and language specification. Technical report CCS-TR-99-157, IDA Center for Computing Sciences (1999)
7. Cray Inc.: Chapel Specification 4 (2005)
8. Datta, K., Bonachea, D., Yelick, K.A.: Titanium performance and potential: an NPB experimental study. In: Ayguadé, E., Baumgartner, G., Ramanujam, J., Sadayappan, P. (eds.) LCPC 2005. LNCS, vol. 4339, pp. 200–214. Springer, Heidelberg (2006)
9. Fatahalian, K., et al.: Sequoia: programming the memory hierarchy. In: Proceedings of the ACM/IEEE SC 2006 Conference on Supercomputing, SC '06 (2006)
10. Garland, M., Kudlur, M., Zheng, Y.: Designing a unified programming model for heterogeneous machines. In: Supercomputing 2012 (2012)
11. Hardwick, J.C.: Practical parallel divide-and-conquer algorithms. Ph.D. thesis, Carnegie Mellon University (1997)
12. Huang, J., Chow, Y.: Parallel sorting and data partitioning by sampling. In: 7th International Computer Software and Applications Conference (1983)
13. Peyton Jones, S.: Harnessing the multicores: nested data parallelism in Haskell. In: Ramalingam, G. (ed.) APLAS 2008. LNCS, vol. 5356, pp. 138–138. Springer, Heidelberg (2008)
14. Kamil, A.: Single program, multiple data programming for hierarchical computations. Ph.D. thesis, University of California, Berkeley (2012)
15. Kamil, A.,Yelick, K.: Concurrency analysis for parallel programs with textually aligned barriers. In: Proceedings of the 18th International Workshop on Languages and Compilers for Parallel Computing (2005)
16. Kamil, A., Yelick, K.A.: Hierarchical pointer analysis for distributed programs. In: Riis Nielson, H., Filé, G. (eds.) SAS 2007. LNCS, vol. 4634, pp. 281–297. Springer, Heidelberg (2007)
17. Kamil, A., Yelick, K.: Enforcing textual alignment of collectives using dynamic checks. In: Proceedings of the 22nd International Workshop on Languages and Compilers for Parallel Computing (2009)

18. Kamil, A., Yelick, K.: Hierarchical additions to the SPMD programming model. Technical report UCB/EECS-2012-20, University of California, Berkeley (2012)
19. Message Passing Interface Forum. MPI: A message-passing interface standard, version 1.1 (1995)
20. Numrich, R., Reid, J.: Co-array Fortran for parallel programming. Technical report RAL-TR-1998-060, Rutherford Appleton Laboratory (1998)
21. Yan, Y., et al.: Hierarchical place trees: a portable abstraction for task parallelism and data movement. In: Proceedings of the 22nd International Workshop on Languages and Compilers for Parallel Computing (2009)
22. Yau, S.M.: Experience in using Titanium for simulation of immersed boundary biological systems. Master's thesis, University of California, Berkeley (2002)
23. Yelick, K., et al.: Titanium: a high-performance Java dialect. In: Workshop on Java for High-Performance Network Computing (1998)

Porting Applications with OpenMP Using Similarity Analysis

Wei Ding[1,2](✉), Oscar Hernandez[1,2], Tony Curtis[1,2],
and Barbara Chapman[1,2]

[1] Department of Computer Science, University of Houston, Houston, USA
[2] Oak Ridge National Laboratory, Oak Ridge, USA
{wding3,tonyc,chapman}@cs.uh.edu,
oscar@ornl.gov

Abstract. Computer architecture has undergone dramatic changes due to technology innovation. Some emerging architectures, such as GPUs and MICs also have been successfully used for parallel computation in the today's HPC field. Nowadays, people frequently have to port application to a new architecture or system and to expand its functionality for a better performance while in the meantime to meet the new hardware environment need. However, many scientific application legacy codes have a relative large size and long development cycle, so it's a very challenging job to port legacy codes to a new environment. And current codes porting process is a manual, time-consuming, expensive and error-prone process, which requires a team of people work together. Barely any useful tools can be used to ease the porting process in High Performance Computing (HPC). In this paper, we present a tool called *Klonos*, which is designed for assisting scientific application porting. Based on similarity analysis of code syntax and cost-model provided metrics, we are able to find codes which can be optimized similarly without the need of profiling the codes. The proposed porting plan can systematically guide users for selecting subroutines in a way which maximizes the reuse of similar porting strategy. We evaluate *Klonos* by applying it to a real scientific application porting to a shared memory environment using OpenMP. According to our experiment result, which shows that *Klonos* is very accurate to detect similar codes which can be ported similarly.

1 Introduction

HPC systems have been continually evolving, driven by technology innovation in computer hardware, operating systems, network protocols, and system libraries. As a result, applications that have been developed and tuned for older systems often require significant code changes to utilize the capabilities of the newer systems. The process of code changes for a new system is called *software porting*.

This work was funded by the ORAU/ORNL HPC grant. This research used resources of the Leadership Computing Facility at Oak Ridge National Laboratory and NICS Nautilus supercomputer for the data analysis.

© Springer International Publishing Switzerland 2014
C. Caşcaval and P. Montesinos (Eds.): LCPC 2013, LNCS 8664, pp. 20–35, 2014.
DOI: 10.1007/978-3-319-09967-5_2

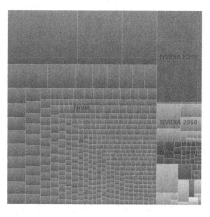

Fig. 1. Accelerator/Co-Processor Treemap of Top500 released in November 2012

In software engineering, *software porting* refers to the process of adapting software originally designed for one computing environment so that an executable program can be created for a different computing environment [28]. This process is a task that frequently arises in HPC, and it poses particular challenges in this domain.

On the roadmap toward exascale computing, a major challenge with respect to supercomputer design is the need to provide higher levels of computational power at dramatically lower rates of power consumption. The use of GPUs as co-processors is rapidly becoming a popular and powerful way to perform parallel computation. In Fig. 1, according to the Treemap (Accelerator/Co-Processor) of the Top500 List [19], released in November 2012, we see that the emerging co-processor such as GPUs and MICs are playing a greatly increased role in the supercomputers listed in the Top500. On the one hand, these co-processor- (or vector processor-) based heterogeneous systems provide more computation and power balance, but on the other hand, complicate programming models, which makes application porting more challenging than ever.

The Titan supercomputer at Oak Ridge National Laboratory is equipped with NVIDIA graphics processing units (Kepler K20x GPUs). In order to migrate codes to Titan, scientists need to know how to exploit not only the large number of CPU cores, but also the GPUs that are configured on the nodes. They will need to create new computational kernels with suitable granularity to exploit the GPUs, while minimizing costly data movement, exploiting complex memory subsystems, and mapping work to balance the overall load. They may need to use a hybrid programming model, such as adding OpenMP [1,3] and accelerator directives [12,13] to MPI applications [27], or they may introduce Pthreads [4] or an API designed for accelerators [22,23].

CUDA and OpenCL are two popular programming APIs specifically used for GPU programming, however programmers often have to restructure and write kernels for running regions of code on GPU. Worse still, the syntax of CUDA or

OpenCL code is quite different from the traditional C and Fortran languages, which makes it almost impossible for programmers with no CUDA or OpenCL background to understand and maintain the code. Directives-based programming models like OpenMP, HMPP, PGI and OpenACC for GPU programming that can greatly increase programming productivity, have been proposed to face such challenges. Reference [14] have explored and compared popular programming models used for GPUs, showing that a directives-based approach is able to achieve similar or even better performance compared to CUDA and OpenCL. By raising the level of abstraction, directives-based models will enable incremental development and increase programming productivity, fast prototyping and retargetability for future new development environment and hardware. Reference [18] summarizes the authors' experience of porting a simulation of turbulent combustion application to a GPU by using OpenACC. Although directives-based programming models to some extent ease the programmability burden, the whole porting process is still manual, time-consuming and error-prone.

Profiling tools are used to find computationally intensive code regions and then offload them to GPUs, followed by either a manual or compiler-driven restructuring for performance tuning. The quality of code porting relies solely on the user's programming experience. There are very few tools that can assist the porting process. The whole process requires a lot of work, and worse still, neither programmers or compilers can reuse previous experience for structurally similar code. In order to ease the process of porting software to a new system, we have created a tool called *Klonos*, which is able to provide a porting plan based on similarity analysis. This tool allows programmers and compilers to reuse porting experience as much as possible during the porting process. In this paper, we use the OpenMP programming model as an example to show how we can apply *Klonos* for porting serial code to a shared-memory programming environment. The main contributions of this paper are that: (1) we adapt cost-model provided metrics to capture code similarity in terms of optimization or porting, which saves the trouble of running the application for profiling information collection; (2) we propose a method for combining syntactic and cost-model-provided metrics clusters which aggregate similar subroutines that can be ported similarly. (3) we validate the *Klonos* tool by applying it to a large scientific application that is in production use. Our experiments shows that *Klonos* is an accurate tool for detecting subroutines that can benefit from similar porting strategies, and which reuse the programmers' or compiler's porting experience as much as possible. For clarity, Table 1 explains terms used in this paper.

This paper is organized as follows: Sect. 2 summarizes related work for the software porting. Section 3 describes the framework of *Klonos* and the cost model metrics which we introduced for detecting subroutine similarity in terms of porting or optimization. Section 4 evaluates *Klonos* tool for porting a real application called GenIDLEST to a shared programming environment by using OpenMP. Section 5 is the conclusion and future work.

Table 1. Terminology used in the Klonos tool

Term	Description
Similarity	A percentage score used to describe the match between a pair of sequences
Similarity distance matrix	A matrix (two-dimensional array) containing the distances, taken pairwise, of a set of subroutines. Matrix size is N×N, N is the number of subroutines
Family distance tree	A tree structure which is constructed based on the similarity distance matrix. Inside the tree, subroutines with similar code structure will be grouped into one sub-tree
Porting strategy	A solution for adapting a program to a different or new platform while guaranteeing program correctness and efficiency
Porting cluster	A group of clusters with subroutines in each cluster share the same syntactic and cost-model provided metrics clusters
Porting plan	A process of making plans for deciding the porting orders among the porting groups to a new platform in order to reuse porting strategies as much as possible

2   Related Work

Various techniques are used to port software from one environment to another. Two of these techniques used in the evolution of legacy codes are software refactoring and re-engineering. Additionally, a directives-based approach is used to guide the compiler while minimizing code changes and retaining the original syntax. With the help of code transformation tools, such restructuring work can be carried out (semi-)automatically, greatly improving work productivity.

Software refactoring is an important technique for the development and evolution of complex software systems. This technology saves development time and effort by reusing much of the existing design and code. Reference [20] uses some design tactics that assist users when evolving code from an existing software system, rather than starting from scratch. However based on their proposed approach, the onus is on the programmer to build a case model and object-oriented design model. The development team must also go manually through a discovery process to determine the structure of the code [8]. The discovery process is difficult and time-consuming, and it also not trivial to determine architecture features from the source code. Software re-engineering is the examination, analysis and alternation of an existing software system to reconstitute it for a new system. But this technique usually comes with extremely high manual re-engineering costs, and it's hard to get a global view for code, data, process re-engineering. Additionally the re-engineered system might perform inadequately. We still needs a tool to accurately provide us a code review.

A directives-based programming approach can be used to increase programmability and keep code concise. OpenMP serves as the de facto directives-based standard for parallel programming on shared memory systems, and is now deployed beyond pure HPC to include embedded systems, real time systems, and accelerators [6]. This directives-based approach greatly increases programming productivity, although it is not easy to write highly efficient code simply by adding directives, as unexpected overheads or side-effects may be introduced. In order to remedy this, several tools have been proposed: [16] develops an environment integrated with a tool called CAPO [5] where the user can navigate through both the program structure and performance data information in order to make efficient optimization decisions during the process of porting sequential applications to parallel computer architectures. ParaWise [15] parallelizes applications, including the automatic insertion of message passing communications and/or OpenMP directives. However, all of those tools are limited to the compiler for the code analysis, no optimization strategies can be reused, and the analysis capability is inaccurate in some cases.

A code transformation technique, [25] describes the porting strategy for translating from COBOL to C/C++ based. However this tool is outdated since COBOL is not used in the HPC field. There are some other tools such as CHiLL [7], POET [30] which provide code transformation for a target system. But the code transformation replies on users to manually write transformation scripts, also it's lack of capability of finding code regions which could apply code transformation. TSF [21] is a pattern matching based code transformation tool only for Fortran code engineering, but it's lack of capability to find how similar of the code regions could be applied for code transformation. Hercules [17] is another code transformation tool that could be used to apply optimizing transformations, but we still need a tool to identify code regions in which these transformations could be applied. The Hercules project from Oak Ridge relies on a transformation recipe and a compiler plug-in infrastructure to apply the transformation processes at compile time. Although early evaluations of Hercules suggest that the pattern matching approach is feasible on current computer resources, the task of defining patterns may become daunting to the programmer, and a tool to assist with the creation of this pattern creation based on similar code is needed.

3   Klonos Framework

Klonos [11] is the tool we designed for assisting software porting. This tool is based on the similarity analysis with the help of the OpenUH [24] compiler. As Fig. 2 shows, the main framework of Klonos is comprised of static, dynamic and cost-model metrics collection and porting planning analysis.

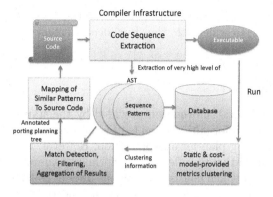

Fig. 2. The KLONOS porting planning system

3.1 Static Metrics

For static metrics collection, we reply on the compiler to collect code syntactic information. Additional functionality to track pattern information in the generated parse tree has been added to OpenUH as part of this work. During the traversal process, each key operator or operand visited by the compiler will be decoded into a unique character, which is defined by a node map that was defined in advance. This maps the hierarchical source code information into a flattened sequence. Next, a sequence alignment is constructed to evaluate the subroutine syntactic similarity for each pair of subroutines. Based on the syntactic similarity score for each pair of subroutines, a family distance tree is built, showing the aggregation of structurally similar subroutines. This aggregation is called a *"syntactic cluster"*. This method is easy to use and quite scalable compared to the graph comparison method. Reference [10] describes these steps in more detail.

3.2 Dynamic Metrics

Syntactic analysis is able to help find similar code quickly, which provides the ability to apply similar optimization strategies to that code. However, similar code structure does not guarantee that similar optimization techniques will apply. For example, the parallelization strategy for a particular loop structure would be totally different if we alternate an array name which might introduce loop-carried dependence. In order to ensure a particular optimization or parallelization strategy can be safely applied for similar codes, code feature metrics such as parallelization, vectorization, and memory access pattern related metrics need to be taken into consideration. In selecting dynamic metrics, we choose metrics that are able to reflect and capture the memory behaviors of an application. In [9], the following hardware counters were collected using AMD Code-Analyst: "DC accesses", "DC misses", "DTLB L1M L2M", "CPU clocks", "Ret branch" and "Ret inst". Once those metrics are available, Weka [2] is used to create "*dynamic clusters*" for subroutines based on these code features, using the K-means algorithm to calculate the Euclidean distance for each pair of subroutines.

3.3 Cost-Model Metrics

The aggregated structural information provided by the static metrics, and the aggregated behavioral information provided by the dynamic metrics combine to identify a viable porting plan for an application. However, it is still impractical to run an entire application to collect the performance sampling data, especially for a large application which consists of millions lines of code. To analyse a very large data set generated by such a run is difficult and time-consuming. Even if it is possible to collect this kind of performance data, the output is sensitive to the content of the input data and sampling information varies significantly between different execution phases. It is also evident that many optimization or code restructuring techniques used during porting are target specific, and lead to variations in performance on different platforms. So different cost-models will be used for different target systems. A cost model is a performance estimation without regard to specific input data, and is used by the compiler to select different optimization algorithms. OpenUH uses a shared memory processor cost model to evaluate different combinations of optimizations and to decide if there is enough work (in processor cycles) to gain from automatic parallelization of a loop. The cost model is essential to evaluate whether it is worth applying static optimizations to loops and consists of three major components: the processor, cache, and parallel overhead [29]. The similarity of code is measured by analysing the similarity of cost-model-based metrics. Sections of code that exhibit the same metrics are likely to benefit from similar optimization and porting strategies. The cost model provided metrics used are: estimated number of iterations, suggested parallelization, loop parallelizable attribute, loop vectorizable attribute, loop vectorized number, loop align peeled, work estimate, loop depth. These metrics are key factors used in the cost model for optimization strategy selection, which can accurately capture the internal code optimization characteristics.

4 Experiments

GenIDLEST is a Fortran program that simulates transitional and turbulent flows in complex geometries [26]. This application features both shared memory (OpenMP) and distributed memory (MPI) parallelism, which leads to a high degree of portability between computer architectures. This application is thus ideal for the porting planning strategy verification that we propose to perform with the *Klonos* tool. First, we use *Klonos* to analyze the serial version of GenIDLEST, and then generate a porting plan for a parallel version of the code using OpenMP. By referring to the optimized GenIDLEST OpenMP code, we are able to verify the accuracy of the proposed OpenMP porting plan with *Klonos*.

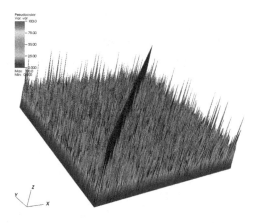

Fig. 3. The subroutine similarities of the GenIDLEST application

4.1   GenIDLEST Similarity Analysis

GenIDLEST has a total of 264 subroutines. Before we perform the syntactic similarity analysis, we pre-process the generated sequence pattern files by excluding subroutines with only one function invocation inside them, since those files only contribute noise through many highly syntactically similar pairs. After the pre-processing steps, next we generate a similarity square matrix by comparing each pair of subroutine sequences until all the subroutines have been consumed. Figure 3 shows the 3D visualization of GenIDLEST subroutines. It lists the overall similarities among all the subroutines. Axes X and Y are subroutines, the Z axis represents the similarity score for each pair of subroutines. The node map legend shows the level of similarity. Red means high similarity and blue means low, or no, similarity. The diagonal shows subroutine self-similarity. Figure 4 is a circular family distance tree with height of 31. It shows the overall relationship of syntactic similarity for GenIDLEST subroutines after pre-processing. The family distance tree lists similarity relationships of 254 subroutines, which the total number of subroutines after preprocessing that excludes subroutines with only one function call inside.

Table 2 summarizes the statistics of the similarities of subroutines after preprocessing. GenIDLEST has 1327 subroutine pairs that maintain syntactic similarity of greater than 50 %, which means a majority of subroutines look similar structurally.

4.2   Syntactic Clustering Analysis

Figure 5 shows the relationship of the number of correct porting similar subroutine pairs with setting different number of clusters based on code syntactic similarity. In Fig. 5(a), we can the see the number of similar subroutine pairs using similar porting directives decreases gradually as the syntactic based cluster number increases. Figure 5(b) shows the ratio of similar subroutine pairs using

Fig. 4. The overall family distance tree for GenIDLEST

Table 2. GenIDLEST subroutines similarity statistics

Similarity range	# of subroutine pairs
Similarity $\geqslant$ 90	47
Similarity $\geqslant$ 80	43
Similarity $\geqslant$ 70	44
Similarity $\geqslant$ 60	208
Similarity $\geqslant$ 50	985
Similarity < 50	30804

Table 3. OpenMP directive encoding code map

Directives	Character map
$!OMP PARALLEL	P
$!OMP DO	D
$!OMP PARALLEL DO	PD

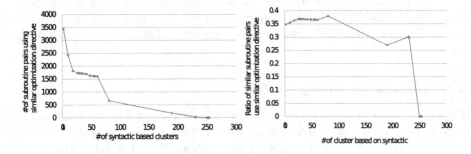

Fig. 5. Syntactic-based cluster for GenIDLEST application

similar porting directives over the total number of similar subroutine pairs from the "syntactic cluster". As we can see, the ratio is less than 40 %, which means the porting accuracy is very low by only using cost-model provided metrics for porting clustering.

To further divide hierarchical clustering into fine-grained *syntactic groups*, we propose three methods to cluster the tree, based on: (A) the user inputs the tree depth value, which is used to divide the tree. (B) a similarity distance value serves as a threshold to divide the tree: if the distance between current the node and its parent is greater than the distance threshold, then the current node and its descendants will be separated into a subtree. (C) a combination of the first two methods; this combination method clusters the tree based on user input of tree depth and similarity distance. Our goal is to find a cluster number that is able to put syntactically similar subroutine pairs into groups as much as possible while maintaining a moderate group size. Based on previous empirical experience, a syntactic value of 50 % is a suitable threshold [9], so in our experiment we use that threshold value and the input depth of the tree for clustering.

4.3   Cost-Model Metrics Clustering Analysis

To better understand the relationship between the cost-model-provided metrics and similar optimization or porting strategy, we only used the cost-model metrics to cluster the subroutines and then check the number of subroutine pairs which use the same optimization directives or strategies. Figure 6(a) depicts the relationship between the number of subroutine pairs that use similar directives and the number of clusters, which is set manually based on the cost-model metrics. When changing the number of clusters based on the cost-model metrics, we can see the number of subroutine pairs using similar directive strategies decreases gradually until it reaches a constant. Figure 6(b) shows the ratio of subroutine pairs using a similar porting strategy over the total number of subroutine pairs that have been clustered with respect to different numbers of clusters. According to this result, we find that relying purely on cost-model provided metrics for clus-

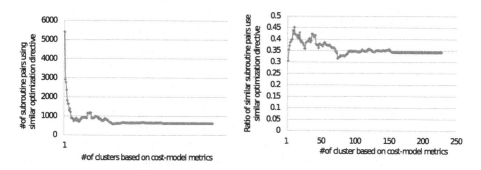

Fig. 6. Cost-model metrics based cluster for GenIDLEST application

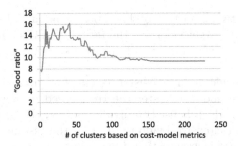

Fig. 7. Cost-model metric based clusters for GenIDLEST

tering subroutines results in low accuracy (below 46 %) for detecting subroutine pairs that can be ported or optimized in the same way. To obtain a reasonable number of clusters for cost-model metrics, we define and use a "Good ratio" to set the number of clusters. "Good ratio a percentage score of the number of subroutine pairs with syntactic similarity greater than 50 % over the total number of subroutine pairs in the clusters. We select a cluster number with highest "Good ratio" to make structurally similar subroutines aggregated as many as possible for similar porting experience reuse.

In Fig. 7, the Y-axis is the percentage of the number of subroutine pairs with syntactic similarity greater than 50 % over the total number of subroutine pairs in the clusters. We use the term "Good ratio" to define this percentage score in the next text. The X-axis is the number of clusters manually set for clustering subroutines based on cost-model metrics In this diagram, we can see that the "Good ratio" is around 16 % when the number of clusters is set to 8 and 41 respectively. When setting up the number of cluster based on cost-model provided metrics, we want to choose a cluster number which could result in "Good ratio" while maintaining a moderate group size to void a scenario of generating too many combined clusters. Considering this, we set the number of cluster for cost-model metrics to 8 in our experiment.

4.4   Combination of Syntactic and Cost-Model Based Clusters

Relying solely on either syntactic or cost-model-provided metrics results in low accuracy when detecting similar subroutine pairs that could be optimized or ported similarly. By incorporating these two metrics we can greatly increase the accuracy of the process of detecting subroutine pairs to be ported in the same way.

In Sect. 4.3, we found that we can get a "Good ratio" by setting cost-model provided cluster number to 8. To discover the relationship between those two clusters, we tried different combinations of numbers of clusters for the syntactic and cost-model-based clusters. To control the size of combined clusters, we set cost-model provided clusters from 1 to 9 in the relationship of syntactic and cost-model cluster analysis. Our goal is to accurately aggregate similar subroutines into groups as much as possible, which provides the opportunity to find

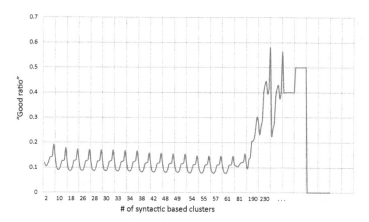

Fig. 8. Combined syntax and cost-model metric clusters for GenIDLEST

subroutines that can be optimized in the same way. In Fig. 8, the X-axis is the ratio of the number of subroutine pairs with syntactic similarity more than 50 % over the total number of subroutine pairs based on current combined clustering methods. The Y-axis is the number of clusters obtained by using different distance values from 0 to 100. Inside each cluster, we vary the number of clusters based on the cost-model metrics, resulting in the "heart-beat" shape diagram. We observe that the ratio reaches a peak in this diagram when setting the cost-model metrics-based cluster to 8, which is exactly the number of cluster we can get peak "Good ratio" value in our cost-model metrics analysis described in Sect. 4.3.

4.5 Improved Verification Methodology

To increase the accuracy of verification, our improved methodology focuses on the syntax of OpenMP directive comparison directly. We add functions into the phase of code sequence extraction (described in Sect. 3.1). If any OpenMP directive is detected in a subroutine, a separate ".opt" file will be generated: this is used to record a loop position index from its corresponding subroutine code sequence, and optimization sequences by encoding OpenMP directives into sequences according to the code map defined in Table 3.

Assume we have subroutines A and B in a combined cluster group. There are three cases that can be classified when comparing their similar optimization or porting strategy: (1) Neither A nor B have corresponding ".opt" files. We treat A and B in the same way, meaning neither of them could be optimized. (2) Only one of A and B has a ".opt" file, which means one was optimized and the other was not. Therefore A and B do not count as similar for optimization, and do not use similar directives for porting. (3) Both A and B have ".opt" files. In this case, we perform code sequence alignments first. We are able to see which loops have been aligned by referring the loop index obtained from a code sequence back to the corresponding ".opt" file. For aligned loops, we check the OpenMP encoded directive sequences directly to check if two similar subroutines can have similar optimization directives applied to them for porting purposes.

4.6   Porting Strategy Verification

Based on analysis of clustering using syntactic and cost-model metrics listed in Figs. 5 and 6, we found that either using syntactic distance or cost-metric metrics only as cluster method will results in inaccurate clustering for making porting planning. Our goal is to minimize the number of clusters while in the meantime to make sure accuracy for clustering similar subroutines using similar porting directives. According to Fig. 8 shows that we can have maximum similar pairs ratios for subroutine pairs fall into the same syntactic and cost-model metrics based cluster So we set up the number of code-model provided metrics cluster (or short for cost-model cluster) to 8 in our experiment and then make a comparison of the accuracy of porting. By setting distance value to 50 and depth to 5 based on the shape of the tree, then we are able to divide the tree into 9 clusters for syntactic cluster. By merging the syntactic and code feature clustering, we divide the 254 subroutines into 25 groups. Subroutines within each group fall into the same syntactic and code-model cluster. After combining syntactic and code-most metric based clusters or combined cluster, next comes to step of verifying the correctness of similar directives used for subroutines fall into combined cluster. The ratio of all subroutine pairs using similar optimization reaches 49.51 % in our experiment. Figure 9(a) shows the relationship of similar optimization ratio over the 254 subroutines with respect to the syntactic similarity for subroutine pairs which fall into the same syntactic and code-model cluster when setting the cost-metrics based cluster number to 8. As the figure shows, the correctness of using similar directive for parallelizing the code is almost 80 % for subroutine pairs who fall into the same syntactic and code-model cluster with syntactic similarity is greater than 50 %. Figure 9(b) shows the number of pairs using similar porting strategy in detail.

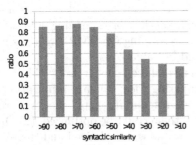

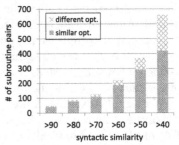

(a)Similar optimization directive verification for GenIDLEST

(b) Similar optimization directive verification for GenIDLEST

Fig. 9. Verification of GenIDLEST porting planning analysis

Higher syntactic similarity will result in using similar directive parallelization strategy for subroutine pairs with the same syntactic and code feature cluster. This result proves that our similarity based methodology is very effective and accurate in detecting similar subroutines which could use similar porting or optimization strategy. Using cost-model based metrics are accurate for capturing code similarity in terms of optimization or porting, which saves the trouble of running applications to collect profiling information.

5   Conclusions and Future Work

In this paper, we have expanded the notion of code similarity analysis to cost-model-provided metrics for detecting similar porting strategies for similar subroutine pairs, thus avoiding the burden of running applications to gather profiling information.

We have validated *Klonos* by applying it to GenIDLEST, a real scientific application, that was originally written as serial code and then parallelized for a shared memory environment using OpenMP. By referring to the optimized OpenMP GenIDLEST code, we discovered that the OpenMP directives proposed by *Klonos* are both accurate and effective. This porting approach is quite easily extended to other directive based approaches for code migration to different architectures (e.g. PGI, OpenACC, HMPP etc.).

Future work will include exploring cost-models for porting code to other accelerators. We will also use data mining techniques to create a framework which can automatically find combinations of syntactic and cost-model clusters to increase porting accuracy. Additionally, we will implement a GUI to visualize the process of generating porting plans.

References

1. OpenMP ARB. Openmp arb. http://openmp.org/wp/about-openmp/
2. Machine Learning Group at University of Waikato. Weka 3: Data mining software in java. http://www.cs.waikato.ac.nz/ml/weka/
3. Jost, G., Chapman, B.M., van der Pas, R.: Using OpenMP: Portable Shared Memory Parallel Programming. The MIT Press, Cambridge (2007)
4. Buttlar, D., Nichols, B., Farrell, J.P.: Pthreads Programming. O'Reilly & Associates Inc., Sebastopol (1996)
5. NASA Ames Research Center. Capo (computer-aided parallelizer and optimizer). http://people.nas.nasa.gov/~hjin/CAPO/index.html
6. Chapman, B., Jost, G., Van Der Pas, R.: Using OpenMP: Portable Shared Memory Parallel Programming, vol. 10. MIT Press, Cambridge (2007)
7. Chen, C., Chame, J., Hall, M.: CHiLL: a framework for composing high-level loop transformations. Technical report, Technical Report 08–897, USC Computer Science Technical Report (2008)
8. Davison, J., Mancl, D., Opdyke, W.: Understanding and addressing the essential costs of evolving systems. Bell Labs Tech. J. 5, 44–54 (2000)

9. Ding, W., Hernandez, O., Chapman, B.: A similarity-based analysis tool for porting OpenMP applications. In: Keller, R., Kramer, D., Weiss, J.-P. (eds.) Facing the Multicore-Challenge III. LNCS, vol. 7686, pp. 13–24. Springer, Heidelberg (2013)

10. Ding, W., Hsu, C.-H., Hernandez, O., Chapman, B., Graham, R.: Klonos: similarity-based planning tool support for porting scientific applications. Concurrency Comput. Pract. Experience **25**, 1072–1088 (2013)

11. Ding, W., Hsu, C.-H., Hernandez, O., Graham, R., Chapman, B.M.: Bioinspired similarity-based planning support for the porting of scientific applications. In: 4th Workshop on Parallel Architectures and Bioinspired Algorithms, Galveston Island, Texas, USA (2011)

12. CAPS Entreprise. HMPP: A Hybrid Multicore Parallel Programming Platform. http://www.caps-entreprise.com/en/documentation/caps_hmpp_product_brief. pdf

13. The Portland Group. PGI accelerator compilers (2010). http://www.pgroup.com/ resources/accel.htm

14. Hernandez, O., Ding, W., Chapman, B., Kartsaklis, C., Sankaran, R., Graham, R.: Experiences with high-level programming directives for porting applications to GPUs. In: Keller, R., Kramer, D., Weiss, J.-P. (eds.) Facing the Multicore - Challenge II. LNCS, vol. 7174, pp. 96–107. Springer, Heidelberg (2012)

15. Johnson, S., Evans, E., Jin, H., Ierotheou, C.: The ParaWise expert assistant - widening accessibility to efficient and scalable tool generated OpenMP code. In: Chapman, B.M. (ed.) WOMPAT 2004. LNCS, vol. 3349, pp. 67–82. Springer, Heidelberg (2005)

16. Jost, G., Jin, H., Labarta, J., Gimenez, J.: Interfacing computer aided parallelization and performance analysis. In: Sloot, P.M.A., Abramson, D., Bogdanov, A.V., Gorbachev, Y.E., Dongarra, J., Zomaya, A.Y. (eds.) ICCS 2003, Part IV. LNCS, vol. 2660, pp. 181–190. Springer, Heidelberg (2003)

17. Kartsaklis, C., Hernandez, O., Hsu, C.H., Ilsche, T., Joubert, W., Graham, R.L.: Hercules: a pattern driven code transformation system. In: 2012 IEEE 26th International Parallel and Distributed Processing Symposium Workshops & PhD Forum (IPDPSW), pp. 574–583. IEEE (2012)

18. Levesque, J., Sankaran, R., et al.: Hybridizing s3d into an exascale application using openacc: an approach for moving to multi-petaflops and beyond. In: Proceedings of the International Conference on High Performance Computing, Networking, Storage and Analysis, p. 15. IEEE Computer Society Press (2012)

19. Top500 List. Treemap - november 2012 (accelerator/co-processor). http://www. top500.org/statistics/treemaps/

20. Mancl, D.: Refactoring for software migration. IEEE Commun. Mag. **39**(10), 88–93 (2001)

21. Mével, Y.: Tsf: an environment for program transformations

22. Munshi, A.: The OpenCL Specification, October 2009

23. NVIDIA Corporation. NVIDIA CUDA Compute Unified Device Architecture Programming Guide Version 3.0, March 2010. http://developer.nvidia.com/cuda

24. The OpenUH compiler project (2005). http://www.cs.uh.edu/~openuh

25. Sampaio do Prado Leite, J.C., Sant'Anna, M., Francisco do Prado, A.: Porting cobol programs using a transformational approach. J. Softw. Maintenance: Res. Pract. **9**(1), 3–31 (1997)

26. Tafti, D.: Genidlest a parallel high performance computational infrastructure for simulating complex turbulent flow and heat transfer. APS Division of Fluid Dynamics Meeting Abstracts, vol. 1 (2002)

27. Vetter, S., Aoyama, Y., Nakano, J.: RS/6000 SP: practical MPI programming, vol. SG24-5380-00 of 0738413658. vervante, August 1999
28. The Wikipedia. Software porting. http://en.wikipedia.org/wiki/Porting
29. Wolf, M.E., Maydan, D.E., Chen, D.-K.: Combining loop transformations considering caches and scheduling. In: Proceedings of the 29th Annual ACM/IEEE International Symposium on Microarchitecture, pp. 274–286. IEEE Computer Society, Washington, DC (1996)
30. Yi, Q., Seymour, K., You, H., Vuduc, R., Quinlan, D.J.: POET: parameterized optimizations for empirical tuning. In: Workshop on Performance Optimization for High-Level Languages and Libraries, March 2007

Tasks

Task-Aware Optimization
of Dynamic Fractional Permissions

Christoph M. Angerer[✉]

IBM Research – Zurich, Rüschlikon, Switzerland
han@zurich.ibm.com

Abstract. Boyland's original work on fractional permissions introduced a mechanism to statically reason about the correct use of shared memory in concurrent programs. Permissions are linear capabilities that can be passed from one task to another. By splitting a permission into fractions, a task can grant multiple other tasks concurrent read access. Because writing data requires the full permission–and by definition at most one task can have the full permission–, fractional permissions prevent read/write conflicts.

This paper presents an optimizing compiler for a dynamic variant of fractional permissions where memory accesses are checked at runtime. In this system, every object is associated with a list of tasks that have read and/or write permission for the object. Tasks can grant read permission to subtasks by splitting their own permission into fractions and later collect those fractions back to re-gain the original permission.

To reduce the time and space overhead associated with permission checks, the compiler uses task-ordering information to minimize the places where permission checks must be inserted. For three of the five benchmarks we have investigated, the fully optimized version is within 10 % of the original version without fractional permissions. The average performance overhead over all benchmarks is 48 % which can be attributed to the poor performance of one particular benchmark. (For the other benchmarks, the average overhead is 15 %.)

With the rise of multithreaded programming, the number of programming errors related to concurrency is constantly growing [1]. One prevalent type of bugs found in concurrent systems are *data races*. A data race occurs when two concurrent accesses to the same memory location are not ordered by happens-before relations and at least one of the accesses is a write. In practice, there are three general approaches to design data-race free programs:

Language-enforced data-race freedom: Some languages guarantee data-race freedom through their type systems [2,3]. From a high-level, the programmer provides program and type annotations that describe how data is shared and accessed by concurrent tasks. The languages' type systems use the annotations to prove that accesses to shared memory are ordered or the type checks fail otherwise. In recent years, much research also went into transactional memory [4–6]. Transactional memory allows programmers to specify code regions that should

© Springer International Publishing Switzerland 2014
C. Caşcaval and P. Montesinos (Eds.): LCPC 2013, LNCS 8664, pp. 39–54, 2014.
DOI: 10.1007/978-3-319-09967-5_3

be atomic; an accompanying runtime system implemented in hard- and/or software protects the accessed memory from concurrent accesses thus preventing data races.

Static verification and model checking: Static verification and model checking of concurrent programs are approaches that—conceptually—exhaustively explore the whole state space of the program to rule out potential data races [7,8]. The major challenge of model checking techniques is the state space explosion: the number of states increases exponentially with the number of possible task interleavings. Numerous approaches exist for reducing the state space that must be effectively explored for guaranteeing data-race freedom.

Dynamic detection and testing: Systems for dynamic data-race detection aim at finding data-races when they happen during program execution or testing. This can be done online, that is, during program execution, or offline, by analyzing a pre-recorded program trace. Dynamic detection cannot generally guarantee the absence of data-races for *all possible* executions; rather, it focusses on data-races in the *observed* execution traces. Dynamic data-race detection systems further fall into two general categories: *Precise* and *imprecise* systems [9]. While precise race detectors never report false positives, they can impose a significant runtime overhead due to the additional bookkeeping they require. Imprecise race detectors increase the performance by giving up precision but—as a result—may report false alarms on data-race free programs.

This paper introduces a dynamic variant of *fractional permissions* [3] in which the programmer explicitly manages task-access permissions for objects. In this system, each object is associated with an access control list (ACL) that contains all the tasks that are allowed to access the object.

A task is allowed to *write* an object if it is the *only* task in the object's ACL and therefore has full permission. In order for a task to *read* the object, however, it is enough if the task is *one* of several tasks in the object's ACL.

Each task in an object's ACL conceptually owns a fraction of the full access permission corresponding to the total number of tasks in the ACL. The system can detect data-races by checking the current task's access permissions on every read and write operation. By imposing restrictions on when and how tasks are allowed to modify an object's ACL, the system further forces the programmer to follow a structured access-right management regime and prevents privilege escalation where a task $\mathcal{A}$ with low privileges tries to grant higher access privileges to another task $\mathcal{B}$.

There are two factors that result in a relatively large overhead for a direct implementation of the dynamic fractional permissions system. First, the memory for storing the ACLs for each object have a negative impact on the memory footprint, memory allocation, cache behavior, and garbage collection. And second, checking whether a task has the correct access rights slows down every single field-read and -write operation.

Because of the imposed runtime overhead, without optimizations dynamic fractional permissions are impractical for real-world applications. We present an optimizing compiler that significantly reduces the runtime overhead by only allocating ACLs for objects that may be shared between concurrent tasks as well as removing access checks on read and write operations that are not conflicting with concurrent accesses. The compiler uses a *schedule analysis* [10, 11] to gather information about possible execution orderings of the program tasks.

Section 1 describes the dynamic fractional permission system and its implementation. The example presented in Sect. 2 illustrates how dynamic fractional permissions can be used to dynamically enforce a data access policy in a MapReduce(). The compiler optimizations are presented in Sect. 3 and evaluated in Sect. 4 before concluding in Sect. 6.

1 Dynamic Fractional Permissions

This section describes the three components of the dynamic fractional permission system: access control lists (ACLs), permissions, and permission management operations.

1.1 Access Control Lists and Permissions

At runtime, each object o is associated with an access control list (ACL). We define a function $ACL(o)$ to return the ACL of object o. The ACL is the set of all task objects that share the full access permission for the object. The fraction $Frac(o, \mathcal{A})$ of the full permission that a task $\mathcal{A}$ owns for an object o directly correlates to the number of tasks that are in o's ACL. $Frac(o, \mathcal{A})$ is defined as:

$$Frac(o, \mathcal{A}) := \begin{cases} \frac{1}{\|ACL(o)\|} & \text{if } \mathcal{A} \in ACL(o) \\ \\ 0 & \text{else.} \end{cases}$$

If $\mathcal{A}$ is in o's ACL, it shares the permission equally with all other tasks in o's ACL. If $\mathcal{A}$ is not in o's ACL, however, $\mathcal{A}$'s fraction of o's access permission is 0.

The system distinguishes the following three types of permissions, depending on the fraction size:

Write Permission: A task $\mathcal{A}$ has write permission (or 'full' permission) for object o if it is the only task in o's ACL. We define the predicate isWritable(o, $\mathcal{A}$) to be true if $Frac(o, \mathcal{A}) = 1$. Because $\mathcal{A}$ has the full permission, no other task can gain access rights to o without $\mathcal{A}$'s involvement. Therefore $\mathcal{A}$ can safely write the fields of o without risking data-races. In addition, certain permission management operations require the performing task to have full permission on the object.

Read Permission: A task $\mathcal{A}$ has read permission (or 'partial' permission) to access object o if $\mathcal{A}$ is an element in the ACL. We define the predicate isReadable(o, $\mathcal{A}$) to be true if $0 < Frac(o, \mathcal{A}) < 1$. A read permission for object o, as the name implies, allows a task $\mathcal{A}$ to read the fields of o but not write them. A task $\mathcal{A}$ with read permission can grant read permission on o to another task $\mathcal{B}$ by adding $\mathcal{B}$ to o's ACL. This reduces the absolute value of the permission fraction that the tasks in o's ACL own. However, adding $\mathcal{B}$ does not change the access rights a third task $\mathcal{C}$ may have on o.

No Permission: A task $\mathcal{A}$ has no permission for object o if it is not an element in o's ACL. We define the predicate noAccess(o,$\mathcal{A}$) to be true if Frac(o, $\mathcal{A}$) = 0. It is legal for $\mathcal{A}$ to own a reference to o but $\mathcal{A}$ is not allowed to read or write o's fields nor can $\mathcal{A}$ change o's ACL in any way.

To implement a dynamic data-race detection, the compiler automatically inserts assertions before all field accesses that check the current task's read and write permissions. If the check fails the program is aborted and an error message is shown, reporting the offending program point, the required permission, and the actual ACL. The detailed information in the error message together with the early program termination helps the programmer to pinpoint the data-race.

1.2   Permission Management Operations

The dynamic fractional permissions system provides a set of operations that allow a task $\mathcal{A}$ to manage the permissions for an object o. Depending on the operation $\mathcal{A}$ wants to perform it must either have the full permission for o or a fractional permission. This section informally describes the management operations and their semantics.

Split Permission: The most common explicit permission management operation is for a task $\mathcal{A}$ to share its access permission on an object o with one or more other tasks $\mathcal{B}$. In order to split the permission, the issuing task $\mathcal{A}$ **must** have at least read permission for o; that is, isReadable(o,$\mathcal{A}$). Otherwise, the program is aborted with an appropriate error message. In terms of o's ACL, the operation o.splitPermission($\mathcal{B}$) checks whether isReadable(o, currentTask) and, if true, simply adds $\mathcal{B}$ to o's ACL.[1]

Yield permission: A task $\mathcal{A}$ can transfer (yield) its permission for an object o to another task $\mathcal{B}$. After the yield, task $\mathcal{B}$ has the same permission (none, read, or write) on o as $\mathcal{A}$ had before the yield. In any case, after the yield, the issuing task $\mathcal{A}$ has no permission on o. In terms of o's ACL, the operation o.yieldPermission($\mathcal{B}$) executed by task $\mathcal{A}$ replaces the occurrence of task $\mathcal{A}$ (if any) in o's ACL with $\mathcal{B}$.

A task can yield its permission *explicitly* in the code by executing the yield() operation. A task can, however, also yield (or 'give back') its fraction of the permission *implicitly*. When a task $\mathcal{A}$ finishes, the runtime system removes $\mathcal{A}$ from all ACLs it is a member of. This automatically increases the absolute values of the permission fractions of the affected objects. For an object that only had two tasks $\mathcal{A}$ and $\mathcal{B}$ in its ACL, removing $\mathcal{A}$ from the ACL promotes task $\mathcal{B}$'s permission to a full permission. Objects where $\mathcal{A}$ was the only task in their ACL become permanently inaccessible (garbage) when $\mathcal{A}$ is removed.

---

[1] The term *split* stems from the notion of *fractional* permissions. The whole permission of size 1 is split between the n elements in the ACL such that each element has $\frac{1}{n}$th of the permission.

As an example where implicitly yielding permissions is helpful, consider the ACL {W1, W2, W3, Join} for an object o. This ACL contains the three worker tasks W1, W2, and W3 as well as a single Join task. While the workers are executing, they can concurrently read o because they all have read permission. Over time, the worker tasks will finish one after the other and each worker will be removed from the ACL. In the end, the Join task is the only task in the ACL. Join has collected the full permission and therefore has full access to o.

Link and unlink permission: By linking the permission of one object dependent to another object master, dependent will share master's ACL. Linking allows the programmer to express *ownership* relations where the ACL for the dependent is always kept in sync with the master's ACL. When the permissions are linked, only master's ACL has to be managed explicitly. For a task 𝒜 to execute the expression dependent.linkToPermission(master) it must have full permission on the dependent object; 𝒜's permission on master is not important, however. After the two permissions have been linked, 𝒜 the same permission for dependent as it had for accessing master.

Linked objects are unlinked with dependent.unlinkPermission-(master). For unlinking, the executing task 𝒜 must have the full permission on the dependent (and therefore the master, since they are linked). After the unlink operation, both objects master and dependent have their own individual ACLs again, each of which only contains 𝒜.

Shared and immutable permission: The dynamic fractional permissions system supports two special types of objects: immutable objects and shared objects. Marking an object as shared or immutable is permanent and cannot be undone. Immutability and sharing is implemented as two special types of ACLs.

The *immutable* ACL grants read access to every task, but no write access. When a task 𝒜 issues the operation o.immutablePermission(), the system checks that 𝒜 has read permission. If so, it replaces o's ACL with the immutable ACL.

The *shared* ACL grants read and write access to every task. By marking an object to be shared, the programmer asserts to the system that he is aware of the concurrent use of the object and manages concurrent accesses manually (e.g., through locks or atomic sections). For shared objects, the system cannot detect data-races. Calling the operation o.sharedPermission() requires the issuing task 𝒜 to have full permission for o. If this is the case, the system replaces o's current ACL with the immutable ACL.

2 Example: Map-Reduce with Dynamic Data-Race Detection

Map-Reduce is a programming model for processing large data sets [12]. A MapReduce program consists of a Map() function that takes a key/value pair as input and produces some intermediate data, and a Reduce() function that merges the intermediate data of multiple `Map()` tasks into either the final result or the key/value inputs for the next Map-Reduce phase.

In a concrete implementation of a MapReduce computation, a detailed access policy must be worked out to manage access to local and shared data structures. For example, what tasks are allowed to read/write the intermediate objects produced by the `Map()` tasks? Can one `Map()`-task access the intermediate result of another `Map()` task? What tasks need read/write access to the results after the MapReduce has finished? Especially larger applications are prone to introduce inconsistencies in the access policies, resulting in potential data races. With the dynamic fractional permission system, the programmer is forced to explicitly manage the permissions a given task has on a given object. When executing the program, dynamic checks will detect if the access permissions are managed inconsistently and report errors accordingly.

In this example, we use the task model with explicit task ordering constraints from [10]. In this model, task objects are ordered explicitly by ordering operations. For example, an expression `compute` $\rightarrow$ `print` in the source code specifies, that the task referenced by the variable `compute` must be finished before the task referenced by `print` can start. The special keyword now gives the programmer access to the currently executing task. By passing task objects to methods and other tasks, programmers can specify complex task orderings in a modular and flexible way while the compiler can use the explicit ordering constraints to infer an abstract execution schedule.

Figure 1 shows one possible implementation of a single MapReduce step using dynamic fractional permissions and tasks with explicit ordering constraints. The program consists of three task methods: `MapReduce()` on line 3, the `Map()` task on line 22, and the `Reduce()` task on line 33.

The MapReduce Task: The public `MapReduce()` task is the entry point to the MapReduce computation. The second parameter `input` is an `ArrayList` of `Strings` that comprises the input in this example. Following the *now happens-before later* pattern described in our earlier work [13], `MapReduce()` expects as its first parameter a task `later` that will continue once the whole MapReduce step is over. On line 10, we use this reference to `later` to schedule the `reduce` sub-task to finish before `later` starts; by the ordering established on line 18, all created `Map()` tasks must happen before `reduce` and thus–transitively– before `later`. This transitive ordering guarantees that the whole Map-Reduce computation has finished before `later` continues execution, for example with a second Map-Reduce step.

On line 6, the `MapReduce()` task creates a new `Vector` object into which the concurrent `Map()` tasks will write their intermediate results. To indicate that this `Vector` will be accessed in parallel, the programmer explicitly sets the permission on the `data` object to be `shared` on line 7.

The data access policy for this example requires, that the `MapReduce()` task has full write access to the `input` list. This means, that the current now task is the only task in `input`'s ACL. For reasons of simplicity, `MapReduce()` further requires that the `this` object is globally shared so that the `Reduce()`

```
 1  public class MapReduce {
 2    public volatile Result result;
 3    public task MapReduce(Task later, ArrayList<String> input) {
 4      assert isShared(this) && isWritable(input, now);
 5      //the map tasks will access data concurrently
 6      Vector<Data> data = new Vector<Data>();
 7      data.sharedPermission();
 8
 9      Task reduce = schedule Reduce(later, input, data);
10      reduce→later;
11      //grant read access to the reduce task
12      input.splitPermission(reduce);
13
14      for(int i = 0; i < input.size(); i++) {
15        Task map = schedule Map(input, data, i);
16        //grant each map task read access to 'input'
17        input.splitPermission(map);
18        map→reduce;
19      }
20    }
21
22    private task Map(ArrayList<String> input, Vector<Data> data, int index) {
23      assert isReadable(input, now) && isWritable(data, now);
24      //perform complex map operation using the input
25      String s = input.get(index);
26      Data mapped = new ComplexData(s);
27      //make the mapped Data follow the same regime as 'input'
28      mapped.linkToPermission(input);
29      data.add(mapped);
30      //implicitly remove 'now' from input's ACL
31    }
32
33    private task Reduce(Task later, ArrayList<String> input, Vector<Data> data) {
34      //all Map tasks gave back their permissions for 'input'; therefore 'now' has write access
35      assert isWritable(input, now) && isReadable(data, now) && isWritable(this, now);
36      //clear input array and compute the result from the data
37      input.removeAll();
38      Result r = new Result(data);
39      //make the result immutable and publish it
40      r.immutablePermission();
41      this.result = r;
42      //give write permission for 'input' to 'later'
43      input.yieldPermission(later);
44    }
45  }
```

Fig. 1. Implementation of a single MapReduce step using dynamic fractional permissions for data-race detection. Assertions are added automatically by the compiler.

task can later simply publish the result by writing the public `result` field declared on line 2. The assertion on line 4, inserted by the compiler, dynamically enforces this access policy. On lines 12 and 17, the `MapReduce()` task splits its write permission for the `input` list and shares it with the `Map()` tasks and the `Reduce()` task. After the `MapReduce()` task has finished it is automatically removed from `input`'s ACL leaving the `Map()` tasks as well as the single `Reduce()` task.

The Map Tasks: The compiler added an assertion on line 23 to check that each `Map()` task has read permission for the `input` list and write permission for the (shared) `data` vector. All `Map()` task instances read from the `input` list on line 25 and use it in the subsequent lines to compute some complex result object mapped which it then stores in the shared data vector on line 29.

By linking the ACL for the mapped data object to the ACL of the input list on line 28, the Map() tasks eventually transfer the full ownership for the intermediate data to the reduce task. This is because whenever a Map() task finishes, it is implicitly removed from the ACL of the input list. Therefore, when finally the Reduce() task starts, it is the last task remaining in input's ACL and thus has re-gained full write permissions on the input list as well as all the linked Data objects.

The Reduce Task: First, a compiler-inserted assertion asserts the correct access rights on line 35. In this example, the Reduce() task then clears the input array on line 37 so that it can be reused again. On line 38 Reduce() computes the result by combining the intermediate data into a Result object r. For illustrative purposes, r is then made immutable on line 40 and published to the world by storing it in a public field on line 41. Equally, we could have decided to pass the full permission from Reduce() to later if later needed to write the data (e.g., in a subsequent MapReduce step).

Finally, line 43 explicitly yields the full write permission on input to later. Note that the entry point MapReduce() required write permission on the input list and therefore later cannot already have been in input's ACL. For this reason, the permission cannot be returned to later implicitly.

3   Task-Aware Optimization of Dynamic Fractional Permissions

The following two sections describe the two general optimization steps the compiler performs: (1) Local optimization to eliminate redundant permission checks; and (2) global optimization to remove space and time overhead associated with permission management.

3.1   Eliminating Redundant Permission Checks

Redundant read and write checks can be eliminated locally by placing them as early as possible in a method and then removing duplicate checks. Imagine, for example, a task T1() that repeatedly accesses an object Obj through a variable v1 without intermediate splits or yields of permission:

```
task T1() {
    v1 = /*some object*/;
    tmp1 = v1.f;
    v1.f = 42;
    tmp2 = v1.g;
}
```

A naïve insertion of permission checks would result in the following transformed code:

```
task T1() {
  v1 = /*some object*/;
  assert isReadable(v1, now);
  tmp1 = v1.f;
  assert isWritable(v1, now);
  v1.f = 42;
  assert isReadable(v1, now);
  tmp2 = v1.g;
}
```

Clearly, such redundant read and write checks on `v1` are unnecessary because no other task can take away the given permission of `T1()`.[2] By moving the checks as early as possible and then choosing the strongest permission check (here `isWritable()`), the example can be transformed into the optimized form with a single permission check:

```
task T1() {
  v1 = /*some object*/;
  assert isWritable(v1, now);
  tmp1 = v1.f;
  v1.f = 42;
  tmp2 = v1.g;
}
```

Handling Permission Operations: A permission operation such as `v1.yield-Permission(v2)` may change the type of permission the current task now has on `v1`. Therefore, subsequent accesses to `v1` require the compiler to insert permission checks again. Consider the following example, which is similar to the example from the previous section:

```
1  task T1() {
2    v1 = /*some object*/;
3    t1 = /*some task, may be ==now!*/;
4    assert isWritable(v1, now);
5    v1.f = 42;
6    v1.yieldPermission(t1);
7    //Need to check permission on v1 again!
8    assert isReadable(v1, now);
9    tmp2 = v1.g;
10 }
```

If `t1 != now`, the assertion on line 8 will always fail; however for the case where `t1 == now`, the same check will succeed. Therefore, the check on line 4 is not sufficient and the compiler must insert the read check on line 8.

To capture the effects of read and write checks in the control-flow graph, the compiler re-writes a permission operation such as `v1.addPermission(t1)` to define a new SSA variable: `v2 = v1.addPermission(t1)`. All subsequent uses of `v1` in the original control-flow graph are replaced by `v2`, inserting Φ-nodes when needed. Through this transformation (treating a permission operation as a definition of a new SSA variable), permission checks can be placed "as early as possible", grouping them directly after the SSA variable definition. After introducing the additional SSA variable definitions, the actual placement of access checks is done by rules INSERTREADCHECK and INSERTWRITECHECK described later in this section.

---

[2] A task may return its permission and make an earlier write check fail while a later check would succeed. For this reason, write checks cannot be moved across synchronization operations and racefully yielding a permission is not guaranteed to succeed.

3.2   Optimizing Permission Management

Permissions only have to be managed for objects that are potentially accessed in parallel. For task-local objects or for objects that are only accessed from tasks ordered by happens-before relationships, the management operations—including the implicit creation of the initial ACLs by new statements—are unnecessary and can be removed. Similarly, read and write checks only have to be performed on objects that may be accessed in parallel. To effectively decide on what a permission management operations are necessary, the compiler uses a schedule analysis to find tasks that may execute in parallel.

Schedule Analysis: The goal of the schedule analysis described in our previous work [10] is to determine whether at runtime two tasks may be executed in parallel or whether they are always ordered by happens-before relationships. Schedule analysis thus computes the relation $Task \times Task \rightarrow Rel$ where Rel is one of the following:

- Ordered: The two tasks are ordered if either all of their possible executions are ordered by (implicit or explicit) happens-before relationships or if they can never co-exist in a single run of the program (e.g., they are scheduled in different branches of a conditional statement).
- Parallel: If two tasks are not ordered, they are considered (potentially) parallel.

Figure 2 shows how the task-ordering information provided by the schedule analysis is combined with traditional points-to and escape information to compute the relation $conflicting(v1, \mathcal{A}, v2, \mathcal{B})$ containing sets of possibly conflicting variable accesses.[3]

Clauses (1a) and (1b) implement a reachability analysis that compute all pairs of tasks $\mathcal{A}$ and $\mathcal{B}$ that may access variables v1 and v2 respectively. The points-to analysis in clauses (2a) and (2b) then checks if the variables may actually reference the same object. If this is the case, clause (3) checks whether the corresponding object(s) can escape its (their) creating tasks. If an object does not escape its creating task it can be considered task-local and no conflicting accesses are possible. If the object may escape, the schedule analysis in clause

MAY-BE-CONFLICTING
$(1a)$ $\mathcal{A}$ MAY ACCESS $v1$
$(1b)$ $\mathcal{B}$ MAY WRITE $v2$
$(2a)$ $v1$ MAY POINT TO Obj
$(2b)$ $v2$ MAY POINT TO Obj
(3) Obj MAY ESCAPE $m1()$ **and** $m2()$
(4) PARALLEL $(\mathcal{A}, \mathcal{B})$
―――――――――――――――
$conflicting(v1, \mathcal{A}, v2, \mathcal{B})$

Fig. 2. Combining points-to, escape, and schedule analysis.

―――――――――――

[3] Note that an analysis-time task $\mathcal{A}$ can be potentially parallel with itself if at runtime several unordered instances of $\mathcal{A}$ may be created.

(4) computes, whether the accessing tasks $\mathcal{A}$ and $\mathcal{B}$ may execute in parallel. Only if all the above clauses are true, the compiler must conservatively assume that the accesses through variables v1 and v2 may conflict.

Auxiliary Rules: The optimizations for removing unnecessary permission operations and for finding optimized locations to insert permission checks make use of the helper functions shown in Fig. 3.

NEEDSREADCHECK–LOCAL

$$\frac{\mathcal{A} \text{ MAY READ } v1.f \quad \mathcal{B} \text{ MAY ACCESS } v2.f \quad conflicting(v1, \mathcal{A}, v2, \mathcal{B})}{needsReadCheck(v1)}$$

NEEDSREADCHECK–PHI

$$\frac{needsReadCheck(v1) \quad v1 = \Phi(\ldots, v2, \ldots)}{needsReadCheck(v2)}$$

NEEDSREADCHECK–GLOBAL

$$\frac{\text{METHOD CALL } v1.m(\ldots, v2, \ldots) \quad v1 \text{ MAY POINT TO } Base \quad f1 \text{ IS FORMAL PARAMETER FOR } v2 \text{ IN IMPLEMENTATION } Base.m(\ldots, f1, \ldots) \quad needsReadCheck(f1)}{needsReadCheck(v2)}$$

NEEDSWRITECHECK–LOCAL

$$\frac{\mathcal{A} \text{ MAY WRITE } v1.f \quad \mathcal{B} \text{ MAY ACCESS } v2.f \quad conflicting(v1, \mathcal{A}, v2, \mathcal{B})}{needsWriteCheck(v1)}$$

NEEDSWRITECHECK–PHI

$$\frac{needsWriteCheck(v1) \quad v1 = \Phi(\ldots, v2, \ldots)}{needsWriteCheck(v2)}$$

NEEDSWRITECHECK–GLOBAL

$$\frac{\text{METHOD CALL } v1.m(\ldots, v2, \ldots) \quad v1 \text{ MAY POINT TO } Base \quad f1 \text{ IS FORMAL PARAMETER FOR } v1 \text{ IN IMPLEMENTATION } Base.m(\ldots, f1, \ldots) \quad needsWriteCheck(f1)}{needsWriteCheck(v2)}$$

Fig. 3. Auxiliary functions used for optimizing dynamic fractional permissions.

The computation of variables that need a read check starts with rule NEEDS-READCHECK–LOCAL which selects all variables $v1$ that may point to objects that may be accessed in parallel by some other task. Rule NEEDSREADCHECK–PHI then propagates this information *backwards* across Φ nodes inside the surrounding method to mark all SSA variables that may reach the reading operation. NEEDSREADCHECK–GLOBAL globally pushes the access information about formal method parameters up to the callers. Placing the checks at the site whether a method is called instead of leaving them inside the called method optimizes the common case where utility functions are used with shared as well as local objects.

The rules for NEEDSWRITECHECK are functionally equivalent to the NEEDS-READCHECK but start from `read` and `write` operations respectively.

Optimization Rules: Figure 4 shows the optimizations for finding unnecessary permission management operations and for deciding on the locations, where read and write checks must be inserted.

UNNECESSARYOBJECTACL

Op_{new} is $v1 = $ **new** C () CREATING Obj
$v2$ MAY POINT TO Obj
not $needsReadCheck(v2)$
not $needsWriteCheck(v2)$
___
$unnecessaryObjectACL(Op_{new})$

UNNECESSARYPERMISSIONOPERATION

Op_1 is $v1.\{yield \mid add\}Permision(v3)$
$v1$ MAY POINT TO Obj
$v2$ MAY POINT TO Obj
not $needsReadCheck(v2)$
not $needsWriteCheck(v2)$
___
$unnecessaryPermissionOperation(Op_1)$

INSERTREADCHECK

Op_1 DEFINES $v1$ ($v1$ IS NOT A Φ **or** A *formal method param*)
not $needsWriteCheck(v1)$
$needsReadCheck(v1)$
___
$insertReadCheck(Op_1)$

INSERTWRITECHECK

Op_1 DEFINES $v1$ ($v1$ IS NOT A Φ **or** A *formal method param*)
$needsWriteCheck(v1)$
___
$insertWriteCheck(Op_1)$

Fig. 4. Rules used by the compiler to remove unnecessary permission operations and to decide where read and write checks must be inserted.

UNNECESSARYOBJECTACL selects operations Op_{new} corresponding to new-statements that create objects Obj that are never accessed in parallel. For unnecessary Op_{new}, the permission system does not need to create an initial access control list, because no permission check is ever done for the corresponding object.

Similarly, UNNECESSARYPERMISSIONOPERATION chooses all operations Op_1 corresponding to permission management that are performed on objects that never appear in permission checks.

The INSERTREADCHECK and INSERTWRITECHECK rules implement the mechanism for grouping permission checks described earlier. Both rules select the earliest operations Op_1 defining an SSA variable $v1$ without Op_1 being a Φ node or formal method parameter. For parameters to task methods, we decided to place the permission checks at the beginning of a task, however, since there is no obvious advantage of pushing those checks to the creating task. As noted earlier, the compiler treats permission operations as defining statements and therefore will add permission checks whenever the corresponding ACLs may have changed.

4   Evaluation

This section presents the performance evaluation of the dynamic fractional permission system. We compare four different optimization configurations with the original versions of the benchmarks that do not use a permission system.

All experiments were run on a machine equipped with a Intel Core 2 Duo 2.8 GHz and 4 Gb of RAM. The compiler implementation is single threaded, however, and therefore only one core is used during the compilation.

The benchmarks are taken from the ERCO project [14] and were chosen because of their object-oriented parallelism where objects are used for inter-task communication as opposed to numeric matrix and vector based applications such as the Java Grande benchmarks [15]. sor (successive over-relaxation over a 2D grid), and `tsp` (traveling salesman problem) are data- and task-parallel applications with data access patterns of scientific codes; threads are synchronized in a fork/join style based on barriers instead of locks. `hedc` is a warehouse for scientific astrophysics data that implements a meta crawler for searching multiple Internet archives in parallel. The individual queries are handled by reusable worker threads. `philo` is a simulation of the dining philosophers problem. `elevator` is a real-time discrete event simulator where elevators are modeled as individual tasks that poll directives from a central control board. Communication through the control board is synchronized through locks.

The effects of the individual optimization parts were evaluated by compiling the benchmarks in four different configurations:

- In the `None` configuration, the compiler has no advanced analysis information and must insert read and write checks on every memory access.
- In the `Grouping` configuration, redundant permission checks are avoided. While being a global optimization, this configuration does neither use escape nor schedule analysis information. This is achieved by removing clauses (3) and (4) of the MAY-BE-CONFLICTING rule in Fig. 2.
- The third configuration `ESC` uses an escape analysis plus a points-to analysis to decide whether two memory accesses executed by different tasks may conflict (clause (3) but not clause (4) of Fig. 2).
- The third configuration `ESC+SA` adds scheduling information to the points-to analysis and escape analysis to make the optimizations task aware.

Figure 5 shows the runtime overhead of the benchmarks compiled with the `None`, `Grouping`, `ESC`, and `ESC+SA` configurations. The baseline of this comparison is the runtime of the original version without the dynamic fractional permission system.

For three of the five benchmarks, the fully optimized version (`ESC+SA`) is within 10 % of the original version. The average performance overhead over all

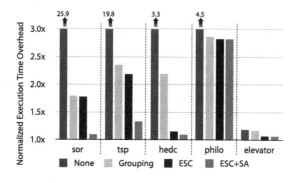

Fig. 5. Runtime overhead of different optimization levels for dynamic fractional permissions compared to the original version without a dynamic fractional permission system.

benchmarks is 48 % which can be attributed to the poor performance of the `philo` benchmark. (Without `philo`, the average overhead is 15 %.)

In the `philo` benchmark, most objects are shared and accessed concurrently and the compiler cannot remove expensive permission checks. This overhead could be reduced significantly by making the compiler aware of `immutable-Permission()` and `sharedPermission()` operations. The compiler does not need to insert read (read/write) permission checks if it knows that an object has been flagged as immutable (shared). The current implementation of the optimizations does not know about immutable and shared permissions, however, and therefore does insert unnecessary read and write checks in the `philo` benchmark.

5   Related Work

Fractional permissions: Boyland's work on fractional permissions [3] introduces a permission system where a single write permission of value 1 can be split into infinitely many read permissions with values < 1. Permission fractions can be distributed to subtasks and later reclaimed. If the system can prove that a task has the original write permission or that it has successfully reclaimed all fractions of the read permissions, the task can write the data. Because fractional permissions guarantee that only one task at a time can have the full write permission, data races are impossible. Terauchi [16,17] and Boyland [18] later presented further improvements for inferring fractional permissions. As opposed to the dynamic fractional permissions presented in this paper, the previous work on fractional permissions focus on static techniques to prove data-race freedom and therefore may statically reject programs that are otherwise safe.

SP-bags: The basic idea behind SP-bags, introduced by Feng and Leiserson's [19] and further refined by Raman et al. [20], is to attach two bags, S and P, to each task. Each bag contains task IDs of descendent tasks that logically precede the task or that operate in parallel respectively. Each memory location is instrumented to contain two additional fields, a reader task ID and a writer task ID. Every time a shared memory location is accessed by a task, the algorithm uses the S and P bags to check whether the current task can interfere with the task that is recorded in the reader and/or writer fields. SP-bags share some similarities with the dynamic fractional permissions but instead of the tasks managing their own bags, dynamic fractional permissions use access control lists on objects. It is an open question, however, whether one approach is more flexible than the other or whether they are equally expressive.

Dynamic data-race detection: Dynamic data-race detectors basically fall into two categories: precise detection, such as the RaceTrack [21] and FastTrack [9] detectors, where every memory operation is checked for data races; and detectors based on sampling, such as LiteRace [22] and Pacer [23]. With sampling, not every memory access is checked but periodic samples are scanned for potential data races. Sampling therefore deliberately introduces some imprecision for the benefit of increased performance. Dynamic fractional permissions do check every memory access and therefore fall under the category of precise detection. However, while the above data-race checkers do not impose any restrictions on the programmer, dynamic fractional permissions do enforce explicit permission management.

6   Concluding Remarks

This paper introduces a dynamic variant of fractional permissions where the programmer manually manages the splitting and recovering of permissions. The manual management forces the programmer to come up with a rigid data management scheme and replaces the common ad-hoc approaches of current languages.

Permissions are maintained and checked at runtime. In the worst case, every read and write access to an object requires checking the permission of the current task, which introduces a significant runtime overhead. The optimizing compiler presented this paper makes use of a combination of points-to, escape, and schedule analysis to remove permission checks whenever possible, significantly reducing the overhead associated with fractional permissions.

References

1. Lu, S., Park, S., Seo, E., Zhou, Y.: Learning from mistakes: a comprehensive study on real world concurrency bug characteristics. SIGOPS Oper. Syst. Rev. **42**, 329–339 (2008)
2. Matsakis, N.D., Gross, T.R.: A time-aware type system for data-race protection and guaranteed initialization. In: OOPSLA '10, pp. 634–651. ACM, New York (2010)
3. Boyland, J.: Checking interference with fractional permissions. In: Cousot, R. (ed.) SAS 2003. LNCS, vol. 2694, pp. 55–72. Springer, Heidelberg (2003)
4. Moir, M.: Transparent support for wait-free transactions. In: Mavronicolas, M. (ed.) WDAG 1997. LNCS, vol. 1320, pp. 305–319. Springer, Heidelberg (1997)
5. Harris, T., Fraser, K.: Language support for lightweight transactions. In: OOPSLA '03, pp. 388–402. ACM, New York (2003)
6. Adl-Tabatabai, A.R., Kozyrakis, C., Saha, B.: Transactional programming in a multi-core environment. In: PPoPP '07, p. 272. ACM, New York (2007)
7. Musuvathi, M., Qadeer, S.: Iterative context bounding for systematic testing of multithreaded programs. In: PLDI '07, pp. 446–455. ACM, New York (2007)
8. Qadeer, S., Wu, D.: Kiss: keep it simple and sequential. In: PLDI '04, pp. 14–24. ACM, New York (2004)
9. Flanagan, C., Freund, S.N.: Fasttrack: efficient and precise dynamic race detection. In: PLDI '09, pp. 121–133. ACM, New York (2009)
10. Angerer, C.M., Gross, T.R.: Exploiting task order information for optimizing sequentially consistent java programs. In: PACT '11, pp. 393–402 (2011)
11. Angerer, C.M., Gross, T.R.: Static analysis of dynamic schedules and its application to optimization of parallel programs. In: Cooper, K., Mellor-Crummey, J., Sarkar, V. (eds.) LCPC 2010. LNCS, vol. 6548, pp. 16–30. Springer, Heidelberg (2011)

12. Dean, J., Ghemawat, S.: Mapreduce: simplified data processing on large clusters. In: OSDI '04, p. 10. USENIX Association, Berkeley (2004)
13. Angerer, C.M., Gross, T.R.: Now happens-before later: static schedule analysis of fine-grained parallelism with explicit happens-before relationships. In: Onward!/SPLASH '10, pp. 3–10. ACM, New York (2010)
14. von Praun, C., Gross, T.R.: Object race detection. SIGPLAN Not. **36**, 70–82 (2001)
15. Smith, L.A., Bull, J.M., Obdrzálek, J.: A parallel java grande benchmark suite. In: Supercomputing '01, p. 8. ACM, New York (2001)
16. Terauchi, T.: Checking race freedom via linear programming. In: PLDI '08, pp. 1–10. ACM, New York (2008)
17. Terauchi, T., Aiken, A.: A capability calculus for concurrency and determinism. ACM Trans. Program. Lang. Syst. **30**, 27:1–27:30 (2008)
18. Boyland, J.T.: Semantics of fractional permissions with nesting. ACM Trans. Program. Lang. Syst. **32**, 22:1–22:33 (2010)
19. Feng, M., Leiserson, C.E.: Efficient detection of determinacy races in cilk programs. In: SPAA '97, pp. 1–11. ACM, New York (1997)
20. Raman, R., Zhao, J., Sarkar, V., Vechev, M., Yahav, E.: Efficient data race detection for async-finish parallelism. In: Barringer, H., et al. (eds.) RV 2010. LNCS, vol. 6418, pp. 368–383. Springer, Heidelberg (2010)
21. Yu, Y., Rodeheffer, T., Chen, W.: Racetrack: efficient detection of data race conditions via adaptive tracking. In: SOSP '05, pp. 221–234. ACM, New York (2005)
22. Marino, D., Musuvathi, M., Narayanasamy, S.: Literace: effective sampling for lightweight data-race detection. In: PLDI '09, pp. 134–143. ACM, New York (2009)
23. Bond, M.D., Coons, K.E., McKinley, K.S.: Pacer: proportional detection of data races. In: PLDI '10, pp. 255–268. ACM, New York (2010)

Near Optimal Work-Stealing Tree Scheduler for Highly Irregular Data-Parallel Workloads

Aleksandar Prokopec[✉] and Martin Odersky

École Polytechnique Fédérale de Lausanne, Lausanne, Switzerland
aleksandar.prokopec@gmail.com, martin.odersky@epfl.ch

Abstract. We present a work-stealing algorithm for runtime scheduling of data-parallel operations in the context of shared-memory architectures on data sets with highly-irregular workloads that are not known a priori to the scheduler. This scheduler can parallelize loops and operations expressible with a parallel reduce or a parallel scan. The scheduler is based on the work-stealing tree data structure, which allows workers to decide on the work division in a lock-free, workload-driven manner and attempts to minimize the amount of communication between them. A significant effort is given to showing that the algorithm has the least possible amount of overhead.

We provide an extensive experimental evaluation, comparing the advantages and shortcomings of different data-parallel schedulers in order to combine their strengths. We show specific workload distribution patterns appearing in practice for which different schedulers yield suboptimal speedup, explaining their drawbacks and demonstrating how the work-stealing tree scheduler overcomes them. We thus justify our design decisions experimentally, but also provide a theoretical background for our claims.

1 Introduction

In data-parallel programming models parallelism is not expressed as a set process interactions but as a sequence of parallel operations on data sets. Programs are typically composed from high-level data-parallel operations, and are declarative rather than imperative in nature, which is of particular interest when it comes to programming the ever more present multicore systems. Solutions to many computational problems contain elements which can be expressed in terms of data-parallel operations [12].

We show several examples of data-parallel programs in Fig. 1. These programs rely heavily on higher-order data-parallel operations such as map, reduce and filter, which take a function argument – they are parametrized by a mapping function, a reduction operator or a filtering predicate, respectively. The first example in Fig. 1 computes the variance of a set of measurements ms. It starts by computing the mean value using the higher-order operation sum, and then maps each element of ms into a set of squared distances from the mean value, the sum of which divided by the number of elements is the variance v. The amount of work executed

© Springer International Publishing Switzerland 2014
C. Caşcaval and P. Montesinos (Eds.): LCPC 2013, LNCS 8664, pp. 55–86, 2014.
DOI: 10.1007/978-3-319-09967-5_4

for each measurement value is equal, so we call this workload *uniform*. This need not be always so. The second program computes all the prime numbers from 3 until N by calling a data-parallel `filter` on the corresponding range. The `filter` uses a predicate that checks that no number from 2 to $\sqrt{i}$ divides i. The workload is not uniform nor independent of i and the processors working on the end of the range need to do more work. This example also demonstrates that data-parallelism can be *nested* – the `forall` can be done in parallel as each element may require a lot of work. On the other hand, the `reduce` in the third program that computes a sum of numbers from 0 to N requires a minimum amount of work for each element. A good data-parallel scheduler must be efficient for all the workloads – when executed with a single processor the `reduce` in the third program must have the same running time as the `while` loop in the fourth program, the data-parallelism of which is not immediately obvious due to its imperative style.

```
1 val sz = ms.size        1 val r = 3 until N      1 val r = 0 until N      1 var sum = 0
2 val a = ms.sum / sz     2 val ps = r filter {    2 val sum = r reduce {   2 var i = 0
3 val ds = ms map {       3   i =>                  3   (acc, i) =>           3 while (i < N) {
4   x => (x - avg)^2      4     2 to ⌈√i⌉ forall {  4     acc + i             4   sum += i
5 }                       5       d => i % d != 0   5 }                       5   i += 1
6 val v = ds.sum / sz     6   }                                             6 }
                          7 }
```

Fig. 1. Data parallel program examples

It has been a trend in many languages to provide data-parallel bulk operations on collections [3–5, 17, 18]. Data-parallel operations are generic as shown in Fig. 1 – for example, `reduce` takes a user-provided operator, such as number addition, string concatenation or matrix multiplication. The computational costs of these generic parts, and hence the workload distribution, cannot always be determined statically, so efficient assignment of work to processors often relies on the runtime scheduling. Scheduling in this case entails dividing the elements into batches on which the processors work in isolation. Work-stealing [1, 7, 8, 15, 20] is one solution to this problem. In this technique different processors occasionally steal batches from each other to load balance the work – the goal is that no processor stays idle for too long.

In this paper we propose and describe a runtime scheduler for data-parallel operations on shared-memory architectures that uses a variant of work-stealing to ensure proper load-balancing. The scheduler relies on a novel data structure with lock-free synchronization operations called the **work-stealing tree**. To show that the work-stealing tree scheduler is optimal we focus on evaluating scheduler performance on uniform workloads with a minimum amount of computation per element, irregular workloads for which this amount varies and workloads with a very coarse granularity.

Our algorithm is based on the following assumptions. There are no fast, accurate means to measure elapsed time with sub-microsecond precision, i.e. there is no way to measure the running time. There is no static or runtime information about the cost of an operation – when invoking a data-parallel operation we do not know how much computation each element requires. There are no hardware-level interrupt handling mechanisms at our disposal – the only way to interrupt a computation is to have the processor check a condition. We assume OS threads as parallelism primitives, with no control over the scheduler. We assume that the available synchronization primitives are monitors and the CAS instruction. We assume the presence of automatic memory management.

The rest of the paper is organized as follows. Section 2 describes related work and alternative schedulers we compare against. Section 3 describes the work-stealing tree scheduler. In Sect. 4 we evaluate the scheduler for different workloads as well as tune several of its parameters, and in Sect. 5 we conclude.

2   Related Work

Per processor (henceforth, worker) work assignment done statically during compile time or linking, to which we will refer to as *static batching*, was studied extensively [13,19]. Static batching cannot correctly predict workload distributions for any problem, as shown by the second program in Fig. 1. Without knowing the numbers in the set exactly, batches cannot be statically assigned to workers in an optimal way – some workers may end up with more work than the others. Still, although cost analysis is not the focus here, we advocate combining static analysis with runtime techniques.

To address the need for load balancing at runtime, work can be divided into a lot of small batches. Only once each worker processes its batch, it requests a new batch from a centralized queue. We will refer to this as *fixed-size batching* [14]. In fixed-size batching the workload itself dictates the way how work is assigned to workers. This is a major difference with respect to static batching. In general, in the absence of information about the workload distribution, scheduling should be *workload-driven*. A natural question arises – what is the ideal size for a batch? Ideally, a batch should consist of a single element, but the cost of requesting work from a centralized queue is prohibitively large for that. For example, replacing the increment `i += 1` with an atomic CAS can increase the running time of a `while` loop by nearly a magnitude on modern architectures. The batch size has to be the least number of elements for which the cost of accessing the queue is amortized by the actual work. There are two issues with this technique. First, it is not scalable – as the number of workers increases, so does contention on the work queue (Fig. 6). This requires increasing batch sizes further. Second, as the granularity approaches the batch size, the work division is not fine-grained and the speedup is suboptimal (Fig. 8, where size is less than 1024).

Guided self-scheduling [16] solves some granularity issues by dynamically choosing the batch size based on the number of remaining elements. At any point, the batch size is R_i/P, where R_i is the number of remaining elements and P is the number of workers – the granularity becomes finer as there is less and less work. Note that the first-arriving worker is assigned the largest batch of work. If this batch contains more work than the rest of the loop due to irregularity, the speedup will not be linear. This is shown in Figs. 8-20 and 9-35.

Factoring [10] and *trapezoidal self-scheduling* [21] improve on guided-self scheduling, but have the same issue with those workload distributions.

One way to overcome the contention issues inherent to the techniques above is to use several work queues rather than a centralized queue. In this approach each processor starts with some initial work on its queue and commonly steals from other queues when it runs out of work – this is known as *work-stealing*, a technique applicable to both task- and data-parallelism. One of the first uses of work-stealing dates to the Cilk language [2,8], in which processors relied on the fast and slow version of the code to steal stack frames from each other. Recent developments in the X10 language are based on similar techniques [20]. Work-stealing typically relies on the use of work-stealing queues [1,7,8,15] and deques [6], implementations ranging from blocking to lock-free. While in the past data-parallel collections frameworks relied on using task-parallel schedulers under the hood [11,17,18], to the best of our knowledge, the tree data structure was not used for synchronization in work-stealing prior to this work, nor for data-parallel operation scheduling.

3   Work-Stealing Tree Scheduler

In this section we describe the work-stealing tree data structure and the scheduling algorithm that the workers run. We first briefly discuss the aforementioned fixed-size batching. We have mentioned that the contention on the centralized queue is one of it drawbacks. We could replace the centralized queue with a queue for each worker and use work-stealing. However, this seems overly eager – we do not want to create as many work queues as there are workers for each parallel operation, as doing so may outweigh the actually useful work. We should start with a single queue and create additional ones on-demand. Furthermore, fixed-size batching seems appropriate for scheduling parallel loops, but what about the reduce operation? If each worker stores its own intermediate results separately, then the reduce may not be applicable to non-commutative operators (e.g. string concatenation). It seems reasonable to have the work-stealing data-structure store the intermediate results, since it has the division order information.

With this in mind, we note that a tree seems particularly applicable. When created it consists merely of a single node – a root representing the operation and all the elements of the range. The worker invoking the parallel operation can work on the elements and update its progress by writing to the node it owns. If it completes before any other worker requests work, then the overhead of the operation is merely creating the root. Conversely, if another worker arrives, it can steal some of the work by creating two child nodes, splitting the elements and continuing work on one of them. This proceeds recursively. Scheduling is thus workload-driven – nodes are created only when some worker runs out of work meaning that another worker had too much work. Such a tree can also store intermediate results in the nodes, serving as a reduction tree.

How can such a tree be used for synchronization and load-balancing? We assumed that the parallelism primitives are OS threads. We can keep a pool of threads [15] that are notified when a parallel operations is invoked – we call these workers. We first describe the worker algorithm from a high-level perspective. Each worker starts by calling the tail-recursive `run` method in Fig. 2. It looks for a node in the tree that is either not already owned or steals a node which some other worker works on by calling `findWork` in line 3. This node is initially a leaf, but we call it a subtree. The worker works on the subtree by calling `descend` in line 5, which calls `workOn` on the root of the subtree to work on it until it is either completed or stolen. In the case of a steal, the worker continues work on one of the children if it can own it in line 11. This is repeated until `findWork` returns ⊥ (`null`), indicating that all the work is completed.

```
struct Ptr              1 def run(): Unit =          7 def descend(leaf: Ptr): Unit =
   child: Node          2   val leaf =               8   val nosteals = workOn(leaf)
struct Node             3     findWork(root)         9   if (¬nosteals)
   left, right: Ptr     4   if (leaf ≠ ⊥)           10     val sub = READ(leaf.child).left
   start, until: Int    5     descend(leaf)         11     if (tryOwn(READ(sub.child)))
   progress: Int        6     run()                 12       descend(subnode)
   owner: Owner
```

Fig. 2. Work-stealing tree data-types and the scheduling algorithm

In Fig. 2 we also present the *work-stealing tree* and its basic data-types. We use the keyword `struct` to refer to a compound data-type – this can be a Java class or a C structure. We define two compound data-types. `Ptr` is a reference to the tree – it has only a single member `child` of type `Node`. Write access to `child` has to be atomic and globally visible (in Java, this is ensured with the `volatile` keyword). `Node` contains immutable references to the `left` and `right` subtree, initialized upon instantiation. If these are set to ⊥ we consider the node a leaf. We initially focus on parallelizing loops over ranges, so we encode the current state of iteration with three integers. Members `start` and `until` are immutable and denote the initial range – for the root of the tree this is the entire loop range. Member `progress` has atomic, globally visible write access. It is initially set to `start` and is updated as elements are processed. Finally, the `owner` field denotes the worker that is working on the node. It is initially ⊥ and also has atomic write access. Example trees are shown in Fig. 3.

Before we describe the operations and the motivation behind these data-types we will define the states work-stealing tree can be in (see Fig. 3), namely its invariants. This is of particular importance for concurrent data structures which have non-blocking operations. Work-stealing tree operations are lock-free, a well-known advantage [9], which comes at the cost of little extra complexity in this case.

INV1. Whenever a new node reference `Ptr` p becomes reachable in the tree, it initially points to a *leaf* `Node` n, such that `n.owner` = ⊥. Field `n.progress` is set to `n.start` and `n.until`≥`n.start`. The subtree is in the AVAILABLE state and its range is ⟨`n.start`,`n.until`⟩.

INV2. The set of transitions of n.owner is $\perp \to \pi \neq \perp$. No other field of n can be written until n.owner $\neq \perp$. After this happens, the subtree is in the OWNED state.

INV3. The set of transitions of n.progress in the OWNED state is $p_0 \to p_1 \to \ldots \to p_k$ such that n.start $= p_0 < p_1 < \ldots < p_k <$ n.until. If a worker π writes a value from this set of transitions to n.progress, then n.owner $= \pi$.

INV4. If the worker n.owner writes the value n.until to n.progress, then that is the last transition of n.progress. The subtree goes into the COMPLETED state.

INV5. If a worker ψ overwrites p_i, such that n.start $\leq p_i <$ n.until, with $p_s = -p_i - 1$, then $\psi \neq$ n.owner. This is the last transition of n.progress and the subtree goes into the STOLEN state.

INV6. The field p.child can be overwritten only in the STOLEN state, in which case its transition is $n \to m$, where m is a copy of n with m.left and m.right being fresh leaves in the AVAILABLE state with ranges $r_l = \langle x_0, x_1 \rangle$ and $r_r = \langle x_1, x_2 \rangle$ such that $r_l \cup r_r = \langle p_i, \text{n.until} \rangle$. The subtree goes into the EXPANDED state.

This seemingly complicated set of invariants can be summarized in a straightforward way. Upon owning a leaf, that worker processes elements from that leaf's range by incrementing the **progress** field until either it processes all elements or another worker requests some work by invalidating **progress**, in which case the leaf is replaced by a subtree such that the remaining work is divided between the new leaves.

Now that we have formally defined a valid work-stealing tree, we provide an implementation of the basic operations (Fig. 4). These operations will be the building blocks for the scheduling algorithm that balances the workload. A worker must attempt to acquire ownership of a node before processing its elements by calling the method **tryOwn**, which returns **true** if the claim is successful. After reading the **owner** field in line 14 and establishing the AVAILABLE state, the worker attempts to atomically push the node into the OWNED state with the CAS in line 15. This CAS can fail either due to a faster worker claiming ownership or spuriously – a retry follows in both cases.

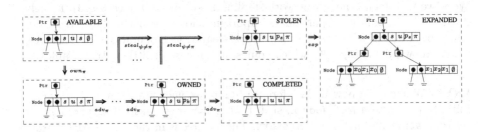

Fig. 3. Work-stealing subtree state diagram

```
13 def tryOwn(n: Node): Boolean =
14   if (READ(n.owner) ≠ ⊥) false
15   else if (CAS(n.owner, ⊥, π)) true
16   else tryOwn(n)
17
18 def tryAdvance(n: Node, p: Int): Int =
19   val q = min(p + STEP, n.until)
20   if (¬CAS(n.progress, p, q)) -1
21   else q - p
22
23 def isLeaf(n: Node): Boolean =
24   n.left == ⊥
25
26 def isEligible(n: Node): Boolean =
27   n.until - READ(n.progress) > 1

28 def trySteal(ptr: Ptr): Boolean =
29   val c_t0 = READ(ptr.child)
30   if (¬isLeaf(c_t0)) true else
31     val p_t1 = READ(c_t0.progress)
32     if (p_t1 == c_t0.until) false
33     else if (p_t1 ≥ 0)
34       val negp = -p_t1 - 1
35       CAS(c_t0.progress, p_t1, negp)
36       trySteal(ptr)
37     else
38       val c_exp = newExpanded(c_t0)
39       if (CAS(ptr.child, c_t0, c_exp))
40         true
41       else trySteal(ptr)
```

Fig. 4. Basic work-stealing tree operations

A worker that claimed ownership of a node repetitively calls `tryAdvance`, which attempts to reserve a batch of size **STEP** by atomically incrementing the **progress** field, eventually bringing the node into the COMPLETED state. If `tryAdvance` returns a nonnegative number, the owner is obliged to process that many elements, whereas a negative number is an indication that the node was stolen.

A worker searching for work must call `trySteal` if it finds a node in the OWNED state. This method returns **true** if the node was successfully brought into the EXPANDED state by any worker, or **false** if the node ends up in the COMPLETED state. Method `trySteal` consists of two steps. First, it attempts to push the node into the STOLEN state with the CAS in line 35 after determining that the node read in line 29 is a leaf. This CAS can fail either due to a different steal, a successful `tryAdvance` call or spuriously. Successful CAS in line 35 brings the node into the STOLEN state. Irregardless of success or failure, `trySteal` is then called recursively. In the second step, the expanded version of the node from Fig. 3 is created by the `newExpanded` method, the pseudocode of which is not shown here since it consists of isolated singlethreaded code. The `child` field in `Ptr` is replaced with the expanded version atomically with the CAS in line 39, bringing the node into the EXPANDED state.

We now describe the scheduling algorithm that the workers execute by invoking the `run` method. There are two basic modes of operation a worker alternates between. First, it calls `findWork`, which returns a node in the AVAILABLE state (line 3). Then, it calls `descend` to work on that node until it is stolen or completed, which calls `workOn` to process the elements. If `workOn` returns **false**, then the node was stolen and the worker tries to descend one of the subtrees rather than searching the entire tree for work. This decreases the total number of `findWork` invocations. The method `workOn` checks if the node is in the OWNED state (line 47), and then attempts to atomically increase **progress** by calling `tryAdvance`. The worker is obliged to process the elements after a successful advance, and does so by calling the `kernel` method, which is nothing more than the `while` loop like the one in Fig. 1. Generally, `kernel` can be any kind of a workload. Finally, method `findWork` traverses the tree left to right and whenever it finds a leaf node it tries to claim ownership. Otherwise, it attempts to steal it until it finds that it is either COMPLETED or EXPANDED, returning ⊥ or descending deeper, respectively. Nodes with 1 or less elements left are skipped.

We explore alternative findWork implementations in Sect. 4. For now, we state but do not prove the following claim. If the method findWork does return ⊥, then all the work in the tree was obtained by different workers that had called tryAdvance except $M < P$ loop elements distributed across M leaf nodes where P is the number of workers. This follows from the fact that the tree grows monotonically.

```
42 def workOn(ptr: Ptr): Boolean =
43   val node = READ(ptr.child)
44   var batch = -1
45   do
46     val p = READ(node.progress)
47     if (p >= 0 ∧ p < node.until)
48       batch = tryAdvance(node, p)
49       if (batch ≠ -1)
50         kernel(p, p + batch)
51     else batch = -1
52   while (batch ≠ -1)
53   if (READ(node.progress) ≥ 0)
54     true
55   else
56     trySteal(ptr)
57   false
```

```
58 def findWork(ptr: Ptr): Node =
59   val node = READ(ptr.child)
60   if (isLeaf(node))
61     if (tryOwn(node)) node
62     else if (¬isEligible(node)) ⊥
63     else if (¬trySteal(ptr))
64       findWork(ptr)
65     else
66       val right = node.right
67       if (tryOwn(READ(right.child)))
68         READ(right.child)
69       else findWork(ptr)
70   else
71     val leftsub = findWork(node.left)
72     if (leftsub ≠ ⊥) leftsub
73     else findWork(node.right)
```

Fig. 5. Scheduling algorithm

Note that workOn is similar to fixed-size batching – the only difference is that an arrival of a worker invalidates the node here, whereas multiple workers simultaneously call tryAdvance in fixed-size batching, synchronizing repetitively. The next section starts by evaluating the impact this has on performance.

4   Evaluation

As hinted in the introduction, we want to evaluate how good our scheduler is for uniform workloads with a low amount of work per element. The reasons for this are twofold – first, we want to compare speedups against an optimal sequential program. Second, such problems appear in practical applications. We thus ensure that the third and fourth program from Fig. 1 really have the same performance for a single processor. We will call the while loop from Fig. 1 the *sequential baseline*.

Parallelizing the baseline seems trivial. Assuming the workers start at roughly the same time and have roughly the same speed, we can divide the range in equal parts between them. However, an assumption from the introduction was that the workload distribution is not known and the goal is to parallelize irregular workloads as well. In fact, the workload may have a coarse granularity, consisting only of several elements.

For the reasons above, we verify that the scheduler abides the following criteria:

C1 There is no noticeable overhead when executing the baseline with a single worker.

C2 Speedup is optimal for both the baseline and typical irregular workloads.

C3 Speedup is optimal when the work granularity equals the parallelism level.

Workloads we choose correspond to those found in practice. Uniform workloads are particularly common and correspond to numeric computations, text manipulation, Monte Carlo methods and applications that involve basic linear algebra operations like vector addition or matrix multiplication. In Fig. 8 we denote this workload as UNIFORM. Triangular workloads are present in primality testing, multiplication with triangular matrices and computing an adjoint convolution (TRIANGLE). In higher dimensions computing a convolution consists of several nested loops and can have a polynomial workload distribution (PARABOLA). Depending on how the problem is formulated, the workload may be increasing or decreasing (INVTRIANGLE, HILL, VALLEY). In combinatorial problems such as word segmentation, bin packing or computing anagrams the problem subdivision can be such that the subproblems corresponding to different elements differ exponentially – we model this with an exponentially increasing workload EXP. In raytracing, PageRank or sparse matrix multiplication the workload corresponds to some probability distribution, modelled with workloads GAUSSIAN and RANDIF. Finally, in problems like Mandelbrot set computation or Barnes-Hut simulation we have large conglomeration of elements which require a lot of computation while the rest require almost no work. We call this workload distribution STEP.

All the tests were performed on an Intel i7 3.4 GHz quad-core processor with hyperthreading and Oracle JDK 1.7, using the server VM. Our implementation is written in the Scala programming language, which uses the JVM as its backend. JVM programs are commonly regarded as less efficient than programs written in C. To show that the evaluation is comparative to a C implementation, we must evaluate the performance of corresponding sequential C programs. The running time of the `while` loop from Fig. 1 is roughly 45 ms for 150 million elements in both C (GNU C++ 4.2) and on the JVM – if we get linear speedups then we can conclude that the scheduler is indeed optimal. We can thus turn our attention to criteria C1.

We stated already that the STEP value should ideally be 1 for load-balancing purposes, but has to be more coarse-grained due to communication costs that could overwhelm the baseline. In Fig. 6A we plot the running time against the STEP size, obtained by executing the baseline loop with a single worker. By finding the minimum STEP value with no observable overhead, we seek to satisfy criteria C1. The minimum STEP with no noticeable synchronization costs is around 50 elements – decreasing STEP to 16 doubles the execution time and for value 1 the execution time is 36 times larger (not shown for readability).

Having shown that the work-stealing tree is as good as fixed-size batching, we evaluate its effectiveness with multiple workers. Figure 6B shows that the mini-

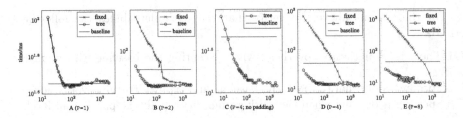

Fig. 6. Baseline running time (ms) vs. STEP size

mum STEP for fixed-size batching increases for 2 workers, as we postulated earlier. Increasing STEP decreases the frequency of synchronization and the communication costs with it. In this case the 3x slowdown is caused by processors having to exchange ownership of the `progress` field cache-line. The work-stealing tree does not suffer from this problem, since it strives to keep processors isolated – the speedup is linear with 2 workers. However, with 4 processors the performance of the naive work-stealing tree implementation is degraded (Fig. 6C). While the reason is not immediately apparent, note that for greater STEP values the speedup is once again linear. Inspecting the number of elements processed in each node reveals that the uniform workload is not evenly distributed among the topmost nodes – communication costs in those nodes are higher due to *false sharing*. Even though the two processors work on different nodes, they modify the same cache line, slowing down the CAS in line 20. Why this exactly happens in the implementation that follows directly from the pseudocode is beyond the scope of this paper, but it suffices to say that padding the node object with dummy fields to adjust its size to the cache line solves this problem, as shown in Fig. 6D, E.

The speedup is still not completely linear as the number of workers grows. Our baseline does not access main memory and only touches cache lines in exclusive mode, so this may be due to worker wakeup delay or scheduling costs in the work-stealing tree. After checking that increasing the total amount of work does not change performance, we focus on the latter. Inspecting the number of tree nodes created at different parallelism levels in Fig. 7B reveals that as the number of workers grows, the number of nodes grows at a superlinear rate. Each node incurs a synchronization cost, so could we decrease their total number?

Examining a particular work-stealing tree instance at the end of the operation reveals that different workers are battling for work in the left subtree until all the elements are depleted, whereas the right subtree remains unowned during this time. As a result, the workers in any subtree steal from each other more often, hence creating more nodes. The cause is the left-to-right tree traversal in `findWork` as defined in Fig. 5, a particularly bad stealing strategy we will call **Predefined**. As shown in Fig. 7B, the average tree size for 8 workers nears 2500 nodes. So, lets try to change the preference of a worker by changing the tree-traversal order in line 70 based on the worker index i and the level l in the tree. The worker should go left-to-right if and only if $(i \gg (l \bmod \lceil \log_2 P \rceil)) \bmod 2 = 1$ where P is the total number of workers. This way, the first path from the root to a leaf up to depth $\log_2 P$ is unique for each worker. The choice of the subtree after a steal in lines 10 and 66 is also changed like this – the detailed implementation of findWork for this and other strategies is shown in the appendix. This strategy, which we call **Assign**, decreases the average tree size at $P = 8$ to 134. Interestingly, we can do even better by doing this assignment only if the node depth is below $\log_2 P$ and randomizing the traversal order otherwise. We call this strategy **AssignTop** – it decreases the average tree size at $P = 8$ to 77. Building on the randomization idea, we introduce an additional strategy called **RandomWalk** where the traversal order in findWork is completely randomized. However, this results in a lower throughput and bigger tree sizes. Additionally randomizing the choice in lines 10 and 66 (**RandomAll**) is even less helpful, since the stealer and the victim clash more often.

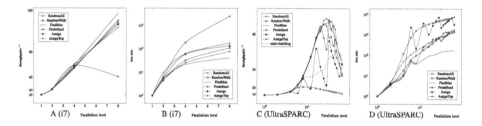

Fig. 7. Comparison of findWork implementations

The results of the five different strategies mentioned thus far lead to the following observation. If a randomized strategy like **RandomWalk** or **AssignTop** works better than a suboptimal strategy like **Predefined** then some of its random choices are beneficial to the overall execution time and some are disadvantageous. So, there must exist an even better strategy which only makes the choices that lead to a better execution time. Rather than providing a theoretical background for such a strategy, we propose a particular one which seems intuitive. Let workers traverse the entire tree and pick a node with most work, only then attempting to own or steal it. We call this strategy **FindMax**. Note that this cannot be easily implemented atomically, but a quiescently consistent implementation may still serve as a decent heuristic. This strategy yields an average tree size of 42 at $P = 8$, as well as a slightly better throughput – we conclude by choosing it as our default strategy. Also, the diagrams in Fig. 7 reveal the postulated inverse correlation between the tree size and total execution time, both for the Intel i7-2600 and the Sun UltraSPARC T2 processor (where STEP is set to 600), which is particularly noticeable for **Assign** when the total number of workers is not a power of two. For some P **RandomAll** works slightly better than **FindMax** on UltraSPARC, but both are much more efficient than static batching, which deteriorates heavily once P exceeds the number of cores.

The results so far go a long way in justifying that C1 is fulfilled. We focus on the C2 and C3 next by changing the workloads, namely the kernel function. Figures 8 and 9 show a comparison of the work-stealing tree and the other

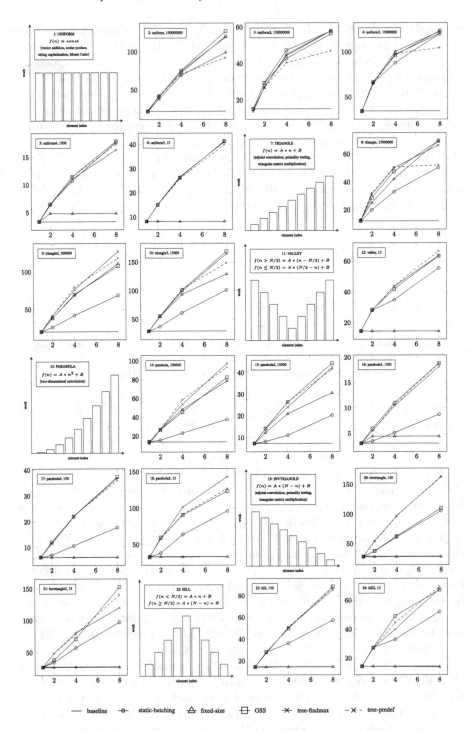

Fig. 8. Comparison of different `kernel` functions I (throughput/s^{-1} vs. #workers)

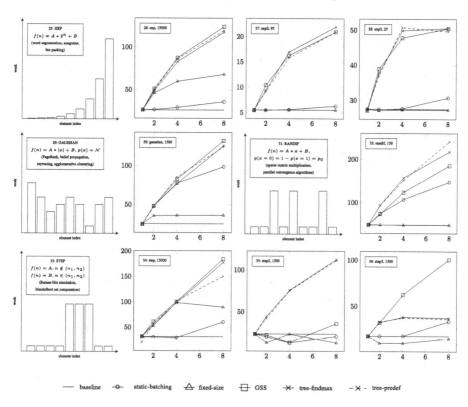

— baseline   -⊖- static-batching   -△- fixed-size   ⊞ GSS   -✕- tree-findmax   - ✕ - tree-predef

Fig. 9. Comparison of different `kernel` functions II (throughput/s^{-1} vs. #workers)

schedulers on a range of different workloads. Each workload pattern is illustrated prior to its respective diagrams, along with corresponding real-world examples. To avoid memory access effects and additional layers of abstraction each workload is minimal and synthetic, but corresponds to a practical use-case. To test C3, in Fig. 8-5, 6 we decrease the number of elements to 16 and increase the workload heavily. Fixed-size batching fails utterly for these workloads – the total number of elements is on the order of or well below the estimated STEP. These workloads obviously require smaller STEP sizes to allow stealing, but that would annul the baseline performance, and we cannot distinguish the two. We address these seemingly incompatible requirements by modifying the work-stealing tree in the following way. A mutable `step` field is added to `Node`, which is initially 1 and does not require atomic access. At the end of the `while` loop in the `workOn` method the `step` is doubled unless greater than some value MAXSTEP. As a result, workers start processing each node by cautiously checking if they can complete a bit of work without being stolen from and then increase the `step` exponentially. This naturally slows down the overall baseline execution, so we expect the MAXSTEP value to be greater than the previously established STEP. Indeed, on the i7-2600, we had to set MAXSTEP to 256 to maintain the baseline performance and at $P = 8$ even 1024. With these modifications work-stealing tree yields linear speedup for all uniform workloads.

Triangular workloads such as those shown in Fig. 8-8, 9, 10 show that static batching can yield suboptimal speedup due to the uniform workload assumption. Figure 8-20 shows the inverse triangular workload and its negative effect on guided self-scheduling – the first-arriving processor takes the largest batch of work, which incidentally contains most work. We do not inverse the other increasing workloads, but stress that it is neither helpful nor necessary to have batches above a certain size.

Figure 9-28 shows an exponentially increasing workload, where the work associated with the last element equals the rest of the work – the best possible speedup is 2. Figure 9-30, 32 shows two examples where a probability distribution dictates the workload, which occurs often in practice. Guided self-scheduling works well when the distribution is relatively uniform, but fails to achieve optimal speedup when only a few elements require more computation, for reasons mentioned earlier.

In the STEP distributions all elements except those in some range $\langle n_1, n_2 \rangle$ are associated with a very low amount of work. The range is set to 25 % of the total number of elements. When its absolute size is above MAXSTEP, as in Fig. 9-34, most schedulers do equally well. However, not all schedulers achieve optimal speedup as we decrease the total number of elements N and the range size goes below MAXSTEP. In Fig. 9-35 we set $n_1 = 0$ and $n_2 = 0.25N$. Schedulers other than the work-stealing tree achieve almost no speedup, each for the same reasons as before. However, in Fig. 9-36, we set $n_1 = 0.75N$ and $n_2 = N$ and discover that the work-stealing tree achieves a suboptimal speedup. The reason is the exponential batch increase – the first worker acquires a root node and quickly processes the cheap elements, having increased the batch size to MAXSTEP by the time it reaches the expensive ones. The real work is thus claimed by the first worker and the others are unable to acquire it. Assuming some batches are smaller and some larger as already explained, this problem cannot be worked around by a different batching order – there always exists a workload distribution such that the expensive elements are in the largest batch. In this adversarial setting the existence of a suboptimal work distribution for every batching order can only be overcome by randomization. We omit the details due to reasons of space, but briefly explain how to randomize batching in the appendix, showing how to improve the expected speedup.

Finally, we conclude this section by comparing the new scheduler with an existing scheduler implementation used in the Scala Parallel Collections [17] in Fig. 10. The Scala Parallel Collections scheduler is an example of an adaptive data-parallel scheduler relying a task-parallel scheduler under the hood [15]. The batching order is chosen so that the sizes increase exponentially. At any point, the largest batch (task) is eligible for stealing – after a steal, the batch is divided in the same batching order. Due to the overheads of preemptively creating batch tasks and scheduling them, Scala Parallel Collections use a bound on the minimum batch size.

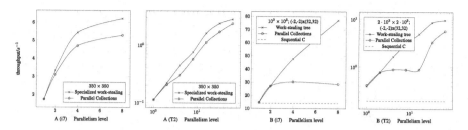

Fig. 10. (A) Matrix multiplication and (B) Mandelbrot sets on i7 and UltraSPARC T2

In Fig. 10 we evaluate the performance of Scala Parallel Collections against the new scheduler against two benchmark applications – triangular matrix multiplication and Mandelbrot set computation. Triangular matrix multiplication has a linearly increasing workload. Scala Parallel Collections scale as the number of processors increases on both the i7 and the UltraSPARC machine, although they are slower by a constant factor. However, in the Mandelbrot set benchmark where we render set in the part of the plane ranging from $(-2, -2)$ to $(32, 32)$, they do not scale beyond $P = 2$ on the i7, and only start scaling after $P = 16$ on the UltraSPARC. The reason is that the computationally expensive elements around the coordinates $(0, 0)$ end up in a single batch and work on them cannot be parallelized. The work-stealing tree offers a more lightweight form of work-stealing with smaller batches and better load balancing.

5   Conclusion

We presented a scheduling algorithm for data-parallel operations that fulfills the specified criteria. Based on the experiments, we draw the following conclusions:

1. Minimum batch size on modern architectures needed to efficiently parallelize the sequential baseline typically ranges from a few dozen to several hundred elements.
2. There is no need to make batches larger than some architecture-specific size `MAXSTEP`, which is independent of the problem size – in fact, the approach employed by guided self-scheduling and factoring can be detrimental.
3. Batching can and should occur in isolation – by having workers communicate only when they run out of work batching can be more fine-grained (Fig. 6).
4. Certain workloads require single element batches, in which case batch size has to be modified dynamically. Exponentially increasing batch size from 1 up to `MAXSTEP` works well for different workloads (Fig. 9).
5. When the dominant part of the workload is distributed across a range of elements smaller than `MAXSTEP`, the worst-case speedup can be 1. Randomizing the batching order can improve the average speedup.

We hinted that the work-stealing tree serves as a reduction tree, and we show the details in the appendix. We give some theoretical background to the conclusions from the experiments in the appendix as well. In the paper, we focused on parallel loops, but arrays, hash tables and trees are also eligible for parallel traversal [3,17,18]. The range iterator state was encoded with a single integer, but the state of other data structure iterators, as well as batching and stealing, may be more complex. While the CAS-based implementation of `tryAdvance` and `trySteal` ensures lock-freedom, CAS instructions in those methods can be replaced with short critical sections for more complicated iterators – the work-stealing tree algorithm is potentially applicable to other data structures in a straightforward way.

A   Appendix

We provide the appendix section to further explain some of the concepts mentioned in the main paper which did not fit there. The information here is provided for convenience and it should not be necessary to read this section, but doing so may give useful insight.

A.1   Work-Stealing Reduction Tree

As mentioned, the work-stealing tree is a particularly effective data-structure for a reduce operation. Parallel reduce is useful in the context of many other operations, such as finding the first element with a given property, finding the greatest element with respect to some ordering, filtering elements with a given property or computing an aggregate of all the elements (e.g. a sum).

There are two reasons why the work-stealing tree is amenable to implementing reductions. First, it preserves the order in which the work is split between processors, which allows using non-commutative operators for the reduce (e.g. computing the resulting transformation from a series of affine transformations can be parallelized by multiplying a sequence of matrices – the order is in this case important). Second, the reduce can largely be performed in parallel, due to the structure of the tree.

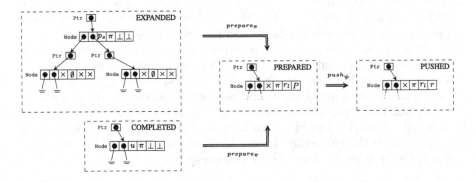

Fig. 11. Reduction state diagram

The work-stealing tree reduce works similar to a software combining tree [9], but it can proceed in a lock-free manner after all the node owners have completed their work, as we describe next. The general idea is to save the aggregated result in each node and then push the result further up the tree. Note that we did not save the return value of the **kernel** method in line 50 in Fig. 5, making the scheduler applicable only to parallelizing **for** loops. Thus, we add a local variable **sum** and update it each time after calling **kernel**. Once the node ends up in a COMPLETED or EXPANDED state, we assign it the value of **sum**. Note that updating an invocation-specific shared variable instead would not only break the commutativity, but also lead to the same bottleneck as we saw before with fixed-size batching. We therefore add two new fields with atomic access to **Node**, namely **lresult** and **result**. We also add a new field **parent** to **Ptr**. We expand the set of abstract node states with two additional ones, namely PREPARED and PUSHED. The expanded state diagram is shown in Fig. 11.

The **parent** field in **Ptr** is not shown in the diagram in Fig. 11. The first two boxes in **Node** denote the left and the right child, respectively, as before. We represent the iteration state (**progress**) with a single box in **Node**. The iterator may either be stolen (p_s) or completed (u), but this is not important for the new states – we denote all such entries with ×. The fourth box represents the owner, the fifth and the sixth fields **lresult** and **result**. Once the work on the node is effectively completed, either due to a steal or a normal completion, the node owner π has to write the value of the **sum** variable to **lresult**. After doing so, the owner announces its completion by atomically writing a special value P to **result**, and by doing so pushes the node into the PREPARED state – we say that the owner prepares the node. At this point the node contains all the information necessary to participate in the reduction. The sufficient condition for the reduction to start is that the node is a leaf or that the node is an inner node and both its children are in the PUSHED state. The value **lresult** can then be combined with the **result** values of both its children and written to the **result** field of the node. Upon writing

```
74 def complete(sum: T, tree: Ptr) =        93    else if (res0 ≠ P)
75    node = READ(tree.child)                94       // already in PUSHED state
76    stolen = READ(node.progress) < 0       95    else
77    if (stolen)                            96       res = ⊥
78       trySteal(tree)                      97       if (isLeaf(node)) res = lresult
79       node = READ(tree.child)             98       else
80       node.lresult = sum                  99          left = READ(node.left.child)
81    else                                   100         right = READ(node.right.child)
82       node.lresult = sum                  101         rl = READ(left.result)
83    while (READ(node.result) == ⊥)         102         rr = READ(right.result)
84       CAS(node.result, ⊥, P)              103         if (rl ≠ ⊥ ∧ rr ≠ ⊥)
85    pushUp(tree)                           104            res = lresult + rl + rr
86    ¬stolen                                105      if (res ≠ ⊥)
87                                           106         if (CAS(node.result, res0, res))
88 def pushUp(tree: Ptr): Unit =             107            if (tree.parent ≠ ⊥)
89    node = READ(three.child)               108               pushUp(tree.parent)
90    res0 = READ(node.result)               109            else tree.synchronized
91    if (res0 == ⊥)                         110               { tree.notifyAll() }
92       // not yet in PREPARED state        111            else pushUp(tree)
```

Fig. 12. Reduction pseudocode

to the `result` field, the node goes into the PUSHED state. This push step can be done by any worker ψ and assuming all the owners have prepared their nodes, the reduction is lock-free. Importantly, the worker that succeeds in pushing the result must attempt to repeat the push step in the parent node. This way the reduction proceeds upwards in the tree until reaching the root. Once some worker pushes the result to the root of the tree, it notifies that the operation was completed, so that the thread that invoked the operation can proceed, in case that the parallel operation is synchronous. Otherwise, a future variable can be completed or a user callback invoked.

Before presenting the pseudocode, we formalize the notion of the states we described. In addition to the ones mentioned earlier, we identify the following new invariants.

INV6. Field `n.lresult` is set to $\perp$ when created. If a worker π overwrites the value $\perp$ of the field `n.lresult` then `n.owner` $= \pi$ and the node n is either in the EXPANDED state or the COMPLETED state. That is the last write to `n.lresult`.

INV7. Field `n.result` is set to $\perp$ when created. If a worker π overwrites the value $\perp$ of the field `n.result` with $\mathbb{P}$ then `n.owner` $= \pi$, the node n was either in the EXPANDED state or the COMPLETED state and the value of the field `n.lresult` is different than $\perp$. We say that the node goes into the PREPARED state.

INV8. If a worker ψ overwrites the value $\mathbb{P}$ of the field `n.result` then the node n was in the PREPARED state and was either a leaf or its children were in the PUSHED state. We say that the node goes into the PUSHED state.

We modify `workOn` so that instead of lines 53 through 57, it calls the method `complete` passing it the `sum` argument and the reference to the subtree. The pseudocodes for `complete` and an additional method `pushUp` are shown in Fig. 12.

Upon completing the work, the owner checks whether the subtree was stolen. If so, it helps expand the subtree (line 78), reads the new node and writes the `sum` into `lresult`. After that, the owner pushes the node into the PREPARED state in line 84, retrying in the case of spurious failures, and calls `pushUp`.

The method `pushUp` may be invoked by the owner of the node attempting to write to the `result` field, or by another worker attempting to push the result up after having completed the work on one of the child nodes. The `lresult` field may not be yet assigned (line 92) if the owner has not completed the work – in this case the worker ceases to participate in the reduction and relies on the owner or another worker to continue pushing the result up. The same applies if the node is already in the PUSHED state (line 94). Otherwise, the `lresult` field can only be combined with the `result` values from the children if both children are in the PUSHED state. If the worker invoking `pushUp` notices that the children are not yet assigned the `result`, it will cease to participate in the reduction. Otherwise, it will compute the tentative result (line 104) and attempt to write it to `result` atomically with the CAS in line 106. A failed CAS triggers a retry, otherwise `pushUp` is called recursively on the parent node. If the current node is the root, the worker notifies any listeners that the final result is ready and the operations ends.

A.2   Work-Stealing Tree Traversal Strategies

We showed experimentally that changing the traversal order when searching for work can have a considerable effect on the performance of the work-stealing tree scheduler. We described these *strategies* briefly how, but did not present a precise, detailed pseudocode. In this section we show different implementations of the `findWork` and `descend` methods that lead to different tree traversal orders when stealing.

Assign. In this strategy a worker with index i invoking `findWork` picks a left-to-right traversal order at some node at level l if and only if its bit at position $l \bmod \lceil \log_2 P \rceil$ is 1, that is:

$$(i \gg (l \bmod \lceil \log_2 P \rceil)) \bmod 2 = 1 \tag{1}$$

The consequence of this is that when the workers descend in the tree the first time, they will pick different paths, leading to fewer steals assuming that the workload distribution is relatively uniform. If it is not uniform, then the workload itself should amortize the creation of extra nodes. We give the pseudocode in Fig. 13.

```
112 def assign.left(p: Ptr, i: Int) =        127 def assign.findWork(ptr: Ptr): Node =
113   val bit = i >> (p.level % log2(P))    128   val node = READ(ptr.child)
114   bit % 2 == 1                           129   if (isLeaf(node))
115                                            130     if (tryOwn(node)) node
116 def assign.choose(p: Ptr, i: Int) =      131     else if (¬isEligible(node)) ⊥
117   if (left(p, i)) READ(p.child).left     132     else if (¬trySteal(ptr)) findWork(ptr)
118   else READ(p.child).right               133     else
119                                            134       val ptr =
120 def assign.descend(leaf: Ptr): Unit =    135         choose(ptr, thisWorker.index)
121   val nosteals = workOn(leaf)            136       if (tryOwn(READ(ptr.child)))
122   if (¬nosteals)                          137         READ(ptr.child)
123     val sub =                             138       else findWork(ptr)
124       choose(leaf, thisWorker.index)     139   else if (left(ptr, thisWorker.index))
125     if (tryOwn(READ(sub.child)))          140     val leftsub = findWork(node.left)
126       descend(subnode)                    141     if (leftsub ≠ ⊥) leftsub
                                              142     else findWork(node.right)
                                              143   else
                                              144     val rightsub = findWork(node.right)
                                              145     if (rightsub ≠ ⊥) rightsub
                                              146     else findWork(node.left)
```

Fig. 13. **Assign** strategy

AssignTop. This strategy is similar to the previous one with the difference that the assignment only works as before if the level of the tree is less than or equal to $\lceil log_2 P \rceil$. Otherwise, a random choice is applied in deciding whether traversal should be left-to-right or right-to-left. We show it in Fig. 14 where we only redefine the method `left`, and reuse the same `choose`, `descend` and `findWork`.

```
147 def top.left(p: Ptr, idx: Int) =        153 def randomall.left(p: Ptr, idx: Int) =
148   if (p.level ≤ log2(P))                 154   coinToss()
149     val bit = i >> (p.level % log2(P)) 155
150     bit % 2 == 1
151   else
152     coinToss()
```

Fig. 14. AssignTop and RandomAll strategies

RandomAll. This strategy randomizes all the choices that the stealer and the victim make. Both the tree traversal and the node chosen after the steal are thus changed in `findWork`. We show it in Fig. 14.

RandomWalk. Here we only change the tree traversal order that the stealer does when searching for work and leave the rest of the choices fixed to victim picking the left node after expansion and the stealer picking the right node. The code is shown in Fig. 15.

```
156 def randomwalk.left(p: Ptr, i: Int) =      170 def rwalk.findWork(ptr: Ptr) =
157   val bit = i >> (p.level % log2(P))       171   val node = READ(ptr.child)
158   bit % 2 == 1                             172   if (isLeaf(node))
159                                            173     if if (tryOwn(node)) node
160 def rwalk.choose(p: Ptr, i: Int) =         174     else if (¬isEligible(node)) ⊥
161   if (left(p, i)) READ(p.child).left       175     else if (¬trySteal(ptr))
162   else READ(p.child).right                 176       findWork(ptr)
163                                            177     else
164 def rwalk.descend(leaf: Ptr) =             178       val r = node.right
165   val nosteals = workOn(leaf)              179       if (tryOwn(READ(r.child)))
166   if (¬nosteals)                           180         READ(r.child)
167     val sub = READ(leaf.child).left        181       else findWork(ptr)
168     if (tryOwn(READ(sub.child)))           182   else if (left(ptr, thisWorker.index))
169       descend(subnode)                     183     val leftsub = findWork(node.left)
                                               184     if (leftsub ≠ ⊥) leftsub
                                               185     else findWork(node.right)
                                               186   else
                                               187     val rightsub = findWork(node.right)
                                               188     if (rightsub ≠ ⊥) rightsub
                                               189     else findWork(node.left)
```

Fig. 15. RandomWalk strategy

FindMax. This strategy, unlike the previous ones, does not break tree traversal early as soon as a viable node is found. Instead, it traverses the entire work-stealing tree in left-to-right order and returns a reference to a node with the most work. Only then it attempts to own or steal that node. As noted before, this kind of search is not atomic, since some nodes may be stolen and expanded in the meantime and processors advance through the nodes they own. However, we expect steals to be rare events so in most cases this search should give an exact or a nearly exact estimate. The decisions about which node the victim and the stealer take after expansion remain the same as in the basic algorithm from Fig. 5. We show the pseudocode for **FindMax** in Fig. 16.

```
190 def findmax.search(p: Ptr): Ptr =       202 def findmax.findWork(ptr: Ptr): Node =
191   if (isLeaf(p.child)) p                 203   val maxp = search(tree)
192   else                                   204   val max = READ(maxp.child)
193     val lp = search(p.child.left)        205   if (remains(max) > 0)
194     val rp = search(p.child.right)       206     if (tryOwn(max)) max
195     val l = READ(lp.child)               207     else if (¬isEligible(max)) ⊥
196     val r = READ(rp.child)               208     else if (trySteal(maxp))
197     if (remains(l) > remains(r)) l       209       val subnode = READ(maxp.right.child)
198     else r                               210       if (tryOwn(subnode)) subnode
199                                          211       else findWork(ptr)
200 def findmax.remains(n: Node) =          212     else findWork(ptr)
201   n.until - READ(n.progress)            213   else ⊥
```

Fig. 16. FindMax strategy

A.3 Speedup and Optimality Analysis

In Fig. 9-36 we identified a workload distribution for which the work-stealing reduction tree had a particularly bad performance. This coarse workload consisted of a major prefix of elements which required a very small amount of computation followed by a minority of elements which required a large amount of computation. We call it coarse because the number of elements was on the order of magnitude of a certain value we called MAXSTEP.

To recap, the speedup was suboptimal due to the following. First, to achieve an optimal speedup for at least the baseline, not all batches can have fewer elements than a certain number. We have established this number for a particular architecture and environment, calling it STEP. Second, to achieve an optimal speedup for ranges the size of which is below STEP·P, some of the batches have to be smaller than the others. The technique we apply starts with a batch consisting of a single element and increases the batch size exponentially up to MAXSTEP. Third, there is no hardware interrupt mechanism available to interrupt a worker which is processing a large batch, and software emulations which consist of checking a volatile variable within a loop are too slow when executing the baseline. Fourth, the worker does not know the workload distribution and cannot measure time. All this caused a single worker obtain the largest batch before the other workers had a chance to steal some work for a particular workload distribution. Justifying these claims requires a set of more formal definitions. We start by defining the context in which the scheduler executes.

Definition 1 (Oblivious conditions). *If a data-parallel scheduler is unable to obtain information about the workload distribution, nor information about the amount of work it had previously executed, we say that the data-parallel scheduler works in* oblivious conditions.

Assume that a worker decides on some batching schedule $c_1, c_2, \ldots, c_k$ where c_j is the size of the j-th batch and $\sum_{j=1}^{k} c_j = N$, where N is the size of the range. No batch is empty, i.e. $c_j \neq 0$ for all j. In oblivious conditions the worker does not know if the workload resembles the baseline mentioned earlier, so it must assume that it does and minimize the scheduling overhead. The baseline is not only important from a theoretical perspective being one of the potentially worst-case workload distribution, but also from a practical one – in many problems parallel loops have a uniform workload. We now define what this baseline means more formally.

Definition 2 (The baseline constraint). *Let the workload distribution be a function $w(i)$ which gives the amount of computation needed for range element i. We say that a data-parallel scheduler respects the baseline constraint if and only if the speedup s_p with respect to a sequential loop is arbitrarily close to linear when executing the workload distribution $w(i) = w_0$, where w_0 is the minimum amount of work needed to execute a loop iteration.*

Arbitrarily close here means that ϵ in $s_p = \frac{P}{1+\epsilon}$ can be made arbitrarily small.

The baseline constraint tells us that it may be necessary to divide the elements of the loop into batches, depending on the scheduling (that is, communication) costs. As we have seen in the experiments, while we should be able to make the ϵ value arbitrarily small, in practice it is small enough when the scheduling overhead is no longer observable in the measurement. Also, we have shown experimentally that the average batch size should be bigger than some value in oblivious conditions, but we have used particular scheduler instances. Does this hold in general, for every data-parallel scheduler? The answer is yes, as we show in the following lemma.

Lemma 1. *If a data-parallel scheduler that works in oblivious conditions respects the baseline constraint then the batching schedule $c_1, c_2, \ldots, c_k$ is such that:*

$$\frac{\sum_{j=1}^{k} c_j}{k} \geq S(\epsilon) \tag{2}$$

Proof. The lemma claims that in oblivious conditions the average batch size must be above some value which depends on the previously defined ϵ, otherwise the scheduler will not respect the baseline constraint.

The baseline constraint states that $s_p = \frac{P}{1+\epsilon}$, where the speedup s_p is defined as T_0/T_p, where T_0 is the running time of a sequential loop and T_p is the running time of the scheduler using P processors. Furthermore, $T_0 = T \cdot P$ where T is the optimal parallel running time for P processors, so it follows that $\epsilon \cdot T = T_p - T$. We can also write this as $\epsilon \cdot W = W_p - W$. This is due to the running time being proportionate to the total amount of executed work, whether scheduling or useful work. The difference $W_p - W$ is exactly the scheduling work W_s, so the baseline constraint translates into the following inequality:

$$W_s \leq \epsilon \cdot W \tag{3}$$

In other words, the scheduling work has to be some fraction of the useful work. Assuming that there is a constant amount of scheduling work W_c per every batch, we have $W_s = k \cdot W_c$. Lets denote the average work per element with $\overline{w}$. We then have $W = N \cdot \overline{w}$. Combining these relations we get $N \geq k \cdot \frac{W_c}{\epsilon \cdot \overline{w}}$, or shorter $N \geq k \cdot S(\epsilon)$. Since N is equal to the sum of all batch sizes, we derive the following constraint:

$$\frac{\sum_{j=1}^{k} c_j}{k} \geq \frac{W_c}{\epsilon \cdot \overline{w}} \tag{4}$$

In other words, the average batch size must be greater than some value $S(\epsilon)$ which depends on how close we want to get to the optimal speedup. Note that this value is inversely proportionate to the average amount of work per element $\overline{w}$ – the scheduler could decide more about the batch sizes if it knew something about the average workload, and grows with the scheduling cost per batch W_c – this is why it is especially important to make the workOn method efficient. We already saw the inverse proportionality with ϵ in Fig. 6. In part, this is why we had to make MAXSTEP larger than the chosen STEP (we also had to increase it due to increasing the scheduling work in workOn, namely, W_c). This is an additional constraint when choosing the batching schedule.

With this additional constraint there always exists a workload distribution for a given batching schedule such that the speedup is suboptimal, as we show next.

Lemma 2. *Assume that $S(\epsilon) > 1$, for the desired ϵ. For any fixed batching schedule $c_1, c_2, \ldots, c_k$ there exists a workload distribution such that the scheduler executing it in oblivious conditions yields a suboptimal schedule.*

Proof. First, assume that the scheduler does not respect the baseline constraint. The baseline workload then yields a suboptimal speedup and the statement is trivially true because $S(\epsilon) > 1$.

Otherwise, assume without the loss of generality that at some point in time a particular worker ω is processing some batch c_m the size of which is greater or equal to the size of the other batches. This means the size of c_m is greater than 1, from the assumption. Then we can choose a workload distribution such that the work $W_m = \sum_{i=N_m}^{N_m + c_m} w(i)$ needed to complete batch c_m is arbitrarily large, where $N_m = \sum_{j=1}^{m-1} c_j$ is the number of elements in the batching schedule coming before the batch c_m. For all the other elements we set $w(i)$ to be some minimum value w_0. We claim that the obtained speedup is suboptimal. There is at least one different batching schedule with a better speedup, and that is the schedule in which instead of batch c_m there are two batches c_{m_1} and c_{m_2} such that c_{m_1} consists of all the elements of c_m except the last one and c_{m_2} contains the last element. In this batching schedule some other worker can work on c_{m_2} while ω works on c_{m_1}. Hence, there exists a different batching schedule which leads to a better speedup, so the initial batching schedule is not optimal.

We can ask ourselves what is the necessary condition for the speedup to be suboptimal. We mentioned that the range size has to be on the same order of magnitude as S above, but can we make this more precise? We could simplify this question by asking what is the necessary condition for the worst-case speedup of 1 or less. Alas, we cannot find necessary conditions for all schedulers because they do not exist – there are schedulers which do not need any preconditions in order to consistently produce such a speedup (think of a sequential loop or, worse, a "scheduler" that executes an infinite loop). Also, we already saw that a suboptimal speedup may be due to a particularly bad workload distribution, so maybe we should consider only particular distributions, or have some conditions on them. What we will be able to express are the necessary conditions on the range size for the existence of a scheduler which achieves a speedup greater than 1 on any workload. Since the range size is the only information known to the scheduler in advance, it can be used to affect its decisions in a particular implementation.

The worst-case speedups we saw occurred in scenarios where one worker (usually the invoker) started to work before all the other workers. To be able to express the desired conditions, we model this delay with a value T_d.

Lemma 3. *Assume a data-parallel scheduler that respects the baseline constraint in oblivious conditions. There exists some minimum range size N_1 for which the scheduler can yield a speedup greater than 1 for any workload distribution.*

Proof. We first note that there is always a scheduler that can achieve the speedup 1, which is merely a sequential loop. We then consider the case when the scheduler is parallelizing the baseline workload. Assume now that there is no minimum range size N_1 for which the claim is true. Then for any range size N we must be able to find a range size $N + K$ such that the scheduler still cannot yield speedup 1 or less, for a chosen K. We choose $N = \frac{f \cdot T_d}{w_0}$, where w_0 is the amount of work associated with each element in the baseline distribution and f is an architecture-specific constant describing the computation speed. The chosen N is the number of elements that can be processed during the worker wakeup delay T_d. The workers that wake up after the first worker ω processes N elements have no more work to do, so the speedup is 1. However, for range size $N + K$ there are K elements left that have not been processed. These K elements could have been in the last batch of ω. The last batch in the batching schedule chosen by the scheduler may include the Nth element. Note that the only constraint on the batch size is the lower bound value $S(\epsilon)$ from Lemma 1. So, if we choose $K = 2S(\epsilon)$ then either the last batch is smaller than K or is greater than K. If it is smaller, then a worker different than ω will obtain and process the last batch, hence the speedup will be greater than 1. If it is greater, then the worker ω will process the last batch – the other workers that wake up will not be able to obtain the elements from that batch. In that case there exists a better batching order which still respects the baseline constraint and that is to divide the last batch into two equal parts, allowing the other workers to obtain some work and yielding a speedup greater than 1. This contradicts the assumption that there is no minimum range size N_1 – we know that N_1 is such that:

$$\frac{f \cdot T_d}{w_0} \leq N_1 \leq \frac{f \cdot T_d}{w_0} + 2 \cdot S(\epsilon) \tag{5}$$

Now, assume that the workload $w(i)$ is not the baseline workload w_0. For any workload we know that $w(i) \geq w_0$ for every i. The batching order for a single worker has to be exactly the same as before due to oblivious conditions. As a result the running time for the first worker ω until it reaches the Nth element can only be larger than that of the baseline. This means that the other workers will wake up by the time ω reaches the Nth element, and obtain work. Thus, the speedup can be greater than 1, as before.

We have so far shown that we can decide on the average batch size if we know something about the workload, namely, the average computational cost of an element. We have also shown when we can expect the worst case speedup, potentially allowing us to take prevention measures. Finally, we have shown that any data-parallel scheduler deciding on a fixed schedule in oblivious conditions can yield a suboptimal speedup. Note the wording "fixed" here. It means that the scheduler must make a definite decision about the batching order without any knowledge about the workload, and must make the same decision every time – it must be deterministic. As hinted before, the way to overcome an adversary that is repetitively picking the worst case workload is to use randomization when producing the batching schedule. This is the topic of the next section.

A.4   Overcoming the Worst-Case Speedup Using Randomization

Recall that the workload distribution that led to a bad speedup in our evaluation consisted of a sequence of very cheap elements followed by a minority of elements which were computationally very expensive. On the other hand, when we inverted the order of elements, the speedup became linear. The exponential backoff approach is designed to start with smaller batches first in hopes of hitting the part of the workload which contains most work as early as possible. This allow other workers to steal larger pieces of the remaining work, hence allowing a more fine grained batch subdivision. In this way the scheduling algorithm is workload-driven – it gives itself its own feedback. In the absence of other information about the workload, the knowledge that some worker is processing some part of the workload long enough that it can be stolen from is the best sign that the workload is different than the baseline, and that the batch subdivision can circumvent the baseline constraint. This heuristic worked in the example from Fig. 9-36 when the expensive elements were reached first, but failed when they were reached in the last, largest batch, and we know that there has to be a largest batch by Lemma 1 – a single worker must divide the range into batches the mean size of which has a lower bound. In fact, no other deterministic scheduler can yield an optimal speedup for all schedules, as shown by Lemma 2. For this reason we look into randomized schedulers.

In particular, in the example from the evaluation we would like the scheduler to put the smallest batches at the end of the range, but we have no way of knowing if the most expensive elements are positioned somewhere else. With this in mind we randomize the batching order. The baseline constraint still applies in oblivious conditions, so we have to pick different batch sizes with respect to the constraints from Lemma 1. Lets pick exactly the same set of exponentially increasing batches, but place consequent elements into different batches randomly. In other words, we permute the elements of the range and then apply the previous scheme. We expect some of the more expensive elements to be assigned to the smaller batches, giving other workers a higher opportunity to steal a part of the work.

In evaluating the effectiveness of this randomized approach we will assume a particular distribution we found troublesome. We define it more formally.

Definition 3 (Step workload distribution). *A* step workload distribution *is a function which assigns a computational cost $w(i)$ to each element i of the range of size N as follows:*

$$w(i) = \begin{cases} w_e, & i \in [i_1, i_2] \\ w_0, & i \notin [i_1, i_2] \end{cases} \tag{6}$$

where $[i_1, i_2]$ is a subsequence of the range, w_0 is the minimum cost of computation per element and $w_e \gg w_0$. If $w_e \geq f \cdot T_d$, where f is the computation speed and T_d is the worker delay, then we additionally call the workload highly irregular. *We call $D = 2^d = i_2 - i_1$ the* span *of the step distribution. If $(N - D) \cdot \frac{w_0}{f} \leq T_d$ we also call the workload* short.

We can now state the following lemma. We will refer to the randomized batching schedule we have described before as the **randomized permutation with an exponential backoff**. Note that we implicitly assume that the worker delay T_d is significantly greater than the time T_c spent scheduling a single batch (this was certainly true in our experimental evaluation).

Lemma 4. *When parallelizing a workload with a highly irregular short step workload distribution the expected speedup inverse of a scheduler using randomized permutations with an exponential backoff is:*

$$\langle s_p^{-1} \rangle = \frac{1}{P} + \left(1 - \frac{1}{P}\right) \cdot \frac{(2^k - 2^d - 1)!}{(2^k - 1)!} \cdot \sum_{i=0}^{k-1} 2^i \frac{(2^k - 2^i - 1)!}{(2^k - 2^i - 2^d)!} \tag{7}$$

where $D = 2^d \gg P$ is the span of the step workload distribution.

Proof. The speedup s_p is defined as $s_p = \frac{T_0}{T_p}$ where T_0 is the running time of the optimal sequential execution and T_p is the running time of the parallelized execution. We implicitly assume that all processors have the same the same computation speed f. Since $w_e \gg w_0$, the total amount of work that a sequential loop executes is arbitrarily close to $D \cdot w_e$, so $T_0 = \frac{D}{f}$. When we analyze the parallel execution, we will also ignore the work w_0. We will call the elements with cost w_e *expensive*.

We assumed that the workload distribution is highly irregular. This means that if the first worker ω starts the work on an element from $[i_1, i_2]$ at some time t_0 then at the time $t_1 = t_0 + \frac{w_e}{f}$ some other worker must have already started working as well, because $t_1 - t_0 \geq T_d$. Also, we have assumed that the workload distribution is short. This means that the first worker ω can complete work on all the elements outside the interval $[i_1, i_2]$ before another worker arrives. Combining these observations, as soon as the first worker arrives at an expensive element, it is possible for the other workers to parallelize the rest of the work.

We assume that after the other workers arrive there are enough elements left to efficiently parallelize work on them. In fact, at this point the scheduler will typically change the initially decided batching schedule – additionally arriving workers will steal and induce a more fine-grained subdivision. Note, however, that the other workers cannot subdivide the batch on which the current worker is currently working on – that one is no longer available to them. The only batches with elements of cost w_e that they can still subdivide are the ones coming after the first batch in which the first worker ω found an expensive element. We denote this batch with c_ω. The batch c_ω may, however, contain additional expensive elements and the bigger the batch the more probable this is. We will say that the total number of expensive elements in c_ω is X. Finally, note that we assumed that $D \gg P$, so our expression will only be an approximation if D is very close to P.

We thus arrive at the following expression for speedup:

$$s_p = \frac{D}{X + \frac{D-X}{P}} \tag{8}$$

Speedup depends on the value X. But since the initial batching schedule is random, the speedup depends on the random variable and is itself random. For this reason we will look for its expected value. We start by finding the expectation of the random variable X.

We will now solve a more general problem of placing balls to an ordered set of bins and apply the solution to finding the expectation of X. There are k bins, numbered from 0 to $k - 1$. Let c_i denote the number of balls that fit into the ith bin. We randomly assign D balls to bins, so that the number of balls in each bin i is less than or equal to c_i. In other words, we randomly select D slots from all the $N = \sum_{i=0}^{k-1} c_i$ slots in all the bins together. We then define the random variable X to be the number of balls in the non-empty bin with the smallest index i. The formulated problem corresponds to the previous one – the balls are the expensive elements and the bins are the batches.

An alternative way to define X is as follows:

$$X = \sum_{i=0}^{k-1} \begin{cases} \text{number of balls in bin } i & \text{if all the bins } j < i \text{ are empty} \\ 0 & \text{otherwise} \end{cases} \tag{9}$$

Applying the linearity property, the expectation $\langle X \rangle$ is then:

$$\langle X \rangle = \sum_{i=0}^{k-1} \langle \text{number of balls in bin } i \text{ given that all the bins } j < i \text{ are empty, and 0 otherwise} \rangle \tag{10}$$

The expectation in the sum is conditional on the event that all the bins coming before i are empty. We call the probability of this event p_i. We define b_i as the number of balls in any bin i. From the properties of conditional expectation we than have:

$$\langle X \rangle = \sum_{i=0}^{k-1} p_i \cdot \langle b_i \rangle \tag{11}$$

The number of balls in any bin is the sum of the balls in all the slots of that bin which spans slots n_{i-1} through $n_{i-1} + c_i$. The expected number of balls in a bin i is thus:

$$\langle b_i \rangle = \sum_{i=n_{i-1}}^{n_{i-1}+c_i} \langle \text{expected number of balls in a single slot} \rangle \qquad (12)$$

We denote the total capacity of all the bins $j \geq i$ as q_i (so that $q_0 = N$ and $q_{k-1} = 2^{k-1}$). We assign balls to slots randomly with a uniform distribution – each slot has a probability $\frac{D}{q_i}$ of being selected. Note that the denominator is not N – we are calculating a conditional probability for which all the slots before the ith bin are empty. The expected number of balls in a single slot is thus $\frac{D}{q_i}$. It follows that:

$$\langle b_i \rangle = c_i \cdot \frac{D}{q_i} \qquad (13)$$

Next, we compute the probability p_i that all the bins before the bin i are empty. We do this by counting the events in which this is true, namely, the number of ways to assign balls in bins $j \geq i$. We will pick combinations of D slots, one for each ball, from a set of q_i slots. We do the same to enumerate all the assignments of balls to bins, but with $N = q_0$ slots, and obtain:

$$p_i = \frac{\binom{q_i}{D}}{\binom{q_0}{D}} \qquad (14)$$

We assumed here that $q_i \geq D$, otherwise we cannot fill all D balls into bins. We could create a constraint that the last batch is always larger than the number of balls. Instead, we simply define $\binom{q_i}{D} = 0$ if $q_i < D$ – there is no chance we can fit more than q_i balls to q_i slots. Combining these relations, we get the following expression for $\langle X \rangle$:

$$\langle X \rangle = D \cdot \frac{(q_0 - D)!}{q_0!} \sum_{i=0}^{k-1} c_i \cdot \frac{(q_i - 1)!}{(q_i - D)!} \qquad (15)$$

We use this expression to compute the expected speedup inverse. By the linearity of expectation:

$$\langle s_p^{-1} \rangle = \frac{1}{P} + \left(1 - \frac{1}{P}\right) \cdot \frac{(q_0 - D)!}{q_0!} \sum_{i=0}^{k-1} c_i \cdot \frac{(q_i - 1)!}{(q_i - D)!} \qquad (16)$$

This is a more general expression than the one in the claim. When we plug in the exponential backoff batching schedule, i.e. $c_i = 2^i$ and $q_i = 2^k - 2^i$, the lemma follows.

The expression derived for the inverse speedup does not have a neat analytical form, but we can evaluate it for different values of d to obtain a diagram. As a sanity check, the worst expected speedup comes with $d = 0$. If there is only a single expensive element in the range, then there is no way to parallelize execution – the expression gives us the speedup 1. We expect a better speedup as d grows – when there are more expensive elements, it is easier for the scheduler to stumble upon some of them. In fact, for $d = k$, with the conventions established in the proof, we get that the speedup is $\frac{1}{P} + \left(1 - \frac{1}{P}\right) \cdot \frac{c_0}{D}$. This means that when all the elements are expensive the proximity to the optimal speedup depends on the size c_0 of the first batch – the less elements in it, the better. Together with the fact that many applications have uniform workloads, this is also the reason why we advocate exponential backoff for which the size of the first batch is 1.

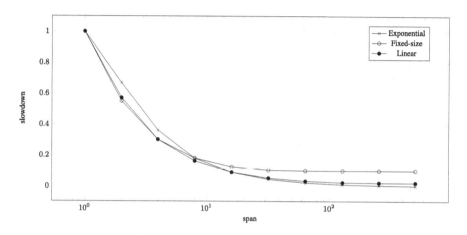

Fig. 17. Randomized scheduler executing step workload – speedup vs. span

We call the term $\frac{(q_0-D)!}{q_0!} \sum_{i=0}^{k-1} c_i \cdot \frac{(q_i-1)!}{(q_i-D)!}$ the *slowdown* and plot it with respect to span D on the diagram in Fig. 17. In this diagram we choose $k = 10$, and the number of elements $N = 2^{10} = 1024$. As the term nears 1, the speedup nears 1. As the term approaches 0, the speedup approaches the optimal speedup P. The quicker the term approaches 0 as we increase d, the better the scheduler. We can see that fixed-size batching should work better than the exponential backoff if the span D is below 10 elements, but is much worse than the exponential backoff otherwise. Linearly increasing the batch size from 0 in some step $a = \frac{2 \cdot (2^k - 1)}{k \cdot (k-1)}$ seems to work well even for span $D < 10$. However, the mean batch size $\overline{c_i} = \frac{S}{k}$ means that this approach may easily violate the baseline constraint, and for $P \approx D$ the formula is an approximation anyway.

The conclusion is that selecting a random permutation of the elements should work very well in theory. For example, the average speedup becomes very close to optimal if less than $D = 10$ elements out of $N = 1024$ are expensive. However, randomly permuting elements would in practice either require a preparatory pass in which the elements are randomly copied or would require the workers to randomly jump through the array, leading to cache miss issues. In both cases the baseline performance would be violated. Even permuting the order of the batches seems problematic, as it would require storing information about where each batch started and left off, as well as its intermediate result – for something like that we need a data structure like a work-stealing tree and we saw that we have to minimize the number of nodes there as much as possible.

There are many approaches we could study, many of which could have viable implementations, but we focus on a particular one which seems easy to implement for ranges and other data structures. Recall that in the example in Fig. 9-36 the interval with expensive elements was positioned at the end of the range. What if the worker alternated the batch in each step by tossing the coin to decide if the next batch should be from the left (start) or from the right (end)? Then the worker could arrive at the expensive interval on the end while the batch size is still small with a relatively high probability. The changes to the work-stealing tree algorithm are minimal – in addition to another field called `rresult` (the name of which should shed some light on the previous choice of name for `lresult`), we have to modify the `workOn`, `complete` and `pushUp` methods. While the latter two are straightforward, the lines 47 through 51 of `workOn` are modified. The new `workOn` method is shown in Fig. 18.

```
def workOn(ptr: Ptr): Boolean =
  val node = READ(ptr.child)
  var batch = -1
  var sum = 0
  do
    val p = READ(node.progress)
    if (notCompleted(p) && notStolen(p))
      if (coinToss())
        batchs = tryAdvanceLeft(node, p)
        if (notStolen(batch)) sum += kernel(p, p + decodeStep(batch))
      else
        batch = tryAdvanceRight(node, p)
        if (notStolen(batch)) sum += kernel(p, p + decodeStep(batch))
    else batch = -1
  while (batch ≠ -1)
  complete(sum, ptr)
```

Fig. 18. Randomized loop method

The main issue here is to encode and atomically update the iteration state, since it consists of two pieces of information – the left and the right position in the subrange. We can encode these two positions by using a long integer field and a long CAS operation to update it. The initial 32 bits can contain the position on the left side of the subrange and the subsequent 32 on the right side. With this in mind, the methods `tryAdvanceLeft`, `tryAdvanceRight`, `notStolen`, `notCompleted` and `decodeStep` should be straightforward.

We evaluate the new scheduler on the distribution from Fig. 9-36 and show the results in Fig. 19. The first two diagrams (STEP2 and STEP3) show that with the expensive interval at the beginning and the end of the range the work-stealing tree achieves a close to optimal speedup. However, there is still a worst case scenario that we have to consider, and that is to have a step workload with the expensive interval exactly in the middle of the range. Intuition tells us that

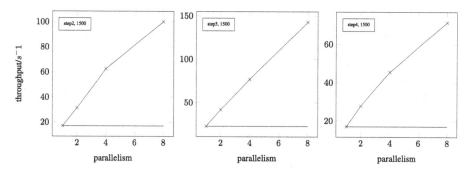

Fig. 19. The randomized work-stealing tree and the STEP3 workload

the probability to hit this interval early on is smaller, since a worker has to progress through more batches to arrive at it. The workload STEP4 in the third diagram of Fig. 19 contains around 25 % expensive elements positioned in the middle of the range. The speedup is decent, but not linear for STEP4, since the bigger batches seem to on average hit the middle of the range more often.

Having shown that randomization does help scheduling both in theory and in practice, we conclude that the problem of overcoming particularly bad workload distributions is an algorithmic problem of finding a batching schedule which can be computed and maintained relatively quickly, leaving this task as future work.

References

1. Arora, N.S, Blumofe, R.D., Plaxton, C.G: Thread scheduling for multiprogrammed multiprocessors. In: Proceedings of the Tenth Annual ACM Symposium on Parallel Algorithms and Architectures, SPAA '98, pp. 119–129. ACM, New York (1998)
2. Blumofe, R.D., Joerg, C.F., Kuszmaul, B.C., Leiserson, C.E., Randall, K.H., Zhou, Y.: Cilk: an efficient multithreaded runtime system. J. Parallel Distrib. Comput. **37**(1), 55–69 (1996)
3. Buss, A., Harshvardhan, Papadopoulos, I., Pearce, O., Smith, T., Tanase, G., Thomas, N., Xu, X., Bianco, M., Amato, N.M., Rauchwerger, L.: STAPL: standard template adaptive parallel library. In: Proceedings of the 3rd Annual Haifa Experimental Systems Conference, SYSTOR '10, pp. 14:1–14:10. ACM, New York (2010)
4. Chakravarty, M.M.T., Leshchinskiy, R., Peyton Jones, S., Keller, G., Marlow, S.: Data parallel Haskell: a status report. In: Proceedings of the 2007 Workshop on Declarative Aspects of Multicore Programming, DAMP '07, pp. 10–18. ACM, New York (2007)
5. Chambers, C., Raniwala, A., Perry, F., Adams, S., Henry, R.R., Bradshaw, R., Weizenbaum, N.: FlumeJava: easy, efficient data-parallel pipelines. In: Proceedings of the 2010 ACM SIGPLAN Conference on Programming Language Design and Implementation, PLDI '10, pp. 363–375. ACM, New York (2010)
6. Chase, D., Lev, Y.: Dynamic circular work-stealing deque. In: Proceedings of the Seventeenth Annual ACM Symposium on Parallelism in Algorithms and Architectures, SPAA '05, pp. 21–28. ACM, New York (2005)

7. Cong, G., Kodali, S.B., Krishnamoorthy, S., Lea, D., Saraswat, V.A., Wen, T.: Solving large, irregular graph problems using adaptive work-stealing. In: ICPP, pp. 536–545 (2008)
8. Frigo, M., Leiserson, C.E., Randall, K.H.: The implementation of the Cilk-5 multithreaded language. In: Proceedings of the ACM SIGPLAN 1998 Conference on Programming Language Design and Implementation, PLDI '98, pp. 212–223. ACM, New York (1998)
9. Herlihy, M., Shavit, N.: The Art of Multiprocessor Programming. Morgan Kaufmann Publishers, San Francisco (2008)
10. Hummel, S.F., Schonberg, E., Flynn, L.E.: Factoring: a method for scheduling parallel loops. Commun. ACM **35**(8), 90–101 (1992)
11. Intel Software Network. Intel Cilk Plus. http://cilkplus.org/
12. JáJá, J.: An Introduction to Parallel Algorithms. Addison-Wesley, Reading (1992)
13. Koelbel, C., Mehrotra, P.: Compiling global name-space parallel loops for distributed execution. IEEE Trans. Parallel Distrib. Syst. **2**(4), 440–451 (1991)
14. Kruskal, C.P., Weiss, A.: Allocating independent subtasks on parallel processors. IEEE Trans. Softw. Eng. **11**(10), 1001–1016 (1985)
15. Lea, D.: A java fork/join framework. In: Java Grande, pp. 36–43 (2000)
16. Polychronopoulos, C.D., Kuck, D.J.: Guided self-scheduling: a practical scheduling scheme for parallel supercomputers. IEEE Trans. Comput. **36**(12), 1425–1439 (1987)
17. Prokopec, A., Bagwell, P., Rompf, T., Odersky, M.: A generic parallel collection framework. In: Jeannot, E., Namyst, R., Roman, J. (eds.) Euro-Par 2011, Part II. LNCS, vol. 6853, pp. 136–147. Springer, Heidelberg (2011)
18. Reinders, J.: Intel Threading Building Blocks, 1st edn. O'Reilly & Associates, Sebastopol (2007)
19. Sarkar, V.: Optimized unrolling of nested loops. In: Proceedings of the 14th International Conference on Supercomputing, ICS '00, pp. 153–166. ACM, New York (2000)
20. Tardieu, O., Wang, H., Lin, H.: A work-stealing scheduler for x10's task parallelism with suspension. In: Proceedings of the 17th ACM SIGPLAN Symposium on Principles and Practice of Parallel Programming, PPoPP '12, pp. 267–276. ACM, New York (2012)
21. Tzen, T.H., Ni, L.M.: Trapezoid self-scheduling: a practical scheduling scheme for parallel compilers. IEEE Trans. Parallel Distrib. Syst. **4**(1), 87–98 (1993)

OpenCL Task Partitioning
in the Presence of GPU Contention

Dominik Grewe$^{(\boxtimes)}$, Zheng Wang, and Michael F.P. O'Boyle

School of Informatics, The University of Edinburgh, Edinburgh, UK
{dominik.grewe,zh.wang}@ed.ac.uk, mob@inf.ed.ac.uk

Abstract. Heterogeneous multi- and many-core systems are increasingly prevalent in the desktop and mobile domains. On these systems it is common for programs to compete with co-running programs for resources. While multi-task scheduling for CPUs is a well-studied area, how to partitioning and map computing tasks onto the heterogeneous system in the presence of GPU contention (i.e. multiple programs compete for the GPU) remains an outstanding problem.

In this paper we consider the problem of partitioning OPENCL kernels on a CPU-GPU based system in the presence of contention on the GPU. We propose a machine learning-based approach that predicts the optimal partitioning of OPENCL kernels, explicitly taking GPU contention into account. Our predictive model achieves a speed-up of 1.92 over a scheme that always uses the GPU. When compared to two state-of-the-art dynamic approaches our model achieves speed-ups of 1.54 and 2.56 respectively.

1 Introduction

Integrated GPUs are becoming ubiquitous for desktop PCs and mobiles. The integrated GPU utilizes a portion of the system's RAM rather than dedicated graphics memory, which shares the same memory space with the CPU. They are less costly when compared to the dedicated GPUs, while still providing parallel computing resources for certain classes of applications. There is an increasing number of applications that make use of the integrated GPU on PCs and mobiles. On these systems it is typical to have multiple programs running at the same time, competing for the shared resources including the GPU. Under such settings, decisions about which computing device (the CPU or the GPU) to use to run the program and how the work should be partitioned across different devices have significant impact on the application's performance.

While multi-task scheduling on the general purpose CPU is a well-studied area, how to partitioning and map tasks onto the underlying platform in the presences of GPU contention remains an outstanding problem. Currently the use of the computing device is statically determine and hard-coded when the application is built. Given that the availability of resources and the behaviours of the workload programs vary in a multi-programmed environment and have a dramatic impact on the correct mapping and scheduling of work, entirely static approaches are likely to

© Springer International Publishing Switzerland 2014
C. Caşcaval and P. Montesinos (Eds.): LCPC 2013, LNCS 8664, pp. 87–101, 2014.
DOI: 10.1007/978-3-319-09967-5_5

fail. What is needed is an approach that can adjust the mapping decision according to the dynamic computing environment by taking into consideration the target program behavior.

Several methods for automatically mapping tasks to devices in a heterogeneous system have been proposed. Luk et al. [14] use offline profiling to determine the best partitioning between the CPU and GPU while Grewe and O'Boyle [6] apply machine learning techniques to predict the optimal partitioning. Both approaches deliver good results but only under the assumption that no other programs are running on the system. Ravi et al. [16] use a dynamic, "task farm" approach for task mapping. They divide the task into a fixed number of chunks and send one chunk to each device. When a device finishes processing it requests a new chunk. As we will show in this paper, this dynamic approach delivers poor performance in the presence of GPU contention.

In this paper a new task partitioning approach is introduced that explicitly takes GPU contention (i.e., multiple programs are competing for the GPU) into account. Unlike most dynamic approaches which require an online searching phase to determine the best partition of work, it uses a machine learning-based predictive model to directly predict the best work partition using code features of the program and runtime information. Unlike previously dynamic approaches, our scheme avoids the potential expensive online searching overhead by directly predicting the best partitioning scheme. The other advantage is that our model is automatically generated off-line at the factory. This avoids the pitfalls of using a hard-wired heuristic that requires human modification whenever the hardware changes.

Across a set of 22 benchmarks and 10 different contention scenarios the predictive model achieves a speed-up of 1.92 over using only the GPU and 1.23 over using only the CPU. When compared to two dynamic approaches our approach achieves speed-ups of 1.54 and 2.56 respectively.

2   Motivation

This section demonstrates the importance of explicitly taking GPU contention into account when mapping programs to heterogeneous systems.

Figure 1 shows the running time of the nbody benchmark in three GPU contention scenarios: no contention, and medium and heavy contention. The medium and heavy contention scenarios are created by running a separate application which uses the GPU alongside the target program to be optimized. More details on which applications were used is given in Sect. 5.1. Along the x axis different static partitioning configurations (represented as the percentage of work mapped to the CPU) are explored. On an idle system (i.e. the no contention scenario) the running time of using only the GPU ($x = 0$) is shorter than the running time of using only the CPU ($x = 100$). This changes, however, when the GPU contention is introduced. Similarly, the optimal partitioning between the devices changes in different contention scenarios. When the system is idle, the best performance is achieved by a 30–70 split but already in medium contention more work should be

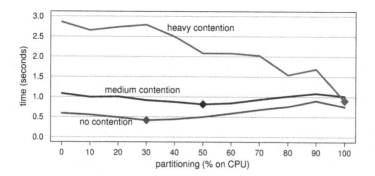

Fig. 1. Running time of the nbody benchmark in multiple GPU contention scenarios for different partitionings. The diamonds indicate the optimal partitioning for the corresponding contention.

assigned to the CPU, namely 50 %. In a heavy contention scenario the runtime of the application increases significantly when some of the work is mapped to the GPU. The best performance is thus achieved when only the CPU is used. The partitioning that is optimal on an idle system ($x = 30$) leads to a $3x$ *slow-down* over the optimal partitioning.

This example demonstrates the need for partitioning techniques that can adapt to contention on the GPU. As the contention information can only be obtained at runtime, any static schemes will fail to achieve good performance on systems being shared by multiple co-running applications. What we need is a dynamic scheme that can adapt to various GPU contention scenarios. The next section will discuss the challenges to be tackled for designing such a dynamic scheme in the presence of GPU contention.

3   Challenges in the Presence of GPU Contention

This work targets OPENCL applications because OPENCL is emerging as a standard for heterogenous computing, which allows the same code to be executed on different computing devices including CPUs and GPUs.

In OPENCL, kernels are launched through command queues. Each time a kernel is being executed it passes through multiple phases, i.e. queueing, ready and execution, as depicted in Fig. 2. Unlike the general purposed CPU where multiple programs can run simultaneously by sharing the CPU time, only one kernel is allowed to execute at a time[1] on the GPU. An OPENCL kernel may therefore have to spend an significant amount of time in the ready phase waiting for the GPU to become available if the GPU is being used by another program. Furthermore, GPU tasks are non-preemptive, i.e. once a task gains access to the GPU no other task can use the GPU until the current task has finished

---

[1] NVIDIA GPUs allow concurrent executions of kernels from the same application but not from different applications.

execution. This means that a kernel scheduled to the GPU may have spent a long time in the ready phase if a different applications has previously launched a long-running kernel. Therefore, non-careful mappings of kernels onto the GPU at the presence of other GPU workload can lead to longer waiting time and result in poor performance. The goal of this work is to determine how the work of OPENCL kernels should be partitioned across the CPU and the GPU to give the best performance by taking the GPU contention into consideration.

The OPENCL API provides an interface for querying the starting and finishing time of each of the phases as indicated by the labels in Fig. 2. This allows one to get insights into the behavior of OPENCL applications in the presence of GPU contention. Figure 3 shows the behavior of the nbody benchmark in the presence of heavy contention. Each bar represents the running time of a kernel launch, divided into the times spent in each of the three phases. During the first few kernel executions the system is idle. Only halfway through the contention is introduced on the respective device. This highlights the difference in behavior on an idle system and one with resource contention.

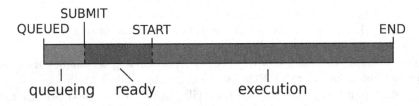

Fig. 2. The three pases of launching and executing an OPENCL kernel. The labels on top correspond to the CL_PROFILING_COMMAND_* parameters passed to the clGetEventProfilingInfo function of the OPENCL API.

When the system is idle the overall running time of each kernel is dominated by the execution phase which is stable across these runs. Time spent in the queueing and ready phases is minimal (they are not even visible in the graphs) because no other applications compete for resources. The behaviour of the application is the same and it takes around 19 ms to run on the GPU. When a competing application is launched, however, the behavior is different. Under such a setting, time spent in the execution phase on the GPU remains the same at 19 ms because the kernel will always have exclusive access to all GPU resources. However, time spent waiting for the GPU to became available (the ready phase) shows dramatic variation. Sometimes it is as low as on the idle system but it can be as high as 120 ms (more than 6 times of the time spent in the execution phase). The variation is due to other applications blocking the GPU. If a long-running kernel has been launched before a kernel is submitted it has to wait for the long-running kernel to finish. If, however, the long-running kernel is just about to finish when the kernel is launched the wait time is small. The total execution time of a kernel launch therefore varies significantly even if the contention is constant, i.e. a fixed co-running applications. In such heavy GPU contention

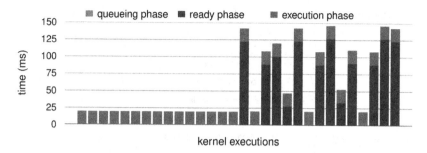

Fig. 3. Profiling of kernel launches in the presence of GPU contention. Each bar shows the total running time of a kernel launch; broken down into queueing, ready and execution times. During the first half the system is idle, then another application is launched competing for resources of the GPU.

it is thus better to use the CPU which provides a much quicker running time (25 ms v.s. 120 ms). This unpredictable behavior of OPENCL applications in the presence of GPU contention provides a big challenge to schedulers trying to find the best partitioning of a kernel across devices. The next section will describe how we build a dynamic scheme that can adapt to the GPU contention using predictive modeling.

4   Predictive Modeling

This section describes how a machine learning-based model can be built for determining a good partitioning for OPENCL tasks in the presence of GPU contention. The input to the predictive model contains information on both the OPENCL kernel and the GPU contention. Its output is a ratio describing the amount of work to map to the CPU and the GPU.

4.1   The Features of the Model

The inputs of model are two sets of numerical values, namely *feature sets*, that represent the input program and the runtime contention. The first set of features describe the OPENCL kernel itself. They are extracted using a static analysis tool based on clang [12]. The second set of features characterize the contention on the GPU device. These features are constructed from information readily available via the OPENCL API.

Program Features. The program features contain information about the number and types of instructions in a kernel. Additionally, the number of coalesced memory accesses is determined. The benchmarks used for this study, as described in Sect. 5.1, often contain vector data types because they were targeted towards both CPUs and GPUs. Another feature is thus the number of vector operations in the code. The full list of program features is shown in Table 1.

Table 1. List of program features used by the predictive model.

Program features
1: # global memory accesses
2: # compute operations
3: # conditionals and loops
4: communication-to-computation ratio
5: percentage of vector operations
6: percentage of coalesced memory accesses
7: # work-items

Contention Features. Contention on the GPU is experienced by increased delays in the ready phase waiting for the device to become available (see Sect. 3). The specific GPU kernel causing the contention does not have any other influence on the remaining programs because access to the GPU is exclusive. The best way to characterize GPU contention is thus to quantify this delay. Since the delay exhibits a significant variance a single observation does not carry much information. Therefore, to characterize the contention the average delay (using the arithmetic mean) is computed over time.

4.2 Building the Model

Machine learning models are built by fitting a mathematical model to *training data*. Training data are observations where both the features (input) and target (output) are known. In our case the training data comprise a set of benchmarks and contention scenarios together with the optimal partitioning in each case. The process of obtaining this data is described in the next section. Once the model has been built predictions for new programs and contention scenarios can be made. This process is depicted in Fig. 4.

In order to model the problem of task partitioning a multi-class classification model is used. Specifically, the model is based on support vectors machines (SVMs) [3]. SVMs try to find hyperplanes in the feature space that separate data points from two different classes. By combining multiple SVMs multi-class problems can be modeled. In order to better find hyperplanes separating the data, kernel functions are used to map the input data into a high-dimensional space. More information on SVMs can be found in [2].

4.3 Collecting Training Data

A set of training programs and "workload" programs are used to collect training data for the predictive model. The workload programs introduce contention on the GPU by either using it for graphics or by executing OPENCL kernels on it. A detailed discussion of which programs were used is given in Sect. 5.1.

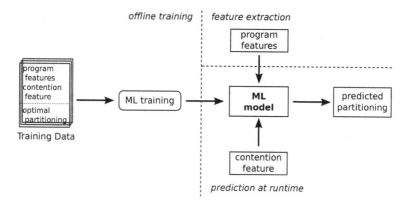

Fig. 4. Building the machine learning (ML) model.

Each combination of training and workload program is executed with different partitionings of the training program. In total eleven different partitionings are evaluated, ranging from CPU-only to GPU-only execution in steps of 10 % as shown in Fig. 1. To ensure a constant degree of contention the workload program is started a few seconds ahead of the training program and input parameters are chosen so that it only finishes after the training program has finished execution.

The best partitioning for each scenario is computed by finding the one with the shortest overall running time. Since some benchmarks contain multiple kernels this computation is done on a per-kernel basis using OPENCL profiling information. The running time of a kernel that is partitioned across the CPU and GPU is defined as the maximum running time across the two devices. The optimal partitions form the targets of the predictive model. The features are collected by performing static analysis on the training program and by recording the incurred delay using the profiling functions provided by OPENCL.

4.4 Deployment of the Model

The model can only be evaluated at run-time because it partially relies on run-time information. On the one hand, the number of work-items needs to be known to compute the program features. This is often only known at run-time. Furthermore, the current GPU contention can obviously only be determined when the program is actually running.

Computing the contention features involves monitoring the waiting times on the GPU and computing the average waiting time as described in Sect. 4.1. Only a window of waiting times of the last few kernel executions should be used, however, to be able to adapt to changes in the contention. This information can either be obtained through previous kernel executions of the program (assuming it launches a sequence of kernels) or by sharing this information across programs.

Table 2. Experimental setup.

	CPU	GPU
Model	Intel Core i5-3570K	Intel HD Graphics 4000
Core clock	3.40 GHz	1.15 GHz
Core count	4	16
Peak performance	108.8 GFLOPS	147.2 GFLOPS
System memory	8 GB	
Operating system	Windows 7 Professional SP 1	
OpenCL SDK	Intel SDK for OPENCL Applications 2013	

5 Experimental Methodology

This section describes the setup used for evaluating the approach presented in this paper. It details how and which aspects of the model were evaluated and describes which other methods it was compared against.

5.1 Experimental Setup

Platform. All experiments were carried out on an Intel IvyBridge platform with a quad-core CPU and an integrated GPU. Full details are shown in Table 2. The aim of this work is to find the best partitionings of OpenCL kernels between the CPU and the integrated GPU. The system was running on Windows 7 and the Intel SDK for OPENCL Applications 2013 [10] was used. Each measured run was repeated 10 times and the average execution time was recorded.

Integrated platforms such as the Intel IvyBridge chip are increasingly common in the desktop and mobile computing space. The trend is to further integrate the CPU and GPU in order to allow close cooperation between the two types of processors.

Benchmarks. We used 22 different benchmarks from the Intel SDK [10] and the AMD SDK [1] to evaluate our approach. These benchmarks were chosen because they are not specifically tuned for GPUs but for use on both CPUs and GPUs, e.g. by using vector data types. They thus provide for more interesting partitioning scenarios. In order to increase the set of training points each benchmark was used with multiple input sizes.

The main computational parts of the benchmarks were executed repeatedly to ensure a minimum running time of around 500 ms. This was done to expose each benchmark to the fluctuations of GPU contention as shown in Sect. 3. It further allows the online search method to find a good partitioning.

Contention Scenarios. To introduce contention to the system a range of applications using GPUs was used. These mainly include OPENCL benchmarks targeting the GPU but also a video player application (VLC). Additionally, the scenario of the idle system, i.e. without any contention, was evaluated. A list of

Table 3. Contention scenarios. Ordered from lowest to highest contention.

Name	Type	Waiting time (μs)
none	no contention	65
vlc	video player	68
sobel-512	OPENCL application	759
monte_carlo	OPENCL application	1,306
sobel-1024	OPENCL application	3,228
aes-512	OPENCL application	8,471
sobel-2048	OPENCL application	12,584
aes-1024	OPENCL application	16,259
aes-2048	OPENCL application	21,944
sort	OPENCL application	36,585

all contention scenarios is given in Table 3. The entries are ordered by how disruptive they are in terms of the average waiting caused as described in Sect. 4.1.

5.2 Comparison

Our approach is compared to three approaches: "oracle", "task farm" and "online search". Unless stated otherwise, performance is shown as the speedup over CPU-only execution.

Oracle. This is a theoretical scheduler that always picks the best static partitioning. It thus provides an estimate of the upper bound performance available in each scenario.

Task farm. This is a dynamic approach which splits each task into a fixed number of chunks. Initially, one chunk is sent to each device and devices request more work after they have finished processing their chunk. For this evaluation we specified the number of chunks to be 8, which leads to the best average performance on the platform we used.

Online search. This dynamic approach finds a good partition over time. For each kernel the scheme keeps track of what the partitioning between the CPU and GPU is. The partition is represented by a *split value* which is the percentage of work mapped to the CPU. The split value is set to 50 % initially, which will be adjusted over time to balance the running times on the CPU and the GPU.

5.3 Evaluation Methodology

We evaluated our approach using the standard *leave-one-out cross-validation* technique. When predicting for a certain benchmark and contention scenario no data from that benchmark, including data from runs with different input sizes, or that contention scenario were used in building the model. It was assumed that

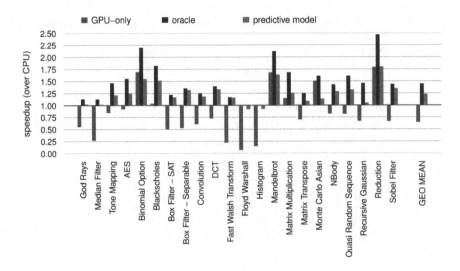

Fig. 5. Speed-up over CPU-only execution averaged across all ten contention scenarios. The GPU-only, oracle and predictive model achieve average speed-ups of 0.61, 1.48 and 1.24 respectively.

information about the GPU contention is available. Section 4.4 provides a brief discussion on how this information can be obtained.

Each benchmark run contains multiple iterations of the main computational phase of the program. This is a common scenario in, for example, linear algebra applications or video processing. Having multiple iterations allows the online search method to find a good partitioning between the CPU and GPU. Furthermore, due to the variable waiting time shown in Sect. 3 it is needed to achieve consistent results.

6   Results

This section evaluates and analyzes the performance of the proposed approach. Firstly, we compare our model and a scheme that uses only the GPU to an oracle scheduler. Then, the performance of the two dynamic schemes is evaluated and compared to our model.

6.1   Comparison to Oracle

Overall. Figure 5 shows the performance of the oracle and the predictive model. Additionally, the performance of a GPU-only approach, which executes all kernels on the GPU, is shown because OPENCL applications typically target the GPU. The performance on each benchmark is shown, averaged across all ten contention scenarios. The numbers are normalized to (parallel) CPU-only execution.

With the exception of five benchmarks, the GPU-only approach leads to on average 1.5x slow downs over CPU-only execution. As shown in Sect. 2 GPU execution can be severely delayed in contention leading to increased running times. The oracle results demonstrate, however, that when using the GPU in the right way significant speed-ups can be achieved. An averaged speed-up of 1.43 (up to 2.47) can be observed across all benchmarks *and* contention scenarios.

Our predictive modeling approach achieves performance close to the oracle for a number of benchmarks, e.g. DCT or Sobel Filter. For all but three benchmarks it outperforms the GPU-only approach and in only two cases can slowdowns over the CPU be observed. On average, the predictive model achieves a speed-up of 1.23 which translates to 86 % of the oracle performance, compared to 45 % and 70 % for the GPU-only and CPU-only approaches, respectively. These results demonstrate that the predictive model manages to adjust well to different contention scenarios.

The overall accuracy of the model is 47.8 %, i.e. in almost half of all cases the model picks the correct partitioning out of the 11 possibilities. A wrong prediction does not necessarily lead to bad performance though. If the prediction is only slightly off, the performance is often close to the optimum (Fig. 1).

Case Studies. To gain a better understanding of the results Fig. 6 shows performance results for 3 of the 10 contention scenarios, namely none, monte_carlo and sort, representing no, medium and heavy contention respectively.

No contention. The average performance of the oracle in no contention is a speed-up of 2.11. The oracle results show, however, that partitioning the work between the CPU and GPU improves performance for all but one benchmark (Floyd Warshall) over using only a single device. When there is no contention on the GPU, the GPU-only approach leads to good performance because the GPU generally outperforms the CPU. On average it achieves a speed-up of 1.64. The predictive model outperforms the GPU-only scheme with an average speedup of 1.74.

Medium contention. When introducing medium contention on the GPU (Fig. 6b) performance of the GPU-only method suffers significantly for some benchmarks, e.g. God Rays and Median Filter, while staying strong for others, e.g. Binomial Option or Reduction. On average, it slows the program down to 0.98 over the CPU execution. By contrast, the predictive modeling approach leads to an average 1.20 speed-up across the benchmarks, which is not far from the 1.42 speed-up of the oracle performance.

Heavy contention. In a heavy contention, the waiting time on the GPU increases significantly. Therefore, in generally, we should avoid to map the program on the GPU. The oracle approach is only able to achieve speedups on 3 out of 22 benchmarks, with an averaged speedup of 1.03 over the CPU-only scheme. It is not supervised that in such a scenario the GPU-only approach performs poorly (Fig. 6c). For only one benchmark, Monte Carlo Asian, an improvement over CPU execution can be observed with some benchmarks have 100x slowdown. On average, the GPU-only method leads to a slow-down of 6 times. Unlike the massive slow-down performance delivered by the GPU-only scheme, the predictive model leads to only minor slow-down over the CPU execution, i.e. 3 %.

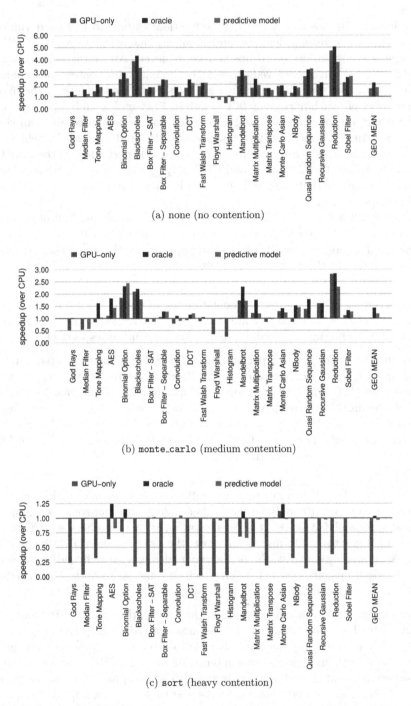

(a) none (no contention)

(b) `monte_carlo` (medium contention)

(c) `sort` (heavy contention)

Fig. 6. Speed-up over CPU-only execution in three different contention scenarios: no contention (a), medium contention with `monte_carlo` as the workload program (b) and heavy contention with `sort` as the workload program (c).

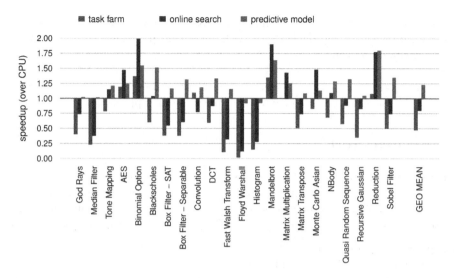

Fig. 7. Speed-up over CPU-only execution averaged across all ten contention scenarios. The task farm, online search and predictive modeling approaches achieve average speed-ups of 0.45, 0.73 and 1.24 respectively.

Summary. The predictive model is able to adapt to contention on the GPU and outperforms single-device approaches. When there is no contention the GPU typically outperforms the CPU but this is reversed when contention is introduced. In all scenarios the predictive model is able to at least match the performance of the fastest single-device strategy. The next section investigates the performance compared to two dynamic mapping approaches (Fig. 7).

6.2 Comparison to State-of-the-Arts

Figure 5 shows the performance of the two dynamic approaches, task farm and online search, as well as that of the predictive model. The performance of each benchmark is shown, averaged across all ten contention scenarios. The numbers are normalized to (parallel) CPU-only execution.

It can be seen immediately that both dynamic approaches fail to achieve good performance in the presence of GPU contention. With a few exceptions, e.g. `Binomial Option` or `Mandelbrot`, both approaches are not able to outperform the CPU-only approach. Especially the task farm mapper leads to slow-downs in most cases. For all but one benchmark, namely `Convolution`, the online search approach beats the task farm mapper. In only 5 of the 22 benchmarks does either of the dynamic approaches outperform the predictive modeling approach.

On average, the task farm method leads to 2.2x slow-down and the online search approach leads to 1.36x slow-down. In other words, both dynamic schemes fail to achieve speedups when there is contention on the GPU. The predictive model, on the other hand, achieves a speed-up of 1.24, demonstrating that using the GPU in the right way can be very beneficial.

The benchmarks where the dynamic approaches, especially the online search method, do well are the ones where GPU execution performs strongly even in heavy contention scenarios, e.g. Binomial Option or Monte Carlo Asian, as can be seen in Fig. 6c. Conversely, benchmarks where a GPU-only approach performs poorly in heavy contention, e.g. Fast Walsh Transform or Floyd Warshall, also show huge slow-downs on the dynamic approaches.

7   Related Work

Programming Frameworks for GPUs. As GPUs become ubiquitous for computing, many programming models [8,9,11] have been proposed for GPU programming. These approaches provide APIs to develop GPU applications. All these approaches implicitly assume the GPU gives the best performance.

Program Mapping for GPUs. A number of approaches have been proposed to partitioning a GPU program kernels across the CPU and the GPU [6,14]. However, those approaches assume the program runs in isolation and do not consider the GPU contention.

Dynamic Task Scheduling. Previous work investigates hardware and operating system based approaches to schedule tasks on CPUs. For examples, symbiotic job scheduling tries to find the best mix of jobs [5,17] on SMT processors; an Parcae is a dynamic tuning framework [15] for CPU execution. Ravi et al. [16] develop a dynamic approach to make task for heterogeneous systems. Their approach searches for the best partition at runtime. However, the searching can lead to significant runtime overhead. Our approach, by contrast, avoids this overhead by directly predicting the portioning setting.

Predictive Modeling. In addition to optimizing sequential programs [4,13], recent studies have shown that predictive modeling is effective in optimizing parallel programs [18,20,21] or scheduling multiple programs on the CPU [7,19]. However, none of the previous research addresses the problem of task mapping in the presence of workload contention on a heterogeneous platform with different computing devices.

8   Conclusion

This paper has investigated the impact of contention for GPU resources on mapping OPENCL programs to CPU-GPU systems. Standard mapping techniques fail to adapt to this type of contention because, unlike on the CPU, kernels have exclusive access to the GPU and cannot be preempted. It is possible, however, to adapt mapping decisions to GPU contention by explicitly taking it into account. We have proposed a machine learning-based approach that uses information of the contention as well as program characteristics to decide how to partition an OPENCL kernel across the CPU and GPU. Across a set of 22 benchmarks and 10 different contention scenarios this method achieved a speed-up of 1.23 over

CPU-only execution. This corresponds to 86 % of the performance of an oracle approach. Two dynamic mappers, task farm and online search, only achieve speed-ups of 0.48 and 0.80 respectively, thus actually slowing down the execution time compared to the CPU-only method.

References

1. AMD. Accelerated parallel processing (APP) SDK (2013)
2. Bishop, C.M.: Pattern Recognition and Machine Learning (Information Science and Statistics). Springer, New York (2006)
3. Boser, B.E., Guyon, I., Vapnik, V.: A training algorithm for optimal margin classifiers. In: Proceedings of the 5th Annual ACM Conference on Computational Learning Theory, pp. 144–152 (1992)
4. Cooper, K.D., Schielke, P.J., Subramanian, D.: Optimizing for reduced code space using genetic algorithms. In: LCTES '99, pp. 1–9 (1999)
5. Eyerman, S., Eeckhout, L.: Probabilistic job symbiosis modeling for SMT processor scheduling. In: ASPLOS '10, pp. 91–102
6. Grewe, D., O'Boyle, M.F.P.: A static task partitioning approach for heterogeneous systems using OpenCL. In: Knoop, J. (ed.) CC 2011. LNCS, vol. 6601, pp. 286–305. Springer, Heidelberg (2011)
7. Grewe, D., Wang, Z., O'Boyle, M.F.P.: A workload-aware mapping approach for data-parallel programs. In: HiPEAC '11 (2011)
8. Han, T.D., Abdelrahman, T.S.: hiCUDA: a high-level directive-based language for GPU programming. In: GPGPU '09
9. Hormati, A., Samadi, M., Woh, M., Mudge, T., Mahlke, S.: Sponge: portable stream programming on graphics engines. In: ASPLOS '11
10. Intel. Intel SDK for OpenCL applications 2013 — intel developer zone (2013)
11. Kim, J., Kim, H., Lee, J.H. Lee, J.: Achieving a single compute device image in OpenCL for multiple GPUs. In: PPoPP '11
12. LLVM. Clang: a C language family frontend for LLVM. http://clang.llvm.org/
13. Long, S., O'Boyle, M.F.P.: Adaptive java optimisation using instance-based learning. In: ICS '04
14. Luk, C.-K., Hong, S., Kim, H.: Qilin: exploiting parallelism on heterogeneous multiprocessors with adaptive mapping. In: MICRO 42 (2009)
15. Raman, A., Zaks, A., Lee, J.W., August, D.I.: Parcae: a system for exible parallel execution. In: PLDI '12, pp. 133–144
16. Ravi, V.T. Ma, W., Chiu, D., Agrawal, G.: Compiler and runtime support for enabling generalized reduction computations on heterogeneous parallel configurations. In: SC, pp. 137–146 (2010)
17. Snavely, A., Tullsen, D.M.: Symbiotic jobscheduling for a simultaneous multithreaded processor. In: ASPLOS-IX, pp. 234–244 (2000)
18. Wang, Z., O'Boyle, M.F.P.: Using machine learning to partition streaming programs. ACM Trans. Archit. Code Optim. **10**(3) (2013)
19. Wang, Z., O'Boyle, M.F.P., Emani, M.K.: Smart, adaptive mapping of parallelism in the presence of external workload. In: CGO '13 (2013)
20. Wang, Z., O'Boyle, M.F.P.: Mapping parallelism to multi-cores: a machine learning based approach. In: PPoPP '09 (2008)
21. Wang, Z., O'Boyle, M.F.P.: Partitioning streaming parallelism for multi-cores: a machine learning based approach. In: PACT '10 (2010)

Heterogeneous Computing

Compiling a High-Level Directive-Based Programming Model for GPGPUs

Xiaonan Tian[✉], Rengan Xu, Yonghong Yan, Zhifeng Yun,
Sunita Chandrasekaran, and Barbara Chapman

Department of Computer Science, University of Houston, Houston, TX 77004, USA
{xtian2,rxu6,yyan3,zyun,schandrasekaran,bchapman}@uh.edu

Abstract. OpenACC is an emerging directive-based programming model for programming accelerators that typically enable non-expert programmers to achieve portable and productive performance of their applications. In this paper, we present the research and development challenges, and our solutions to create an open-source OpenACC compiler in a main stream compiler framework (OpenUH of a branch of Open64). We discuss in details our loop mapping techniques, i.e. how to distribute loop iterations over the GPGPU's threading architectures, as well as their impacts on performance. The runtime support of this programming model are also presented. The compiler was evaluated with several commonly used benchmarks, and delivered similar performance to those obtained using a commercial compiler. We hope this implementation to serve as compiler infrastructure for researchers to explore advanced compiler techniques, to extend OpenACC to other programming languages, or to build performance tools used with OpenACC programs.

1 Introduction

Computational accelerators that provide massive parallelism such as NVIDIA GPGPUs and Intel Xeon Phi, or those that provide special-purpose application engines such as DSP have become viable solutions to build high performance supercomputers, as well as special-purpose embedded systems. However, one of the critical challenges to fully exploit the hardware computation capabilities is the need for productive programming models. OpenCL and CUDA are widely-used low-level programming models designed for programming GPGPUs. These two programming models require rewriting of most of the application program from its CPU version that users want to offload to accelerators. This has been known to be a non-productive approach.

OpenACC [5] is an emerging standard for programming accelerators in heterogeneous systems. The model allows developers to mark regions of code for acceleration in a vendor-neutral manner. It is built on top of prior efforts adopted by several compiler vendors (notably PGI and CAPS Enterprise). OpenACC is intended to enable programmers to easily develop portable applications to maximize performance and power efficiency of the hybrid CPU/GPU architecture.

© Springer International Publishing Switzerland 2014
C. Cascaval and P. Montesinos (Eds.): LCPC 2013, LNCS 8664, pp. 105–120, 2014.
DOI: 10.1007/978-3-319-09967-5_6

Compiler implementation and enhancement in the model are underway by several industry compilers, notably from Cray, PGI and CAPS. However, their source codes are mostly inaccessible to researchers and they cannot be used to gain an understanding of the OpenACC compiler technology or to explore possible improvements and suggest language extensions to the model.

In this paper, we present our experience of constructing an OpenACC compiler in the OpenUH open source compiler framework [10], with goals to enable a broader community participation and dialog related to this programming model and the compiler techniques to support it. We also hope this implementation to serve as compiler infrastructure for researchers that are interested in improving OpenACC, extending the OpenACC model to other programming languages, or building tools that support development of OpenACC programs. Specifically, the features of the compiler and our contributions are summarized as follows:

1. We constructed a prototype open-source OpenACC compiler based on a branch of main stream Open64 compiler. Thus the experiences could be applicable to other compiler implementation efforts.
2. We provide multiple loop mapping strategies in the compiler on how to efficiently distribute parallel loops to the threading architectures of GPGPU accelerators. Our findings provide guidance for users to adopt suitable loop mappings depending on their application characteristics.
3. OpenUH compiler adopts a source-to-source approach and generates readable CUDA source code for GPGPUs. This gives users opportunities to understand how the loop mapping mechanism are applied and to further optimize the code manually. It also allows us to leverage the advanced optimization features in the backend compilation step by the CUDA compiler.

We evaluate our compiler with several commonly used benchmarks, and showed the similar performance results to those obtained using a commercial compiler. The remainder of this paper is organized as follows: Sect. 2 gives an overview of OpenACC model. Section 3 presents implementation details of the OpenACC compiler. Section 4 shows the detail of runtime support. Section 5 discusses the results and evaluation. Section 6 provides a review of the related work. Conclusion and future work are presented in Sect. 7.

2   Overview of OpenACC Programming Model

OpenACC is a high-level programming model that can be used to port existing HPC applications on different types of accelerators with minimum amount of effort. It provides directives, runtime routines and environment variables as its programming interfaces. The execution model assumes that the main program runs on the host, while the compute-intensive regions of the program are offloaded to the attached accelerator. The accelerator and the host have separate memory, and the data movement between them need to be handled explicitly. OpenACC provides different types of data transfer clauses and runtime call in its standard. To reduce the performance impacts of data transfer latency, OpenACC also allows asynchronous data transfer and asynchronous computation with the CPU code to enable overlapping of data movement and computation.

Figure 1 shows a simple OpenACC vector addition example. The `acc data` directive, which identifies a data region, will create a and b in device memory and then copy the respective data into device at the beginning of the data region. The array c will be copied out after finishing the code segment of the region. The `acc kernels` directive means the following block is to be executed on device. The `acc loop` directive causes the distributions of loop iterations among the threads on the device.

```
#pragma acc data copyin( a[0:n], b[0:n] ), copyout( c[0:n] )
{
  #pragma acc kernels
  {
    #pragma acc loop independent
    for ( i = 0; i < n; i++ ) {
      c[i] = a[i] + b[i];
    }
  }
}
```

Fig. 1. OpenACC vector addition example

3   Compiler Implementation

The creation of an OpenACC compiler requires both innovative research solutions to the challenges of mapping high-level loop iterations to low-level threading architectures of the hardware, and also large amount of engineering work in compiler development to handle parsing, transformation and code generations. It also requires runtime support for handling data movement and scheduling of computation on the accelerators. The compiler framework we are using is OpenUH compiler, a branch of the open source Open64 compiler suite. Figure 2 shows the components of the OpenUH framework. The compiler is implemented in highly component-oriented way and composed of several modules, each of which operates on a multi-level IR called WHIRL. From top, each module translates the current level of WHIRL to its lower-level form.

We have identified the following challenges that must be addressed to create an OpenACC implementation. First, it is very important that we create an extensible parsing and IR systems to facilitate addition of new features of future language revisions and to support aggressive compiler transformation and optimizations. Fortunately, the extensibility of OpenUH framework and WHIRL IR allow us to easily add those extensions with decent amount of work. Secondly, we need to design and implement an effective means for the distribution of loopnest across thread hierarchy of GPGPUs. We discuss in more details of our solutions in Sect. 3.1. Thirdly, we need to create a portable runtime to support data handling, reductions operations, and GPU kernel launching. Runtime support will be discussed in more details in Sect. 4.

We decide to use the source-to-source approach, as shown in Fig. 2. WHIRL2C tool has been enhanced to output compilable C program from the CPU portion

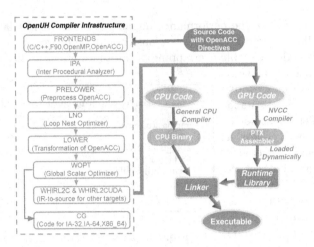

Fig. 2. OpenUH compiler framework for OpenACC

of the original OpenACC code, and we have created a WHIRL2CUDA tool that will produce NVIDIA CUDA kernels after the transformation of offloading code regions. Compared to binary code generation, the source-to-source approach gives much more flexibilities to users. It allows to leverage advanced optimization features in the backend compilation step by nvcc. It also gives user options to manually optimize the generated CUDA code for further performance improvement.

3.1   Loop Transformation

Programmers usually offload the computation intensive loopnest to massive parallel accelerators. One of the major challenges of compiler transformation is to create a uniformed loop distribution mechanism that can effectively map loopnest iteration across the GPU parallel system. As an example, NVidia GPGPUs has two level of parallelisms: block-level and thread-level. Blocks can be organized as multi-dimensional in a grid and threads in a block can also be multi-dimensional. How to distribute iterations of multi-level loopnest across the multi-dimensional blocks and threads is a nontrivial problem.

OpenACC provides three level of parallelisms for mapping loop iterations to the accelerators' thread structures: coarse grain parallelism "gang", fine grain parallelism "worker" and vector parallelism "vector". OpenACC standard gives the flexibility of interpreting them to the compiler. For NVIDIA GPU, some compilers map each gang to a thread block, and vector to threads in a block and ignore worker [6]; other compilers map gang to the x-dimension of a grid block, worker to the y-dimension of a thread block, and vector to the x-dimension of a thread block [2]. There are also compilers that map each gang to a thread block, worker to warp and vector to SIMT group of threads [7].

Table 1. OpenACC and CUDA terminology mapping

OpenACC clause	CUDA	Comment
gang (integer expression)	block	If there is an integer expression for this gang clause, it defines the number of blocks in one dimension of grid
vector (integer expression)	thread	If there is an integer expression for this vector clause, it defines the number of threads in one dimension of block

In our implementation, we evaluated 8 loopnest mapping algorithms covering single loop, double nested loop, and triple nested loop as shown in Figs. 3, 6, 7. If the depth of the nested loop is more than 3, the OpenACC `collapse` clause will be used. More specifically, gangs are mapped to blocks and vectors are mapped to threads in each block. Both gang and vector can be multi-dimensional. The worker clause is omitted in current OpenUH compiler. Table 1 shows the mapping terminology we used between OpenACC and CUDA.

Memory coalescing is an important part that needs to take into careful consideration in compiler loop transformation. Different mapping can heavily affect the application's performance. Adjacent threads (in x-dimension of a block) taking consistent memory space can improve performance. Therefore we need to make sure the loop iteration mapped to vector x-dimension operates the continuous memory operands. The single loop and the inner loop iteration in double nested loop are mapped to x-dimension of threads. For triple nested loop, we selected three examples that are typically encountered in the OpenACC program. We mapped the innermost loop of Map3_1 and Map3_2 to operate on the continuous memory, but in Map3_3 it is mapped to the outmost loop to compute continuous memory. The reason of this mapping for Map3_3 is because we have a particular stencil application requiring the pattern likes this.

Single Loop. N iterations are equally distributed among gangs and vectors. Both gang and vector are one dimension. It means the grid and thread-block are also one dimension. Each thread takes one iteration at a time and then moves ahead with $blockDim.x * gridDim.x$ stride. Figure 3 show the mapping and transformation for this single loop.

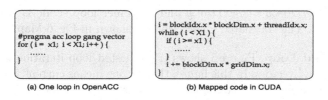

Fig. 3. One loop transformation.

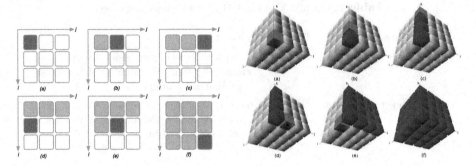

Fig. 4. Double nested loop iteration distribution (color figure online).

Fig. 5. Triple nested loop iteration distribution (color figure online).

Double Nested Loop. Figure 4 shows the double nested loop iteration distribution across gangs and vectors. The red one means current working area, green one means the finished computation, and white means untapped. The axises i and j represent the outer and inner loop iterations. Figure 4(a) shows the first working area, and the next status is in Fig. 4(b). After finishing the last one in j axis, working area moves ahead into another i iteration. The computation is not finished until all the rectangles turn to be green. The stride (length of the rectangle) in i and j depends on different mapping algorithms.

There are four different double nested loop cases, and the mapping algorithms are different from each other. Figure 6 shows the mapping for each case:

- Both gangs and vector are one dimension. The outer loop is distributed across the gang and inner loop is executed among threads in each gang. The stride in i and j axis are $gridDim.x$ and $blockDim.x$. The translated CUDA code from this case is shown in Fig. 6 Map2_1.
- One dimensional gang, two dimensional vector. After the mapping, the outer loop stride is $gridDim.x*blockDim.y$ and the inner loop stride is $blockDim.x$. The translated CUDA code is shown in Fig. 6 Map2_2.
- Two dimensional gangs and one dimensional vectors. After the mapping, the outer loop stride is $gridDim.y$ and the inner loop stride is $gridDim.x * blockDim.x$. The translated CUDA code is shown in Fig. 6 Map2_3.
- Both grid and block are two dimensions. After the mapping, the outer loop stride is $gridDim.y * blockDim.y$ and the inner loop stride is $gridDim.x * blockDim.x$. The translated CUDA code is shown in Fig. 6 Map2_4.

Triple Nested Loop. Figure 5 shows triple nested loop iteration distribution across gangs and vectors. In this figure, the red one means current working area, blue one means the finished computation, and green means untapped. The axises i, j, and k represent the outermost, middle and innermost loop iterations. At the first step, GPU takes computation from axis k in Fig. 5(a). When finishing, working area moves ahead along the k axis Fig. 5(b) until all the computation

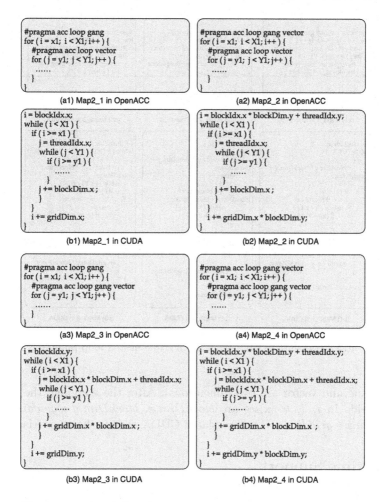

Fig. 6. Translated CUDA code from double nested loop mappings

in k axis is done Fig. 5(c). After this, the computation will move to the next j Fig. 5(d). Repeat the first step until j reaches the boundary. Once all the computation on the j, k space are done, i moves a stride ahead, and reset j, k axises Fig. 5(e). The computation repeats until all the computation is done Fig. 5(f).

For the three different triple nested loops, Fig. 7 shows the mapping:

- Both gang and vector are two dimensional. After the mapping, the outmost loop stride in i, j, k axises are $griddim.x$, $blockDim.y * griddim.y$ and $blockDim.x$. The translated CUDA code is shown in Fig. 7 Map3_1.
- Two dimensional gang and three dimensional vector. After the mapping, the outmost loop stride in i, j, k axises are $blockDim.z$, $blockDim.y * griddim.y$ and $blockDim.x * griddim.x$. The translated CUDA code is shown as Map3_2.

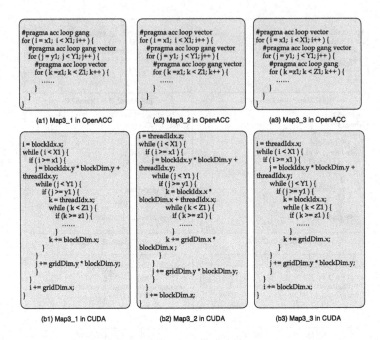

Fig. 7. Translated CUDA code from triple nested loop mappings

– Both gang and vector are two dimensional. After the mapping, the outmost loop stride in i, j, k axises are $blockDim.x$, $blockDim.y * griddim.y$ and $gridDim.x * griddim.x$. The translated CUDA code is shown as Map3_3.

4   Runtime Support

The OpenACC annotated source code is parsed by the compiler to extract the device kernels and translate the OpenACC directives into runtime calls. Then two parts of the code are generated: one part is the host code compiled by the host compiler, another part is the kernel code compiled by the accelerator compiler. The runtime is responsible for handling data movement and managing the execution of kernels from the host side.

4.1   Runtime Library Components

The runtime library consists of three modules: context module, memory manager, and kernel loader. The context module is in charge of creating and managing the virtual execution environment. This execution environment is maintained along the lifetime of all OpenACC directives. All context and device related runtimes, such as `acc_init()` and `acc_shutdown()`, are managed by this module.

The memory manager helps to control the data movement between the host and device. The compiler will translate the clauses in **data** and **update** directives into corresponding runtime calls in this module. OpenACC provides a `present` clause that indicates the corresponding data list are already on the device, in order to avoid unnecessary data movement. To implement this feature, the runtime creates a global hash map that stores all the device data information. Whenever a compiler parses a `present` clause, it will translate this clause to the runtime call to check if the data list in the `present` clause are in the map. If the data exists in the map, then there is no need for data movement. If the data does not exist in the map, the compiler will issue a compilation error. Each data structure in the map includes the host address, device address and the data size so that we can find the device address given a host address or vice versa. Note that the data allocated from `acc_malloc()` and the data in the `deviceptr` clause do not have a corresponding host address since they are only allowed to use on the device.

The purpose of kernel loader module is to launch the specified kernel from the host. After the kernel file is compiled by the accelerator compiler, the runtime loads the generated file, setups the threads topology and pushes the corresponding arguments list into the kernel parameter stack space, then launch the specified kernel. Since different kernels have different number of parameters, a vector data structure is created to store the kernel arguments to guarantee that the kernel argument size is dynamic. Another work to do before launching a kernel is to specify the threads topology. The compiler parses the loop mapping strategy and then generates the corresponding thread topology. The recommended threads value in the topology is described in Sect. 4.2.

4.2 Gang and Vector Topology Setting

The threads topology is an important factor affecting application performance. Since we map gangs to blocks in grid and vector into threads within each block, the values of blocks and threads need to be chosen carefully. Too many blocks and threads may generate potential scheduling overhead, and too few threads and blocks cannot take advantage of the whole GPU hardware resources such as cache and registers. The threads topology setting should consider exposing enough parallelism in each multiprocessor and balancing the workload across all multiprocessors. Different threads topology affects the performance differently. Some results with different topology values are discussed in Sect. 5. In OpenUH, if the user did not specify the gang and vector number, the default value will be used. The default vector size is 128 because the Kepler architecture has quad warp scheduler that allows to issue and execute four warps (32 threads) simultaneously. The default gang number is 16 since Kepler allows up to 16 thread blocks per multiprocessor.

4.3 Execution Flow in Runtime

Figure 8 gives a big picture of the execution flow at runtime. In the beginning, `acc_init()` is called to setup the execution context. This routine can be either called explicitly by the user or implicitly generated by the compiler. Next the

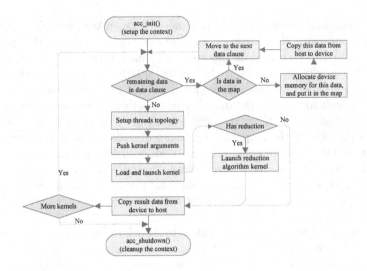

Fig. 8. Execution flow with OpenACC runtime library

data clauses will be processed. There are different kinds of data clauses (e.g. `copyin`, `copyout` and `copy`) and these data clauses may be in either of `data`, `parallel` or `kernels` directive. If the data needs to be accessed from the device, for instance those in `copyin` or `copy` or `update device` clauses, then they are transferred from the host to device. These data clauses will be scanned and processed. The purpose of this step is to make the data ready before launching the kernels. After the data is ready, we will setup the threads topology and push the corresponding arguments to the kernel. So far everything is ready and we can safely load and launch the kernel. If the kernel needs to do some reduction operation, after this kernel is finished a separate reduction algorithm kernel will be launched. The result data, for instance those in `copyout` or `copy` or `update host` clauses, will be transferred from the device to host. Finally `acc_shutdown()` is called to release all the resources and destroy the context.

5   Preliminary Results

We evaluated OpenUH OpenACC compiler implementation using performance test suite from [3], Stencil benchmark from [13] and DGEMM written by ourselves. The double precision numerical algorithms in these examples are on either 2D or 3D grids, and therefore they are highly suitable to test different loop mapping strategies. The experimental machine has 16 cores Intel Xeon x86_64 CPU with 32 GB main memory, and a NVIDIA Kepler GPU card (K20). OpenUH translates the original OpenACC program into host code and device code. The host code is compiled by gcc 4.4.7 with -O0 and the device code is compiled by nvcc 5.0 with "-arch=sm_35", and then they are linked into an executable.

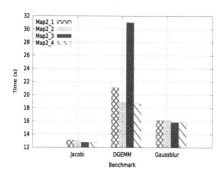

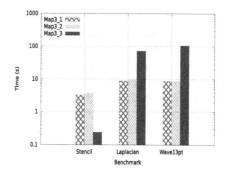

Fig. 9. Double nested loop mapping.   **Fig. 10.** Triple nested loop mapping.

Table 2. Threads used in each loop with double loop mappings

Benchmark	Double loop	Map2_1	Map2_2	Map2_3	Map2_4
Jacobi (2048×2048)	Outer loop	2048	1024×2	2046	1023×2
	Inner loop	128	128	16×128	16×128
DGEMM (8192×8192)	Outer loop	8192	4096×2	8192	4096×2
	Inner loop	128	128	64×128	64×128
Gaussblur (1024×1024)	Outer loop	1024	512×2	1020	510×2
	Inner loop	128	128	8×128	8×128

5.1 Performance for Double Nested Loop Mapping

In the first stage, we compile these benchmarks with OpenUH compiler and compare the performance difference among different loop mappings. Figure 9 shows the performance comparison in different benchmarks with different double nested loop mappings. All of Jacobi, DGEMM and Gaussblur have double nested parallel loops but they show different performance behavior. In Jacobi, the data accessed from the inner loop are contiguous in memory while they are non-contiguous when accessed from the outer loop. In all of our four double nested loop mappings, the inner loop uses **vector** which means the threads executing the inner loop are consecutive. In both **vector** and **gang vector** cases, the threads are consecutive and the only difference is the length of concurrent threads. In Jacobi inner loop, consecutive threads access aligned and consecutive data and therefore the memory access is coalesced. In this case the memory access pattern and the loop mapping mechanism match perfectly. That is why the performance using all of the four loop mappings are close. Table 2 shows the number of threads used in each loop mapping. Because Map2_1 and Map2_2 have less threads than Map2_3 and Map2_4 in the inner loop, the execution time is slightly longer. Map2_1 and Map2_2 have the same performance since their threads are the same in both the outer loop and inner loop. The performance behavior of Gaussblur is similar to Jacobi because their memory access pattern and threads management are similar.

In DGEMM, the performance of Map2_2 and Map2_4 are better than the other two mappings which is because they both have enough parallelism in each block to hide memory access latency. The performance penalty in Map2_1 is due to less parallelism in each block. Map2_3 has the worst performance as it does not have enough parallelism in each block and has many thread blocks. Too many blocks means more scheduling overhead as a block cannot be started until all resources for a block is available.

5.2   Performance for Triple Nested Loop Mapping

Figure 10 shows the performance comparison in different benchmarks with different triple nested loop mappings. In Stencil, the data is stored in memory in $x \rightarrow y \rightarrow z$ order which means the data is firstly stored in x dimension, then y dimension and lastly z dimension. The computation kernel, however, access the data in $z \rightarrow y \rightarrow x$ order which means the data accessed in the innermost loop (z dimension) are not contiguous in memory but the data accessed in the outermost loop (x dimension) are contiguous in memory. The loop Map3_3 uses vector in the outermost loop and therefore the global memory access are coalesced. This follows the most important rule when mapping the loop: consecutive threads access consecutive data in memory. Hence the performance with Map3_3 is much better than the other two loop mappings. Note that the loop Map3_2 also used vector in the first loop, but its performance is worse than Map3_3. This is because the threads in this vector are in z dimension and not consecutive in CUDA context. The loop Map3_1 uses gang in the first loop and this also indicates that the threads are not consecutive in this level, as the stride between each thread pair is $gridDim.x$ rather than 1. Table 3 shows the threads in each loop of different benchmarks. In Stencil note that although the total number of threads in Map3_1 is much more than that of Map3_3, its performance is still

Table 3. Threads used in each loop with triple loop mappings

Benchmark	Triple loop	Map3_1	Map3_2	Map3_3
Stencil ($512 \times 512 \times 64$)	outermost loop	510	2	128
	middle loop	255×2	255×4	255×2
	innermost loop	128	16×64	62
Laplacian ($128 \times 128 \times 128$)	outermost loop	63	2	128
	middle loop	126×2	32×4	2
	innermost loop	128	2×64	126
Wave13pt ($128 \times 128 \times 128$)	outermost loop	64	2	128
	middle loop	124×2	31×4	2
	innermost loop	128	2×64	124

poorer which is just because the memory access is uncoalesced. Laplacian and Wave13pt have similar performance patterns in which the performance with loop Map3_1 and 3_2 are much better than loop Map3_3. The reason is that their data layout in memory matches the data memory access pattern indicated by the loop mapping mechanism. For instance, in Laplacian the data accessed in the inntermost loop are consecutive in memory and the threads specified by loop Map3_1 and 3_2 are also consecutive, as a result the data accesses are coalesced in GPU and high performance can be achieved. With loop Map3_3, however, the used loop clause is gang and the stride between threads is larger than 1 which means the threads are not consecutive. As a consequence, the non-consecutive threads try to access consecutive data and therefore the data access is not coalesced, and finally the performance is penalized. The loop Map3_1 and 3_2 are similar and the only difference is the thread increment stride. That can be explained why the performance using these two loop mapping mechanisms are close.

5.3   Performance Comparison Between OpenUH and PGI OpenACC

We also compared the performance for all benchmarks with PGI commercial compiler. PGI 13.6 was used and both -O0 and -O3 optimization flags were experimented, respectively. OpenUH only used -O0 since it has not applied any optimization in generated GPU code. Figure 11(a) shows the performance difference between OpenUH and PGI compiler in double nested loop mapping. Since PGI compiler always converts Map2_1 to 2_3 and Map2_2 to 2_4, we only compare the performance between 2_3 and 2_4 loop mappings. We measured the kernel time which indicates the efficiency of the kernel code generated by compiler, and the total time which includes the kernel time, data transfer time and the runtime overhead. The result shows that OpenUH is slightly better than PGI compiler in the total time of Jacobi, DGEMM and Gaussblur. By profiling all benchmarks, we found that the performance difference is due to PGI compiler always creates two contexts to manage asynchronous data transfer even though the async clause was not specified in the program. As a result, the runtime has more overhead of creating another context and managing the synchronization of all asynchronous activities. For the kernel time, OpenUH is still slightly better than PGI in Jacobi and DGEMM, but slightly worse in Gaussblur. Overall the performance in PGI compiler with -O0 and -O3 has no much difference, and the performance variance between OpenUH and PGI is within a very small range and OpenUH performance is very competitive comparing to PGI compiler.

Figure 11 (b) shows the performance comparison between OpenUH and PGI compiler in triple nested loop mappings. It is observed that in Stencil the performance of OpenUH is much worse than PGI compiler in loop Map3_2. We believe that PGI did some memory access pattern analysis and can automatically adjust its loop mapping mechanism, thus delivering better performance than ours. Briefly speaking, in the outermost loop of Stencil, the data access is not coalesced in OpenUH implementation as OpenUH assumes the data accessed only from the innermost loop are contiguous in memory, whereas in this program

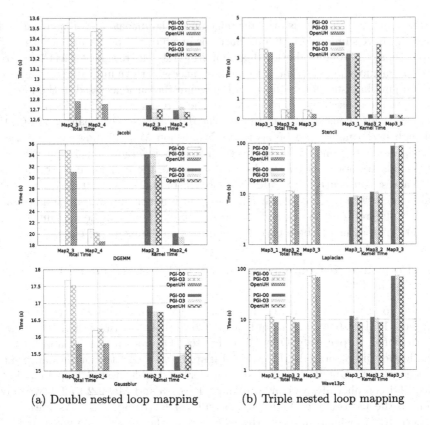

(a) Double nested loop mapping   (b) Triple nested loop mapping

Fig. 11. Performance comparison with different loop mappings

the data accessed only from the outermost loop are contiguous in memory. We believe PGI compiler did data flow analysis which can automatically detect this and change the loop mapping, so that the access to the outermost loop are coalesced by threads. So far OpenUH has implemented the same loop mapping techniques, but it requires a memory access analysis model to dynamically change the loop mapping, which is one of our ongoing work.

6   Related Work

There are both commercial OpenACC compiler and academic compiler efforts to support high-level programming models for GPGPUs. CAPS compiler [1] also uses the same source-to-source translation approach as ours. PGI OpenACC accelerator compiler [4] use binary code generation approach. Cray compiler [7] is another OpenACC compiler that can only be used in Cray supercomputers. These three compilers have different mapping mechanisms as we discussed in early section. Since both CAPS and Cray have different interpretations of **gang**, **worker** and **vector**, we did not compare our results with these compilers for fairness reason. accULL [12] is another OpenACC compiler written in python script. KernelGen [11] can port the existing code into Nvidia GPU without the need of adding any directives. It requires the GPU to support dynamic parallelism, so it is not as portable as OpenACC. OpenMPC [9] translates OpenMP code to cuda and HiCUDA [8] is another directive-based model which is similar to OpenACC but the user still needs to manage almost everything.

7 Conclusion

In this paper, we presented our effort of creating an OpenACC compiler in our OpenUH compiler framework. We have designed loop mapping mechanisms of single, double nested, and triple nested loops that are used in the compiler transformation. These mechanisms will be helpful for users to adopt suitable computation distribution techniques according to their application's characteristics. Our open-source OpenUH compiler can generate readable CPU code and CUDA code, which allows user to further tune the code performance. The experiments show that our compiler can generate code with competitive performance to commercial OpenACC compiler.

Since this is our first baseline version, advanced features such as multidimensional array movement, loop collapse, parallel construct and async, etc. are under development. All the executions currently implemented are on synchronization mode. Advanced compiler analysis and transformation techniques will also be explored to further improve the quality of generated kernel codes.

Acknowledgements. This work was supported in part by the NVIDIA and Department of Energy under Award Agreement No. DE-FC02-12ER26099. We would also like to thank PGI for providing the compilers and support for the evaluation.

References

1. CAPS Enterprise OpenACC Compiler Reference Manual, June 2013. http://www.openacc.org/sites/default/files/HMPPOpenACC-3.2_ReferenceManual.pdf
2. CAPS OpenACC Parallism Mapping (2013). http://kb.caps-entreprise.com/what-gang-workers-and-threads-correspond-to-on-a-cuda-card
3. Performance Test Suite, June 2013. https://hpcforge.org/plugins/mediawiki/wiki/kernelgen/index.php/Performance_Test_Suite
4. PGI Compilers, June 2013. http://www.pgroup.com/resources/accel.htm
5. The OpenACC Standard, June 2013. http://www.openacc-standard.org
6. Brent Leback, M.W., Miles, D.: The PGI Fortran and C99 OpenACC Compilers. Cray User Group (2012)
7. Cray, C.: C++ Reference Manual (2003)
8. Han, T.D., Abdelrahman, T.S.: hiCUDA: high-level GPGPU programming. IEEE Trans. Parallel Distrib. Syst. **22**, 78–90 (2011)
9. Lee, S., Eigenmann, R.: OpenMPC: extended openMP programming and tuning for GPUs. In: Proceedings of the 2010 ACM/IEEE International Conference for High Performance Computing, Networking, Storage and Analysis, pp. 1–11. IEEE Computer Society (2010)

10. Liao, C., Hernandez, O., Chapman, B., Chen, W., Zheng, W.: OpenUH: an optimizing, portable OpenMP compiler. Concurrency Comput. Pract. Experience **19**(18), 2317–2332 (2007)
11. Mikushin, D., Likhogrud, N.: KERNELGEN - a toolchain for automatic GPU-centric applications porting (2012). https://hpcforge.org/scm/viewvc.php/checkout/doc/sc_2012/sc_2012.pdf?root=kernelgen
12. Reyes, R., López-Rodríguez, I., Fumero, J.J., de Sande, F.: accULL: an OpenACC implementation with CUDA and OpenCL support. In: Kaklamanis, C., Papatheodorou, T., Spirakis, P.G. (eds.) Euro-Par 2012. LNCS, vol. 7484, pp. 871–882. Springer, Heidelberg (2012)
13. Stratton, J.A., Rodrigues, C., Sung, I.-J., Obeid, N., Chang, L.-W., Anssari, N., Liu, G.D., Hwu, W.: Parboil: a revised benchmark suite for scientific and commercial throughput computing. Center for Reliable and High-Performance Computing (2012)

Separate Compilation in a Language-Integrated Heterogeneous Environment

Mike Murphy[1]($\boxtimes$), Jaydeep Marathe[1], Girish Bharambe[2], Sean Lee[1],
and Vinod Grover[1]

[1] NVIDIA Corporation, Santa Clara, USA
[2] NVIDIA Corporation, Pune, India
{mmurphy,jmarathe,gbharambe,selee,vgrover}@nvidia.com

Abstract. Heterogeneous computing platforms are becoming more common in recent years. Effective programming languages and tools will play a key role in unlocking the performance potential of these systems. In this paper, we present the design and implementation of separate compilation and linking support for the CUDA programming platform. CUDA provides a language-integrated environment for writing parallel programs targeting hybrid systems with CPUs and GPUs (Graphics Processing Unit). We present a novel linker that allows linking of multiple subsets of GPU executable code. We also describe a link time optimization of GPU shared memory layout. Finally, we measure the impact of separate compilation with real world benchmarks and present our conclusions.

Keywords: Separate compilation · Linker · Heterogeneous · GPU

1 Introduction

Heterogeneous computing platforms are becoming widespread in recent years. Such platforms are not just limited to supercomputing systems, but also being deployed in personal computing environments. NVIDIA introduced CUDA for programming CPU-GPU heterogeneous computing platforms in 2007 [1]. Since then, the CUDA ecosystem has grown rapidly [10] and has spurred language and tools development for effectively exploiting the performance potential of such systems. OpenACC [11], OpenCL [6], and Microsoft AMP [14] are a few other programming systems for heterogeneous computing.

With widespread increase in size and complexity of programs, it is important to provide a programming environment that is intuitive to developers who are used to creating software on non-heterogeneous systems. CUDA's *language-integrated heterogeneous parallel programming* approach is key for this goal. CUDA modules contain code that executes on the CPU, GPU or on both processors. Functions and variables are annotated with execution spaces (CPU/GPU). CPU code can create work on the GPU using an extended call syntax.

Our *language-integrated* approach is distinct from other frameworks such as OpenCL, where the GPU program is embedded in a character string that is explicitly passed to compiler API functions invoked by the CPU program.

© Springer International Publishing Switzerland 2014
C. Caşcaval and P. Montesinos (Eds.): LCPC 2013, LNCS 8664, pp. 121–135, 2014.
DOI: 10.1007/978-3-319-09967-5_7

Early versions of CUDA tools required the whole program at compile time. This represented a significant hurdle from a software development and porting perspective. In this paper, we describe our work to enable *separate compilation* for CUDA in release 5.0, which removes this limitation. *We believe this to be the first language-integrated heterogeneous programming environment that provides separate compilation and linking support.*

In the rest of the paper, we use the terms *device* and *host* to refer to the GPU and the CPU, respectively. By extension, *device code* and *host code* refer to code entities that execute on the GPU and CPU, respectively. There are several motivations for enabling separate compilation for device code:

Incremental Compilation Speedup: Requiring all device code to be in a single translation unit increases the compile time and memory requirements for the compiler toolchain. Incremental compilation is also not possible; if any part of the device code is changed, the entire device code must be compiled again. This slows down the edit-build-debug cycle during software development. Separate compilation solves this problem by allowing code refactoring into multiple translation units. A change to one translation unit requires only that translation unit to be re-compiled, and the application to be re-linked. This reduces the incremental compilation overhead, allowing faster code development.

Ease of Porting: Most large applications have code factored into tens or even hundreds of translation units. Separate compilation support eases the process of porting such applications to the GPU.

Library Support: Separate compilation support enables linking against third party libraries, allowing *modular* program development. User code may now link against one or more libraries with device code, where the library and user code are independently compiled, including the possibility of libraries calling user-defined device callback functions.

In this paper, we make the following contributions:

– We present our design for separate compilation in the CUDA programming environment. We introduce the *device linker* for linking separately compiled device code objects.
– We describe how *host-visible device entities* are supported under separate compilation.
– We present a novel *device sub-link* mechanism that allows groups of objects to be linked separately, and co-exist in the generated program.
– We describe a device link time resource allocation algorithm for allocating device shared memory.
– We evaluate the optimization tradeoffs in separate compilation mode compared to the older whole-device-program compilation mode.
– We present performance metrics with real applications, comparing programs built under separate compilation versus the whole-device-program mode.

2 CUDA

CUDA consists of a programming language, a compiler and a runtime for heterogeneous parallel computing [1,10]. A typical target platform has two different kinds of processors - the CPU and the GPU. The GPU can execute many threads in parallel using multiple processors that contain local memories.

Figure 1 shows a simple CUDA program that multiples two vectors element wise, in parallel.

```
__constant__ int factor = 0.5;
__device__ float multiply (float a, float b) { return a * b * factor; }

__global__ void vectorMultiply(float *A, float *B, float *C)  {
  C[threadIdx.x] = multiply (A[threadIdx.x], B[threadIdx.x]);
}

void hostFunc(void) {
  float *A, *B, *C;
  // allocate device memory for A, B, C and initialize A and B with data
  // (not shown to save space)

  vectorMultiply<<< 1, vectorLength>>>(A, B, C);  // launch kernel on device

  // copy C to host memory.
}
```

Fig. 1. An example CUDA program fragment

Functions annotated with __device__ keyword execute on the GPU. Functions annotated with __global__ keyword are the entry point for GPU code execution (*kernel* function). A function with no explicit annotation or marked with the __host__ keyword execute on the CPU. Thus, multiply is a device function, hostFunc is a host function and vectorMultiply is an entry function for GPU code execution.

Kernel functions can be launched from host code using the triple angle bracket syntax ("<<<...>>>"). Namespace scope variables can be allocated in specific GPU memory regions with annotations (e.g., __constant__).

3 Heterogeneous Separate Compilation

Figure 2 shows the CUDA separate compilation and linking framework. For each translation unit, the CUDA frontend splits the host and device code into separate parts. The device code is passed to the device compiler, generating a "fatbinary". A fatbinary contains the device machine code for one or more GPU architectures in ELF format [5]. The fatbinary is transformed into a data array and embedded in the host part of the CUDA source file generated by the frontend. This combined program is then processed by the host compiler to produce an object

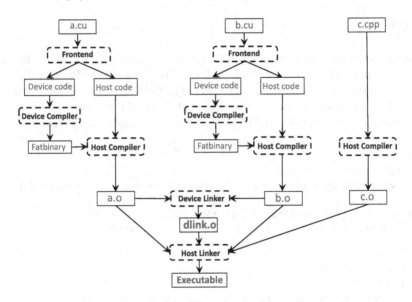

Fig. 2. Separate compilation and device linking

file. The object file can be linked against other objects on the host system to produce a host executable or library.

Previous versions of CUDA did not support separate compilation of device code, *i.e.,* all device code entities accessed during a kernel launch had to be in the same translation unit. The separate compilation framework described in this paper removes this restriction, by using a new *device linker* that links the device code entities from multiple object files.

The device linker extracts the device code embedded in the object files, carries out the linking process, and generates another object file embedding the linked device code image. The generated object also contains synthesized definitions for host functions that are invoked during host startup (see Sect. 5). The synthesized object file is presented to the host linker along with the original object files to produce a host executable or library[1]. The device linker may be invoked explicitly, it is also invoked implicitly by the compiler driver when the target is a host executable[2].

4   Host-Visible Device Entities

In a heterogeneous computing environment like CUDA, certain device entities can be directly referenced in host code. For example, kernel functions can be

---

[1] Original objects are required during host linking, since they may define host entities (e.g., functions) with external linkage that are referenced from host code in other objects.

[2] In this case, the device linker ignores any object files without device code.

launched from the host, but these functions contain code that executes on the GPU. In this section, we detail how such "host-visible" device entities are supported under separate compilation.

The host-visible entities are __global__ (kernel) functions, namespace scope variables allocated in __device__ or __constant__ address space, textures and surfaces. With separate compilation, the definition and reference to these entities may be in different translation units. For example, consider the program below, where the host-visible entities are defined in first.cu and referenced in second.cu.

```
first.cu:
__global__ void foo(void) { ....}        // kernel
__device__ int devVar;                    // variable
__constant__ int constVar;                // variable
texture<float> tex;                       // texture
surface<void, 2> surf;                    // surface

second.cu:
extern __global__ void foo(void);         // kernel
extern__device__ int devVar;              // variable
extern __constant__ int constVar;         // variable
extern texture<float> tex;                // texture
extern surface<void, 2> surf;             // surface

void host_func(void) {
foo<<<1,1>>>();                           // launch kernel
cudaGetSymbolAddress(..., devVar);        // get address
cudaGetSymbolAddress(..., constVar);      // get address
cudaBindTexture(...,tex,...);             // bind texture
cudaBindSurfaceToArray(surf,...);         // bind surface
}
```

As described in Fig. 2, the host code and device code are processed by different backend compilers. As a result, host-visible device entities need special handling in the code passed to the host backend compiler. For each host-visible entity defined in the current translation unit, the compiler frontend will create a *shadow* entity (function, variable, etc.) with the same linkage, in the code passed to the host compiler. References in the host code to the original device entity will be updated to refer to the *shadow* entity. In addition, the compiler frontend will insert *registration code* to be run during host start up. The registration code creates a mapping from the *shadow* entity to the name of the original device entity[3]. This mapping enables the CUDA driver to retrieve the device entity being referenced from the host code. For example, the compiler frontend would insert the following code for "foo" when generating the host-side code for first.cu above:

---

[3] Names of entities with static linkage are mangled with a unique translation unit specific prefix.

```
void foo(void) { } // shadow function
// host code from first.cu
....
```

```
attribute((constructor)) __init(void) {
__register(&foo, "foo"); // map shadow entity to device entity
}
```

5 Multiple Device Links

5.1 Motivation

Existing separate compilation environments typically have a single link step. Objects are combined into a single executable by the link step. In the CUDA environment, linking device code in a single link step may negatively impact the performance of the final linked code. The entry point for device execution is a kernel function. Before a kernel is launched, the runtime ensures that the all resources required by the kernel are available. The runtime requires that the compiler toolchain provide upper bounds on the resources used by the kernel and any functions transitively invoked from the kernel. Examples of the resources that need to be tracked are the maximum amount of __shared__ memory needed by the kernel and the maximum number of physical registers needed during the kernel's execution. To compute this information, the CUDA linker builds a callgraph for each kernel function. However, in the presence of indirect function calls, the call graph information may be conservative. As a result, the computed resource usage values may be overly pessimistic. This may cause the kernel launch to fail at runtime or to artificially restrict the number of parallel units of work that are run simultaneously on the processor, degrading the throughput of the executing programs[4].

For example, consider the following two source files:

```
first.cu:
__device__ void first(void) {
__shared__ int arr \cite{bib4096};
...
 }
__device__ void (*func_ptr)(void) = first;
```

```
second.cu:
__device__ void second(void (*fp)(void)) {
  __shared__ int local \cite{bib1024};
  fp();
  ...
}
```

---

[4] Thus, it may reduce the the *occupancy* [7] of the GPU.

The functions *first* and *second* are never invoked during the execution of the same kernel. However, since the address of *first* is taken, the linker may assume that *first* is invokable from the indirect call site in *second*. As a result, the __shared__ memory requirement for a kernel invoking *second* includes allocations for both variables *arr* and *local*. If the entities from first.cu and second.cu never interact, one solution is for the user to put the objects created from first.cu and second.cu in different *sub-linked* object groups. The device linker is invoked multiple times, with disjoint sets of objects participating in each link step. Since the linker call-graph only considers objects participating in the current link step, the call graph will be more precise and the __shared__ memory requirement calculations will therefore be more accurate.

This *multiple device link* facility is very useful for library writers, because it enables *performance isolation* of library code from the user's code. Objects in the library that contain device code, and that are not supposed to directly interact with the user's device code, can be device-linked before the library is shipped. This insulates the user's device code and the library's device code from each other, with respect to the per-kernel resource requirement computation in the linker. It may also lead to shorter device link times for the user's code, since objects from the pre-linked library will not participate in the user's device link step.

5.2   Constraints

The design for the multiple device link mechanism must support the following constraints:

- As described in Sect. 4, registration code for host-visible device entities needs a handle to the linked device image. The device linker must define a function that provides this handle.
- The same object cannot be allowed to link in multiple device links. The object file may contain definition of host-visible entities such as kernel functions; if the entity is referenced in host code, the CUDA runtime would not be able to uniquely determine the device entity being referenced if the object participates in multiple device links. This restriction is consistent with the "one-definition-rule" (ODR) semantics of the CUDA C language, derived from C++ [8].
- The device linker design places a restriction that host objects created by the compiler cannot be modified by the device linker. This eliminates the possibility of patching the object file, e.g., to insert a function call to the linker generated function that returns a handle to the linked image[5].

---

[5] Patching object files during linking may also complicate "rule-based" build environments. These define rules to produce a "result" given one or more inputs, and the input entities are not expected to be modified in the user-provided implementation of the rule. Also, the object files may not be modifiable, e.g., because of file permissions or because they contain objects that are part of multiple programs, such as a system provided library.

5.3 Design

Each object is associated with a unique identifier, called the *module-id*. The *module-id* uniquely identifies the object among all objects that participate in any device link step. The *module-id* is computed by the device compiler and embedded in the generated object file. The device compiler also synthesizes a call to an externally defined function (*"init-function"*) in the generated object. The *init-function's* name is derived from the *module-id*, and is unique per object. The *init-function* returns a handle to the linked device image, and the handle is used to register host-visible device entities (Sect. 4). During device linking, the linker synthesizes the definition for the *init-function* for every object, using the embedded *module-id*.

How does the device compiler generate the *module-id*? It leverages the ODR semantics of the CUDA C source language. ODR semantics require that a function or variable with extern linkage be defined exactly once in the complete program[6]. If such a function or variable definition is present in the current translation unit, its name is used to derive the *module-id*, along with the file name and path[7].

Figure 3 shows an example with multiple device links. a.o and b.o participate in the first device link, c.o and d.o participate in another one. The object files generated from the source (.cu) files contains the *module-id* and the call to the

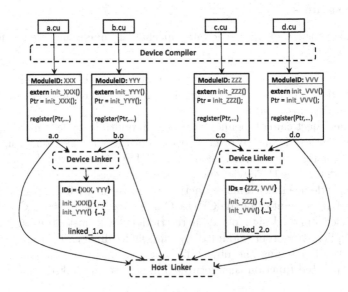

Fig. 3. Multiple Device Link Example

---

[6] Some exceptions are template instantiations and inline function definitions. These are ignored for *module-id* calculation.

[7] In uncommon cases where no such function or variable is available, the current time value is used along with the file name and path.

init-function (e.g., *init_XXX*). The object file generated by each device link step contains the *module-ids* and the *init-function* definitions. The host linker binds the *init-function* calls to the definitions present in the objects created by the device link steps.

5.4 Detecting Error Scenarios

The above design ensures that the program will fail to build for some error cases:

- **Object in Multiple Sub-links**: If an object is involved in multiple device links, the device linker will create the *init-function* definition for that object multiple times. When the host linker is invoked, the program will fail to link because of ODR semantics (a function with extern linkage can be defined exactly once).
- **Device Link Step Missing**: As described above, the device compiler synthesizes a call to the uniquely named *init-function* in every object. If this object does not participate in any device link step, and is presented to the host linker, the program will fail to link because of the missing definition of the *init-function*.

6 No-Cloning Under Separate Compilation

Typical host programs have a single entry point (usually called "main") which is the starting point for execution. Under CUDA, each kernel represents an entry point in the device code; there can be multiple kernels in a complete device program. The kernel functions may call common device functions or reference common data. Under the legacy compilation mode (*i.e.*, without separate compilation), the entire device code was compiled as a single translation unit. In this case, a compiler optimization would *clone* the common device functions and __shared__ memory variables, per kernel. Thus, each kernel could be separately optimized, for example:

- Since each kernel gets its own cloned version of the __shared__ memory variable, the __shared__ memory layout can be computed independently of other kernels. This has two benefits. First, the __shared__ memory addresses can be fixed before code generation, allowing optimizations such as constant folding. Second, the total size of the __shared__ memory addressed by the kernel may be reduced, since there is more freedom in assigning offsets to __shared__ memory variables.
- Global inter-procedural register allocation is possible for each kernel and the versions of the device functions cloned for it; this allows better code generation, and can reduce the maximum number of registers used by the kernel.

Decreasing the resource requirements of the kernel (total registers and __shared__ memory used) can increase GPU performance by increasing GPU occupancy [7], *i.e.*, by reducing the number of cycles the GPU is stalled without work.

Unfortunately, with separate compilation, this optimization is no longer possible, since device function definitions may now be in a different translation unit. We measure the impact of disabling this optimization in Sect. 8[8].

7 Optimizing Shared Memory Layout at Link Time

GPUs have limited memory space for shared memory, so it is important to allocate shared memory objects in an optimal manner. This is complicated by the fact that device code can have multiple kernels (entry points in device code), and different kernels may access different shared memory objects. If a user declares the shared memory variables local to a kernel, then it is obvious where they are used, but typically users allocate the shared memory in global scope so that it can be shared by multiple functions[9]. This provides us with an opportunity to reduce the space requirements by overlapping shared memory objects that are used in different kernels.

Consider the following example:

```
__shared__ int X[1000],  Y[1000], Z[100];
__global__ void E() {  .... X;   .... Z;   }
__global__ void F() {  .... Y;   .... Z;   }
```

There are two kernels E and F, and three shared memory objects X, Y and Z; if E uses X and Z, while F uses Y and Z, then we can overlap the allocation of X and Y, thus only using 4400 bytes rather than 8400 bytes. However, this requires doing data allocation at link time rather than having each object allocate its own memory. This also requires the use of a link-time callgraph with multiple roots (kernel functions). Determining the optimal allocation of such shared memory can be thought of as a graph coloring algorithm. Graph coloring is commonly used in the context of register allocation. In this case we apply it to data allocation, and use the set of kernels reached as the interference graph. The algorithm works as follows:

1. Search the relocations [5] to find all uses of shared objects.
2. Use the callgraph to find which shared objects are used by each kernel (so if a non-kernel function F references a shared object, find all kernels that reach F).
3. If no one uses the shared object, remove it. If only one kernel uses shared object, move it to be local to kernel.
4. Build interference graph where each node represents the shared memory object, and has edge between nodes when the sets of kernels they reach intersect.

---

[8] Disallowing device function cloning reduces overall program size. We found that this significantly reduces overall compile time for a few large files in our repository (up to 7x reduction).

[9] Shared memory variables can have extern specifiers and be in different translation units.

5. Sort the list of nodes so largest-size objects are allocated first.
6. Go through interference graph and assign each node to an allocation group such that edges are always in a different group (color the graph).
7. Assign offsets to each allocation group (a group is set of overlapping objects).

The above scheme is not always optimal. Graph coloring assumes equal-size registers; in our case the objects are not all equal sized. We allocate the largest objects first to minimize the wasted space, but there can be situations where several smaller objects that conflict with each other but not with a larger object could all fit within the space of the larger object, in essence by doing a nested allocation of the smaller objects. This situation requires completely independent sub-graphs. We may modify our algorithm to account for this case, but so far we have not seen this be an issue in the code we have processed, and thus have refrained from the additional complexity. The algorithm is very effective for the benchmarks we evaluated, as shown in Sect. 8. Typically all the shared objects can be fit into just two allocation groups, the most complicated case we have seen so far in real code has required only 4 allocation groups.

8   Results

Table 1 describes the benchmarks used for performance measurements. The Lawa sources may be configured to be compiled as single file containing all the device source code, or as separate files. We contrast the two build modes to illustrate the potential advantages of separate compilation. The three other benchmarks (Cublas, Cufft, Thrust) contain legacy CUDA code sources that put all device code in a single file. We use these benchmarks to measure the impact of toggling the cloning optimization (Sect. 6) and for measuring the effectiveness of the link time shared memory allocation scheme (Sect. 7).

All measurements are done with the CUDA 5.0 release, running on a 64bit Linux system with default full optimization. The separate compilation support is also implemented on Windows and Mac systems, but the results are independent of host platform so we only show the results for one platform.

8.1   Lawa

Figure 4 plots the compilation time for each source file in seconds, with Lawa built in separate compilation mode. All except one file take less than 6 s to

Table 1. Benchmarks

Name	Description	#Files	#Kernels	#Lines
Lawa	Library for adaptive wavelet applications	151	4	47 K
Cublas	BLAS library	330	2178	90 K
Cufft	Fast Fourier Transforms library	85	644	35 K
Thrust	Parallel Algorithms library	111	1588	75 K

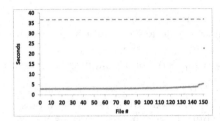

Table 2. Lawa run time for kernels K1–K4 (microseconds)

	K1	K2	K3	K4	Total
Separate compilation	146759	14263	975	38	162036
Whole program compilation	147355	6360	977	38	154732

Fig. 4. Lawa compile time

compile. The combined host and device link times were less than a second. The dotted line in the same graph shows the build time when the Lawa device code is compiled as a single translation unit $(36\,\mathrm{s})$[10]. Doing a full build from scratch is significantly slower with separate compilation, due to invoking the both the host and device compilers multiple times, but incremental compilation where only part of the program is rebuilt (which is typical of the edit-build-debug cycle and one of the goals of separate compilation) is significantly faster (6 vs 36 s).

Table 2 compares the program runtime when built under separate compilation versus the entire device code in a single file ("whole program compilation"). The second kernel slows down significantly due to the lack of inlining when the file is split. However, other kernels have comparable runtime, such that the overall run time only degrades by 4.5 % in the separate compilation mode. To get better performance with separate compilation, a user should look for hot spots and potentially inline code in that area.

8.2   Impact of No-Cloning Versus Cloning

Figure 5 shows performance metrics when the benchmarks were built in no-cloning mode, relative to the values for cloning mode[11]. Compile times for Cufft and Thrust show little impact from no-cloning. The effect for Cublas is less clear. Compilation time for some files decreased significantly, while it increased for other files, though it remains almost unchanged for the vast majority.

The runtime impact of no-cloning was minimal for most tests, but did show some negative impact on about 25 % of the Cublas tests. As described in Sect. 6, disabling cloning inhibits certain optimizations that seem to impact these tests.

For all three benchmarks, the per-kernel shared memory does not change significantly with no-cloning, for the vast majority of the kernels[12]. This indicates that the link time shared memory layout optimization (Sect. 7) effectively places the shared memory variables such that the per-kernel sizes approach the

---

[10] 90 % of Lawa's compilation time is spent on device code so any improvements are predominantly due to changes on the device side.

[11] No run time reported for Thrust, since we don't have performance tests for this benchmark.

[12] Only kernels with non-zero shared memory sizes are reported here.

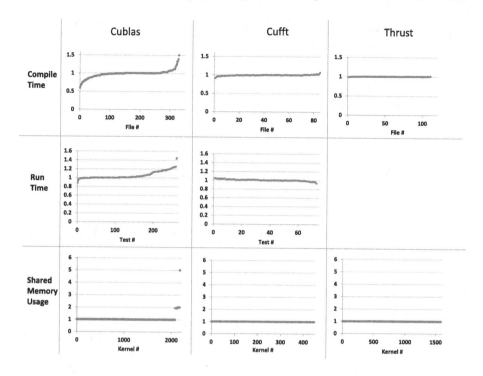

Fig. 5. Performance metrics for No-Cloning relative to Cloning.

"best case" sizes possible with cloning. Alternately, the benchmarks may predominantly contain shared memory variables accessed only by a single kernel, in which case the layout optimization is not applicable. This is further explored in Sect. 8.3 below.

As legacy CUDA code is recompiled under separate compilation mode, the cloning optimization will be disabled. The fact that compile time, run time and shared memory usage did not change significantly for the vast majority of the cases should smooth the initial transition to separate compilation mode for legacy CUDA programs.

8.3 Impact of Shared Memory Layout Optimization

Figure 6 shows the per kernel shared memory sizes with the link time layout optimization discussed in Sect. 7. The values are relative to the sizes with the optimization disabled and compiled under no-cloning mode. So 1.0 means there was no change, 0.2 means that the optimized code reduced the space usage to 20 % of the original. The figure shows that the link time optimization is extremely effective for Cublas and Thrust kernels, while there was no impact for Cufft. For Cublas, the optimized layout was less than a quarter of the size of the non-

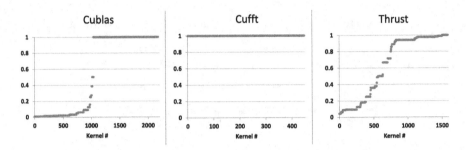

Fig. 6. Per kernel shared memory size with link time layout optimization, relative to size with optimization disabled.

optimized layout, for almost half of the kernels. Similarly dramatic results can be seen for the Thrust kernels.

9 Related Work

Several heterogeneous parallel programming systems have been developed over recent years. OpenACC [11], OpenCL [6], Microsoft AMP [14], Cell [16], PGI Accelerator [13] and PGI CUDA Fortran [12] are some of the prominent examples. OpenACC and PGI Accelerator provide pragma directives to control code generation and variable placement for the associated heterogeneous co-processor. AMP and CUDA Fortran provide a language-integrated environment similar to CUDA. However, none of these environments currently allow separate compilation and linking of device code.

OpenCL 1.2 adds support for separate compilation and linking of device code fragments. This is quite different from our approach:

- Language integration: In OpenCL, the device code is represented as a string embedded in host code. In CUDA, host and device code entities are part of the same source program where kernel functions and device variables may be accessed in host code. This makes programming simpler, but is challenging to implement.
- Explicit (OpenCL) versus Implicit (CUDA) linking: OpenCL provides APIs to explicitly link device code. In CUDA, the linking is implicit - it is orchestrated by the compiler driver. This model is easier to use because it is similar to existing host environments.
- Device Sub-linking (CUDA): The CUDA linker allows linking sub-groups of device code. This feature is important for shipping pre-linked library code.

Cell supports device code link, in a similar manner to ours but the host and device sources are compiled and linked separately.

Levine gives a short history of linking and suggests that the idea has been around since 1947 [2].

10   Conclusion

In this paper, we presented our design for separate compilation and linking of embedded device code, in a language-integrated heterogeneous environment. Separate compilation provides many advantages - the ability to support third party libraries, compile time speedups with incremental builds and ease of porting legacy programs to the heterogeneous environment. We described the linker extensions for sub-linking subsets of device code objects. We also described a link time scheme for optimizing shared memory layout. Finally, we evaluated the cost of disabling cloning in separate compilation mode, and the effectiveness of the shared memory layout optimization.

References

1. Buck, I.: GPU computing: programming a massively parallel processor. In: International Symposium on Code Generation and Optimization (2007)
2. Levine, J.R.: Linkers and Loaders. Morgan-Kaufman, San Francisco, CA (1999)
3. Presser, L., White, J.R.: Linkers and loaders. ACM Comput. Surv. 4(3), 149–167 (1972)
4. Taylor, I.L.: Part 1 of 20 on linkers (2007). http://www.airs.com/blog/archives/38
5. ELF specification: System V Application Binary Interface (2010). http://www.sco.com/developers/gabi/latest/contents.html
6. Khronos OpenCL Working Group: OpenCL Specification version 1.2 (2011). http://www.khronos.org/registry/cl/specs/opencl-1.2.pdf
7. NVIDIA Corporation: NVIDIA CUDA programming guide (2012)
8. The C++ Standards Committee ISO/IEC JTC1/SC22/WG21: 14882:2011(E), Programming Languages C++ (2011)
9. Top500 Project: TOP500 Supercomputer Sites (2012). http://i.top500.org/overtime
10. Clavel, M., Durán, F., Eker, S., Lincoln, P., Martí-Oliet, N., Meseguer, J., Talcott, C.: Introduction. In: Clavel, M., Durán, F., Eker, S., Lincoln, P., Martí-Oliet, N., Meseguer, J., Talcott, C. (eds.) All About Maude - A High-Performance Logical Framework. LNCS, vol. 4350, pp. 1–28. Springer, Heidelberg (2007)
11. OpenACC Corporation: The OpenACC Application Programming Interface (2012). http://www.openacc.org/sites/default/files/OpenACC.1.0_0.pdf
12. The Portland Group: PGI CUDA Fortran Compiler (2012). http://www.pgroup.com/resources/cudafortran.htm
13. The Portland Group: PGI Accelerator Compilers with OpenACC Directives (2012). http://www.pgroup.com/resources/accel.htm
14. Microsoft Corporation: C++ AMP: Language and Programming Model (2012). http://msdn.microsoft.com/en-us/library/hh265137.aspx
15. Intel Corporation: Intel Array Building Blocks (2012). http://software.intel.com/en-us/articles/intel-array-building-blocks
16. Chow, Alex Chunghen: Programming the Cell Broadband Engine (2012). http://www.gamasutra.com/view/feature/130278/programming_the_cell_broadband_.php
17. LLVM: LLVM gold plugin (2013). http://llvm.org/docs/GoldPlugin.html

Parametric GPU Code Generation
for Affine Loop Programs

Athanasios Konstantinidis[1]([⊠]), Paul H.J. Kelly[1],
J. Ramanujam[2], and P. Sadayappan[3]

[1] Imperial College London, London, UK
{ak807,p.kelly}@imperial.ac.uk
[2] Louisiana State University, Baton Rouge, USA
ram@cct.lsu.edu
[3] The Ohio State University, Columbus, USA
saday@cse.ohio-state.edu

Abstract. Partitioning a parallel computation into finite-sized chunks
for effective mapping onto a parallel machine is a critical concern for
source-to-source compilation. In the context of OpenCL and CUDA,
this translates to the definition of a uniform hyper-rectangular partitioning of the parallel execution space where each partition is subject to
a fine-grained distribution of resources that has a direct yet hard to estimate impact on performance. This paper develops the first compilation
scheme for generating parametrically tiled codes for affine loop programs
on GPUs, which facilitates run-time exploration of partitioning parameters as a fast and portable way of finding the ones that yield maximum
performance. Our approach is based on a parametric tiling scheme for
producing wavefronts of parallel rectangular partitions of parametric size
and a novel runtime system that manages wavefront execution and local
memory usage dynamically through an inspector-executor mechanism.
An experimental evaluation demonstrates the effectiveness of our approach for wavefront as well as rectangularly-parallel partitionings.

1 Introduction and Related Work

The diverse and evolving hardware organization of modern GPUs highlights the
importance of search-based performance tuning in finding the right set of execution parameters for best software performance. The benefits of performing such
tuning at runtime (as opposed to iterative compilation), is that we can minimize
total compilation cost, simplify code generation and therefore enable fast design-
space exploration through parameterized OpenCL/CUDA programs that can be
reused across different GPU devices. Parametric tiling (also referred to as parameterized tiling in the literature) can realise these benefits as it produces tiled
loop nests with parametric tile sizes amenable to runtime search [12,16,17,20].

One of the fundamental properties of tileable loop nests, i.e., loop nests for
which tiling is a semantics-preserving transformation, is that it allows parallel execution of tiles through wavefront (also known as pipeline) parallelism

© Springer International Publishing Switzerland 2014
C. Caşcaval and P. Montesinos (Eds.): LCPC 2013, LNCS 8664, pp. 136–151, 2014.
DOI: 10.1007/978-3-319-09967-5_8

[15,25,26]. However, being able to produce wavefronts of parametric tiles is challenging. Solutions have been proposed for OpenMP targets by Hartono et al. [13] and Baskaran et al. [4]. In particular, the first solution [13] constructs a space of non-aligned rectangular tiles of parametric sizes proposed earlier [12] and then utilizes an inspector-executor runtime that packs intra-wavefront tiles into bins for parallel execution. On the other hand, Baskaran et al. [4] relies on a uniform space of rectangular parametric tiles and proposes a relaxed Fourier-Motzkin elimination algorithm in order to derive parameterized wavefronts of parallel tiles statically.

In the context of GPU code generation, fixed-size tiling (i.e., tile sizes are known at compilation time) remains the dominant approach [5,21,24,27]. With fixed-size tiling, loop tiling can be modeled as an affine transformation [7,8] and GPU code can be effectively produced by means of polyhedral code generation [3,6]. Nonetheless, Yang et al. [27] showed that a syntax-based non-polyhedral method for fixed-size tiling for GPUs can also be effective for dense linear algebra programs.

To the best of our knowledge, this paper is the first to present a code generation strategy that enables parametric tiling for GPUs. In order to achieve this, we address three main challenges. First, extracting and mapping parameterized tile wavefronts for GPU execution can lead to significant load imbalance if wavefronts are not mapped precisely to the hyper-rectangular execution space of GPUs. Secondly, the intra-tile space needs to be parallelised as well in a manner that efficiently exploits the fine-grained SIMD capabilities of GPUs. Finally, the parametric nature of the produced code requires a dynamic local memory management mechanism that would allow us to allocate and use local memory buffers dynamically. In this paper we provide solutions to these technical issues and develop the first code generation algorithm that produces parametric GPU code amenable to runtime tuning.

In some cases, avoiding wavefront parallelism altogether is possible [18] and has motivated alternative parametric [14,19] and non-parametric [11] code-generation schemes for GPUs. However, wavefront parallelism is a more general method and therefore is the focus of our work.

2 Background

2.1 Compilation Flow

This paper focuses on a specific class of programs which are those that conform to the restrictions of the affine transform theory [1,9,10]. These restrictions guarantee that the control behavior of a computation as well as the data access patterns involved, are precisely determinable at compile-time. In the rest of the paper we will refer to such programs as *Affine Loop Programs* or *ALPs*.

Our compilation flow (Fig. 1) begins with a compilation unit written in a sequential imperative language (e.g., C) that contains at least one ALP, annotated with a preprocessor directive (e.g., *#pragma*). Those ALPs are then extracted from the original program and enter a pre-processing stage embodied

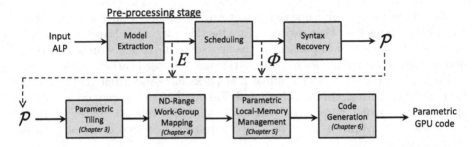

Fig. 1. Code generation flow, where E is a set of polyhedral dependences, Φ a set of multi-dimensional affine transformations and $\mathcal{P}$ a syntactic form of a tilable program.

by an abstract affine transformation framework that consists of a model extraction, scheduling and syntax recovery module as shown in Fig. 1. Such frameworks can be used in finding combinations of loop-nest transformations—in the form of affine scheduling functions—that enable tiling [8]. This issue though goes beyond the scope of this paper; we consider our input to be already sufficiently transformed to enable tiling. Therefore, let Φ be a multi-dimensional affine transformation that enables tiling and $\mathcal{P}$ the transformed syntax-tree of the program based on Φ.

2.2 The OpenCL/CUDA Paradigm

The OpenCL[1] platform model defines a central control processor called *Host*, that coordinates a vector of parallel *Devices*. Each individual device is defined as a set of functionally independent *Compute Units* and each compute unit as a set of *Processing Elements*. We will refer to this abstract device model as the *physical processor space* of a device.

Each device executes a *Device Code* following a data-parallel *SIMT* (Single Instruction Multiple Threads) concurrency model. The device code is written as special C-style functions called *Kernels* or *Device Functions* that are invoked by the Host. The SIMT concurrency model indicates that a single Kernel is executed concurrently across a set of threads called *work-items*. Work-items are organized into uniform hyper-rectangular partitions called *Work-Groups* that are further organized into an *ND-Range* – a hyper-rectangular space of Work-Groups. We will refer to a work-group and nd-range configuration as the *Virtual Processor Space*.

The OpenCL memory model exposes a 3-level abstract memory hierarchy associated with each device. In particular, there is a *Global Memory* randomly accessed by all threads, a software-managed *Local Memory* with a work-group scope and a *Private Memory* (typically a register file), dedicated to each thread separately. In this paper we are not considering the management of global memory which we assume to be an abundant resource.

---

[1] In order to facilitate the generality of the definitions presented and used in the rest of the paper, the OpenCL terminology will be primarily adopted.

3   Parametric Tiling

The proposed code generation scheme relies on two independent preprocessing steps corresponding to Sects. 3.1 and 3.2. The first step (see Sect. 3.1) utilizes well-known techniques [4] for determining a parametric tile space for the input program in the form of perfectly nested loops that scan a uniform space of rectangular tiles with parametric sizes (see Fig. 2).

The second step (see Sect. 3.2) focuses on the intra-tile space, i.e., on the rectangular execution space enclosed within each tile. The objective of these two steps is to expose coarse-grained and fine-grained parallelism respectively either through wavefronts (see dotted lines in Fig. 2) or through rectangularly parallel loop dimensions if any (the trivial case).

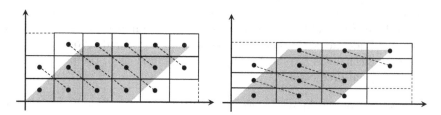

Fig. 2. Two variations of a uniform space of rectangular tiles each one characterized by different tile-sizes. The dotted lines indicate wavefront instances. Notice that the total number of wavefront instances and the number of tiles for each wavefront instance depend on the tile-size parameters.

3.1   The Tile Space

Our first step towards generating parametrically tiled code is to derive a set of d_t perfectly nested loops $L_i : i \in [1 \cdots d_t]$—where d_t denotes the innermost tileable dimension of the program—that would scan the space of uniform rectangular tiles of parametric sizes. For an imperfectly nested loop program, this space corresponds to the convex hull of all execution domains. More specifically, we begin by acquiring the new transformed domains D'_{S_i} for each statement S_i in the transformed syntactic tree $\mathcal{P}$ and then use a polyhedral library [23] in order to get the convex hull D_{CH} of the d_t innermost dimensions of all D'_{S_i}. In the case of imperfectly nested programs, we add semantics-preserving one-time-loops on $\mathcal{P}$ prior to extracting D'_{S_i}. Note that D_{CH} is a convex polyhedron by definition, and therefore is represented by a single integer coefficient matrix where each row represents a loop-bound expression. For the next step, we need different data structures since parametric tiling cannot be represented in the polyhedral model i.e., using integer coefficient matrices. For that purpose, we convert D_{CH} into a list of symbolic polynomial fractions as proposed by [4] and then apply the following algebraic operations in order to get our tiled execution space $\mathbb{S}_T$:

Introduce tile coordinates: Each coordinate x_i of the original execution space D_{CH}, is expressed in terms of tile coordinates t_i, intra-tile coordinates u_i and tile sizes T_i as follows: $x_i = t_i \cdot T_i + u_i$ for $0 \leq u_i < T_i$. Finally, $\mathbb{S}_T$ takes the form: $\mathbb{S}_T : lb_i \leq t_i \cdot T_i + u_i \leq ub_i$ for $i \in [1..d_t]$.

Eliminate intra-tile coordinates: The intra-tile coordinates u_i can be eliminated by making sure we include all non-empty tiles: $\mathbb{S}_T : \binom{lb_i \leq t_i \cdot T_i + T_i - 1}{ub_i \geq t_i \cdot T_i}$ for $i \in [1..d_t]$.

Get final tile loop-bounds: The resulting expressions though require additional processing since the tile coordinate variables appear as part of a product (i.e., $t_i \cdot T_i$) that prevents us from constructing tile loops. We overcome this by dividing all terms with T_i and since tile coordinates can only take integer values, we enclose the resulting symbolic fractions into *floor*[2] operators: $\mathbb{S}_T : \binom{\text{floor}(lb_i/T_i) + \text{floor}(1/T_i) - 1 \leq t_i}{\text{floor}(ub_i/T_i) \geq t_i}$ for $i \in [1..d_t]$. The introduction of *floor* operations though has an important impact on the resulting tile loops. In particular, they produce a number of empty tiles, i.e., tiles that do not include any valid points. These tiles are eliminated by our inspector-executor mechanism (see Sect. 4) using the expressions of the previous step as conditional predicates.

Given a set $\mathbb{S}_T$ of tile loops L_i, we either determine a subset $\mathbb{S}_{TP} \subseteq \mathbb{S}_T$ of parallel tile loops that can be mapped directly to a GPU or we resort to wavefront parallelism. In the latter case, we utilize the relaxed Fourier-Motzkin elimination (RSFME) algorithm proposed by Baskaran et al. [4] and get an outer wavefront loop $\mathcal{W}$ surrounding d_t parallel tile loops $\mathbb{S}_{WT}$. Because the shape of the parallel tile space produced by RSFME is inherently non-rectangular and depends on the wavefront instance $w \in \mathcal{W}$, mapping it to a GPU device is challenging. In Sect. 4 we present our method for mapping $\mathbb{S}_{WT}(w)$ into a GPU execution environment through a runtime inspector-executor mechanism.

3.2 The Intra-tile Space

The situation within each tile appears to be simpler as it is just a rectangular execution space. Nevertheless, in order to preserve the legality of tiling we need to respect the multi-dimensional affine transformations Φ embodied by the transformed syntax $\mathcal{P}$. Furthermore, we need to also identify parallelism within each tile, which might come from parallel intra-tile dimensions or wavefront parallelism.

In either case, parallel intra-tile points will be captured by the work-group configuration (see Sect. 4) and executed by the device code in a SIMT fashion. Since the respective work-group configuration will inherently respect the tile bounds of the parallel intra-tile dimensions, we only need to replace the respective syntactic loop bounds of $\mathcal{P}$ with if-guards and adjust non-parallel loop bounds to be:

---

[2] A *floor* operator returns the largest integer that is not greater than the actual result of the fraction.

$$\mathbb{S}_{I_{seq}} : \max(lb_i, t_i \cdot T_i) \leq x_i \leq \min(ub_i, t_i \cdot T_i + T_i - 1)$$

The result is a transformed syntax tree $\mathcal{P}'$ that will be embedded into the device code (see Sect. 6 and Fig. 6).

In the case of wavefront parallelism, the situation is rather straightforward. In particular, since the intra-tile space is essentially a rectangular bounding box of size T_i across each dimension $i \in [1..d_t]$, the wavefront loops can be generated for the intra-tile space using a loop-skewing transformation thanks to CLooG, a polyhedral code generation tool [6]. We can then wrap these loops around $\mathcal{P}$ and replace all but the outer wavefront loop with if-guards. In Sect. 4 we will see that the wavefront conditions can actually be hoisted to the host code and evaluated once using an inspector-executor mechanism. Therefore, $\mathcal{P}'$ in case of intra-tile wavefront parallelism, is actually produced by replacing all loops in $\mathcal{P}$ with if-guards and surrounding them with the sequential wavefront loop. Keep in mind that in case of full-tile separation the if-guards corresponding to parallel intra-tile dimensions (wavefront or rectangularly-parallel) are completely avoided.

Sometimes, the derived affine transformation functions Φ will result in a maximally fused loop-nest in an attempt to minimize sequential execution (or scanning) overhead. However, in a GPU execution context this approach is not always ideal as we see from the Jacobi-2d example of Fig. 3. In particular, we notice that the affine transformations derived from the well-known Pluto scheduling algorithm [8] resulted in a maximally fused program, where inter-statement dependences carried by the transformed space dimensions i and j, prevent the respective space loops (i.e., loops i and j) from being parallel. This situation forces us to resort to wavefront parallelism on the intra-tile space as well. However, avoiding an intra-tile wavefront, whenever possible, can be highly beneficial since the lightweight nature of GPU cores makes them particularly vulnerable to the additional control overhead incurred due to wavefront parallelism.

```
for( t=0; i<T; ) {
    for( j=2t+2; j<2t+N-1; )
        S1(t,2,j-2t);
    for( i=2t+3; i<2t+N-1; ) {
        S1(t,i-2t,2);
        for( j=2t+3; j<2t+N-1; ) {
            S2(t,i-2t-1,j-2t-1);
            S1(t,i-2t,j-2t);
        }
        S2(t,i-2t-1,N-2);
    }
    for( j=2t+3; j<2t+N; )
        S2(t,N-2,j-2t-1);
}
```

```
for( t=0; i<T; ) {
    for( i=2; i<N-1; )
        for( j=2; j<N-1; )
            S1(t,i,j);
    for( i=2; i<N-1; )
        for( j=2; j<N-1; )
            S2(t,i,j);
}
```

```
for( t=0; t<N; )
    for( i=2t+2; i<2t+N-2; )
        for( j=2t+2; j<2t+N-2; )
            S1(t,i-2t,j-2t);
    for( i=2t+3; i<2t+N-1; )
        for( j=2t+3; j<2t+N-1; )
            S2(t,i-2t-1,j-2t-1);
}
```

(a)   (b)   (c)

$S1(x_1, x_2, x_3) : b[x_2][x_3] = 0.2 \cdot (a[x_2][x_3] + a[x_2][x_3 - 1] + a[x_2][x_3 + 1] + a[x_2 + 1][x_3] + a[x_2 - 1][x_3])$

$S2(x_1, x_2, x_3) : a[x_2][x_3] = b[x_2][x_3]$

Fig. 3. (a) The original Jacobi-2d kernel, (b) transformed Jacobi-2d kernel from the Pluto scheduling algorithm [8], (c) proposed fusion structure derived from Algorithm 1.

In order to overcome this problem, we develop Algorithm 1 which is applied on Φ prior to acquiring $\mathcal{P}$, in order to eliminate such inter-statement dependences. Figure 3 (c) shows the result for the Jacobi-2d example. Note that Algorithm 1 does not alter the affine transformations per se, but only the fusion structure of the program by decoupling the strongly connected components scc of the data-dependence graph ddg in an attempt to avoid wavefront parallelism – a process similar to classic vectorization algorithms [2]. Furthermore, if the condition of Line 5 is false, then the rest of the scheduling dimensions are unfused (an operation equivalent to loop fission) and marked parallel. Therefore, in order to ensure correctness of the respective parallel program, the decoupling of scc imposed by Line 6 must be accompanied by intra-tile synchronization in between those components.

Algorithm 1. Elimination of intra-statement dependences that can result in unecessary intra-tile wavefronts. Let ddg be the directed dependence graph of a d-dimensional program derived from a set of polyhedral dependence edges $e \in E$ each involving a source (src_e) and a sink ($sink_e$) statement.

```
 1: procedure INTRADEPELIMINATION(Φ,ddg,E)
 2:     scc[1...n] ← ddg                          ▷ Calculate scc with well-known algorithms
 3:     mark[1...d] ← parallel                    ▷ All loops marked parallel
 4:     for each i ∈ [1..d] do
 5:         if (∄e ∈ E for which scc[src_e] = scc[sink_e]) then
 6:             CUTSCC(i,scc)                      ▷ Add scc values to Φ on position i
 7:             return mark
 8:         end if
 9:         if (ISPARALLEL(i,Φ)=false) then
10:             mark[i] = non-parallel
11:             update E,ddg and scc              ▷ Remove satisfied dependences
12:             if (E = ∅) return mark             ▷ Exit if no dependences left
13:         end if
14:     end for
15:     return mark
16: end procedure
```

---

4   ND-Range and Work-Group Mapping

The ND-Range and Work-Group mapping process involves the task of mapping parallel tiles and parallel intra-tile points on to the virtual processor space of an OpenCL device, embodied by the ND-Range and Work-Group configurations. For that, we introduce the concepts of *Tile-Buckets* and *Thread-Buckets* defined as follows:

Definition 1. *A* Tile-Bucket *is denoted by $\mathcal{B}_T$ and contains the coordinates of all parallel tile instances to be mapped into an ND-Range and it is of size $\mathcal{B}_{Tsize}(w) = |\mathbb{S}_{WT}(w)|$ or $\mathcal{B}_{Tsize} = |\mathbb{S}_{TP}|$ for wavefront or rectangularly parallel tiles respectively.*

Definition 2. *A* Thread-Bucket *is denoted by* $\mathcal{B}_I$ *and contains the coordinates of all parallel intra-tile points to be executed by each work-group.*

Each bucket is populated dynamically by an inspector-executor mechanism running on the host while each bucket entry (i.e., tile and intra-tile coordinates) can be recovered from the device code using the built-in index variables.

With respect to the tile-bucket, in Sect. 3.1 we defined our parallel tiled execution space as a vector of loop-bound expressions resulted from rectangularly parallel tile dimension – $\mathbb{S}_{TP}$ – or wavefront parallelism – $\mathbb{S}_{TW}(w)$. These loops can now be executed in any order from the host environment and can populate the tile-bucket $\mathcal{B}_T$ with tile coordinates. Note that the chosen execution order will effectively define the layout of the mapping. This layout could be an arbitrary permutation of the respective loops or a more complex layout like a diagonal reordering [22] to avoid partition camping.

On the intra-tile level, if the number of parallel transformation dimensions $d_{par} \leq d_t$ is non-zero (see *mark* vector of Algorithm 1), then we have a d_{par}-dimensional rectangle containing parallel execution instances that can be mapped directly into a Work-Group (without the use of thread-buckets).

In case of intra-tile wavefront parallelism, bucket $\mathcal{B}_I$ is split into multiple buckets, each one corresponding to a wavefront instance $w \in \mathcal{W}_I$ and containing the parallel execution instances of w. Therefore, $\mathcal{B}_I$ is defined as $\mathcal{B}_I[\mathcal{W}_{Isize}][\mathcal{B}_{Isize}]$ with $\mathcal{W}_{Isize}$ and $\mathcal{B}_{Isize}$ being defined as the maximum number of wavefronts and the maximum number of points within a wavefront respectively. Both $\mathcal{W}_{Isize}$ and $\mathcal{B}_{Isize}$ are symbolic expressions depending on tile sizes and can be calculated with polyhedral tools. In fact, since they are the same for each problem dimensionality, they could be derived once and then reused for any program.

Notice that $\mathcal{B}_{Isize}$ reflects the maximum number of intra-wavefront points across all wavefront instances. We will use it for the work-group configuration as it denotes the total amount of work-items per work-group. This means that for wavefront instances with fewer intra-wavefront points, we will have idle work-items. These work-items can be identified by a negative coordinate since all valid intra-tile coordinates are non-negative by default.

5 Parametric Local Memory Management

The total number of work-groups is typically larger than the number of compute units; therefore, local memory can be shared among multiple active work-groups. If the collective demand for local memory exceeds its physical capacity, the number of active work-groups per compute unit is reduced. This highlights the tight balance between locality and parallelism. In particular, if the number of local memory buffers per work-group is reduced, then the number of active work-groups can be increased. On the other hand, if the local memory usage of a single work-group exceeds the physical capacity, then the kernel invocation will fail completely. In a tuning environment where tile sizes can take arbitrary values, this situation can unnecessarily restrict the tuning space. We attempt to overcome these problems by introducing the concept of *Buffer Buckets*:

Definition 3. *A Buffer-Bucket denoted by $\mathcal{B}_B$, is a collection of local-memory buffers accompanied by a kernel descriptor mapping the respective buffer-bucket to a specific device function.*

Each buffer-bucket is characterized by a tunable capacity parameter called the *Local Memory Window* $\mathcal{L}_w$, that represents the per-work-group availability of local memory. In particular, local memory buffers can be added to a buffer-bucket by the host at runtime as long as its contents do not exceed $\mathcal{L}_w$. If $\mathcal{L}_w$ is exceeded, the respective buffer-bucket is closed and no more additions to it can be performed; hence the order of addition matters. Furthermore, each addition is accompanied by a kernel descriptor mapping the contents of the respective buffer-bucket to a specific device function. The complete process is outlined in Fig. 4. Note that the kernel invocation (on Line 8) requires a buffer-bucket argument that specifies the device function to call and the total amount of local memory to be allocated dynamically. In other words a buffer-bucket constructs an execution environment in which the contained buffers are available for use.

```
1: initBufferBucket(𝓑_B,𝓛_w,Kernel(0))
2:
3: addBuffer(𝓑_B,B_1,Kernel(1))
4: addBuffer(𝓑_B,B_2,Kernel(2))

5:          ⋮
6: addBuffer(𝓑_B,B_n,Kernel(n))

7:          ⋮
8: invokeKernel(𝓑_B,𝓑_T,𝓑_I)
```

Fig. 4. Mechanism for adding n buffers $B_i : i \in [1..n]$ to a buffer-bucket $\mathcal{B}_B$ which is subsequently used for the kernel invocation. Note that the device function specified by the Kernel(0) descriptor will not use any of the buffers.

We have developed a dynamic local memory management policy that ranks the set of candidate local memory buffers and then utilizes the buffer-bucket abstraction and the associated population mechanism (Fig. 4) to construct an execution environment. This implies that $n+1$ kernel versions are needed, where n is the total number of buffers; $kernel_n$ will use all n buffers, $kernel_{n-1}$ will use the best $n - 1$ buffers according to their rank, etc. In other words, buffers are added incrementally according to their rank and if the addition of buffer $B_i : i \in [1..n]$ results in exceeding $\mathcal{L}_w$, then all subsequent additions will fail and the kernel using $i - 1$ buffers – indicated by the Kernel($i - 1$) descriptor – will be invoked. The ranking of the candidate local memory buffers is based on temporal reuse, group reuse and self-spatial reuse.

Each buffer entry contains the total size of the respective buffer and a set of parameters that are transferred to read-only constant memory and then used by pre-defined data-movement procedures to move data in and out of the buffers. More details on this will be discussed in Sect. 5.2.

5.1 Buffer Definition

Let $\mathcal{F}_i$ be the multi-dimensional access function of array i, ignoring any constant terms. Furthermore, let C_i^t be a set of integers denoting the absolute distance between the maximum and the minimum constant terms across all textual references to array i for each dimension. We define buffer B_i of i to be the rectangular bounding box of $\mathcal{F}_i$ enlarged by the elements of C_i^t along each dimension; it is characterized by two sets of symbolic expressions namely the *footprint origins* $O_i(t, T)$ and the *footprint extents* $E_i(T)$, where t and T denote the vectors of tile coordinates and tile sizes respectively. Figure 5 illustrates how buffer B_A is defined for the *Seidel-2D* kernel of Fig. 5(a), based on O_A, E_A and C_A^t. The O_i and E_i expressions can be derived using lexicographic minimum and maximum operations of $\mathcal{F}_i$ under the tile domain using existing polyhedral tools [23].

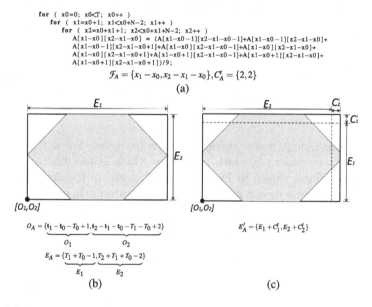

```
for ( x0=0; x0<T; x0++ )
   for ( x1=x0+1; x1<x0+N-2; x1++ )
      for ( x2=x0+x1+1; x2<x0+x1+N-2; x2++ )
         A[x1-x0][x2-x1-x0] = (A[x1-x0-1][x2-x1-x0-1]+A[x1-x0-1][x2-x1-x0]+
         A[x1-x0-1][x2-x1-x0+1]+A[x1-x0][x2-x1-x0-1]+A[x1-x0][x2-x1-x0]+
         A[x1-x0][x2-x1-x0+1]+A[x1-x0+1][x2-x1-x0-1]+A[x1-x0+1][x2-x1-x0]+
         A[x1-x0+1][x2-x1-x0+1])/9;
```

$$\mathcal{F}_A = \{x_1 - x_0, x_2 - x_1 - x_0\}, C_A^t = \{2, 2\}$$

(a)

$$O_A = \{\underbrace{t_1 - t_0 - T_0 + 1}_{O_1}, \underbrace{t_2 - t_1 - t_0 - T_1 - T_0 + 2}_{O_2}\}$$

$$E_A = \{\underbrace{T_1 + T_0 - 1}_{E_1}, \underbrace{T_2 + T_1 + T_0 - 2}_{E_2}\}$$

(b)

$$E_A' = \{E_1 + C_1^t, E_2 + C_2^t\}$$

(c)

Fig. 5. (a) A skewed Seidel-2d kernel (b) global view of the access foorptint of A coinciding with the buffer view for $O_A = \{0, 0\}$ and all constant terms being ignored (c) buffer view of the access footprint of A if we consider all constant terms.

Note that we only consider a single access function for each array implying that we ignore any arrays that have multiple linearly independent access functions for any dimension.

5.2 Moving Data in and Out of the Buffers

Since the buffer extents as well as the work-group configuration are parametric, the movement of data in and out of the buffers need to be parametric as well, i.e., data movement is carried out without any assumption about the relation between the layout of threads in a work-group and the buffer extents. Consequently, we predefine a set of data-movement procedures that are used as runtime API functions and can be incrementally optimized based on certain assumptions pertaining to the thread and buffer layouts. For a 2-dimensional array, the basic data movement procedures are presented in Algorithm 2, in which C_i^{neg} denote the absolute value of the minimum negative constant term across all textual references of array i for each dimension, and b_i a set of global bounds associated with i.

Algorithm 2. The basic move-in procedure of a 2-dimensional buffer B_i executed on the device code by each thread.

```
1: procedure MOVEINOUT2DGENERIC(O_i,C_i^neg,B_i,b_i,F_i(l_i))
2:     l_i ← recover new thread layout with B_i params      ▷ Using modulo and division
3:     g_i ← (O_i − C_i^neg + l_i)                          ▷ recover global coordinates
4:     for (g_1 : [0..b_i[1]]) and (l_1 : [0 : E_i[1]])     ▷ Height traversal
5:         for (g_2 : [0..b_i[2]]) and (l_2 : [0 : E_i[2]]) ▷ Width traversal
6:             if (F_i(l_i))                                ▷ For Move-Out only
7:                 buffer[l_1][l_2] = global[g_1][g_2]      ▷ Reverse for Move-Out
8: end procedure
```

Note that in Line 2, a new thread layout is recovered. For a 2D buffer, this layout is characterized by a width parameter which is specified by the buffer allocation procedures shown in Fig. 4 and then stored in the device's constant memory for fast access by the data-movement procedures. In our current implementation of the buffer allocation runtime, we assume that the total number of threads in a work-group is always greater than or equal to the buffer width; thus we can effectively avoid the width traversal of Line 6.

The main difference between the move-in and move-out procedures is in Line 6. The condition on Line 6 involves $F_i(l_i)$, a conditional expression that depends on the buffer coordinates l_i and restricts the move-out procedures to operate only on the elements that have actually been written by the respective tile (the gray area in Fig. 5). Therefore, in order to determine $F_i(l_i)$, we examine the write accesses of the program and derive a conditional expression denoting their convex hull for the domain of the buffer, i.e., a tile domain in which $O_i(t, T)$ is zero across all dimensions.

6   Code Generation

The code generation algorithm developed in this paper produces two pieces of code: (i) the inspector-executor code that runs on the host side, and (ii) the $n + 1$ kernels (where n is the total number of buffers used in the program) that are executed on the device. Figure 6 shows a generic form of the produced code that provides a clear outline of the code generation algorithm.

```
1:  Inspector-Executor Host-Code
2:  INITBUFFERBUCKET($\mathcal{B}_B$,$\mathcal{L}_w$,Kernel(0))
3:  INITTHREADBUCKET($\mathcal{B}_I$)
4:  if (Intra-tile wavefront) then
5:      SETINTRAWAVE($\mathcal{B}_I$,$d_t$)
6:  else
7:      SETRECTANGULARLAYOUT($\mathcal{B}_I$,$T_1$,...,$T_{d_{par}}$)
8:  end if
9:  ADDBUFFER($\mathcal{B}_B$,$E_1[1]$,...,$E_1[d]$,Kernel(1))

10:     :
11: ADDBUFFER($\mathcal{B}_B$,$E_n[1]$,...,$E_n[d]$,Kernel(n))
12: if (Tile wavefront) then
13:     for each $w \in \mathcal{W}$ do
14:         for each loop $L_{wi}$ in $S_{WT}(w)$ do
15:             POPULATETILEBUCKET($\mathcal{B}_T$,$t_i \in L_{wi}$)
16:         end for
17:         INVOKEKERNEL($\mathcal{B}_T$,$\mathcal{B}_I$,$\mathcal{B}_B$)
18:     end for
19: else
20:     for each loop $L_i$ in $S_{TP}$ do
21:         POPULATETILEBUCKET($\mathcal{B}_T$,$t_i \in L_i$)
22:     end for
23:     INVOKEKERNEL($\mathcal{B}_T$,$\mathcal{B}_I$,$\mathcal{B}_B$)
24: end if
```

```
1:  Rectangularly Parallel Intra-Tile Execution
2:  RECOVERTILECOORDINATES
3:  RECOVERINTRATILECOORDINATES  ▷ The parallel ones
4:  for each sequential tile loop do
5:      SYNCHRONIZE
6:      MOVEIN(1,$O_1$,$C_1^{neg}$,$b_1$)

7:      :
8:      MOVEIN(n,$O_n$,$C_n^{neg}$,$b_n$)
9:      SYNCHRONIZE
10:     Computation ...     ▷ $\mathcal{P}'$
11:     SYNCHRONIZE
12:     MOVEOUT(1,$O_1$,$C_1^{neg}$,$b_1$,$F_1$)

13:     :
14:     MOVEOUT(n,$O_n$,$C_n^{neg}$,$b_n$,$F_n$)
15: end for
16:
17: Intra-Tile Wavefront Execution
18: RECOVERTILECOORDINATES
19: MOVEIN(1,$O_1$,$C_1^{neg}$,$b_1$)

20:     :
21: MOVEIN(n,$O_n$,$C_n^{neg}$,$b_n$)
22: for each intra-tile wavefront instance $w$ do
23:     if (current thread is valid) then
24:         RECOVERINTRATILECOORDINATES
25:         Computation ...     ▷ $\mathcal{P}'$
26:     end if
27:     SYNCHRONIZE
28: end for
29: MOVEOUT(1,$O_1$,$C_1^{neg}$,$b_1$,$F_1$)

30:     :
31: MOVEOUT(n,$O_n$,$C_n^{neg}$,$b_n$,$F_n$)
```

Fig. 6. Generic output of the proposed code-generation algorithm

All the functions whose names are in uppercase in Fig. 6 constitute the platform-independent runtime environment[3] that supports the inspector-executor mechanisms as well as the data-movement procedures and the tile/intra-tile recovery methods that reside on the device code. In particular, the latter are using the built-in work-group and nd-range index variables to access the tile and thread-bucket entries which have been transferred to concurrent data structures by the host code. More specifically, the tile-bucket entries are stored in global memory and the thread-bucket entries are stored in image-memory while the buffer-bucket entries are stored in constant memory. The condition in Line 23 in the intra-tile wavefront code simply checks whether the corresponding thread-bucket entry is negative.

The simplicity and robustness of the code generation algorithm indicates that manual code generation is also possible and sensible since the code is produced once and then used for runtime tuning across any GPU device. The parameterized benchmarks that were used for our experimental evaluation along with the inspector-executor runtime are publicly available[4].

---

[3] Currently supporting CUDA targets.
[4] http://www.doc.ic.ac.uk/~phjk/LCPC13

7 Experimental Evaluation

The purpose of our experimental evaluation is to assess two main properties of the produced parameterized code. First of all, in the presence of rectangular parallel tile spaces that do not require wavefront parallelism, we would like to evaluate the effectiveness of our code in matching the performance of a statically partitioned GPU code. Secondly, in the presence of wavefront parallelism, we would like to assess the effectiveness of the proposed inspector-executor mechanism in mapping wavefronts of tile and intra-tile instances onto a GPU execution environment. For both experiments we compared our solution to *PPCG* [24] (version c7179a0), which is a state-of-the-art C-to-CUDA compiler that utilizes polyhedral analysis and code-generation for producing statically partitioned CUDA code, i.e., the tile-sizes are compile-time constants. In both systems, the Pluto [8] scheduling algorithm is used to enable tiling through affine transformations. The devices used for our experiments were the following NVIDIA GPUs: (a) GT540M(CUDA 4.2), (b) GTX580(CUDA 4.2), (c) M2070(CUDA 4.2) and (d) K20c(CUDA 5).

With respect to our first assessment, we used the well-known matrix multiplication example as a representative of rectangular parallel programs. Figure 7

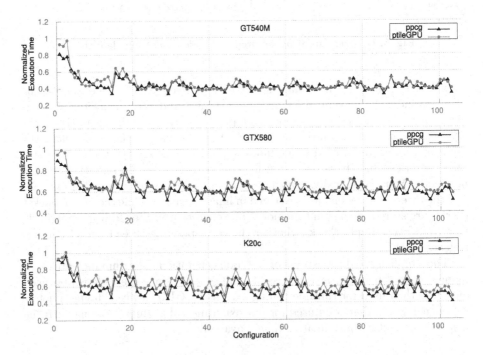

Fig. 7. Comparison of execution time profiles for matrix-multiplication between static (i.e., *PPCG*) and runtime partitioning (i.e., ptileGPU). Each diagram is normalized based on worst execution time which was 2.467 s for GT540M, 0.234 s for GTX580 and 0.191 s for K20c.

shows that for a given set of tile size configurations (horizontal axis), our parameterized code can successfully match the performance profile of *PPCG* while yielding more than 5 times faster search time. On the other hand, Fig. 8 demonstrates the effectiveness of the inspector-executor framework in mapping wavefront parallelism across a collection of stencil benchmarks. From those benchmarks, ADI (Alternating Direction Implicit) and Seidel-2d utilize the thread-bucket feature while Jacobi-1d, Jacobi-2d and FDTD-2D (Finite Difference Time Domain) utilize Algorithm 1 to eliminate intra-tile wavefronts. All bars denote the best performance within a given search space[5] while the additional bars per-benchmark show the respective performance when using less local memory buffers (the far

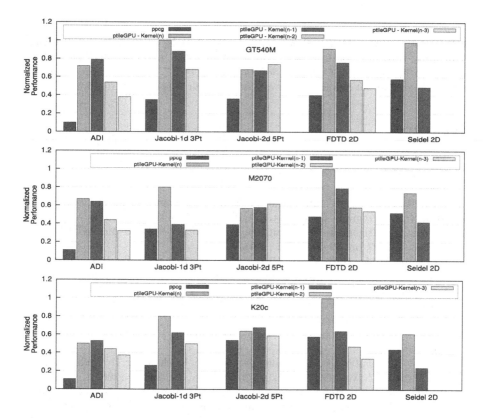

Fig. 8. Comparison of best performance within a given search space of partitioning parameters (i.e., tile-sizes) between *PPCG* and ptileGPU. Each performance bar is normalized based on best performance which was 4.13 GFLOPS for GT540M and Jacobi-2d, 25.11 GFLOPS for M2070 and FDTD 2D and 33.03 GFLOPS for K20c and FDTD 2D.

---

[5] We used tile sizes ranging from 8 to 32 with a stride of 4 while on Jacobi-1d we searched up to time tile sizes of 256.

right bar denote the performance when no buffers are used) which highlights the importance of the locality/parallelism trade-off discussed in Sect. 5.

8 Conclusions

In this paper, we have presented the first code generation algorithm that produces parameterized GPU code (using parametric tiling) for effective runtime auto-tuning of affine programs. Experimental evaluation shows that the our compilation and runtime system is effective in mapping wavefronts of parallel parametric tiles, exploiting parametric intra-tile parallelism and managing local memory dynamically.

Acknowledgments. This work was supported in part by the U.S. National Science Foundation through awards 0811457, 0904549, 1059417 and 1205682. The authors would also like to thank Codeplay Software and EPSRC for their support as well as Louis-Noël Pouchet and Sanket Tavarageri for their valuable contributions.

References

1. Aho, A., Lam, M., Sethi, R., Ullman, J.: Optimizing for parallelism and locality. In: Compilers: Principles, Techniques, and Tools. Pearson/Addison Wesley, Boston (2007)
2. Allen, R., Kennedy, K.: Automatic translation of fortran programs to vector form. ACM Trans. Program. Lang. Syst. (TOPLAS) 9(4), 491–542 (1987)
3. Ancourt, C., Irigoin, F.: Scanning polyhedra with DO loops. In: ACM Sigplan Notices, vol. 26, pp. 39–50. ACM (1991)
4. Baskaran, M.M., Hartono, A., Tavarageri, S., Henretty, T., Ramanujam, J., Sadayappan, P.: Parameterized tiling revisited. In: CGO. ACM (2010)
5. Baskaran, M.M., Ramanujam, J., Sadayappan, P.: Automatic C-to-CUDA code generation for affine programs. In: Gupta, R. (ed.) CC 2010. LNCS, vol. 6011, pp. 244–263. Springer, Heidelberg (2010)
6. Bastoul, C.: Code generation in the polyhedral model is easier than you think. In: PACT (2004)
7. Bastoul, C., Feautrier, P.: Improving data locality by chunking. In: Hedin, G. (ed.) CC 2003. LNCS, vol. 2622, pp. 320–334. Springer, Heidelberg (2003)
8. Bondhugula, U., Hartono, A., Ramanujam, J., Sadayappan, P.: A practical automatic polyhedral parallelizer and locality optimizer. In: PLDI. ACM (2008)
9. Feautrier, P.: Some efficient solutions to the affine scheduling problem. Part i. One-dimensional time. Int. J. Parallel Prog. 21(5), 313–347 (1992)
10. Feautrier, P.: Some efficient solutions to the affine scheduling problem. Part II. Multidimensional time. Int. J. Parallel Prog. 21(6), 389–420 (1992)
11. Grosser, T., Cohen, A., Kelly, P.H., Ramanujam, J., Sadayappan, P., Verdoolaege, S.: Split tiling for GPUs: automatic parallelization using trapezoidal tiles. In: GPGPU. ACM (2013)
12. Hartono, A., Baskaran, M.M., Bastoul, C., Cohen, A., Krishnamoorthy, S., Norris, B., Ramanujam, J., Sadayappan, P.: Parametric multi-level tiling of imperfectly nested loops. In: Supercomputing, pp. 147–157. ACM (2009)

13. Hartono, A., Baskaran, M.M., Ramanujam, J., Sadayappan, P.: DynTile: parametric tiled loop generation for parallel execution on multicore processors. In: IPDPS. IEEE (2010)
14. Holewinski, J., Pouchet, L.N., Sadayappan, P.: High-performance code generation for stencil computations on GPU architectures. In: Proceedings of the 26th ACM International Conference on Supercomputing, pp. 311–320. ACM (2012)
15. Irigoin, F., Triolet, R.: Supernode partitioning. In: POPL. ACM (1988)
16. Kim, D., Rajopadhye, S.: Parameterized Tiling for Imperfectly Nested Loops
17. Kim, D., Renganarayanan, L., Rostron, D., Rajopadhye, S., Strout, M.M.: Multilevel tiling: M for the price of one. In: Proceedings of the 2007 ACM/IEEE Conference on Supercomputing, p. 51. ACM (2007)
18. Krishnamoorthy, S., Baskaran, M., Bondhugula, U., Ramanujam, J., Rountev, A., Sadayappan, P.: Effective automatic parallelization of stencil computations. In: ACM Sigplan Notices, vol. 42, pp. 235–244. ACM (2007)
19. Meng, J., Skadron, K.: Performance modeling and automatic ghost zone optimization for iterative stencil loops on GPUs. In: Supercomputing. ACM (2009)
20. Renganarayanan, L., Kim, D., Rajopadhye, S., Strout, M.M.: Parameterized tiled loops for free. ACM SIGPLAN Not. **42**(6), 405–414 (2007)
21. Rudy, G., Khan, M.M., Hall, M., Chen, C., Chame, J.: A programming language interface to describe transformations and code generation. In: Cooper, K., Mellor-Crummey, J., Sarkar, V. (eds.) LCPC 2010. LNCS, vol. 6548, pp. 136–150. Springer, Heidelberg (2011)
22. Ruetsch, G., Micikcvicius, P.: Optimizing matrix transpose in CUDA. NVIDIA CUDA SDK Application Note (2009)
23. Verdoolaege, S.: An integer set library for the polyhedral model. In: Fukuda, K., Hoeven, J., Joswig, M., Takayama, N. (eds.) ICMS 2010. LNCS, vol. 6327, pp. 299–302. Springer, Heidelberg (2010)
24. Verdoolaege, S., Juega, J.C., Cohen, A., Gómez, J.I., Tenllado, C., Catthoor, F.: Polyhedral parallel code generation for CUDA. ACM Trans. Archit. Code Optim. (TACO) **9**(4), 54 (2013)
25. Wolfe, M.: Loops skewing: the wavefront method revisited. Int. J. Parallel Prog. **15**(4), 279–293 (1986)
26. Wolfe, M.: More iteration space tiling. In: Proceedings of the 1989 ACM/IEEE Conference on Supercomputing, pp. 655–664. ACM (1989)
27. Yang, Y., Xiang, P., Kong, J., Zhou, H.: A GPGPU compiler for memory optimization and parallelism management. In: ACM Sigplan Notices, vol. 45, pp. 86–97. ACM (2010)

Power

OSCAR Compiler Controlled Multicore Power Reduction on Android Platform

Hideo Yamamoto[1]([✉]), Tomohiro Hirano[1], Kohei Muto[1], Hiroki Mikami[1],
Takashi Goto[1], Dominic Hillenbrand[1], Moriyuki Takamura[2], Keiji Kimura[1],
and Hironori Kasahara[1]

[1] Green Computing Systems Research and Department Center,
Waseda University Tokyo, Tokyo, Japan
{hideo,hirano,kmuto,mikami,tgoto,dominic,
kimura,Kasahara}@kasahara.cs.waseda.ac.jp
http://www.kasahara.elec.waseda.ac.jp/
[2] Fujitsu Laboratories Ltd., Kawasaki, Japan
takamura.moriyu@jp.fujitsu.com

Abstract. In recent years, smart devices are transitioning from single core processors to multicore processors to satisfy the growing demands of higher performance and lower power consumption. However, power consumption of multicore processors is increasing, as usage of smart devices become more intense. This situation is one of the most fundamental and important obstacle that the mobile device industries face, to extend the battery life of smart devices. This paper evaluates the power reduction control by the OSCAR Automatic Parallelizing Compiler on an Android platform with the newly developed precise power measurement environment on the ODROID-X2, a development platform with the Samsung Exynos4412 Prime, which consists of 4 ARM Cortex-A9 cores. The OSCAR Compiler enables automatic exploitation of multigrain parallelism within a sequential program, and automatically generates a parallelized code with the OSCAR Multi-Platform API power reduction directives for the purpose of DVFS (Dynamic Voltage and Frequency Scaling), clock gating, and power gating. The paper also introduces a newly developed micro second order pseudo clock gating method to reduce power consumption using WFI (Wait For Interrupt). By inserting GPIO (General Purpose Input Output) control functions into programs, signals appear on the power waveform indicating the point of where the GPIO control was inserted and provides a precise power measurement of the specified program area. The results of the power evaluation for real-time Mpeg2 Decoder show 86.7% power reduction, namely from 2.79[W] to 0.37[W] and for real-time Optical Flow show 86.5% power reduction, namely from 2.23[W] to 0.36[W] on 3 core execution.

Keywords: Smart device · Automatic parallelization · API · Power control · Power reduction · Multicore processor · Android · WFI

© Springer International Publishing Switzerland 2014
C. Caşcaval and P. Montesinos (Eds.): LCPC 2013, LNCS 8664, pp. 155–168, 2014.
DOI: 10.1007/978-3-319-09967-5_9

1   Introduction

Multicore processors have been attracting much attention and applied into a wide variety of systems, such as personal computers, high performance computers, cloud servers and even embedded systems including smartphones, tablets and automobiles [1–3]. In recent years, smart devices such as smartphones and tablets have already been transitioning from single core processors to multicore processors to satisfy the growing demands of higher performance and lower power consumption. However, power consumption of multicore processors on the smart devices is increasing, as usage of these devices become more intense. This situation is one of the most fundamental and important obstacle that the mobile device industries face. Extending the battery life is a crucial problem for current smart devices. To avoid the increasing power consumption, low power architectures like big.LITTLE [4] from ARM [5] have been introduced in the mobile device industries. Some of the multicore processors that apply these architectures are the NVIDIA Tegra3 [6] and the Samsung Exynos 5 Octa [7].

Although recent smart devices apply multicore processors in an attempt to gain higher performance and lower power consumption, the anticipated results require further advancement of cooperative hardware-software environment. To realize such an environment, parallelization of software is crucial to fully utilize the capability and potential of multicore processors. Current methods of parallelization include OpenMP and MPI; however, manual optimization of software lowers productivity and become extremely difficult when complexity of software heightens. In order to ease software optimizations for multicore processors, automatic parallelization compilers are needed. Previous and current works of compilers include the SUIF Compiler [8], Polaris Compiler [9], PLUTO [10], and the OSCAR Automatic Parallelizing Compiler [11,12]. Especially in the works of the OSCAR Compiler, it has realized an automatic power reduction scheme using DVFS, clock gating, and power gating [13,14]. The significance of this compiler lies in the fact that it can both automatically parallelize an application and control power at the same time. As for power reduction, other works propose a compile-time static approach using detailed information of the program behavior from compiler analysis [15–18]. Moreover, dynamic compiler approaches using the information obtained at runtime and compile-time, have also been proposed on a single processor execution [18,19].

This paper evaluates the power reduction control by the OSCAR Automatic Parallelizing Compiler on ODROID-X2 [20], an Android [21] development platform using real-time applications. Furthermore, by using WFI (Wait For Interrupt) instructions, a pseudo clock gating method was developed, which enables clock gating at an 500[us] interval. Compared to the power control of current Android platforms, this method proves higher power reduction. To attain precise power measurements, a new power measurement method was developed utilizing the GPIO. This proposed method allows synchronization between the program and the waveforms in the power measurements, which no other work has done before to the best of the author's knowledge.

This paper gives an overview of the current power control on Android platforms in Sect. 2, the methodology in Sect. 3, an overview of the evaluation environment Sect. 4, evaluation results in Sect. 5, and the conclusion of this paper in Sect. 6.

2   Power Control on Current Android Platforms

This section provides an overview of the current power control on Android platforms. The base of Android is made of Linux, and power control on Android is realized through `cpufreq`, `cpuidle`, and `hotplug` [22].

CPUFreq. The `cpufreq` architecture allows frequency scaling of a target CPU and is a basic driver installed in the Linux kernel. Controlling of frequency and its corresponding voltage results in lower power of the target device. On the Android device, dynamic frequency scaling is realized by using the `ondemand` governor. This governor monitors the current usage on each core at certain time intervals. When the load exceeds or falls below the threshold, frequencies are made higher or lower dynamically.

CPUIdle. Many CPUs on Android devices support multiple idle levels, which are differentiated by power consumption and the exit latencies from that idle level. The `cpuidle` manages the level of idle on each core of the CPU and realizes low power on the device. Linux determines to go idle when no processes are there to execute. The levels of idle state is determined by the number of function units that go to sleep on the CPU. Power consumption is very low when many function units go to sleep, but returning from sleep takes much time. On the other hand, when small amounts of function units go to sleep, power consumption is not lessened much, but returning from sleep is very quick. When the idle state continues for a certain time period, the depth of the idle state goes deeper by default.

HotPlug. The `hotplug` is an extended function of `cpufreq`, which was developed specifically for the power control of multicore processors. When `cpufreq` sets a core to the maximum frequency that runs for a certain period of time, the `hotplug` adds another core to distribute the load. Similarly, when `cpufreq` sets a core to the minimum frequency and the load stays low, the `hotplug` shuts down excess cores to reduce power consumption.

However, utilizing these assets as power control inside applications takes some to some tens of milliseconds, which is not suited for fine power control by a compiler.

3   Power Reduction Control by the OSCAR Compiler

This section provides an overview of the power reduction scheme realized in the OSCAR Automatic Parallelizing Compiler and the OSCAR API. Furthermore, an explanation of the pseudo clock gating method controlled by the OSCAR Compiler and the precise power measurement method will be given.

3.1 Multigrain Parallel Processing and Low Power Optimization by the OSCAR Compiler

The OSCAR (Optimally Scheduled Advanced multiprocessor) Compiler exploits multigrain parallelism, which consists of coarse grain task parallelism, loop iteration level parallelism, and statement level near-fine grain parallelism. In order to exploit multigrain parallelism, OSCAR compiler first decomposes a sequential C or Fortran program into coarse grain tasks named macro tasks(MTs), such as basic block(BB), loop(RB), and subroutine call(SB). Using these MTs, the OSCAR compiler would then analyze both the control flow and the data dependencies among them, creating a macro-flow-graph (MFG). After creating the MFG, the compiler applies the earliest executable condition analysis [23], which can exploit parallelism among MTs associated with both the control dependencies and the data dependencies. The analysis result is represented as a macro-task-graph (MTG).

If a MT is a subroutine call or a loop that has coarse grain task parallelism, the OSCAR compiler hierarchically generates inner MTs inside that MT. Also, loop iteration level parallelism is translated into coarse grain task parallelism by loop decomposition.

These MTs are assigned to the processor cores, which is grouped into processor groups (PG) logically and hierarchically considering the parallelism in each layer of the hierarchical MTG. If the MTG fluctuates at runtime or has conditional branches, dynamic scheduling is applied. Otherwise, static scheduling is applied to the MTG [24].

If there are idle or busy-waiting periods between MTs in a statically scheduled MTG, the compiler tries to minimize total power dissipation by prolonging the execution time of MTs with DVFS or applying clock gating and power gating during the idle periods. This execution mode is named as the fastest execution mode [14]. Note that the OSCAR compiler carefully controls DVFS, clock gating and power gating not to prolong the program execution time in the case of the fastest execution mode.

Similarly, if the deadline of an MTG is given and there are sufficient idle periods until the deadline, the compiler also applies DVFS over MTs on the critical path and applies its clock gating and power gating over idle periods not on the critical path, so that total energy consumption can become as little as possible. This execution mode is named as the realtime execution mode [14].

For example, a power-optimized MTG with a deadline is processed iteratively as in the case of a movie player, this execution mode is called as real-time execution mode. The experimental evaluations in this paper use the real-time execution mode.

3.2 OSCAR Application Programming Interface

The OSCAR API (Application Programming Interface) is a parallel API for executing the optimized code generated by the OSCAR compiler on various shared memory multiprocessor and multicore systems, including server, desktop computers and embedded systems [13].

The OSCAR API consists of a set of compiler directives based on a subset of OpenMP. The OSCAR API employs user-level power control in addition to thread creation and memory allocation considering local memory and distributed shared memory. The OSCAR compiler generates a parallelized program by inserting these compiler directives. Then, an OpenMP compiler compile this parallelized program into executable binary in the case of server platforms.

The standard API translator, which translates directives of OSCAR API into runtime library calls, has been also developed especially for embedded systems. In this case, an ordinary sequential compiler like gcc finally generates the parallelized executable binary for the target system.

For power control, the OSCAR API provides `fvcontrol` and `get_fv_status` directives. The `fvcontrol` directive sets the power status of a hardware module in a target system to a specified value. The `get_fv_status` acquires the current power status from a specified hardware module.

The power status notation used in these directives is an integer value ranging from -1 to 100. The value from 0 to 100 represents the percentage of clock frequency of the specified hardware module. For example, 0 represents clock gating, 100 is the maximum clock frequency, and 50 is half of the maximum clock frequency. In addition, -1 denotes power gating.

The standard API translator translates `fvcontrol` and `get_fv_status` directives into `oscar_fvcontrol()` and `oscar_get_fv_status()` functions, respectively. These functions wrap the runtime library calls for the target system.

3.3 Pseudo Clock Gating Method Using WFI

This section explains the newly developed pseudo clock gating method that has been implemented in `oscar_fvcontrol` for the OSCAR API.

The current power control method that can be utilized on consumer Android devices is the `cpufreq`. However, this method require millisecond level latency, which prevents high power reduction using the OSCAR compiler. In order to reduce as much power consumption as possible on the Android platform, a new clock gating method was developed. This method utilizes the WFI (Wait For Interrupt) instruction, which is supported by the ARM architecture. The WFI instruction gives a signal to the processor as a hint that there is no process to be executed. This instruction suspends the execution on the processor core and stops the clock. Specifically, the WFI instruction shuts down any instruction issue of a new process until an interrupt or a debug event occurs [5]. To utilize the characteristics of WFI as a low power optimization, additional functions were inserted in the Linux Kernel to enable the WFI instruction to be issued directly

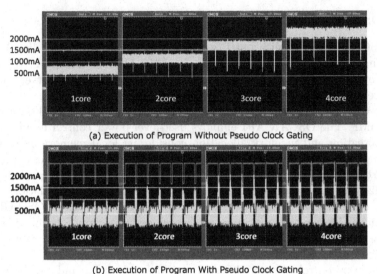

(a) Execution of Program Without Pseudo Clock Gating

(b) Execution of Program With Pseudo Clock Gating

Fig. 1. Comparison of power waveform with/without pseudo clock gating

from the applications. Furthermore, this clock gating method is able to stop the clock at a 500[us] interval.

Figure 1(a) shows the measurements of the electric current on each number of cores without the implementation of the pseudo clock gating method. The graph shows that as number of cores in usage increase, the electric current consumed on the board increases from 500[mA] for 1 core to 2000[mA] for 4 cores. However, by implementing the pseudo clock gating method, as shown in Fig. 1(b), the electric current stays just below 500[mA] even if the number of cores in usage increase. Figure 1(b) also shows that the proposed method stops the clock at an interval of 500[us]. Compared to the power gating method using `cpufreq`, which requires over 10[ms], the new pseudo clock gating method is higher in precision and speed. By implementing this new method into the runtime library, higher power reduction can be obtained on an Android platform by the OSCAR Compiler.

3.4   Precise Power Measurement Method Using GPIO

This section explains the development of the precise power measurement method using the GPIO (General Purpose Input Output) [25] pins on the ODROID-X2. GPIO pins on chips are usually used for debugging or testing on embedded systems by inputting commands and triggering interrupts. The Linux kernel driver can control these GPIO pins. A state of a GPIO pin can be seen as an event rising up and down on the voltage measurements.

A GPIO control function is prepared to change the state of GPIO from user applications. The GPIO control function changes the state of the GPIO by

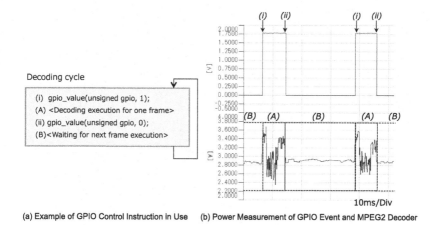

(a) Example of GPIO Control Instruction in Use   (b) Power Measurement of GPIO Event and MPEG2 Decoder

Fig. 2. Example of GPIO control functions

setting 1 or 0 as a parameter. Figure 2 shows how the GPIO is utilized on the power measurements. Figure 2(a) shows a program example of inserting GPIO control functions inside the MPEG2 Decoder program. Function `gpio_value` changes the state of GPIO from the application. Variable `gpio` specifies the GPIO pin number and the second argument specifies the value to write into the GPIO register. Figure 2(b) shows the waveforms of the GPIO and the MPEG2 Decoder in execution. The top voltage waveform shows the output state of the GPIO. Similarly, the bottom power waveform shows the power consumption of MPEG2 Decoder. This figure shows how precise and efficient the usage of GPIO is in power measurements. The marks on the voltage waveform, (i) and (ii), corresponds to the exact location of where the GPIO control functions were processed. On the other hand, the precise power consumption can be measure by expliciting the waveform for MPEG2 Decoder between GPIO signals rising up and down. This precise measurement method using GPIO allows a causal relationship and synchronization between the program and the power measurements.

4   Evaluation Environment

This section provides an overview of the environment used for power measurements. Although there are many different kinds of smart devices with different chips, a platform which enables power measurements are very rare, or do not exist in the consumer market. Therefore, to take power measurements on an Android platform, the evaluation environment itself had to be developed.

4.1   The Development of the Evaluation Environment

The ODROID-X2 [20] is a development board, which has the Samsung Exynos4412 Prime chip. Within the Exynos4412 Prime [26], there are 4 ARM

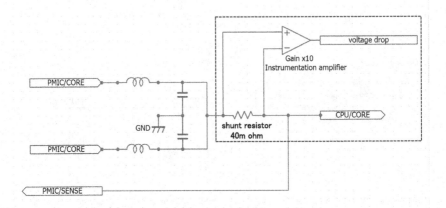

Fig. 3. Modified circuit diagram of ODROID-X2

Cortex-A9 cores each with a maximum clock frequency of 1.7 GHz with 1 MB shared L2 cache memory, 2 GB of dual channel LPDDR2 RAM is equipped on the board. The frequency and voltage scaling cannot be controlled differently on individual cores of this chip, but on all cores at the same time.

The ODROID-X2 development board is originally not designed for measuring power consumption of any parts of the board. In order to measure the power consumption of the cores on a chip some modifications are applied around the PMIC (Power Management IC) [27], which acts as the controller of power source of the CPU. PMIC on ODROID-X2 controls each power supply of the following function units on the CPU: battery, cores, memory, interrupt controller, accelerators, and so on. The modification of the circuit connected to the PMIC is shown in the dotted line of Fig. 3. The modifications applied to the development board are the following: altering the power source circuit of cores connected to the PMIC, adding a 40[mΩ] shunt resistor, and placing a 10x gain instrumentation amplifier. By placing an amplifier with 10x gain, the measurement of voltage difference between both ends of the shunt resistor become precise. This newly developed environment enables measurements of electrical current on cores from tens of milliampere to thousands of milliampere.

4.2   Evaluated Applications on ODROID-X2

This section explains two real-time applications used for the power evaluations on the ODROID-X2.

MPEG2 Decoder. MPEG2 Decoder is a standard video coding application from MediaBench [28].

The OSCAR compiler exploits slice level parallelism from the program. The deadline set for the MPEG2 Decoder is set to 60[fps] (16.6[ms] per frame).

Optical Flow. The Optical Flow is a benchmark application referenced from OpenCV [29]. This real-time application tracks 16×16 blocks between two images by calculating the velocity fields.

OSCAR compiler exploits parallelism among calculations of velocity fields from each block in two images. The deadline for Optical Flow is set to 30[fps] (33[ms] per frame).

5 Evaluation of Power Reduction on ODROID-X2

This section presents the results of power evaluations on the modified ODROID-X2. Power consumption for each evaluation is exploited by the proposed power measurement method using GPIO mentioned in Sect. 3.4. The power reduction control parameters set in the OSCAR Compiler for frequencies are FULL (1700[MHz]), MID(900[MHz]), and LOW(400[MHz]). Moreover, the cpufreq governor on Android is set to ondemand for benchmark applications without power control and userspace for benchmark applications with power control.

5.1 Power Consumption of MPEG2 Decoder on ODROID-X2

Figure 4 shows the power consumption results of MPEG2 Decoder for each number of processor element (PE). The power consumption of 1PE with power reduction controls consumed 0.63[W] (power reduced to 75.7 %) compared to 0.97[W] on 1PE without power reduction controls. The power consumption of 2PE with power reduction controls consumed 0.46[W] (power reduced to 24.5 %) compared to 1.88[W] on 2PE without power reduction controls. The power consumption of 3PE with power reduction controls consumed 0.37[W] (power reduced to 13.3 %) compared to 2.79[W] on 3PE without power reduction controls. The 0.37[W] for 3PE with power control resulted in 86.7 % power reduction against the ordinary 1PE execution without power control.

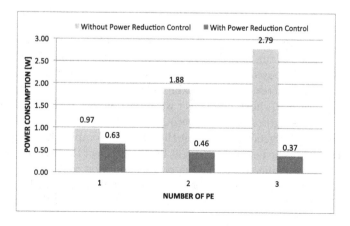

Fig. 4. Power consumption of MPEG2 decoder on ODROID-X2

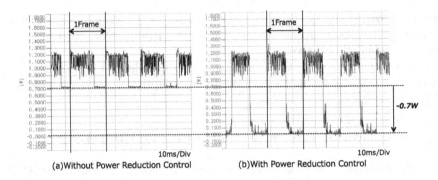

Fig. 5. Power waveform of MPEG2 decoder for 1PE

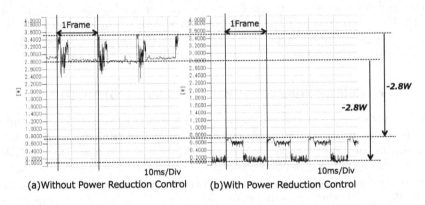

Fig. 6. Power waveform of MPEG2 decoder for 3PE

Figure 5(a) shows the power waveform of 1PE without power reduction control. MPEG2 Decoder in this figure is running at maximum frequency (1700[MHz]) and the **ondemand** governor seems to automatically lower the frequency when waiting for the deadline. Figure 5(b) shows the power waveform of 1PE with power reduction control. This figure shows that the OSCAR Compiler had analyzed 1PE of MPEG2 Decoder to run at FULL to meet the deadline time. Furthermore, by implementing the proposed pseudo clock gating method mentioned in Sect. 3.3, power consumption decreases to approximately 0[W] when waiting for the deadline. Similarly, Fig. 6(a) shows the power waveform of 3PE without power reduction control. In this figure, MPEG2 Decoder is running at maximum frequency using 3PE. However, Fig. 6(b) shows that the OSCAR Compiler had analyzed 3PE of MPEG2 Decoder is fast enough to run at LOW and meet the deadline time. This figure exhibits the significance of having power reduction controls at an application level on Android platforms. Furthermore, as explained in Fig. 5(b), the pseudo clock gating lowers the power consumption to approximately 0[W] when waiting for the deadline time.

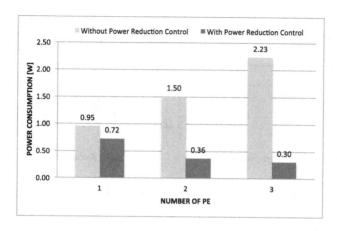

Fig. 7. Power consumption of optical flow on ODROID-X2

5.2 Power Consumption of Optical Flow on ODROID-X2

Figure 7 shows the power consumption results of Optical Flow for each number of processor element (PE). The power consumption of 1PE with power reduction controls consumed 0.72[W] (power reduced to 75.8 %) compared to 0.95[W] on 1PE without power reduction controls. The power consumption of 2PE with power reduction controls consumed 0.36[W] (power reduced to 24.0 %) compared to 1.50[W] on 2PE without power reduction controls. The power consumption of 3PE with power reduction controls consumed 0.30[W] (power reduced to 13.5 %) compared to 2.23[W] on 3PE without power reduction controls. The 0.30[W] for 3PE with power control resulted in 86.5 % power reduction against the ordinary 1PE execution without power control.

Figure 8(a) shows the power waveform of 1PE without power reduction control. Optical Flow in this figure is running at maximum frequency (1700[MHz]) and the **ondemand** governor seems to lower the frequency when waiting for the deadline similar to Fig. 5. Figure 8(b) shows the power waveform of 1PE with power reduction control. This figure shows that the OSCAR Compiler had analyzed 1PE of Optical Flow to run at FULL to meet the deadline time. Power consumption decreases to approximately 0[W] when waiting for the deadline using the pseudo clock gating. Figure 9(a) shows the power waveform of 3PE without power reduction control. In this figure, Optical Flow is running at maximum frequency using 3PE. However, Fig. 9(b) shows that the OSCAR Compiler had analyzed 3PE of Optical Flow is fast enough to run at LOW and meet the deadline time. This figure exhibits the significance of having power reduction controls at an application level on Android platforms. Furthermore, as explained in Fig. 8(b), the pseudo clock gating lowers the power consumption to approximately 0[W] when waiting for the deadline time.

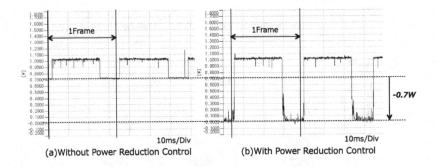

(a)Without Power Reduction Control   (b)With Power Reduction Control

Fig. 8. Power waveform of optical flow for 1PE

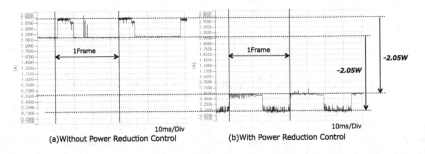

(a)Without Power Reduction Control   (b)With Power Reduction Control

Fig. 9. Power waveform of optical flow for 3PE

6 Conclusion

This paper evaluated the power reduction controls by the OSCAR Compiler on an Android platform, ODROID-X2. A pseudo clock gating method was developed using WFI to realize a low-overhead, or 100[us] transition time, power control by the compiler. All measurements in the evaluation were taken with the precise power measurement environment using the GPIO. For the evaluation, MPEG2 Decoder showed 86.7 % power reduction on 3PE from 2.79[W] on ordinary execution to 0.37[W] on execution with power control by the OSCAR compiler. Similarly, Optical Flow showed 86.5 % power reduction on 3PE from 2.23[W] on ordinary execution to 0.30[W] on execution with power control. The results exibit that the proposed pseudo clock gating method and the low power optimizations by the OSCAR Compiler enables significant power reduction on the Android platform.

References

1. Taylor, M., Kim, J., Miller, J., Wentzlaff, D.: The raw microprocessor: a computational fabric for software circuits and general-purpose programs. IEEE Micro **22**(2), 25–35 (2002)

2. Hammond, L., Hubbert, B., Siu, M.: The Stanford Hydra CMP. IEEE Micro **20**(2), 71–84 (2000)
3. Friedrich, J., McCredie, B.: Design of the Power6 microprocessor, pp. 96–97 (2007)
4. Jeff, B.: Advances in big. LITTLE Technology for power and energy savings, pp. 1–11, (September) (2012)
5. ARM Corporation: Cortex-A9 Technical Reference Manual http://infocenter.arm. com/help/topic/com.arm.doc.ddi0388i/DDI0388I_cortex_a9_r4p1_trm.pdf
6. NVIDIA Corporation: Whitepaper NVIDIA Tegra Multi-processor Architecture, pp. 1–12
7. Samsung Electronics Co. Ltd.: White Paper of Exynos 5. vol. 1(1) (April 2011) pp. 1–8
8. Amarasinghe, S., Anderson, J.: An overview of the SUIF compiler for scalable parallel machines, vol. 667 (1995)
9. Blume, W., Doallo, R., Eigenmann, R.: Parallel programming with polaris. Computer **29**(12), 78–82 (1996)
10. Bondhugula, U., Ramanujam, J., Sadayappan, P.: Pluto: A practical and fully automatic polyhedral parallelizer and locality optimizer. Technical Report OSU-CISRC-10/07-TR70, The Ohio State University (October 2007)
11. Kasahara, H., Obata, M., Ishizaka, K.: Automatic coarse grain task parallel processing on SMP using openMP. In: Midkiff, S.P., Moreira, J.E., Gupta, M., Chatterjee, S., Ferrante, J., Prins, J.F., Pugh, B., Tseng, C.-W. (eds.) LCPC 2000. LNCS, vol. 2017, pp. 189–207. Springer, Heidelberg (2001)
12. Obata, M., Shirako, J., Kaminaga, H., Ishizaka, K., Kasahara, H.: Hierarchical parallelism control for multigrain parallel processing. In: Pugh, B., Tseng, C.-W. (eds.) LCPC 2002. LNCS, vol. 2481, pp. 31–44. Springer, Heidelberg (2005)
13. Kimura, K., Mase, M., Mikami, H., Miyamoto, T., Shirako, J., Kasahara, H.: OSCAR API for real-time low-power multicores and its performance on multicores and SMP servers. In: Gao, G.R., Pollock, L.L., Cavazos, J., Li, X. (eds.) LCPC 2009. LNCS, vol. 5898, pp. 188–202. Springer, Heidelberg (2010)
14. Shirako, J., Oshiyama, N., Wada, Y., Shikano, H., Kimura, K., Kasahara, H.: Compiler control power saving scheme for multi core processors. In: Ayguadé, E., Baumgartner, G., Ramanujam, J., Sadayappan, P. (eds.) LCPC 2005. LNCS, vol. 4339, pp. 362–376. Springer, Heidelberg (2006)
15. Hsu, C.H., Kremer, U.: The design, implementation, and evaluation of a compiler algorithm for CPU energy reduction. In: Proceedings of the ACM SIGPLAN 2003 Conference on Programming Language Design and Implementation - PLDI '03, p. 38 (2003)
16. Chen, G., Malkowski, K., Kandemir, M., Raghavan, P.: Reducing power with performance constraints for parallel sparse applications. http://ieeexplore.ieee.org/lpdocs/epic03/wrapper.htm?arnumber=1420150
17. Xie, F., Martonosi, M., Malik, S.: Compile-time dynamic voltage scaling settings: Opportunities and limits. In: ACM SIGPLAN Notices (2003)
18. Martonosi, M., Clark, D., Reddi, V., Connors, D., Brooks, D.: Dynamic-compiler-driven control for microprocessor energy and performance (January 2006). http://ieeexplore.ieee.org/lpdocs/epic03/wrapper.htm?arnumber=1603505
19. Azevedo, A., Cornea, R., Issenin, I., Gupta, R., Dutt, N., Nicolau, A., Veidenbaum, A.: Architectural and compiler strategies for dynamic power management in the COPPER project. In: Innovative Architecture for Future Generation High-Performance Processors and Systems IWIA-01, pp. 25–34 (2001)
20. Hardkernel: ODROID-X2. http://www.hardkernel.com/renewal_2011/products/prdt_info.php?g_code=G135235611947

21. Google: Android Developers. http://developer.android.com/index.html
22. Linux: CPU hotplug Support in Linux(tm) Kernel. https://www.kernel.org/doc/Documentation/cpu-hotplug.txt
23. Honda, H., Kasahara, H.: Coarse grain parallelism detection scheme of a fortran program. Syst. Comput. Jpn. **22**(12), 24–36 (1991)
24. Obata, M., Shirako, J., Kaminaga, H.: Hierarchical parallelism control for multi-grain parallel processing, pp. 31–44 (2005)
25. ARM Information Center: GPIO Interfaces. https://www.kernel.org/doc/Documentation/gpio.txt
26. SAMSUNG ELECTRONICS: Samsung Exynos 4 Quad (Exynos 4412) RISC Microprocessor User's Manual. (October) (2012)
27. SAMSUNG ELECTRONICS: Samsung Semiconductors Global Site. https://www.samsung.com/global/business/semiconductor/product/poweric/overview
28. Lee, C., Potkonjak, M., Mangione-Smith, W.: MediaBench: A Tool for Evaluating and Synthesizing Multimedia and Communications Systems, pp. 330–335 (1997)
29. Opencv. http://www.opencv.org

Folklore Confirmed: Compiling for Speed = Compiling for Energy

Tomofumi Yuki[1][(⊠)] and Sanjay Rajopadhye[2]

[1] INRIA, Rennes, France
tomofumi.yuki@inria.fr
[2] Colorado State University, Fort Collins, USA
Sanjay.Rajopadhye@colostate.edu

Abstract. As we move towards exa-scale computing, energy is becoming increasingly important, even in the high performance computing arena. However, the simple equation, Energy = Power × Time, suggests that optimizing for speed already optimizes for energy, under the assumption that Power is constant. When power is not constant, a strategy that achieves energy savings at the cost of slower execution is Dynamic Voltage and Frequency Scaling (DVFS). However, DVFS is currently applicable only to the processor, and the entire system has many other sources of power dissipation. We show that there is little to gain in compilers by trying to trade off speed for energy using DVFS. It is best to produce code that runs full-throttle, completing as quickly as possible, an approach called "race to sleep." Our result is based on analyses of a high-level energy model that characterizes energy consumption, related to survey of power consumption trends of recent processors for both desktop and server, as well as Cray supercomputers.

1 Introduction

The main motivations behind the arrival of multi-core processors were power and energy considerations. Increasing power density coupled with heat problems rendered untenable the premise that steadily increased performance could be achieved merely by steadily increasing processor clock speed. Multi-core processors were introduced based on the observation that multiple processors with lower frequency consume less total power, while preserving performance throughput [8]. Power and energy have been of great interest in the embedded systems community, where they were constrained by limited power capacity or battery life.

Even in the High Performance Computing (HPC) community, where the term "performance" had previously been synonymous with speed, power and energy are becoming more and more important. The annual cost for powering supercomputers, including their associated cooling systems, is now reaching 50 % of the purchase cost of the machines and is expected to grow even further [24]. Power and energy are acknowledged to be the most difficult and pervasive challenges in order to achieve exa-scale computing [6]. In fact, if current hardware

© Springer International Publishing Switzerland 2014
C. Caşcaval and P. Montesinos (Eds.): LCPC 2013, LNCS 8664, pp. 169–184, 2014.
DOI: 10.1007/978-3-319-09967-5_10

trends hold, there will remain a significant gap (a factor of 10–100) between predicted and required performance per watt, even under optimistic assumptions. It is therefore natural to explore possible compiler optimizations for power/energy efficiency.

It is known that current compiler optimizations also reduce total energy cost [29,32]. Since the basic optimizations seek to speed up the computation, the equation, Energy = Power × Time, implies that optimizing for speed also optimizes energy, provided the average power remains constant. Moreover, many of the speed enhancing optimizations have a second order benefit that also reduces the power. For example, locality improving transformations like tiling increase the number of references that access local memory, such as caches, rather than off-chip memory. In addition to the low latency, caches also consume less power per access. Many authors have made this observation, and there seems to be a view in the folklore that in order to optimize for energy, compilers need to do no more than what they have always been doing—optimize for speed.

However, this naïve analysis assumes that power remains constant, which may not be true. Dynamic Voltage and Frequency Scaling (DVFS) is a technique that allows to dynamically change the operating frequency and voltage. As we shall see, DVFS implies that energy can be minimized by running as *slowly* as possible, or at least, as slow as one can get away with, until the response time becomes unacceptable and/or the components of the system, *not* governed by DVFS rules, come into play.

A number of studies [7,14,17,27,31] show that a significant fraction of the total power (more than 30 %) comes from various components of the system that are not influenced by DVFS, such as motherboard, power supply unit, and memory. Moreover, around half of the power consumed by the processor comes from leakage power, where DVFS is significantly less effective. Thus, the effectiveness of DVFS must be considered with the energy consumption of the entire system included in the picture.

These considerations lead to the question whether there is any trade-off, where compilers need to perform any "special" optimizations that solely target energy savings, *without* necessarily reducing, or possibly even *increasing* execution time. We want to answer the question whether "is compiling for speed also compiling for energy," with respect to the use of DVFS. In this paper, we present analyses based on a high-level energy model that characterize this trade-off.

The main focus of our work is compute-bound programs, including as a limiting case, compute-I/O balanced programs and DVFS for processors. For these class of programs, we identify conditions under which using the highest frequency is most energy efficient. We show that on a large number of recent machines this condition is met. Therefore, we conclude that compilers should simply work on optimizing for speed.

2   Background

We first present an overview of various power/energy related aspects of processors that influence our model and analyses. Energy (E), Power (P), and Time

(T) are related by the equation: $E = PT$ (more precisely, it is the integral over T when P changes over time). If an optimization keeps P unchanged, and reduces T, total energy consumption will decrease. The claim that optimizing for speed implicitly optimizes for energy comes from this observation.

Equation 1 below gives the simplified model of power dissipation of CMOS circuits [8]. The first term models the *dynamic* power consumption, where C is the total capacitance, V is the supply voltage, f is the clock frequency, and α is the "activity rate." The second term is the *static* power consumption (the power dissipated regardless of switching activity) where I_0 is the leakage current.

$$P_{proc} = \alpha C f V^2 + I_0 V \qquad (1)$$

Dynamic Voltage and Frequency Scaling (DVFS) is an architectural feature that allows the supply voltage, and the corresponding running frequency to be changed at run time. Voltage and frequency are known to be linearly related. From Eq. 1, power dissipation increases quadratically with voltage and linearly with operating frequency, DVFS can lead to cubic improvement in power dissipation. However, because of the linear relationship between voltage and frequency, there is also a linear degradation in speed. But reduction in power dissipation is cubic, and the degradation in execution time is only linear. To a first approximation, this leads to a quadratic reduction of energy as supply voltage is reduced.

Only the dynamic power component is amenable to DVFS optimization, the static power component decreases only linearly, and there is no net energy savings (in fact it is worse as we shall see later). Previously, dynamic power dominated the power consumption by processors, and thus power/energy optimizations focused on this component. It was predicted, and now observed, that static power consumption would reach 50 % of the total power [14,23].

3   Energy Model and Implications

We now present our energy consumption model, starting from a base model and progressively enhancing it. The following equation gives the energy consumption at maximum voltage and frequency:

$$E_{base} = (\alpha C f_{max} V_{max}^2 + I_0 V_{max} + P_c)T_{min} = (P_d + P_s + P_c)T_{min} \qquad (2)$$

where the variables are defined as follows:

- P_d: maximum frequency dynamic power consumption of the processor,
- P_s: maximum frequency static power consumption of the processor,

- P_c: constant power; power consumed by various system components not influenced by DVFS, but excluding those due to program activity (such as memory/disk accesses), and
- T_{min}: is the execution time at the maximum frequency.

The energy consumed per access to memory/disk is not included in the model, since the number of accesses to memory/disk does not change as a result of frequency scaling. This is essentially a combination of $E = P \times T$ and Eq. 1.

The above is a crude approximation as DVFS may indirectly influence energy consumption of various system components. For example, frequency of disk accesses may change, which in turn make the disk to switch between active and idle states more often, leading to larger energy consumption and vice versa.

Although we mentioned that the energy is the integral over time, product is sufficiently precise for our analysis. This is because when applying DVFS, programs are separated into relatively large regions where the frequency is fixed for each region. Since changing the frequency via DVFS comes with a cost in terms of both energy and time, frequent changes are not desirable.

3.1   Normalized Energy Model for DVFS

Under DVFS, let the operating voltage be $V = x_v v_{max}$, where x_v is the scaling factor, $0 < x_v, \leq 1$. Similarly, for frequency, let the operating frequency be $f = x_f f_{max}$, with $0 < x_f \leq 1$. Finally, let the increased execution time be $T = x_t T_{min}$, with $x_t \geq 1$. We express energy as a function of the three scaling factors

$$E(x_f, x_v, x_t) = (\alpha C(x_f f_{max})(x_v V_{max})^2 + I_0(x_v V_{max}) + P_c)x_t T_{min}$$
$$= \left(x_f x_v^2 P_d + x_v P_s + P_c\right) x_t T_{min}$$

We now normalize this by dividing by $P_d T_{min}$ to obtain the normalized energy consumption,

$$E_n(x_f, x_v, x_t) = \left(x_f x_v^2 + x_v R_s + R_c\right) x_t \tag{3}$$

where

- R_s: ratio of static power with respect to dynamic power, and
- R_c: ratio of constant power with respect to dynamic power.

3.2   Relationship Between Voltage and Frequency Scale Factors

Although voltage and frequency are linearly related, a few subtle issues arise when we precisely model their combined effect. The two scale factors are related as given below. The widely accepted formula is based on a study of recent processors, by a number of authors [16,20,30].

$$x_v = \frac{2}{3}x_f + \frac{1}{3} \tag{4}$$

We use this to eliminate x_v in Eq. 3 to obtain:

$$E_n(x_f, x_t) = \left(x_f \left(\frac{2}{3}x_f + \frac{1}{3} \right)^2 + \left(\frac{2}{3}x_f + \frac{1}{3} \right) R_s + R_c \right) x_t \qquad (5)$$

3.3   Properties of the Energy Model

For now, we let the slowdown factor, be $x_t = \frac{1}{x_f}$. For compute-bound programs, execution time scales directly proportional to scaling of frequency [14]. Since x_f is normalized, execution time for such programs can be expressed as $\frac{1}{x_f}$ (a more nuanced analysis is provided in Sect. 3.4).

Let us show some of the important properties of our model that give insights to how dynamic, static, and constant powers influence overall energy consumption. Distributing $\frac{1}{x_f}$ and further expanding x_v^2 gives:

$$E_n(x_f) = \left(\frac{4}{9}x_f^2 + \frac{4}{9}x_f + \frac{1}{9} \right) + \left(\frac{2}{3} + \frac{1}{3}x_f^{-1} \right) R_s + R_c x_f^{-1} \qquad (6)$$

Taking the derivative of the above with respect to x_f yields:

$$\frac{dE_n}{dx_f}(x_f) = \left(\frac{8}{9}x_f + \frac{4}{9} \right) - \frac{1}{3}R_s x_f^{-2} - R_c x_f^{-2}$$

Further taking the second derivative with respect to x_f yields:

$$\frac{d^2 E_n}{dx_f^2}(x_f) = \frac{8}{9} + \frac{2}{3}R_s x_f^{-3} + 2R_c x_f^{-3}$$

The second derivative is always positive if $R_s, R_c > 0$, which leads to:

- $\frac{dE_n}{dx_f} = 0$ will give the frequency with minimal energy consumption, and
- optimal frequency is less than 1 iff $\frac{dE_n}{dx_f} > 0$ when $x_f = 1$.

Based on the above, we compute the condition for optimal frequency being 1 (f_{max}):

$$\frac{dE_n}{dx_f}(1) \leq 0$$

$$\implies \left(\frac{8}{9} + \frac{4}{9} \right) - \left(\frac{1}{3}R_s + R_c \right) \leq 0$$

$$\implies 4 \leq R_s + 3R_c$$

When static power is 50 % of the processor power, $R_s = 1$, we obtain $R_c \geq 1$ as the solution, indicating that if components of the system unaffected by DVFS consume about as much as the dynamic power of processors, then executing at the highest frequency level is the optimal choice.

One additional remark we make is that the static power also works against DVFS, and its degree is related to the fraction of voltage that do not scale along with frequency in Eq. 4. This is because its linear power saving is cancelled by the linear increase in execution time.

3.4   Reducing the Impact on Execution Time

In the above, the influence of x_f on execution time was expressed as $x_t = \frac{1}{x_f}$. One may argue that many programs do not slow down as rapidly as frequency is scaled. Although accurate modeling of the impact on execution time is out of our scope, we provide additional analysis to show the implications of reduced impact on execution time. As mentioned earlier, the impact on execution time as a direct inverse of the normalized frequency may seem too steep for some programs that frequently access memory. In this section, we extend our model in Eq. 3 and add a variable to control the speed degradation.

We use a variable x, $0 \le x \le 1$ and let $x_t = 1 + x(\frac{1}{x_f} - 1)$. The variable x controls the speed degradation as frequency is scaled in a linear fashion. At $x = 1$, $x_t = \frac{1}{x_f}$, which is what we used in the above, and at $x = 0$, $x_t = 1$, no degradation as frequency scales. We substitute x_t in Eq. 3 to obtain:

$$E_n^x(x_f, x_v, x) = \left(x_f x_v^2 + x_v R_s + R_c\right)\left(1 + x(\frac{1}{x_f} - 1)\right)$$

To simplify our analysis, we write the energy as $E_n^x = E_n^A + E_n^B$, the sum of two different sub-functions:

$$E_n^A(x_f, x_v) = \left(x_f x_v^2 + x_v R_s + R_c\right)$$

$$E_n^B(x_f, x_v, x) = \left(x_f x_v^2 + x_v R_s + R_c\right)\left(\frac{x}{x_f} - x\right)$$

The respective derivatives[1] after eliminating x_v with Eq. 4 are:

$$\frac{dE_n^A}{dx_f}(x_f) = \left(\frac{12}{9}x_f^2 + \frac{8}{9}x_f + \frac{1}{9}\right) + \frac{2}{3}R_s$$

$$\frac{d^2E_n^A}{dx_f^2}(x_f) = \left(\frac{24}{9}x_f + \frac{8}{9}\right)$$

$$\frac{dE_n^B}{dx_f}(x_f, x) = x\left[\left(\frac{8}{9}x_f + \frac{4}{9}\right) - \frac{1}{3}R_s x_f^{-2} - R_c x_f^{-2}\right]$$
$$- x\left[\left(\frac{12}{9}x_f^2 + \frac{8}{9}x_f + \frac{1}{9}\right) + \frac{2}{3}R_s\right]$$

$$\frac{d^2E_n^B}{dx_f^2}(x_f, x) = x\left(\frac{2}{3}R_s x_f^{-3} + 2R_c x_f^{-3} - \frac{24}{9}x_f\right)$$

We can again observe that the second derivative of $E_n^x(x_f, x)$, $\frac{d^2E_n^x}{dx_f^2}(x_f, x) = \frac{d^2E_n^A}{dx_f^2}(x_f) + \frac{d^2E_n^B}{dx_f^2}(x_f, x)$, is always positive if $R_s, R_c > 0$, $0 < x \le 1$, and $0 \le$

---

[1] Derivations are not shown, as they are similar (but slightly more complicated) to the derivation from Eq. 3.

$x_f \leq 1$. The second derivative also always positive if $R_s, R_c > 0$, $0 < x \leq 1$, and $0 \leq x_f \leq 1$. Thus, the optimal frequency is 1 (f_{max}) when:

$$\frac{dE_n^x}{dx_f}(1, x) \qquad\qquad \leq 0$$

$$\implies \left(\frac{21}{9} + \frac{2}{3}R_s\right) + x\left(\frac{12}{9} - \frac{1}{3}R_s - R_c\right) - x\left(\frac{21}{9} + \frac{2}{3}R_s\right) \qquad \leq 0$$

$$\implies \left(\frac{7}{3} + \frac{2}{3}R_s\right) - x\left(1 + R_s + R_c\right) \qquad\qquad \leq 0$$

The above leads to the following remarks:

– As expected, the above indicates that as x decreases, which means as penalty on execution time with DVFS decreases, the inequality is less likely to be satisfied.
– Static power (R_s) work for DVFS when $x < \frac{2}{3}$. This is when the linear decrease in static power dissipation by DVFS starts to benefit overall energy consumption.
– With lower x, especially below $\frac{2}{3}$, much larger R_c will be required to satisfy the condition for f_{max} to be optimal.

The key implication is that as the program is less and less penalized by scaling the operating frequency, the ratio of constant power (R_c) to processor must become larger for the "go as fast as possible" strategy to hold, but the general property is unchanged.

When the program execution time is not dominated by processor speed, we can expect that other system components, such as the memory or network card, are stressed, and therefore ratio of processor power in the total system load to decrease [7,17,28].

Therefore, the behavior when degradation in speed is scaled is largely dependent on the application characteristics. When the x is small, it is likely that slowing the processor will be beneficial, since it is approaching memory-bound programs. For relatively large x, required R_c will become larger, but it is probable that going as fast as possible is still optimal. We also note that some of the recent machines have R_c much larger than 1 as we show in Sect. 4, further increasing the likelihood of this being the case.

3.5   Parallelism

So far, our analysis was completely independent of parallelism, although energy is intimately tied to parallelism. Indeed, the advent of multi-core and many-core processors was dictated by the needs of energy efficiency. We now tie the results to parallelization. Our main message remains that energy efficiency is attained by optimizing for speed, and that using DVFS to slow down the application to achieve total energy gains will yield limited benefits at best. However, optimizing for speed is not necessarily the same as maximizing parallelism, and hence there are a few special considerations.

Let us first assume that the program is perfectly parallelizable on an N-core processor. Even in this optimistic situation, some of the components of the processor, like cache or other on-chip memory, are shared among the cores. In addition, regardless of the number of cores, the thermal envelope/budget is usually allocated for a processor chip, and therefore, R_c is computed for a processor chip, and not on a per-core basis. Therefore, if only one of the N cores is being used, it is likely that the constant power is greater than $\frac{1}{N}$. This leads to the conclusion that utilizing all the cores if possible, is the optimal strategy, unless parallel efficiency is low.

Now consider the situation where the program is not perfectly parallelizable. The question of whether or not to parallelize, and if so, how aggressively, is beyond the scope of this paper, and we do not attempt to answer it. Rather, let us suppose that the decision to use some number p out of the N cores has been made. Our analysis indicates that now, the best strategy is to make the program execute as fast as possible. Basically, if a processor cannot save energy by slowing down in sequential case, then trying to slow down processors in parallel case cannot save energy as well. Note that one may apply our analysis to each core, if per-core DVFS is supported, but the result remains the same.

The choice of the optimal p may involve a trade-off similar to that pointed out by Cho and Melhem [10,11], but is also related to the application itself and how scalable its parallelization is. If the program has poor parallel speedup, and the decision is nevertheless to allocate an increasing number of processors to it, then some of the other, non-energy related issues (i.e., the response time of the program) are deemed to be important enough, to possibly override the gains of energy savings by using fewer cores. This means that any compiler (and possibly the programmer) should seek to provide the maximally scalable parallelization possible.

4   Trends in Recent Machines

In this section, we present trends in recent machines based on a survey ranging from desktop processors to Cray supercomputers. The goal of this section is to verify the observation based on previous studies that the constant power is around $\frac{1}{3}$ of the total power consumption under load, so that even if a significant fraction of the remaining $\frac{2}{3}$ is used by processor, $R_c \geq 1$ would still be true, satisfying the condition for f_{max} to be the optimal frequency for energy efficiency [7,17,27,31].

For desktop and server processors, we show that, even with conservative estimates, ratio of constant power in the total system power under load is close to $\frac{1}{3}$. We also show that the ratio of constant power has been relatively constant over the last 5+ years. This is to be expected, since designers of different components of the system try and fit their component to the same thermal envelope as previous generations. Therefore, if the ratio of static power consumption increases in processor power, then R_c will also increase.

For Cray supercomputers, we present estimates of R_c for two recent machines, and show that they are highly likely to exceed 1, also satisfying the condition.

4.1   Sources of Constant Power

Let us first describe various sources of constant power we use to estimate the lower bound. Constant power is power consumed under high load that are not affected by DVFS. Although there may be some relationship, it is not closely related to idle power. Especially with recent architectures, where aggressive power-gating is performed, idle power is likely to be much less than the constant power.

Stand-By Memory Power Consumption. One of the sources of constant power consumption is stand-by memory power. Recent study show that a 4 GB DDR3 memory consume around 4 W in stand-by state [13]. Although memory can also be put into low-power states that consume less power, unless the program does not use memory at all, it cannot be put into low-power states for long under heavy load. Therefore, we count 1 W per 1 GB of memory as part of the constant power consumption.

Power Supply Unit. When a system draws power, alternate current must be transformed to direct current, and significant amount of power may be lost during this process. Efficiency varies greatly depending on the quality of Power Supply Unit (PSU) and load, and it is considered efficient if the efficiency is higher than 80 % [1]. We assume 85 % efficiency for commodity desktop machines, 90 % for servers, and 95 % for supercomputers.

Chipsets and Fans. Prior studies show that older chipsets consuming 20–30 W, while some new designs reduce its consumption to 6 W [12,15,28]. Fans also consume 10–15 W when active [15,28]. For the purpose of our estimation, we consider 20 W per chip for processors with 45 nm or older process, and 10 W for 32 nm and 22 nm processors as constant power for both chipset and fan combined. We believe this to be a safe lower bound based on the numbers above.

4.2   Desktop and Server Processors

We have collected a number of power consumption measurements for desktop and server processors under heavy load. We show that the ratio of conservative estimate of constant power; the sum of memory stand-by power, efficiency loss by PSU, and estimated power consumption by chipsets and fans; is more than 30 % in most cases. This means that even if most of the remaining power is used by the processor, the value of R_c will be around 1. Since there are other sources of power consumption that are not included, such as accesses to memory/HDD, and network cards, it is highly likely that R_c is well above 1 in most cases.

We collected total system power consumption measurements from Anand Tech [2], an online hardware review site, for various desktop processors. They provide measurements under compute-intensive workload (x264 encoding), and many components are kept consistent across different processors (e.g., same memory and video card, but not motherboard). Since GPUs consume significant amount of idle power, we exclude GPU idle power (25 W) from the measured power consumption (the benchmark does not use GPU). The data set contains 46 data points, with Intel and AMD processors from 2008 to 2012. All machines measured were equipped with 4 GB of memory.

The data set for server processors are from published SPECpower_ssj2008 results [4]. The data set contains 255 data points, with Intel and AMD processors from 2007 to 2012; excluding results that are either for a system with multiple nodes, labeled non-compliant, or with imprecise processor name (i.e., only Xeon with out specifying which model). The benchmark models server applications with large number of user requests ("ssj" in the name stands for "Server Side Java"). The metric we use from the published results is Average Active Power (W) with 100 % target load, where the target load is calibrated to be the maximum throughput of the server computed as part of the benchmark run. Due to the nature of the work load, 100 % load does not necessarily mean 100 % processor utilization.

Figure 1 shows individual data points and means for each year for both desktop and server processors. The means are more than 30 % in all cases, where

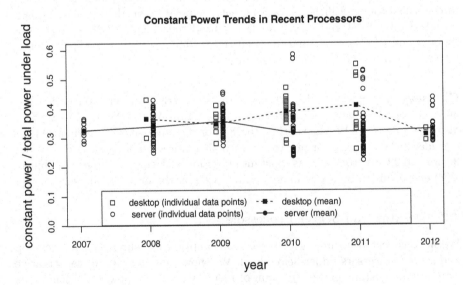

Fig. 1. Constant power in recent machines. Constant power is more than 30 % of the total power under load in many cases. Also, the fraction of estimated constant power in total system power is staying flat at the same level for both cases. Therefore, increase in static power will gradually increase R_c used in our model.

79 % of desktop processors, and 69 % of server processors have more than 30 % of constant power. This is an indication that the constant power is large enough such that R_c will exceed 1. Moreover, we emphasize that our estimate of constant power is conservative, and that actual constant power is likely to be higher than our estimate.

Also, the benchmark used for server processors stress both disk and memory to a great extent. In addition to our assumption that servers use more efficient PSU, the difference in work is another explanation that we can provide for the estimated constant power to consist lesser fraction of the total power in server machines.

4.3   Cray Supercomputers

We also show that R_c is likely to be higher than 1 for Cray supercomputers. Since precise power breakdown of supercomputers are not available, our analysis is based on specifications of recent Cray supercomputers, summarized in Table 1. Thermal Design Power (TDP) is the thermal envelope assigned to the Opteron processor used within Cray, and we use TDP as the upper bound on power dissipation by the processor.

We assume that Cray machines have PSU with 95 % efficiency, and only 5 % is counted towards constant power. We further assume that 10 % of the power is used for cooling fans, based on the measurements from Cray XT5 in Oak Ridge National Laboratory [33].

In Table 2, we present estimates of R_c based on Table 1. Since the total system power is specified as range, we compute the percentages for 2 scenarios, highest and lowest total power. For each scenario, we estimate R_c where constant power is memory + PSU (5 %) + cooling fans (10 %) and dynamic power is 50 % of the total chip TDP. The estimate on R_c is further divided into 2 cases, one with largest memory and the other with smallest memory. Finally, we compute how much additional constant power (as a percentage of the total power) is required to make $R_c \geq 1$, when smallest memory size, which alway give the smallest R_c, is used.

In the newer machines (XT6 and XE6), power consumed by processor as a fraction of total power is lower than the previous generation. Although the higher

Table 1. Power consumption of a recent Cray supercomputer cabinet, based on manufacturer specifications [3]. All these machines use AMD Opteron processors.

Cray	Nodes	Chips per node	Memory per node	Total system power	TDP per chip	Total chip TDP	Memory stand-by power
XT5	96	2	16–32 GB	32–42.7 kW	95 W	18.24 kW	1.54–3.07 kW
XT6	96	2	32–64 GB	45–54.1 kW	115 W	22.08 kW	3.07–6.14 kW
XE6	96	2	32–128 GB	45–54.1 kW	115 W	22.08 kW	3.07–12.29 kW

Table 2. Estimated R_c for Cray machines assuming different total system power. R_c is computed by assuming dynamic processor power is 50 % of the TDP, constant power is the sum of memory stand-by power, cooling fan (10 %), and PSU loss (5 %). The last column is the fraction of total power that must be additionally included as constant power for $R_c \geq 1$ to hold, assuming the Cray was configured with smallest memory size.

Cray	Assumed system power	Percentage CPU TDP	Percentage memory (min)	Percentage memory (max)	R_c max memory	R_c min memory	Additional P_s for $R_c \geq 1$
XT5	32 kW	57 %	5 %	10 %	0.86	0.69	8.70 %
	42.7 kW	43 %	4 %	7 %	1.04	0.87	2.76 %
XT6	45 kW	49 %	7 %	14 %	1.17	0.89	2.71 %
	54.1 kW	41 %	6 %	11 %	1.29	1.01	0.00 %
XE6	45 kW	49 %	7 %	27 %	1.72	0.89	2.71 %
	54.1 kW	41 %	6 %	23 %	1.85	1.01	0.00 %

total power consumption is likely to be a combined effect of various factors, part of the increase may be attributed to increase in memory capacity. As a result, R_c is at least 0.89 for the new generation of machines.

For the earlier generation (XT5), the processor power can dominate up to 57 of the total power, and R_c can be as low as 0.69. However, the first scenario assuming lowest total system power is likely to be too strong, since we assume processor is running at its TDP. When we assume the highest total system power and largest memory, all of the three machines exhibit $R_c \geq 1$.

Moreover, we have not included power consumed by the network among nodes and other cabinets, which is likely to add another few percent to constant power. Thus, we conclude that current generations of Cray supercomputers is highly likely to have R_c greater than 1, satisfying the conditions for the optimal frequency to be f_{max}.

5   Related Work

Our work is definitely not the first to show that simply going as fast as possible can also be energy efficient. Cho and Melhem [10,11] developed an analytical model of energy consumption under DVFS with multiple processors. They identify that there are cases where slowing the processor may not lead to reduced energy consumption, and that it is related to the fraction of total power unaffected by DVFS. We distinguish our work in three key aspects:

- (i) we tie our analysis results back to current machines, to verify that the constant power is significant enough for running as fast as possible to be optimal,
- (ii) our model separates the influence of dynamic and static power consumption of the processor, since the ratio of the two is also important, and

– (iii) we also extend the model to gain some insights for the case when execution time does not linearly degrade as frequency is scaled.

Dawson et al. [14] have empirically shown that constant power dominates (50 %–80 %) total power by measuring power consumption of two processors. They also conclude that running as fast as possible and then going to sleep is likely to be energy efficient. However, they do not have a model of how much constant power is required for "racing-to-sleep" to be optimal. We complement their work by showing that it holds for large range of more recent processors, and also with Cray supercomputers. Our estimate of constant power is much more conservative, since we do not include GPU idle power, and assume much lower power consumption for chipsets. They have included 50 W for chipset and GPU as constant power, whereas we only include 10–20 W for chipset and cooling fan combined.

Our work focus on compute-bound (including compute-I/O balanced) applications. For memory-bound programs, where DVFS is considered more beneficial due to reduced degradation in speed as frequency is scaled, the work by Le Sueur and Heiser [25] had shown that the benefits of DVFS is also diminishing. One of the observations was also that the constant power of the full system, which has been overlooked in some energy optimizations based on DVFS, plays a significant roll in the overall picture.

When DVFS Can Help

In this paper, we show that trading off speed with energy with DVFS is not possible in most cases. However, there are a number of prior work that use DVFS to save energy without increasing the execution time [9,18–22,26]. The common idea behind these work is to utilize load imbalance across components of the system.

For example, memory-bound computations allow processors to be slowed down without affecting the execution time [19,20]. Similarly, different components such as disks [18], or link interconnects [22,26] that are not utilized all the time, can be turned off for energy efficiency. Load imbalance in parallel applications [9,21] is another candidate for saving energy.

All of the above corresponds to techniques to bring programs into compute-I/O balanced state in our terms, and are still useful optimizations to improve energy efficiency. However, these techniques should be applied as a "last resort", after optimizing for speed. For instance, it does not make sense to make a program (more) memory-bound such that DVFS can be applied. Efficient access to memory will reduce the execution time and energy consumption. Similarly, it does not make sense to increase load imbalance of parallel applications such that DVFS can be applied. Developing methods for better load balancing will simultaneously improve speed and energy efficiency.

In addition to the above, recent processors employ sophisticated frequency/voltage scaling themselves, such as the Turbo Boost on Intel processors [5] These hardware controls are likely to be able to detect memory-bound regions of programs, and employ scaling themselves. Therefore, even such opportunities for energy saving by compilers may also be diminishing.

Another domain where DVFS may help is embedded systems, where you have much more flexibility than general purpose processors. Although the analysis in this paper remains the same, the significance of processor power with respect to the whole system power can vary widely between applications.

For some applications, the processor may be the dominant source of power usage, and hence DVFS is more effective. However, the opposite is also true. For example, screen and wireless card are the dominant power consumers in a smartphone, making DVFS even less interesting.

6 Conclusion

We have presented our analysis based on our high-level model of power consumption under DVFS. When the constant power in a system is comparable to the dynamic power consumption of the processor, using DVFS to trade speed with energy efficiency cannot be done, and it is best to run as fast as possible to completion.

We showed through a survey of number of recent machines that it is highly likely that most machines today fall under the condition where running as fast as possible wins in terms of energy.

Therefore, we confirm the "folklore" we have been hearing regarding energy optimization, and conclude that simply compiling for speed will also give better overall energy efficiency.

Our analysis is based on a high-level model, and it is possible that some class of problems can still benefit from DVFS. However, in this paper we have ignored the cost of changing DVFS states, and also assumed that arbitrary frequency/voltage can be selected. In practice, the cost of transition is not negligible, and available frequency/voltage configurations are limited, further limiting the applicability of DVFS.

Our result may seem negative, but from compilers' perspective, the problem has been made simpler. We can focus on speed, and the resulting code will be energy efficient. Until the time when the leakage power becomes a negligible component again, which is when the game entirely changes, invalidating many analyses including ours, compilers should focus on speed.

References

1. 80plus power supplies. www.plugloadsolutions.com/80PlusPowerSupplies.aspx
2. Anandtech. www.anandtech.com
3. Cray products. www.cray.com/Products/Products.aspx
4. Specpower, published at www.spec.org as of 6 May 2012. SPEC and the benchmark name SPECpower_ssj2008 are registered trademarks of the Standard Performance Evaluation Corporation. For more information about SPECpower_ssj2008. www.spec.org/power_ssj2008/

5. Intel® Turbo Boost Technology in Intel® Core™ Microarchitecture (Nehalem) based processors. White paper, November 2008

6. Bergman, K., Borkar, S., Campbell, D., Carlson, W., Dally, W., Denneau, M., Franzon, P., Harrod, W., Hill, K., Hiller, J., et al.: Exascale computing study: technology challenges in achieving exascale systems. Technical report, Defense Advanced Research Projects Agency Information Processing Techniques Office (DARPA IPTO) (2008)

7. Bircher, W., John, L.: Complete system power estimation: a trickle-down approach based on performance events. In: Proceedings of the IEEE International Symposium on Performance Analysis of Systems & Software, pp. 158–168 (2007)

8. Chandrakasan, A., Sheng, S., Brodersen, R.: Low-power CMOS digital design. IEEE J. Solid-State Circ. **27**(4), 473–484 (1992)

9. Chen, G., Malkowski, K., Kandemir, M., Raghavan, P.: Reducing power with performance constraints for parallel sparse applications. In: Proceedings of the 19th IEEE International Parallel and Distributed Processing Symposium, p. 8 (2005)

10. Cho, S., Melhem, R.: Corollaries to Amdahl's law for energy. IEEE Comput. Archit. Lett. **7**(1), 25–28 (2008)

11. Cho, S., Melhem, R.: On the interplay of parallelization, program performance, and energy consumption. IEEE Trans. Parallel Distrib. Syst. **21**(3), 342–353 (2010)

12. Chun, B., Iannaccone, G., Iannaccone, G., Katz, R., Lee, G., Niccolini, L.: An energy case for hybrid datacenters. ACM SIGOPS Oper. Syst. Rev. **44**(1), 76–80 (2010)

13. David, H., Fallin, C., Gorbatov, E., Hanebutte, U., Mutlu, O.: Memory power management via dynamic voltage/frequency scaling. Memory **300**, 400 (2011)

14. Dawson-Haggerty, S., Krioukov, A., Culler, D.: Power optimization - a reality check, Technical Report UCB/EECS-2009-140. Technical report, EECS Department, University of California, Berkeley (2009)

15. Fan, X., Weber, W., Barroso, L.: Power provisioning for a warehouse-sized computer. ACM SIGARCH Comput. Archit. News **35**, 13–23 (2007)

16. Freeh, V., Kappiah, N., Lowenthal, D., Bletsch, T.: Just-in-time dynamic voltage scaling: exploiting inter-node slack to save energy in MPI programs. J. Parallel Distrib. Comput. **68**(9), 1175–1185 (2008)

17. Ge, R., Feng, X., Song, S., Chang, H., Li, D., Cameron, K.: Powerpack: energy profiling and analysis of high-performance systems and applications. IEEE Trans. Parallel Distrib. Syst. **21**(5), 658–671 (2010)

18. Heath, T., Pinheiro, E., Hom, J., Kremer, U., Bianchini, R.: Application transformations for energy and performance-aware device management. In: Proceedings of the 2002 International Conference on Parallel Architectures and Compilation Techniques, pp. 121–130 (2002)

19. Hsu, C., Feng, W.: A power-aware run-time system for high-performance computing. In: Proceedings of the 2005 ACM/IEEE Conference on Supercomputing, p. 1 (2005)

20. Hsu, C., Kremer, U.: The design, implementation, and evaluation of a compiler algorithm for CPU energy reduction. In: Proceedings of the ACM SIGPLAN 2003 Conference on Programming Language Design and Implementation, p. 48 (2003)

21. Kadayif, I., Kandemir, M., Chen, G., Vijaykrishnan, N., Irwin, M., Sivasubramaniam, A.: Compiler-directed high-level energy estimation and optimization. ACM Trans. Embed. Comput. Syst. (TECS) **4**(4), 850 (2005)

22. Kim, E., Yum, K., Link, G., Vijaykrishnan, N., Kandemir, M., Irwin, M., Yousif, M., Das, C.: Energy optimization techniques in cluster interconnects. In: Proceed-

ings of the 2003 International Symposium on Low Power Electronics and Design, pp. 459–464 (2003)

23. Kim, N., Austin, T., Blaauw, D., Mudge, T., Flautner, K., Hu, J., Irwin, M., Kandemir, M., Narayanan, V.: Leakage current: Moore's law meets static power. Computer **36**(12), 75 (2003)

24. Koomey, J.G., Belady, C., Patterson, M., Santos, A., Lange, K.D.: Assessing trends over time in performance, costs, and energy use for servers. Technical report, Lawrence Berkeley National Laboratory, Stanford University, Microsoft Corpotation, Intel Corporation, Hewlett-Packard Corporation (2009)

25. Le Sueur, E., Heiser, G.: Dynamic voltage and frequency scaling: the laws of diminishing returns. In: Proceedings of the 2010 International Conference on Power Aware Computing and Systems, pp. 1–8 (2010)

26. Li, F., Chen, G., Kandemir, M.: Compiler-directed voltage scaling on communication links for reducing power consumption. In: Proceedings of the 2005 IEEE/ACM International Conference on Computer-Aided Design, p. 460 (2005)

27. Mahesri, A., Vardhan, V.: Power consumption breakdown on a modern laptop. In: Falsafi, B., VijayKumar, T.N. (eds.) PACS 2004. LNCS, vol. 3471, pp. 165–180. Springer, Heidelberg (2005)

28. Meisner, D., Gold, B.T., Wenisch, T.F.: Powernap: eliminating server idle power. In: Proceedings of the 14th International Conference on Architectural Support for Programming Languages and Operating Systems, pp. 205–216 (2009)

29. Seng, J.S., Tullsen, D.M.: The effect of compiler optimizations on pentium 4 power consumption. In: Proceedings of the 7th Workshop on Interaction Between Compilers and Computer Architectures, pp. 51–56 (2003)

30. Sinha, A., Chandrakasan, A.: Jouletrack-a web based tool for software energy profiling. In: Proceedings of the 38th Design Automation Conference, pp. 220–225 (2001)

31. Subramaniam, B., Feng, W.: Understanding power measurement implications in the green500 list. In: Green Computing and Communications, 2010 IEEE/ACM International Conference on & International Conference on Cyber, Physical and Social Computing, pp. 245–251 (2010)

32. Tiwari, V., Singh, D., Rajgopal, S., Mehta, G., Patel, R., Baez, F.: Reducing power in high-performance microprocessors. In: Proceedings of the 35th Design Automation Conference, p. 737 (1998)

33. Wenning, T., MacDonald, M.: High performance computing data center metering protocol. Federal Energy Management Program, US Department of Energy, Resources on Data Center Energy Efficiency (2010)

Debugging

Effectively Recognize Ad hoc Synchronizations with Static Analysis

Le Yin[(✉)]

Institute of Computing Technology, Beijing, China
yinle@ict.ac.cn

Abstract. Ad hoc synchronizations are ubiquitous in multi-threaded programs. They can cause data race detection tools to report a lot of false warnings. The existing tools for automatically recognizing ad hoc synchronizations limit their recognizing patterns to spin loops. In this paper for the first time we give a formal definition of ad hoc synchronization. Based on the definition we have implemented a static analysis to recognize them. Compared with the best existing analysis tool, the static analysis we have proposed has the same capability of recognizing spin loop synchronizations; in addition to that, the analysis can recognize ad hoc synchronizations which do not belong to the spin loop pattern. We have applied the analysis to a suite of middle scale multi-threaded Java programs. The experiment shows the analysis is effective and fast.

Keywords: Synchronization primitive · Ad hoc synchronization · Data race detection · Static analysis

1 Introduction

Data races are generally thought as programming errors. When two threads access the same memory location at the same time without synchronization, and at least one of the accesses is a write, a data race happens. However, apart from the data races that occur because of programmers' carelessness, some data races are introduced *intentionally* by programmers to implement user-defined synchronizations among threads. Those data races are not errors but integral parts of parallel algorithms. In this paper we call these user-defined synchronizations *ad hoc synchronizations*.

Figure 1 presents two instances of ad hoc synchronization. Fig. 1(a) is a spin loop synchronization used for enforcing the execution order between two threads: thread 2 will not jump out of the spin loop until the value of Flag is set to one by thread 1. The write and read on the variable Flag, which is called a *sync variable* by Xiong et al. [14], form a true but harmless data race. Fig. 1(b) is a simplified version of Dekker's algorithm. The two sync variables Flag1 and Flag2 are used as *flags* between threads to implement a critical region synchronization.

Ad hoc synchronizations are ubiquitous in multi-threaded programs [4,5,13,14]. Programmers will implement and use their own synchronization

© Springer International Publishing Switzerland 2014
C. Caşcaval and P. Montesinos (Eds.): LCPC 2013, LNCS 8664, pp. 187–201, 2014.
DOI: 10.1007/978-3-319-09967-5_11

mechanisms either because the synchronizations provided by libraries are slow or because some synchronization structures (e.g. barriers) they need are not supported by libraries. The existing data race detection tools [6,9–12,15] generally are not aware of ad hoc synchronizations and a large part of the false warnings reported by these tools come from this unawareness [13]. It is useful to automatically recognize ad hoc synchronizations to make race detectors treat them correctly to reduce false warnings. Krena et al. [5], Tian et al. [13] and Jannesari et al. [4] have developed dynamical tools to detect ad hoc synchronizations by analyzing run-time traces. The static tool SyncFinder proposed by Xiong et al. [14] achieves the same target through analyzing source code. All these methods identify spin loops checking conditions as the basic pattern of ad hoc synchronizations.

X is not initialized, but Flag is initialized to 0.

Thread 1	Thread 2
X=1;	while(Flag != 1) {;}
Flag=1;	... = X;

(a)

Initially, Flag1 = Flag2 = 0;

Thread 1	Thread 2
Flag1 = 1;	Flag2 = 1;
if (Flag2 == 0) {	if (Flag1 == 0) {
data = ...;	data = ...;
Flag1 = 0;	Flag2 = 0;
}	}

(b)

Fig. 1. Two examples of ad hoc synchronizations.

However, not all ad hoc synchronizations obey the spin loop pattern. For example, the critical region synchronization in Fig. 1(b) is not implemented by spin loops. It cannot be recognized by the existing static or dynamic tools.

To recognize ad hoc synchronizations like that, we present a formal definition of ad hoc synchronization, which specifies more ad hoc synchronizations than the spin loop pattern does. To our knowledge, it is the first formal definition of ad hoc synchronization. Based on the definition, we have implemented a static recognition analysis in a static data race detection tool, Chord [9]. Compared with the best existing analysis tool, SyncFinder [14], the static analysis we have proposed has the same capability of recognizing spin loop synchronizations. We have applied the analysis to a suite of middle scale multi-threaded Java programs. The experiment shows our analysis can recognize all spinning-based ad hoc synchronizations[1]; it also has identified other ones which do not belong to the spin loop pattern. The ad hoc synchronizations recognized by our analysis are all harmless data races.

2   Ad hoc Synchronization: Formal Definitions

In this section we give formal definitions of *synchronization primitive* and *ad hoc synchronization*. We use the examples in Fig. 1 to illustrate each definition.

---

[1] We have checked the data races reported by Chord manually and verified that no spinning-based ad hoc synchronization in those data races is missed by our analysis.

Figure 2 represents the code in Fig. 1 in the form of memory accesses. W_v^t (R_v^t) means a write (read) in thread t which accesses variable v. RC_v^t is a special read operation; it is defined formally in Definition 1. The racing memory accesses x and y are recorded as (x, y).

Thread 1	Thread 2		Thread 1	Thread 2
			W_{Flag1}^1	W_{Flag2}^2
W_X^1	RC_{Flag}^2		RC_{Flag2}^1	RC_{Flag1}^2
W_{Flag}^1	R_X^2		W_{data}^1	W_{data}^2
			$W`_{Flag1}^1$	$W`_{Flag2}^2$
(a)				(b)

Fig. 2. The code in Fig. 1 in the form of memory accesses.

2.1 The Key Idea

In a program, when a variable's value is used to compute some condition to determines which branch governed by the condition will be executed, the variable carries *control information*. The purpose of synchronization is cooperation among threads. To achieve this purpose control information need be communicated from one thread to another to trigger particular processing logic of the receiver.

When a shared variable is used to communicate control information between two threads, it is first written by one thread and then subsequently read and tested by another thread to see whether a certain condition has been satisfied. Different outcome of the test determines different branch of code to be executed. Such communication underpins ad hoc synchronization programming idioms. It is based on this insight that we develop the definition of ad hoc synchronization.

2.2 Synchronization Primitive

Definition 1. Synchronization primitive: *A synchronization primitive is a racing pair* $(W_v^{t_1}, RC_v^{t_2})$ *where v is a shared variable and t_1 and t_2 are two different threads such that*

- $W_v^{t_1}$ *is a write on v by thread t_1.*
- $RC_v^{t_2}$ *is a read on v by thread t_2 and the value read is used to evaluate a branch condition to determine whether the branch it guards in t_2 will be taken. RC stands for "Read for a Condition Test".*

Example: In Fig. 2(a) the racing pair $(W_{Flag}^1, RC_{Flag}^2)$ is a synchronization primitive. In Fig. 2(b) reads on Flag1 and Flag2 are all RC operations, so the data races on these two variables are all synchronization primitives.

Note in Fig. 2(a) the variable Flag carries control information, while the variable X does not, since no execution of any branch of code is dependent on its value. So although X is written by Thread 1 and then read by Thread 2 just like Flag, the racing pair (W_X^1, R_X^2) is not a synchronization primitive.

Synchronization primitives are the most fundamental synchronization facilities. They can be combined to implement complex synchronization functions. However, a single synchronization primitive might or might *not* be enough for a self-contained synchronization task. The case for the former situation is Fig. 1(a), in which $(W_{Flag}^1, RC_{Flag}^2)$, the only synchronization primitive, constitutes the spin loop synchronization. The case for the latter situation is Fig. 1(b), in which four synchronization primitives *together* constitute the Dekker's critical region synchronization. For the latter situation, any single synchronization primitive is just a part of the whole synchronization algorithm.

So we need a synchronization conception which is higher than synchronization primitive. That is *ad hoc synchronization*. An ad hoc synchronization is supposed to perform a self-contained synchronization task; it consists of one or multiple *related* synchronization primitives.

2.3   Ad hoc Synchronization

In this subsection, we at first introduce the definition of an equivalence relation to describe the relatedness among synchronization primitives. Then we define ad hoc synchronization on top of it.

Let $\mathbb{M}$ be the set of memory accesses in the program. Let $\mathbb{R}$ be the set of data races. Let $\mathbb{R}_{sp}$ be the set of synchronization primitives. And let $\mathbb{R}_n$ be the set of *normal data races* which are not synchronization primitives. We have $\mathbb{R} = \mathbb{R}_{sp} \cup \mathbb{R}_n$.

Definition 2. $\sim$ *is an equivalence relation defined on* $\mathbb{R}$. *It consists of five rules*:

$$x, y, z, w, u, v, W, RC \in \mathbb{M}; \qquad (x, y), (z, w), (u, v) \in \mathbb{R}; \qquad (W, RC) \in \mathbb{R}_{sp};$$

[REL 1] $(x, y) \sim (x, y)$.
[REL 2] $(x, y) \sim (z, w)$ if $(z, w) \sim (x, y)$.
[REL 3] $(x, y) \sim (u, v)$ if $(x, y) \sim (z, w) \wedge (z, w) \sim (u, v)$.
[REL 4] $(x, y) \sim (W, RC)$ if $x \propto RC$.
[REL 5] $(x, y) \sim (W, RC)$ if $\mathcal{L}_{exit} \propto RC \wedge x \xrightarrow{po} W \wedge \mathcal{L}_{exit} \xrightarrow{po} y$

If two racing pairs satisfy the relation $\sim$, they are called to be *related* to each other. The rule [REL 1] means the relation $\sim$ is reflexive: any racing pair is related to itself. The rule [REL 2] means $\sim$ is symmetric. The rule [REL 3] means the relation $\sim$ is transitive: if (x, y) is related to (z, w) and (z, w) is related to (u, v), then (x, y) and (u, v) are related. Because it is reflexive, symmetric, and transitive, $\sim$ is an *equivalence relation*.

The rule [REL 4] says if, in the control flow graph of the program, the basic block containing x is *control-dependent* [7] on the basic block containing RC (it is recorded as $x \propto RC$), then the racing pairs (x, y) and (W, RC) are related.

The rule [REL 5] says if, in the control flow graph of the program, the basic block containing some exit statement of loop $\mathcal{L}$ is control-dependent on the basic block containing RC ($\mathcal{L}_{exit} \propto RC$), x precedes W in the *program order*[2] ($x \xrightarrow{po}$ W), and $\mathcal{L}_{exit}$ precedes y in the program order ($\mathcal{L}_{exit} \xrightarrow{po} y$), then (x,y) and (W,RC) are related to each other.

Example:

For Fig. 2(a), according to [REL 5] we have $(W_X^1, R_X^2) \sim (W_{Flag}^1, RC_{Flag}^2)$.

For Fig. 2(b), the procedure of applying the rules is as follows.

Step 1: $W_{data}^1 \propto RC_{Flag2}^1 \xrightarrow{[REL\ 4]} (W_{data}^1, W_{data}^2) \sim (RC_{Flag2}^1, W_{Flag2}^2)$

Step 2: $(W_{data}^1, W_{data}^2) \sim (RC_{Flag2}^1, W_{Flag2}^2) \xrightarrow{[REL\ 2]} (RC_{Flag2}^1, W_{Flag2}^2) \sim (W_{data}^1, W_{data}^2)$

Step 3: $W_{data}^2 \propto RC_{Flag1}^2 \xrightarrow{[REL\ 4]} (W_{data}^1, W_{data}^2) \sim (RC_{Flag1}^2, W_{Flag1}^1)$

According to [REL 3], from the results of step 2 and step 3 we have $(RC_{Flag2}^1, W_{Flag2}^2) \sim (RC_{Flag1}^2, W_{Flag1}^1)$.

An ad hoc synchronization consists of one or multiple synchronization primitives. If α is a synchronization primitive contained in an ad hoc synchronization $\mathbb{S}$, then the ad hoc synchronization can be recorded as $\mathbb{S}_\alpha$.

Definition 3. Ad hoc synchronization: *An ad hoc synchronization $\mathbb{S}_\alpha$ is an equivalence class of α in $\mathbb{R}_{sp}$ with respect to the relation $\sim$[3]. It can be formally presented as follows:*

$$\text{For } \alpha \in \mathbb{R}_{sp}, \mathbb{S}_\alpha = \{\beta \mid \beta \in \mathbb{R}_{sp} \wedge \beta \sim \alpha\}.$$

Since an ad hoc synchronization is an equivalence class of $\mathbb{R}_{sp}$, all ad hoc synchronizations in the program form a partition of $\mathbb{R}_{sp}$: each synchronization primitive belongs and only belongs to one ad hoc synchronization.

Example:

In Fig. 2(a) $(W_{Flag}^1, RC_{Flag}^2)$ is not related to any other synchronization primitive; it itself forms a spinning-based ad hoc synchronization. The four synchronization primitive in Fig. 2(b) are related to one another; they form an equivalence class. So data races on Flag1 and Flag2 form Dekker's critical region synchronization.

With synchronization primitives, programmers can build ad hoc synchronizations of varying complexities, from simple ones with just one IF statement to sophisticated ones with multiple IF and/or LOOP statements. Definition 3 includes more ad hoc synchronizations than the spin loop pattern, which is used in the existing tools [4,5,13,14], can specify.

The property of equivalence class has two indications. First, related synchronization primitives come together to form a stand-alone ad hoc synchronization which is meant to have *complete* logic for synchronizing. In Fig. 4(b) Dekker's

---

[2] Program order is the order among statements statically specified in the source code.

[3] $\sim$ is an equivalence relation in $\mathbb{R}$. $\mathbb{R}_{sp}$ is a subset of $\mathbb{R}$, so $\sim$ is also an equivalence relation in $\mathbb{R}_{sp}$.

algorithm contains four synchronization primitives, none of which can solely synchronize two conflicting accesses on `data`. It is the four synchronization primitives as a whole that can guarantee W_{data}^1 and W_{data}^2 are correctly synchronized.

Second, different ad hoc synchronizations are independent to one another. An ad hoc synchronization can only synchronize conflicting accesses which are related to it. For example, in the program containing the code of Fig. 4(a) and (b), Dekker's critical region synchronization only synchronize the accesses on `data`; it does not synchronize accesses on X, which are not related to it.

It is based on these two indications that related synchronization primitives are *grouped* as an ad hoc synchronization to see whether correct logic for synchronization is implemented. How to judge the correctness of ad hoc synchronizations is detailed in the next subsection.

2.4   The Correctness of Ad hoc Synchronizations

After Recognize ad hoc synchronizations in the program, how can we judge whether they are implemented correctly? Since our analysis is implemented in the tool Chord and Chord is targeted to Java programs, we resort to Java memory model for this question. Java memory model [8], which is based on *data-race-free model* [1], prescribes that a data race free program is correctly-synchronized. So we have the following criterion:

Criterion 1. *Ad hoc synchronizations are correctly implemented if, after all synchronization primitives in the program are labeled as standard synchronization operations, the program becomes data-race-free.*

Java language specification [16] specifies that all the accesses on *volatile* variables are standard synchronization operations. So we can label synchronization primitives by declaring variables accessed by them as volatile. In the rest of this paper, we talk about the correctness of ad hoc synchronizations under the condition that synchronization primitives are labeled.

To judge whether the program is data-race-free we should guarantee that in any execution of the program there is no conflicting memory accesses occurring adjacently: they are always separated by synchronization operations[4]. An *execution* of the program is a sequence of operations of the program. For a real application containing hundreds of thousands of lines code, the number of its executions is very large, and it is impractical to enumerate all the executions to see whether conflicting accesses occur adjacently in them.

But in fact we do not need to check all executions of the program. Data races are divided into groups according to their *relatedness*: related data races are put into the same group. Note that the equivalence relation $\sim$ is used to judge whether two data races are related to each other. We use Fig. 2 as examples.

---

[4] Here we can not use the criterion that all conflicting accesses are under the guard of the same lock to judge the program is data-race-free. For example, in Fig. 2(a) W_X^1 and R_X^2 are not guarded by any lock, but they are synchronized by the spin loop. The same is true of the accesses of `data` in Fig. 2(b).

Suppose the code in Fig. 2(a) and (b) are in the same program, then there are two groups of data races in that program: one group is the data races in Fig. 2(a), the other is the data races in Fig. 2(b).

After data races are divided into groups, we only need to check the executions of memory accesses in each group. For a given group $\mathbf{G}$, an execution of $\mathbf{G}$ is a sequence of memory accesses in $\mathbf{G}$, which is a subsequence of some execution of the whole program. If two conflicting accesses x and y in $\mathbf{G}$ are always separated by synchronization operations in any execution of $\mathbf{G}$, we say x and y are correctly synchronized within $\mathbf{G}$. In other words, if there is no execution of $\mathbf{G}$ in which x and y occur adjacently, we say x and y are correctly synchronized within $\mathbf{G}$.

Theorem 1. *If any two conflicting memory accesses in the program are correctly synchronized within the group which contains them, the program is data-race-free.*

Proof. Assume any two conflicting memory accesses in the program are correctly synchronized within the group they belong to, but there is still a data race (x,y) in the program. The group contains (x,y) is $\mathbf{G}_{(x,y)}$. We have following results:

(1) Since x and y are correctly synchronized within $\mathbf{G}$, x and y are separated by synchronization operations in each execution of $\mathbf{G}$.
(2) Since (x,y) is a data race, there must be an execution $\mathcal{S}$ of the program, in which x and y occur adjacently. Removing all the operations in $\mathcal{S}$ except those belonging to $\mathbf{G}$, we get a sub-sequence $\mathcal{S}'$, which is an execution of $\mathbf{G}$. The result that x and y occur adjacently in $\mathcal{S}'$ contradicts (1). So the assumption is not right.

For Fig. 2(a), the possible execution sequences are as follows (we use '$x*$' to mean the access x occurs zero or multiple times), in which $\mathbf{W}_{\mathbf{X}}^{1}$ and $\mathbf{R}_{\mathbf{X}}^{2}$ are always separated by $\mathbf{W}_{Flag}^{1} \rightarrow \mathbf{RC}_{Flag}^{2}$. So $\mathbf{W}_{\mathbf{X}}^{1}$ and $\mathbf{R}_{\mathbf{X}}^{2}$ are correctly synchronized in the group containing them.

$$\mathbf{RC}_{Flag}^{2}* \rightarrow \mathbf{W}_{\mathbf{X}}^{1} \rightarrow \mathbf{RC}_{Flag}^{2}* \rightarrow \mathbf{W}_{Flag}^{1} \rightarrow \mathbf{RC}_{Flag}^{2} \rightarrow \mathbf{R}_{\mathbf{X}}^{2}$$

For Fig. 2(b), there are executions in which $\mathbf{W}_{data}^{1}$ and $\mathbf{W}_{data}^{2}$ do not occur at the same time. For example, in the sequence $\mathbf{W}_{Flag1}^{1} \rightarrow \mathbf{RC}_{Flag2}^{1} \rightarrow \mathbf{W}_{Flag2}^{2} \rightarrow \mathbf{RC}_{Flag1}^{2} \rightarrow \mathbf{W}_{data}^{1} \rightarrow \mathbf{W}_{Flag1}^{1}$, only $\mathbf{W}_{data}^{1}$ occurs. In the sequence $\mathbf{W}_{Flag1}^{1} \rightarrow \mathbf{W}_{Flag2}^{2} \rightarrow \mathbf{RC}_{Flag2}^{1} \rightarrow \mathbf{RC}_{Flag1}^{2}$ both of them do not appear.

However, for all the executions they both occur, $\mathbf{W}_{data}^{1}$ and $\mathbf{W}_{data}^{2}$ are always separated by some synchronization primitive. Those executions are as follows.

$$\cdots \rightarrow \mathbf{W}_{data}^{1} \rightarrow \mathbf{W}_{Flag1}^{`1} \rightarrow \mathbf{RC}_{Flag1}^{2} \rightarrow \mathbf{W}_{data}^{2} \rightarrow \cdots$$
$$\cdots \rightarrow \mathbf{W}_{data}^{2} \rightarrow \mathbf{W}_{Flag2}^{`2} \rightarrow \mathbf{RC}_{Flag2}^{1} \rightarrow \mathbf{W}_{data}^{1} \rightarrow \cdots$$

Since there is no execution in which $\mathbf{W}_{data}^{1}$ and $\mathbf{W}_{data}^{2}$ occur adjacently, they are correctly synchronized within the group containing them.

If conflicting accesses in a group are not correctly synchronized within the group, it might indicate the ad hoc synchronization in the group is not implemented correctly, and the program still has data races even after all synchronization primitives are labeled as synchronization operations.

2.5 Discussion

The definition of synchronization primitives can capture structures that clearly are not used for synchronization. A case is demonstrated in the following Figure.

Thread 1	Thread 2	Thread 1	Thread 2
	if (x > y)		RC_x^2
...	$\quad$ max = x;	W_x^1	
x = 100;	else		R_x^2
...	$\quad$ max = y;		
(a)		(b)	

Fig. 3. A buggy data race recognized as a synchronization primitive.

Figure 3(a) is the example code and Fig. 3(b) is its representation of memory accesses. Thread 1 writes x and Thread 2 computes the maximum of x and y. (W_x^1, RC_x^2) is a synchronization primitive according to Definition 1. But in fact the data race (W_x^1, RC_x^2) occurs because of the programmer's carelessness: he or she does not use x for synchronization.

However, the over-broadness of Definition 1 can be compensated by Definition 3. Related data races should be grouped together to see whether the ad hoc synchronization is correctly implemented. The data races in Fig. 3(a) form a group: $G = \{(W_x^1, RC_x^2), (W_x^1, R_x^2)\}$. In the execution of G, $RC_x^2 \rightarrow W_x^1 \rightarrow R_x^2$, W_x^1 and R_x^2 occur adjacently. The code is not correct according to Criterion 1. In a short word, if after marking synchronization primitives as standard synchronization operations there are still data races in the program, it indicates that some errors exist. At that time the programmer should review the racy code and do some modifications.

3   The Static Analysis Algorithms

We have implemented the analysis for recognizing ad hoc synchronizations in the tool Chord [9]. Chord statically checks whether two conflicting memory accesses in a Java program are guarded by a common lock by analyzing source code statically. Data races are at first detected by Chord, and then our analysis is applied to them.

3.1   The Comes-from Analysis

To recognize synchronization primitives, RC operations must be identified at first. The challenge of recognizing RC operations can be demonstrated by the example in Fig. 4: the value of the variable a is read and assigned to another variable b; it is b, not a, that occurs directly in the branch condition expression.

Furthermore, the accesses on a and b are located in different methods in the Java program. To recognize the read on a is a RC operation (since its value can affect some branch's execution), the algorithm must perform inter-procedure analysis to compute the information that b's value comes from the read on a.

```
void foo()              int bar()
{                       {
    int b = bar();          ...
    if (b>0)                // a is a shared variable
        ...                 return a; // Rda
}                       }
```

Fig. 4. Recognize Rd_a as a RC operation.

To solve this problem, we use a value propagating algorithm to systematically compute *comes-from set* for each variable. Rd_u signifies a read operation on a variable u. $cf(v)$ signifies the comes-from set of a variable v. $Rd_u \in cf(v)$ means v's value can come from Rd_u. For Fig. 4 we have $cf(b)=\{Rd_a\}$. The algorithm is an extension of Andersen points-to analysis [2]. Because the points-to analysis is also a value propagating problem: the value of the address of a heap object is propagated from one variable to another by some assignment. So what we need is to extend Andersen points-to analysis on address value propagation to the analysis on all types of value propagation.

Two rules are used to compute the comes-from set for each variable in the program. $\mathbb{T}$ is the set of all *thread-escape entities*[5] [3] in a multi-threaded program. $v \in \mathbb{T}$ means v is a shared variable accessed by multiple threads. The assignment $v_1 \rightarrow v_2$ means v_1's value is assigned to v_2.

$$[\text{CF 1}] \quad \frac{v_1 \rightarrow v_2 \quad v_1 \notin \mathbb{T}}{cf(v_1) \subseteq cf(v_2)} \qquad [\text{CF 2}] \quad \frac{v_1 \rightarrow v_2 \quad v_1 \in \mathbb{T}}{cf(v_1) \subseteq cf(v_2) \quad Rd_{v_1} \in cf(v_2)}$$

The rule [CF 1] says, for the assignment $v_1 \rightarrow v_2$, if v_1 is *not* thread-escape, then all the reads in $cf(v_1)$ are included into $cf(v_2)$; the rule [CF 2] says, if v_1 is thread-escape, then both Rd_{v_1} in the assignment $v_1 \rightarrow v_2$ and all the reads in $cf(v_1)$ are included into $cf(v_2)$.

The comes-from set for each variable v in the program are initialized to $\emptyset$. When the rules are applied, only reads on fields in thread-escape objects and reads on static variables will be added into comes-from sets; those entities which are local in one thread will not be involved in communications among threads and so will not be added into comes-from sets.

---

[5] Only thread-escape entities, which are accessed by multiple threads, will be involved in the computation of the come from sets, because an object which is local to some thread has nothing to do with communications among threads.

For the following code segment, assume a and c are thread-local variables while r and b are thread-escape variables, and $cf(\mathtt{r})=\emptyset$.

$$\mathtt{a=r;\ \ b=a;\ \ c=b;\ \ if(c>0)\{\ldots\}}$$

The procedure of applying the rules for comes-from analysis to the code is as follows.

[CF 2]: $cf(\mathtt{a}) = cf(\mathtt{r}) \cup \{\mathrm{Rd_r}\} = \{\mathrm{Rd_r}\}$
[CF 1]: $cf(\mathtt{b}) = cf(\mathtt{a}) = \{\mathrm{Rd_r}\}$
[CF 2]: $cf(\mathtt{c}) = cf(\mathtt{b}) \cup \{\mathrm{Rd_b}\} = \{\mathrm{Rd_r}, \mathrm{Rd_b}\}$

Note r and b are thread-escape and hence reads on them are added into comes-from sets.

3.2   Recognizing RC operations and Synchronization Primitives

After the comes-from set for each variable is computed, the rules [RC 1], [RC 2] and [SYNC] are used to compute synchronization primitives, where $\mathbb{B}$ is the set of variables that occur directly in condition expressions and $\mathbb{D}$ is the set of reads that occur in condition expressions; $\mathbb{C}$ is the set of RC operations; $\mathbb{R}_{sp}$ is the set of synchronization primitives and $\mathbb{R}$ is the set of data races.

[RC 1]   [RC 2]   [SYNC]

$$\dfrac{\mathrm{Rd} \in \mathbb{D}}{\mathrm{Rd} \in \mathbb{C}} \qquad \dfrac{v \in \mathbb{B} \quad \mathrm{Rd} \in cf(v)}{\mathrm{Rd} \in \mathbb{C}} \qquad \dfrac{\mathrm{Rd} \in \mathbb{C} \quad (\mathrm{Wr,Rd}) \in \mathbb{R}}{(\mathrm{Wr,Rd}) \in \mathbb{R}_{sp}}$$

The rule [RC 1] says that reads occurring directly in condition expressions are RC operations. The rule [RC 2] says that, if the variable v appears in some branch condition expression ($v \in \mathbb{B}$), and its value comes from Rd, then Rd is a RC operation. The rule [SYNC] says that if Rd is a RC operation, then the racing pair (Wr,Rd) is a synchronization primitive.

The three rules are applied to the code in previous subsection as follows: $\mathrm{Rd_c} \in \mathbb{D}$, so $\mathrm{Rd_c}$ is a RC operation by the rule [RC 1]. $\mathtt{c} \in \mathbb{B}$ and $cf(\mathtt{c}) = \{\mathrm{Rd_r}, \mathrm{Rd_b}\}$, so $\mathrm{Rd_r}$ and $\mathrm{Rd_b}$ are RC operations by the rule [RC 2]. Assume in the program there exists a data race $(\mathrm{Wr_b}, \mathrm{Rd_b})$, then it is a synchronization primitive by the rule [SYNC].

3.3   Group Related Synchronization Primitives

The rules in Definition 2 are used to group related data races. Synchronization primitives in the same group form a stand-alone ad hoc synchronization.

The rules [REL 4] and [REL 5] plays a core role in finding related synchronization primitives and the control dependency information is computed by using the standard algorithm described by Steven S. Muchnick [7]. When applying the rule [REL 5], we use dominator/post-dominator information to judge whether one memory access precedes another in program order: if in the control flow graph the block containing access x dominates the block containing access y or the block containing access y post-dominates the block containing access x, then x precedes y in program order. If x and y are in the same basic block, it is trivial to judge their order.

4   Experimental Results

In this paper we focus on recognizing ad hoc synchronizations. Our analysis does not judge whether an ad hoc synchronization it finds will cause errors. We run our analysis on a suite of real Java applications and have found dozens of ad hoc synchronizations. We verified manually those ad hoc synchronizations are all harmless data races.

4.1   The Benchmarks and Platform

The first two programs are tsp, a traveling salesman problem solver and jtpcc, a TPC-C benchmark [20]. Java Grande Benchmark Suite [17] contains eleven programs, most of which are of scientific computation. raja is ray tracer with graphic user interface [18]; jbb is the benchmark SPEC JBB2000 [19]. avrora is AVR micro controller simulation program, it comes from Dacapo Benchmarks [21]. Jigsaw is W3C's leading-edge Web server [22][6]. All the experiments were done on a machine with a 3.2 GHZ quad-core Intel Xeon CPU with 8 GB memory.

4.2   The Summary of The Experiments

The experimental results are presented in Table 1. Column "SP" and "AS" give the numbers of *Synchronization Primitives* and *Ad hoc Synchronizations* respectively, where "AS" is further divided into two sub-columns "spin" (synchronizations of spin loop pattern) and "non-spin" (synchronizations not belonging to spin loop pattern).

Table 1. The number of synchronization primitives.

Program	LOC	SP	AS		Time	
			spin	non-spin	T1(secs)	T2(%)
tsp	706	11	0	11	81	0.90
jtpcc	4,462	1	1	0	7056	1.01
Grande	8,615	8	6	2	988	1.09
raja	10,692	1	1	0	5312	2.35
jbb	30,486	45	1	0	2029	6.21
avrora	114,361	9	4	2	7140	1.27
jigsaw	160,618	55	10	31	10080	0.97

SP: Sync Primitive   **AS**: Ad hoc synchronization

There are 130 synchronization primitives reported; they form 59 ad hoc synchronizations, in which there are 23 spin loop synchronizations. Most ad hoc

---

[6] Chord can not process dynamic class loading in Java, which is used by jbb, avrora and jigsaw. We modified these programs to make them analyzable to Chord.

synchronizations only contain one synchronization primitive, except in the program jbb an ad hoc synchronization contains multiple synchronization primitives, which will be discussed in detail in the following subsection. All the ad hoc synchronizations are harmless races.

The last two columns are time data. The "T1" column is the total time in seconds of data race detection and ad hoc synchronization recognition. The "T2" column is the percentage of the recognition time vs the total time. Our recognition analysis is fast: for most program it accounts for about one percent of the total time.

4.3   Effectiveness of Recognition

Our ad hoc synchronization recognition is based on the result of data race detection in Chord. We have checked the data races reported by Chord [9] manually and have verified no synchronization primitive is missed by our analysis. In the rest of this subsection, we will discuss ad hoc synchronizations recognized in detail.

There are four programs (barrier, lufact, moldyn, raytracer) in Java Grande benchmark suite using the array IsDone[] to implement a tournament barrier. For two threads $myid_1$ and $myid_2$ such that $myid_1 = myid_2 + i*spacing$, thread $myid_2$ will wait at S1 until thread $myid_1$ reverses the value of IsDone[$myid_1$] at S2. The program sor in Grande benchmark suite uses array sync[][] to implement barrier synchronism. The worker thread id increments sync[id][0] to signal its work has been finished and wait for its "neighboring" threads id-1 and id+1 to finish.

Reads on IsDone[] and sync[][] are all recognized as RC operations, and those races on IsDone[] and sync[][] are recognized as synchronization primitives, which are illustrated in Fig. 5.

```
        public void DoBarrier(int myid) {
            ...
S1:         while(IsDone[myid+i*spacing] != donevalue){...}
S2:         IsDone[myid] = donevalue;
            ...
        }
```

(a) The user-defined tournament barrier used by programs **barrier, lufact, moldyn, raytracer**.

```
        ...
S1:     sync[id][0]++;
        if (id>0)
S2:         while(sync[id-1][0] < sync[id][0]);
        if (id<JGFSORBench.nthreads-1)
S3:         while(sync[id+1][0] < sync[id][0]);
```

(b) The user-defined barrier used by program **sor**.

Fig. 5. Ad hoc synchronizations in user-defined barriers.

The most complex ad hoc synchronization recognized by our analyses is that in the program jbb, which is showed in Fig. 6(a). There are five writes on the variable mode in main thread and eight RCs[7] on it in a loop in transaction manager thread. Together there are 40 (5 × 8) synchronization primitives, which are

---

[7] There are five statements of 'if (mode==RECORDING)' in the loop, only one of which is showed in Fig. 6(a) because of space limit.

related to one another and form a single ad hoc synchronization: main thread sets `mode` to different value to represent different states in the transaction processing; `mode`'s value is read and tested by transaction manager thread to do corresponding jobs. Our analysis can correctly recognize and group these synchronization primitives.

Main Thread	Transaction Manager	Main Thread	ImageDisplay Thread
S1: **mode**=RAMP_UP;	S6: while (**mode** != STOP) {	synchronized	void run() {
	if (**mode**==DEFAULT_MODE)	void setUpdating(boolean b)	while (true) {
S2: **mode**=RECORDING;	...	{	...
	S7: if (**mode**==RECORDING)	if (updaingRunning && !b)	if (**updatingRunning**)
S3: **mode**=RAMP_DOWN;	...	repaint();	repaint();
	...		...
S4: **mode**=STOP;	if (**mode**==DEFAULT_MODE)	**updatingRunning** = b;	}
...	...	notify();	}
S5: **mode**=DEFAULT_MODE;	} // end of while	}	
(a) **jbb**		(b) **raja**	

Fig. 6. Ad hoc synchronizations in `jbb` and `raja`.

The ad hoc synchronization recognized in `raja` is showed in Fig. 6(b). The main thread sets `updateRunning` after finishing graphics computation. An image display thread is checking `updateRunning` constantly in a spin loop to re-paint the graphics.

It is common in multi-threaded programs that a shared variable is always written under the guard of a lock, but freely read without any synchronization. Data race in `raja` (Fig. 6(b)) is a case of this kind. Figure 7 shows another two races caused by this reason.

For Fig. 7(a), different threads in `tsp` write `MinTourLen` under the protection of the lock, but read it freely. For Fig. 7(b), working threads in `jigsaw` increment `loadedStore` in a synchronized way, while collect thread reads it freely.

```
static void set_best(int best, int[] path) {      synchronized void incrLoadedStore() {
    if (best >= MinTourLen) return;                   loadedStore++;
    synchronized(MinLock) {                           checkMaxLoadedStore();
        if (best < MinTourLen) {                   }
            MinTourLen = best;
            for (int i = 0; i < Tsp.TspSize; i++)  void collect() {
                MinTour[i] = path[i];                 ...
        }                                             while ( loadedStore > maxload )
    }                                                     synchronized(entry) {...}
}                                                  }
```

(a) low lock in **tsp**   (b) low lock in **jigsaw**

Fig. 7. Low-locks in `tsp` and `jigsaw`.

Races in `sync` (on field `shared_counter`), `tsp` (on fields `prefix_weight`, `last`), `jtpcc` (on field `terminalsStarted`) and many other races in `jigsaw` are caused by this programming paradigm. All the reads in the races are RC operations. These races are harmless synchronization primitives.

5   Related Work

Some tools have been proposed to automatically recognize ad hoc synchronizations of the spin loop pattern. The tools proposed by Krena et al. [5] and Tian et al. [13] dynamically recognize in programs spin loops whose condition variables do not change during three iterations. If the spin loop is not executed repeatedly, it can not be recognized. To overcome this drawback, Jannesari et al. [4] instrument code on writes and reads of condition variables to make them dynamically detectable. However condition variables may be data-dependent or control-dependent on other variables (they are called *Exit Dependent Variables, EDVs*, by Xiong et al. [14]). The signaling thread can *indirectly* modify the loop exit condition in the signaled thread by modifying some EDV, which cannot be recognized by the method proposed by Jannesari et al.. The static tool SyncFinder proposed by Xiong et al. recognizes EDVs as sync variables through data flow and control flow analyses [14]. It can recognize very complicated spin loops in real world large-scale programs with few false positives.

```
for (deleted=0;;) {              while (1) {
    ...                              int oldcount =
    if (dbmfp->ref == 1)                 global->barrier.count;
        deleted = 1;                 ...
    ...                              if (updatecount == oldcount) break;
    if (deleted) break;              ...
}                                }

    (a) control dependency          (b) data dependency
```

Fig. 8. Two complex spin loops recognized by SyncFinder.

For recognizing complex spin loops containing EDVs, our analysis has the same ability as SyncFinder. The two spin loops in Fig. 8 are Fig. 1(c) and Fig. 5(a) in the paper of Xiong et al. [14] respectively. Our analysis can recognize them as can SyncFinder.

The variable `dbmfp->ref` is a EDV on which a loop exit condition is control-dependent, while `global->barrier.count` is a EDV of data-dependency. The variable `dbmfp->ref` is referenced directly in a branch condition expression and the read on it is recognized as a RC operation. `oldcount` is referenced in a branch condition and its value comes from `global->barrier.count`, so the read on `global->barrier.count` is a RC operation too. If there exist racing writes for these RC operations, the writes and corresponding RC operations are recognized as synchronization primitives by our analysis.

Nevertheless, SyncFinder will miss the Dekker's synchronization in Fig. 1(b). It also will miss some synchronization primitives in the Fig. 6(a), such as the synchronization primitive formed by the statements 'mode=RECORDING' and 'if (mode==RECORDING)', even though the condition 'if (mode== RECORDING)' is located in a spin loop. Those ad hoc synchronizations can be recognized correctly by our analysis.

6   Conclusion and Future Work

In this paper for the first time we give a formal definition of ad hoc synchronization. Based on it a static analysis has been implemented and applied to a suite of middle scale Java multi-threaded programs. The experiment shows the analysis is fast and can recognize ad hoc synchronizations more than the spin loop pattern used by the existing tools can specify.

References

1. Adve, S.V., Hill, M.D.: Weak ordering - a new definition. In: ISCA, pp. 2–14 (1990)
2. Andersen, L.O.: Program analysis and specialization for the C programming language. Ph.D thesis, DIKU, University of Copenhagen, May 1994
3. Lee, K., Midkiff, S.P.: A two-phase escape analysis for parallel Java programs. In: PACT, pp. 53–62 (2006)
4. Jannesari, A., Tichy, W.F.: Identifying ad-hoc synchronization for enhanced race detection. In: IPDPS. IEEE (2010)
5. Krena, B., Letko, Z., Tzoref, R., Ur, S., Vojnar, T.: Healing data races on-the-fly. In: PADTAD, pp. 54–64 (2007)
6. O'Callahan, R., Choi, J.-D.: Hybrid dynamic data race detection. In: PPoPP, pp. 167–178 (2003)
7. Muchnick, S.S.: Advanced Compiler Design and Implementation. Morgan Kaufmann Publisher, San Francisco (1997)
8. Manson, J., Pugh, W., Adve, S.V.: The Java memory model. In: POPL, pp. 378–391 (2005)
9. Naik, M., Aiken, A., Whaley, J.: Effective static race detection for Java. In: PLDI, pp. 308–319 (2006)
10. von Praun, C., Gross, T.R.: Object race detection. In: OOPSLA, pp. 70–82 (2001)
11. Perkovic, D., Keleher, P.J.: Online data-race detection via coherency guarantees. In: OSDI, pp. 47–57 (1996)
12. Savage, S., Burrows, M., Nelson, G., Sobalvarro, P., Anderson, T.: Eraser: a dynamic data race detector for multi-threaded programs. In: SOSP, pp. 27–37 (1997)
13. Tian, C., Nagarajan, V., Gupta, R., Tallam, S.: Dynamic recognition of synchronization operations for improved data race detection. In: ISSTA, pp. 143–154 (2008)
14. Xiong, W., Park, S., Zhang, J., Zhou, Y., Ma, Z.: Ad hoc synchronization considered harmful. In: OSDI, pp. 1–8 (2010)
15. Xie, X., Xue, J.: ACCULOCK: accurate and efficient detection of data races. In: CGO, pp. 201–212 (2011)
16. Subsection 8.3.1.4 in The Java Language Specification, Third Edition. http://java.sun.com/docs/books/jls/third_edition/html/j3TOC.html
17. Java grande benchmark. http://www.epcc.ed.ac.uk/research/java-grande/
18. Raja raytracer program. http://raja.sourceforge.net/
19. SPEC2000 Java Business Benchmark. http://www.spec.org/osg/jbb2000/
20. JTPCC TPC-C benchmark. http://jtpcc.sourceforge.net/
21. Dacapo Benchmarks. http://dacapobench.org/
22. W3C web server jigsaw. http://www.w3.org/Jigsaw/

AntSM: Efficient Debugging for Shared Memory Parallel Programs

Jae-Woo Lee and Samuel P. Midkiff(⊠)

School of Electrical and Computer Engineering, Purdue University,
West Lafayette, IN 47907, USA
{jaewoolee,smidkiff}@purdue.edu

Abstract. This paper describes AntSM, a system that uses the inherent parallelism of multi-threaded programs to reduce the overhead of statistical and invariant violations detection-based debugging tools. The runtime monitoring of these tools leads to high overheads. The key insight of the AntSM system is that this overhead can be reduced in parallel programs by performing sampled monitoring across parallel regions of the program that are performing similar actions. AntSM implements this sampling using a combination of static and dynamic analyses to determine similar parts of the program executing in parallel and the number of threads executing those parts of the program. Experimental results, performed using the C-DIDUCE (a variant of DIDUCE for C) debugging tool on eleven Pthreads benchmarks from the PARSEC suite, show monitoring overhead is reduced by up to 18.14 times (and on average 8.73 times) on an eight-core machine relative to a naive port that performs no sampling.

Keywords: Pthreads · Parallel program debugging · Anomaly detection · DIDUCE

1 Introduction

Writing correct sequential programs is a difficult task – bugs in these programs cost the software industry billions of dollars in lost productivity each year [1]. Using more complicated parallel programming models will not reduce the number of sequential bugs, and may increase their number by adding to the overall complexity of programming. Tools exist that identify statements that may be related to sequential bugs and that allow the bugs to be identified quickly and fixed. Because sequential bugs will continue to exist in parallel programs, these tools will continue to be useful in parallel programming environments.

An important class of these tools detects *invariant violations*, and includes tools such as DIDUCE [2], C-DIDUCE [3] and AccMon [4][1] that, in sequential programs, have runtime overheads of up to 20X, 1.21X and 3X, respectively.

---

[1] AccMon uses special hardware.

© Springer International Publishing Switzerland 2014
C. Caşcaval and P. Montesinos (Eds.): LCPC 2013, LNCS 8664, pp. 202–216, 2014.
DOI: 10.1007/978-3-319-09967-5_12

A second class of debugging tools (e.g., [5–7]) looks for statistical variations in program behaviors between correct and incorrect runs, and can also have high runtime overheads. These overheads result from needing to monitor fine grained program actions at runtime.

While a naive port of these tools to a parallel, shared memory platform is possible, doing so is inefficient. The tools often rely on having a single data item monitored for each program point of interest (e.g., every reference of a non-floating point variable). The key insight of this paper is that different instances of the same code executing in parallel in different threads are likely to behave similarly, and that sampled monitoring over that code can reduce overheads with only a small impact on accuracy.

The Ant Shared Memory (or AntSM) system exploits this key observation to reduce the overhead of debugging tools when used with shared memory parallel programs. AntSM uses the parallelism of the multi-threaded shared memory program being monitored to reduce the overhead of the debugging tool, while maintaining a high level of accuracy. It does this by first instrumenting the program with calls to AntSM runtime library to collect and maintain information about parallelism in the program. The program is then instrumented with monitoring and other calls for the bug detection technique being used. At runtime, the parallel structure of the program and the number of threads executing some region of the program are used to perform an intelligently sampled monitoring.

We measure the effectiveness of AntSM with a case study using multi-threaded, parallel Pthreads programs from the PARSEC benchmark suite [8] with injected bugs like those in the Siemens Benchmark Suite [9]. Our debugging tool is C-DIDUCE [3], an implementation of DIDUCE [2] targeting C instead of Java. AntSM reduces the running time of the monitored program by up to 18.14 times (and on average 8.73 times) on an eight-core machine relative to a naive port that performs no sampling, with an accuracy that is close to monitoring all accesses.

To summarize, this paper presents the following technical contributions:

- It describes a debugging framework that allows sequential debugging tools to be efficiently used with shared memory parallel programs;
- It describes in detail the AntSM runtime that maintains information about parallelism to enable sampled monitoring;
- It describes a case study of AntSM using the C-DIDUCE [3] value invariant tool with parallel C/C++ Pthreads programs;
- It provides experimental results showing the usefulness of AntSM.

The rest of the paper is organized as follows. Section 2 provides an overview of the AntSM strategy. Section 3 discusses the AntSM runtime and instrumentation techniques. Section 4 describes a case study of our framework, and Sect. 5 presents an experimental evaluation of the case study. Section 6 discusses related work, and Sect. 7 provides our conclusions.

2   Overview of the AntSM Strategy

To provide insights into AntSM's strategy, we now contrast how it, and a straightforward port of a monitoring-based debugging tool, function. In this paper, we use a statistical and invariance based debugging tool called C-DIDUCE (a variant of DIDUCE for C) that asserts the value invariant hypothesis. The value invariant hypothesis states that a given variable takes on a small set of values during its lifetime, even with different input data, and rarely occurring deviations from this set of values indicate buggy or anomalous behavior.

DIDUCE and other invariance based tools typically have a training phase and a checking phase. During the training phase, the program being debugged is run with data that gives a correct answer. Each action of interest is monitored and the outcome of that action is recorded. For DIDUCE, each variable reference is monitored and the value seen is recorded in a compressed form. These outcomes form an invariant set of outcomes that are true for correct executions. During checking runs, each action of interest is monitored and the outcomes that are deviations from the invariant set are monitored and recorded. This monitoring and recording often incurs a high overhead, and it is this overhead that we seek to reduce with our techniques. After the program executes, the deviations from the invariant set are ranked. Frequently occurring deviations are considered more likely to be invariants that simply were not seen during the training runs, and are ranked lower. Rarely occurring deviations are considered more likely to be signs of a bug, and are ranked higher.

A straightforward port of a tool would simply instrument a parallel program as if it were a sequential program, and monitor all actions of interest in the program. Ignoring overheads induced by the tool running in a parallel environment and needing to be thread-safe, this would produce the same overhead as a sequential execution of the program that executed the same number of monitored actions. Thus each thread executes all of the monitoring, a mode that we call *replicated* monitoring.

One way to reduce the overhead of replicated monitoring is to have each of the T threads executing the program monitor $\frac{1}{T}$ of the events. This performs a *distributed* sampled monitoring across all T threads. This significantly reduces the monitoring overhead but can lead to less accuracy in detecting anomalous events that indicate a bug, as shown in Sect. 5.4. The loss of accuracy results from each thread only sampling $\frac{1}{T}$ events, even in program regions that are not executed by all T threads. This leads to some actions being severely under-monitored or completely missed by monitoring.

AntSM takes a more intelligent approach, and by doing so achieves nearly the low overhead of distributed monitoring and accuracy close to that of replicated monitoring. A typical Pthreads program either spawns threads that directly call a function that performs the thread's share of the computation, or spawns threads (i.e., a thread pool) that check a work queue, and invoke a function implied by the queue entry to perform the computation. We call all these functions that specify the computation *root* functions. By instrumenting and analyzing the thread spawning points and the root functions, and tracking when threads enter and exit root functions, the exact number of threads performing the computation associated with the root function can be determined. This count, T_c, can be used to perform sampling of $\frac{1}{T_c}$ actions rather than $\frac{1}{T}$ actions, and avoid severely undersampling program actions of interest. Moreover, because the functions associated with a given root function are engaged in the same operation on different data, sampling within these functions is more likely to be sampling from a set of similar actions than simply randomly sampling across the entire program, which should lead to higher accuracy. Within loops, this sampling is implemented by each thread executing $\frac{1}{T_c}$ iterations, and within straight-line code, by each thread executing each $\frac{1}{T_c}$ statements in the textual representation of the program.

3   AntSM Runtime and Instrumentation

We now describe how code is analyzed and instrumented to enable AntSM's intelligent sampling strategy (see Fig. 1.)

First, root functions must be identified directly from the *start_routine* argument to the `pthread_create` function. Programs using a thread pool require instrumenting all functions to log when the function is entered and exited, and printing the function name and system thread ID. From this, a simple script

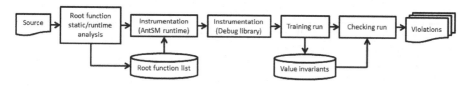

(a) Overview of the AntSM debugging system.

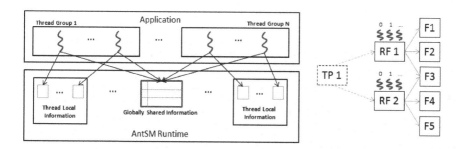

(b) AntSM Runtime and a runtime call graph. `RF` is a root function and the `F`s represent other functions. `TP1` shows the case with a thread pool. Squiggly lines represent threads, numbered by thread group ID.

Fig. 1. Steps performed by AntSM and the AntSM runtime system.

can extract root function names. The logging of function names with the thread id incurs about a 20X runtime overhead, but this task is required only once at the time the root functions are identified. This is unnecessary if the programmer already knows what functions are used for the root functions, by having the programmer provide the function name list to the AntSM. Even when this is not the case, we could identify the root functions within a few minutes to an hour at most.

After root functions are identified, they are instrumented with calls to the AntSM runtime library to monitor when a thread starts and finishes executing the root function. This information is made available to any code that is executed within the root function or any function called (directly or indirectly) from the root function. We refer to this code as a *root reachable code*, and the threads executing it as a *thread group*. Each thread in the program is given a "*thread_id*" by the system. AntSM also maintains for each thread a local ID, called the "*group_id*", where $0 \leq group\_id < T_c$ and T_c is the number of threads executing a particular root function. AntSM also maintains a mapping between *thread_id*s and *group_id*s. This allows the thread to test if it should perform a particular monitoring operation. Next, the program is instrumented with calls to the debugging tool's library to perform sampling. A training run is then performed to build the initial invariant sets, and then one or more checking runs are performed to identify potentially buggy program points. We now describe these operations in more detail.

Algorithm 3.1. AntSM runtime library, antsm_enter_root

Input: *root_addr* - an address of a root function
Output: Set of thread-local variables and thread-global variables

```
 1: // thread-local: each thread keeps own copy of these variables
 2:    thread_id ← syscall(SYS_gettid) // system thread ID
 3:    group_id // unique thread ID in its thread group assigned by AntSM
 4:    my_root_addr ← root_addr // root function address
 5: // thread-global: all threads share these variables
 6:    root_map // thread_id → root function address used by antsm_exit_root
 7:    group_id_map // thread_id → thread ID in its thread group
 8:    thread_cnt_map // my_root_addr → runtime threads count
 9: root_map[thread_id] ← my_root_addr
10: if thread_cnt_map[my_root_addr] is not set then
11:    // this is the first thread that enters the function
12:    group_id_map[thread_id] ← group_id ← 0
13:    thread_cnt_map[my_root_addr] ← 1
14: else
15:    group_id_map[thread_id] ← group_id ← thread_cnt_map[my_root_addr]
16:    thread_cnt_map[my_root_addr] ← thread_cnt_map[my_root_addr] +1
17: end if
```

3.1   Code Instrumentation with AntSM Runtime Calls

To maintain the information about parallelism, i.e., how many threads are executing some root reachable code, the AntSM runtime provides two library functions - *antsm_enter_root* and *antsm_exit_root*. One purpose of this instrumentation is to track when a thread begins executing a particular root function, and when a thread stops executing a root function. This allows the AntSM runtime to know how many threads are executing each root function, i.e., the value T_c for each root function. The second purpose of this instrumentation is to ensure that all *group_ids* lie between 0 and $T_c - 1$. When the thread that finishes executing a root function is not the thread with the highest valued *group_id*, it is necessary to adjust the *group_ids* of the remaining threads to maintain the constraint that all *group_ids* lie between 0 and $T_c - 1$.

A call to *antsm_enter_root*, described in Algorithm 3.1, is inserted at the beginning of each root function. The *thread_id* and root function address are captured in thread-local variables (lines 2 and 4). Line 9 associates the root function's address with the current thread. Because parallelism information is kept for each root function, line 10 checks if another thread is already executing the root reachable code. If not, in line 12 the current thread is given the *group_id* of 0 in the current thread group (the set of threads executing this root reachable code) and the thread count is set to 1 (line 13). If other threads are executing code from this root, the *group_id* for this group is set to the number of threads that were already executing code from the root (line 15) and the thread count for this root is incremented (line 16). At this point, each thread executing a root reachable code has access to its position within its thread group, and the total number of threads in the thread group. Note that thread-local variables are used to avoid unnecessary synchronization for better performance in the AntSM runtime. In Algorithm 3.1, all the accesses to the thread-global data structures must be guarded by the proper synchronization techniques. The hashmap variables (*root_map*, *group_id_map* and *thread_cnt_map*) may be accessed by multiple entering/exiting threads at the same time. Pthreads mutexes and condition variables with the read/write counters are used to synchronize the accesses.

A call to *antsm_exit_root*, described in Algorithm 3.2, is inserted at the exit points of each root function. This function updates the count of threads executing a root reachable code, and ensures the *group_id* have values between 0 and $T_c - 1$. The function first decrements the thread count for the current thread group (lines 4 and 5) and nulls out its entry in the *group_id* map and the root function map (lines 7, 8, 13 and 14) since the thread is no longer active in executing a root reachable code. Because of the way the monitoring code is generated (as described below), the *group_id* must always be in the range, $0 \leq group\_id < thread\_cnt$. Thus, if the current thread's *group_id* is less than the decremented thread count (line 9), then the thread with the highest *group_id* in its group will have a *group_id* equal to the thread count in its group. In this case, the thread with its *group_id* equal to thread count is found (line 10), and assigned the current thread's *group_id* in its group (line 12). As in Algorithm 3.1, all accesses to the thread-global data structures (*root_map*, *group_id_map* and *thread_cnt_map*)

Algorithm 3.2. AntSM runtime library, antsm_exit_root

Input: *root_addr* - an address of a root function
Output: Set of thread-local variables and thread-global variables

```
1: // thread local and global variables are as in antsm_enter_root in Algorithm 3.1
2: // local (automatic) variable:
3:    thread_cnt
4: thread_cnt ← thread_cnt_map[my_root_addr] −1
5: thread_cnt_map[my_root_addr] ← thread_cnt
6: if group_id_map[thread_id] = thread_cnt then
7:    group_id_map[thread_id] ← NULL
8:    root_map[thread_id] ← NULL
9: else if group_id_map[thread_id] < thread_cnt then
10:    find group_id_map[thread_idᵢ] where root_map[thread_idᵢ] = root_addr
       and group_id_map[thread_idᵢ] = thread_cnt
11:    // i between 0 and size[group_id_map] −1
12:    group_id_map[thread_idᵢ] ← group_id_map[thread_id]
13:    group_id_map[thread_id] ← NULL
14:    root_map[thread_id] ← NULL
15: end if
```

must be also protected by the synchronization techniques. The same Pthreads mutexes and condition variables with the read/write counters that are used in the *antsm_enter_root* function are also used to synchronize these accesses.

For example, in the runtime call graph of Fig. 1, when an initial thread enters a root function, RF1, the *group_id* of 0 in its thread group, is assigned and the associated thread's count is increased by one (line 12 and 13 of Algorithm 3.1). If three more threads execute the RF1 root function, each will execute lines 15 and 16 of Algorithm 3.1 (i.e., thread_cnt_map[RF1] is 4). If a thread with *group_id*, 2, exits RF1 (giving a "true" condition in line 9 of Algorithm 3.2), the thread with *group_id*, 3, is found and its *group_id* is replaced with the leaving thread's *group_id*, 2 (lines 10 and 12 of Algorithm 3.2). Therefore, the range of thread IDs in this group is maintained within the updated thread count of 3. The *group_id* for each thread group, set in lines 12 and 15 of Algorithm 3.1, is also used to distribute monitoring as described in Sect. 3.2.

3.2   Instrumentation with Calls to the Debug Library

With AntSM, the sampled monitoring of program points is done within a thread group. If the program point is in straight-line code (Fig. 2(b)), AntSM generates the conditional statement:

if ($group\_id$ == pgm_pt_id % T_c),

where $group\_id \in \{0, \ldots, T_c - 1\}$ and pgm_pt_id is the numerical ID given for the current program point. Sampling in loops (Fig. 2(c)) is done by iteration using an inserted loop iteration count, with $\frac{1}{T_c}$ iterations monitored by each

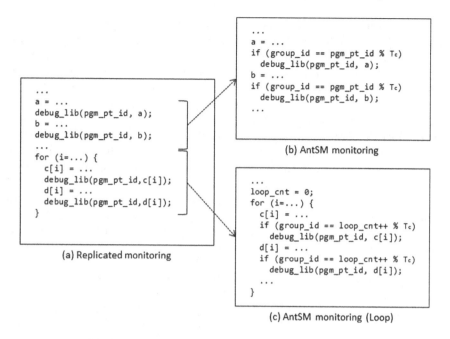

Fig. 2. Debugging library instrumentation example.

thread. *antsm_enter_root* and *antsm_exit_root* cause the number of threads, T_c, to change dynamically as threads enter and exit the root function, as was described in Sect. 3.1. AntSM performs replicated monitoring (Fig. 2(a)) on code that is never executed in parallel, i.e., not reachable from a root function.

4   A Case Study with C-DIDUCE and Value Invariant Detection

We now present a case study of the AntSM system using the C-DIDUCE [3] value invariant detection (VID) technique [2]. We note that AntSM can be used with two large classes of debugging tools, as both allow sampled monitoring. The first class contains *invariant violation detection* tools (e.g., [2–4,10]), which look for violations of program invariants, of which DIDUCE and C-DIDUCE[2] are two examples. They assert the *value invariant hypothesis*, which states that a given variable takes on a small set of values (the *invariant set*) across different program runs with different input data sets. Rarely occurring deviations from this set of values are indicative of buggy or anomalous behavior. The second class contains tools that find statistical variations in program behaviors that are correlated to bugs (e.g., [5–7]) between correct and incorrect runs.

---

[2] The differences between DIDUCE and C-DIDUCE come from the former targeting Java and the latter C. These differences are explained in [3].

VID tools first perform a training run to form an approximation to the invariant set. DIDUCE associates each reference of a variable with an invariant $I = \langle M_t, V \rangle$, where V is the variables' initial value, and M_t is the value of an *invariant mask* after the t-th access. V is initialized to the variable value that is seen when the reference is first executed, and M is initialized to be all 1's. Let w_t be the t-th value of V observed at the program point.

As each value w_t is observed, the test $(w_t \otimes V) \wedge M_t \neq 0$ is performed, where $\otimes$ is the bitwise XOR operation. If the test is true, the invariant is relaxed by updating the mask so that $M = M_{t+1} \leftarrow M_t \wedge \overline{(w_t \otimes V)}$. Intuitively, each update of the mask results in the mask having a value of '0' in bit positions where both a '0' and a '1' have been previously seen. A mask position containing a '1' indicates that all previous values only had a '1' in that position, or that all previous values only had a '0' in that position. Whether only a '0' or '1' value was seen is determined by inspecting the corresponding bit of V. Thus the test determines if the value w_t differs in one or more bits from all previously seen values, and if it does, the mask is relaxed to indicate this.

In a production run with a different input (which presumably exhibits the buggy behavior), values not in the (approximate) set of seen values are detected by applying the invariant violation test. However, not all invariant violations are treated equally. In particular, violations with values that are seen many times are treated as being less important than violations with values that occur only a few times, as they likely are values that should have been in the invariant set. At the end of the run, the different violations are ranked, and a listing of violations, in rank order, is produced. As with other debugging and anomaly detection tools, the assumption is that lower ranked violations are less likely to correlate to a bug, and that a programmer debugging a program will examine the highly ranked violations, fix any indicated errors, and then either re-execute the program, or re-train and re-execute the program.

4.1 Using C-DIDUCE with AntSM

When using AntSM with C-DIDUCE and Pthreads programs, a runtime initialization call is inserted at the beginning of the program to initialize the C-DIDUCE runtime. This initialization records whether the run is a training or checking run, allocates memory and initializes the invariant data structures. Upon exiting the program, the invariant information is written to an output file. In training mode, the output files contain the value invariant set for all monitored points. In checking mode, the output files contain invariant violation information.

5 Experimental Results

5.1 Implementation and Experimental Setup

Static root function analysis and instrumentation, described in Sect. 3, are implemented in the LLVM compiler, v 3.1 [11]. When a thread pool is used, we find

Table 1. Summary of the PARSEC benchmark characters: "LOC" is lines of code; "Monitored Points" is the number of static program points monitored; "Thread Pool" says if the benchmark uses a thread pool; "Injected Bugs" is the number of bugs injected; and "Original Speedup" is the speedup of the un-instrumented benchmark going from 1 to 8 threads.

Name	Application Domain	LOC	Monitored Points	Thread Pool	Injected Bugs	Original Speedup
blackscholes	Financial Analysis	408	180	No	8	4.63
bodytrack	Computer Vision	3066	6544	Yes	15	5.62
canneal	Engineering	371	207	No	7	1.37
dedup	Enterprise Storage	398	553	Yes	8	2.03
ferret	Similarity Search	8940	9141	Yes	5	2.86
fluidanimate	Animation	2733	1329	No	6	4.02
raytrace	Visualization	3553	2757	Yes	7	1.28
streamcluster	Data Mining	1720	978	No	6	3.46
swaptions	Financial Analysis	994	898	No	14	7.98
vips	Media Processing	98940	21168	No	10	7.63
x264	Financial Analysis	26437	14705	No	15	5.71

root functions as described in Sect. 3. All memory loads, stores, and return values from function calls are monitored. We use eleven programs from the PARSEC Pthreads benchmark suite [8] described in Table 1. Two programs from this suite are not used: *freqmine*, which uses OpenMP, not Pthreads[3], and *facesim*, which LLVM cannot compile.

The bugs which are injected into our benchmark programs are the same kind as those used in the original DIDUCE and C-DIDUCE studies and in the Siemens bug benchmarks [9]. Five to fifteen bugs were injected into each benchmark, with each bug injected into a different copy of the benchmark. To allow an accurate comparison of our technique with C-DIDUCE, bugs are injected at frequently executed program points. If a program point is not frequently executed, it is possible that our sampling will miss "noise" and capture relatively more buggy actions. This in turn makes our sampled executions appear better than full monitoring. Because of this, the number of injected bugs is not proportional to the lines of code in Table 1.

We used machines with two quad core Intel Xeon 2.33 GHz processors, 16 GB of memory, and Linux 2.6.32 for the performance and accuracy experiments; machines with 48 AMD Opteron 6176, 2.3 GHz processors, 256 GB of memory, and Linux 2.6.32 were used for the scalability test. For the performance and accuracy experiments, training runs were done using 2 threads and the small dataset. Checking runs were done using 8 threads and the large dataset.

---

[3] No significant technical challenge prevents us from using OpenMP.

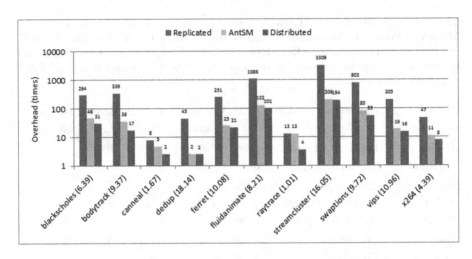

Fig. 3. Comparison of C-DIDUCE execution time overhead in checking mode. The baseline is the execution time of the original benchmark with large dataset and no instrumentation. Note that the vertical axis is on a log scale. The data label on each bar shows the overhead (times) rounded to the nearest one. The number next to each benchmark's name represents the overhead reduction from *Replicated* to *AntSM*.

5.2   Performance of C-DIDUCE with AntSM

Figure 3 compares the overhead of different monitoring schemes. The baseline is the original benchmark execution time (without any monitoring). The bars labeled "Replicated", "AntSM" and "Distributed" are for the naive replicated monitoring scheme, AntSM's sampled monitoring, and the distributed monitoring scheme, respectively. Note that the vertical axis is on a log scale. The benchmark names are labeled with the reduction in overhead going from the replicated scheme to the AntSM scheme ("Replicated" to "AntSM"). AntSM shows up to 18.14 times overhead reduction (*dedup*) and an average reduction of 8.73 times.

Two benchmarks with low overhead reduction are *canneal* (1.67X) and *raytrace* (1.01). As shown in Table 1, these benchmarks have a low original speedup, indicating little parallelism and few opportunities for AntSM to perform sampled monitoring. In particular, the *raytrace* benchmark executes almost entirely sequentially. Measuring overhead in only the parallel section of *raytrace* gives an overhead reduction of 2.17 for AntSM. The naive "Distributed" scheme gives the best performance because this scheme performs a $\frac{1}{T}$, where T is the number of threads, sampling even in sequential areas of the program. As shown in Sect. 5.4, "Distributed" has a lower accuracy than the other two schemes.

Training runs were done with 2 threads and the overhead reductions from "Replicated" to "AntSM" (measured as with the checking runs) are 4.40X for *blackscholes*, 3.55X for *bodytrack*, 1.39X for *canneal*, 0.97X for *dedup*, 2.17X for *ferret*, 4.23X for *fluidanimate*, 1.08X for *raytrace*, 2.46X for *streamcluster*, 3.86X

Table 2. Scalability of C-DIDUCE with AntSM's analysis and instrumentation.

Number of threads	4	8	16	32
blackscholes	6.94	11.64	22.49	44.16
bodytrack	5.96	10.54	13.81	15.59
canneal	2.25	2.48	2.59	2.64
dedup	2.81	3.13	3.58	5.48
ferret	9.03	20.69	35.67	45.51
fluidanimate	9.44	17.35	28.03	35.25
raytrace	1.03	1.05	1.06	1.07
streamcluster	9.17	29.48	71.52	127.77
swaptions	7.15	18.39	39.80	72.96
vips	10.25	25.37	52.64	98.03
x264	6.96	11.92	13.27	16.22

for *swaptions*, 1.78X for *vips*, and 1.80X for *x264*. Low overhead reductions occur because the initial AntSM startup overhead is not amortized on a small number of threads and smaller data set used for some benchmarks.

5.3   Scalability Results

We now present experimental data showing the scalability of AntSM when monitoring value invariants. Table 2 presents the speedup of AntSM with an increasing number of threads. The baseline case is the execution of C-DIDUCE with AntSM in checking mode, executing with a single thread. As the table shows, AntSM scales in most benchmarks as the number of threads increases. There are three benchmarks showing low scalability (*raytrace*, *canneal*, and *dedup*) but as shown in Table 1, the original speedup of those benchmarks are low, resulting in the low scalability in AntSM as well.

5.4   Accuracy of C-DIDUCE with AntSM

Figure 4 shows the accuracy measurements for C-DIDUCE in a checking mode run with "Replicated", "AntSM" and "Distributed" monitoring. We injected 5 to 15 bugs into each benchmark. Each bug is a form of *Value Mutation*, which changes an assignment like "a = x" into "a = x + c", where c is an integer constant. DIDUCE and C-DIDUCE rank anomalies as to how likely they are to be a bug, and we report the rates for bugs occurring in the top 5, 10, 20, or 50 ranked anomalies. Top X in Fig. 4 means that only bugs ranked in the top X violations are considered to be successfully detected. Figure 4 shows that "AntSM" has accuracy similar to "Replicated" in most cases while providing much better performance. "AntSM" accuracy is equal to, or better than (5 cases) "Distributed" in all cases. In particular, "AntSM" has higher accuracy than "Distributed" for

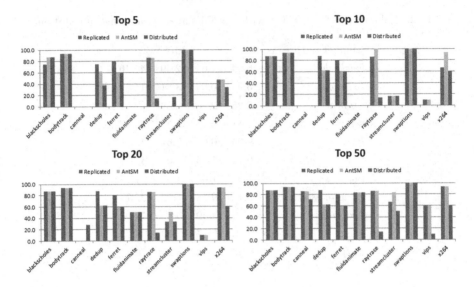

Fig. 4. The comparison of accuracy among *Replicated*, *AntSM*, and *Distributed*.

the two benchmarks with a large sequential portion (*raytrace* and *vips*) in Top 50 because the "AntSM" checking uses replicated monitoring in the sequential parts of the program while "Distributed" uses sampling.

Note that sometimes the sampling schemes ("AntSM" and "Distributed") are ranked higher than "Replicated" as with *streamcluster* of Top 5, *raytrace* and *x264* of Top 10, *canneal* and *streamcluster* of Top 20, and *streamcluster* of Top 50. This is because the "Replicated" scheme performs more monitoring, and thus can see more violation data, which may lower the ranking of detected violations. The same reason holds between "AntSM" and "Distributed."

6   Related Work

In [12], we discuss the Ant debugging framework for distributed memory programs. Although this framework has similar goals to our current work, it uses very different techniques. In particular, it attempted to find program regions executed by *all* processes by analyzing if statements involving the process id. Monitoring was sampled within these regions. In this work, we sample within any code that is executed in parallel, even when executed with a subset of threads. This led to entirely different analysis techniques.

There is previous work on extending traditional debuggers to parallel programs. TotalView [13], Mantis [14], and Prism [15], and DETOP [16] support traditional debugging techniques such as breakpoints for specifying the processes or threads of interest. The work of Stringhini et al. [17] and Cheng et al. [18] group similar MPI processes for targeting with traditional debugging actions.

AntSM differs from these by exploiting the application's parallelism to reduce the overhead of value invariant detection and statistical debugging tools.

Other tools look for outliers in the behavior of processes. These tools often use statistical techniques to find clusters of similarly behaving processes based on communication patterns, volumes, stack traces, and so forth. Outlier processes are identified as they are likely to be exhibiting buggy behavior. Work in this area includes that of Mirgorodskiy et al. [19], DMTracker [20], Arnold et al. [21,22] and Hermes [23]. In contrast, AntSM uses analysis and runtime information to improve the performance of the sequential debugging tools, and is orthogonal to these approaches.

There are sequential program debugging tools, and we have mentioned some of these earlier [2–4,6,7,10]. These tools are developed for sequential programs, and a direct port will be equivalent to the "Replicated" technique.

7   Conclusions

This paper describes AntSM, a system for improving the performance of sequential debugging tools in parallel, shared memory Pthreads programs. AntSM uses a combination of compile-time analysis and instrumentation, and runtime monitoring, to intelligently sample events of interest for these tools. Our techniques lead to significant performance improvements over a naive porting of these tools and much better accuracy than a less intelligently applied sampling. This work allows sequential bugging tools to be efficiently used to create more reliable and robust parallel programs.

References

1. Software errors cost U.S. economy $59.5 billion annually. NIST News Release 2002–10
2. Hangal, S., Lam, M.S.: Tracking down software bugs using automatic anomaly detection. In: Proceedings of the 24th International Conference on Software Engineering, pp. 291–301 (2002)
3. Fei, L., Midkiff, S.P.: Artemis: practical runtime monitoring of applications for execution anomalies. In: PLDI '06, pp. 84–95, New York, NY, USA (2006)
4. Zhou, P., Liu, W., Fei, L., Lu, S., Qin, F., Zhou, Y., Midkiff, S.P., Torrellas, J.: AccMon: automatically detecting memory-related bugs via program counter-based invariants. In: Proceedings of MICRO'04 (2004)
5. Liblit, B., Naik, M., Zheng, A.X., Aiken, A., Jordan, M.I.: Scalable statistical bug isolation. In: PLDI '05 (2005)
6. Liblit, B., Aiken, A., Zheng, A.X., Jordan, M.I.: Bug isolation via remote program sampling. In: PLDI '03, pp. 141–154 (2003)
7. Liu, C., Yan, X., Fei, L., Han, J., Midkiff, S.P.: Sober: statistical model-based bug localization. In: ESEC/FSE-13: 10th European Software Engineering Conference Held Jointly with 13th International Symposium on Foundations of Software Engineering (2005)
8. The PARSEC Benchmark Suite. http://parsec.cs.princeton.edu

9. Hutchins, M., Foster, H., Goradia, T., Ostrand, T.: Experiments of the effectiveness of dataflow- and controlflow-based test adequacy criteria. In: International Conference on Software Engineering, ICSE '94, pp. 191–200, Los Alamitos, CA, USA (1994)

10. Ernst, M.D., Czeisler, A., Griswold, W.G., Notkin, D.: Quickly detecting relevant program invariants. In: Proceedings of the 22nd International Conference on Software Engineering, pp. 449–458 (2000)

11. The LLVM Compiler Infrastructure. http://llvm.org

12. Lee, J.-W., Bachega, L.R., Midkiff, S.P., Hu, Y.C.: Ant: a debugging framework for MPI parallel programs. In: Kasahara, H., Kimura, K. (eds.) LCPC 2012. LNCS, vol. 7760, pp. 220–233. Springer, Heidelberg (2013)

13. Totalview user guide. Accessed 28 Sept 2012

14. Lumetta, S.S., Culler, D.E.: The mantis parallel debugger. In: SPDT '96: Proceedings of the SIGMETRICS Symposium on Parallel and Distributed Tools, pp. 118–126, New York, NY, USA (1996)

15. Sistare, S., Dorenkamp, E., Nevin, N., Loh, E.: MPI support in the Prism programming environment. In: Supercomputing '99, pp. 22 (1999)

16. Wismuller, R., Oberhubera, M., Krammera, J., Hansenb, O.: Interactive debugging and performance analysis of massively parallel applications. Parallel Comput. 22(3), 415–442 (1996)

17. Stringhini, D., Navaux, P., de Kergommeaux, J.C.: A selection mechanism to group processes in a parallel debugger. In: Proceedings of 2000 International Conference on Parallel and Distributed Processing Techniques and Applications (PDPTA'00), June 2000

18. Cheng, D., Hood, R.: A portable debugger for parallel and distributed programs. In: Supercomputing '94, pp. 723–732, November 1994

19. Mirgorodskiy, A.V., Maruyama, N., Miller, B.P.: Problem diagnosis in large-scale computing environments. In: SC '06, pp. 88. ACM (2006)

20. Gao, Q., Qin, F., Panda, D.K.: DMTracker: finding bugs in large-scale parallel programs by detecting anomaly in data movements. In: SC '07. ACM (2007)

21. Arnold, D.C., Ahn, D.H., de Supinski, B.R., Lee, G.L., Miller, B.P., Schulz, M.: Stack trace analysis for large scale debugging. Parallel and Distributed Processing Symposium, p. 64 (2007)

22. Lee, G.L., Ahn, D.H., Arnold, D.C., de Supinski, B.R., Legendre, M., Miller, B.P., Schulz, M., Liblit, B.: Lessons learned at 208k: towards debugging millions of cores. In: SC '08, pp. 1–9, Piscataway, NJ, USA (2008)

23. Strom, R.E., Bacon, D.F., Goldberg, A.P., Lowry, A., Yellin, D.M., Yemini, S.A.: Hermes: A Language for Distributed Computing. Prentice-Hall Inc., Upper Saddle River (1991)

DRIFT: Decoupled CompileR-Based Instruction-Level Fault-Tolerance

Konstantina Mitropoulou[1]([⊠]), Vasileios Porpodas[1], and Marcelo Cintra[1,2]

[1] School of Informatics, University of Edinburgh, Edinburgh, UK
K.Mitropoulou@sms.ed.ac.uk, v.porpodas@ed.ac.uk
[2] Intel Labs Braunschweig, Braunschweig, Germany
mc@staffmail.ed.ac.uk

Abstract. Compiler-based error detection methodologies replicate the instructions of the program and insert checks wherever it is needed. The checks evaluate code correctness and decide whether or not an error has occurred. The replicated instructions and the checks cause a large slowdown. In this work, we focus on reducing the error detection overhead and improving the system's performance without degrading fault-coverage. DRIFT achieves this by *decoupling* the execution of the code (original and replicated) from the checks.

The checks are compare and jump instructions. The latter ones sequentialize the code and prohibit the compiler from performing aggressive instruction scheduling optimizations. We call this phenomenon *basic-block fragmentation*. DRIFT reduces the impact of basic-block fragmentation by breaking the synchronized execute-check-confirm-execute cycle. In this way, DRIFT generates a scheduler-friendly code with more ILP. As a result, it reduces the performance overhead down to $1.29\times$ (on average) and outperforms the state-of-the-art by up to 29.7% retaining the same fault-coverage. The evaluation was done on an Itanium2 by running MediabenchII and SPEC2000 benchmark suites.

Keywords: Compiler error detection · Fault tolerance

1 Introduction

The current techniques to improve performance and to reduce energy consumption have made transistors more vulnerable to errors [6,24,29]. Soft Error Rate (SER) increases as we move to small transistor technologies. In addition, techniques like voltage scaling require transistors to operate at their voltage limit. This increases SER further. An important class of hardware errors is transient errors (a.k.a. soft errors) which occur only once and do not persist [28]. Although transient errors are temporal phenomena, they can alter the program's execution. For instance, in 2000, Sun Microsystems received several complaints from customers such as America On-line, eBay, and Los Alamos Labs, who experienced system failures because of transient errors [18].

This work was supported in part by the EC under grant ERA 249059 (FP7).

© Springer International Publishing Switzerland 2014
C. Caşcaval and P. Montesinos (Eds.): LCPC 2013, LNCS 8664, pp. 217–233, 2014.
DOI: 10.1007/978-3-319-09967-5_13

Hardware redundancy based error detection techniques are used in high-availability systems and mission critical environments. Typical examples are IBM's G4 and G5 processors [26] and HP NonStop series processors [4]. Not all systems can afford the cost of the extra hardware and design complexity of hardware-based error detection. Compiler-based error detection might be preferable instead. There are several reasons: 1. It is more flexible and cheaper than the hardware design and it can be applied on-the-fly on any system. 2. It operates at a higher abstraction level restricting the error detection only to errors that might affect application's output. 3. It gives the designer the flexibility to choose the program region that he wants to protect. Its main drawback is that code duplication has negative impact on performance.

High fault-coverage compiler-based error detection (ED) methodologies face the challenge of effectively managing the error detection overhead without sacrificing reliability. There are two approaches to this. **Synchronized** techniques require that the original and redundant code execute in sync such that the execution is checked in strict intervals. In this way, the strict synchronization guarantees fail/stop behavior, but it has negative impact on the code's performance. On the other hand, **decoupled** approaches remove the strict synchronization between the original and the redundant code, and they let them slip against one another, while performing the checks slightly later, when convenient. Thus, the program runs faster. However, the system looses its fail-stop capability since the synchronization points are removed.

Compiler-based ED techniques increase the code size since they generate redundant and checking code. This extra code can be executed either on the same processor as the original code (**single-core** techniques) or on a separate core (**dual-core** techniques). Each scheme is suited for different use scenarios. On one hand, if there are spare cores and no energy restrictions (all the cores are turned on), then the dual-core technique is the best option. On the other hand, if there are no free cores, or the application is one that benefits from using multiple cores, then wasting multiple cores for running the redundant code is not wise. Under these circumstances, it might be preferable to apply the single-core ED scheme on each thread of the multi-threaded application or each program of a multi-programmed workload. DRIFT is an improved single-core technique.

Our work is based on the observation that the frequent checking of the synchronized scheme becomes a performance bottleneck. This is a phenomenon we refer to as **basic-block fragmentation**. The checks break the code into very small basic-blocks with two exiting control edges (Fig. 1.1.b). The resulting complex control flow acts as a barrier for aggressive compiler optimizations at the instruction scheduling level, even for the most aggressive schedulers. For example, in Fig. 1.1, the original basic-block BB1 (Fig. 1.1.a) splits into three basic-blocks. The scheduler cannot easily move the instructions among basic-blocks to improve ILP because it strictly must respect the program semantics. This is an important restriction that prohibits the compiler from generating high performance code for synchronized single-core ED. **DRIFT** introduces a novel decoupled single-core technique that avoids the basic-block fragmentation and

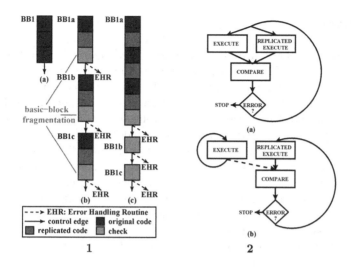

Fig. 1. 1. Control-flow graph for (a) code without ED, (b) synchronized ED (SWIFT) and (c) decoupled ED code (DRIFT). 2. (a) Synchronized ED and (b) Decoupled ED.

improves the performance considerably by relaxing the synchronization between original, replicated code and checks. It achieves this by clustering the checks (Fig. 1.1.c) so as to keep the basic-blocks big. In this way, the code is not fragmented into many basic-blocks and can be scheduled more efficiently.

We note that, strictly speaking, our code generation scheme does modify the code semantics. This, however, takes advantage of knowledge of ED semantics (which are not available to a standard compiler) and does affect the semantics of the original (non-ED) program. Therefore, the aggressive code motion that we perform in DRIFT, could not have been done automatically by any compiler optimization since the compiler is restricted to always preserving the program semantics.

Our contributions are:

- This work is the first to point out a major performance bottleneck in synchronized ED caused by basic-block fragmentation.
- DRIFT overcomes the basic-block fragmentation bottleneck by being the first decoupled single-core ED scheme.
- DRIFT outperforms the state-of-the-art by up to 29.7 % reducing the performance overhead down to 1.29× while retaining high fault-coverage.

The rest of the paper is organized as follows: Sect. 2 presents basic-block fragmentation problem and the proposed solution. Section 3 describes DRIFT algorithm. Section 4 shows the experimental set-up. Section 5 discusses performance and fault-coverage results. Section 6 overviews the related work. Section 7 concludes this paper.

2 Motivation

Synchronized VS Decoupled: In compiler-based error detection, decoupling was first used in DAFT [32] so as to remove the overhead of synchronizing between the main and the checker thread. In that case the main and checker threads are decoupled and allowed to slip between each other. In synchronized single-core error detection, checks are synchronization points where the code is checked for errors and a control point is inserted in the code. In Fig. 1.2.a, it is shown that the execution of the program is interrupted by the checks, which are in the critical path of the program. Therefore, the need to synchronize very often is a significant slowdown factor for compiler-based error detection. The solution is to remove these synchronization points by decoupling the execution of the code (original, replicated) from the checks. In Fig. 1.2.b, we see that the program does synchronize since the checks can be executed some time later. This boosts the performance of the program and reduces the error detection overhead. Such performance improvement may come at the expense of reduced fault coverage. However, as shown previously (e.g., [32]), the impact on fault-coverage is not serious. This is further discussed in the Decoupled Single-Core (DRIFT) Section.

Synchronized Single-Core limitations: In the Synchronized ED (Fig. 1.1.b), all original, replicated and checking code is placed on the same thread. A check is placed right before a non-replicated instruction. Every check compares the original and the replicated code using a compare (CMP) instruction. If the check succeeds, then the code continues executing (no jump), otherwise the control jumps (JMP) to the appropriate error handling routine.

The performance bottleneck of this scheme due to such synchronization, shows up as what we call *basic-block fragmentation*. This problem has two main factors: *1. The complicated Control Flow:* The frequent checks (CMP + JMP) break the original code into a sequence of small basic-blocks with two outgoing edges each. For example BB1 in Fig. 2.a gets split by ED into five basic-blocks (Fig. 2.b). *2. Instruction scheduling:* The complex control flow due to the checks acts as a scheduling barrier for the instruction scheduling optimization (e.g., trace scheduling). Even with a speculative scheduler that schedules regions of multiple basic-blocks, the control edges (due to the checks) limit the scheduler's ability to hoist instructions and extract adequate amounts of ILP. Any state-of-the-art region-based instruction scheduler has some *limitations* in hoisting instructions across basic-blocks: *1.* It cannot hoist instructions with side-effects over branches since this can break the program semantics. This restricts the hoisting of system calls, and store instructions [11,14]. *2.* If there is no hardware support for deferring exceptions then dangerous instructions such as loads and divisions cannot be hoisted either [15]. As a result, the scheduler generates poorly performing schedules, with low ILP.

Decoupled Single-Core (DRIFT): In this paper we propose DRIFT, an ED scheme that addresses the shortcomings of the Single-Core Synchronized scheme, as described earlier. DRIFT is based on three ideas: *1. Optimized Control Flow:*

Fig. 2. The code before and after instruction scheduling for (a) code without ED, (b) synchronized ED and (c) DRIFT where four checks are executed together.

Modifying the control flow of the application can enhance the ability of the instruction scheduler to optimize the code. Since instruction schedulers are not as effective across basic-blocks as within basic-blocks, larger basic-blocks are better. This can be done by decoupling the execution of checks and by executing them later together as a group. By contrasting Fig. 2.b versus Fig. 2.c, we observe that DRIFT generates a much more instruction-scheduler friendly code than the Synchronized scheme. *2. It is acceptable to break the semantics of the combined original and replicated code, as long as the semantics of the original code are respected.* This unawareness of normal compilers to the semantics of ED code is the main reason why the compiler cannot automatically generate decoupled code (like the one DRIFT generates) out of the synchronized code. Therefore the code of Fig. 2.c cannot have been generated by any compiler optimization. Breaking the semantics in a controlled way is required for modifying the code in such an aggressive way. *3. DRIFT's decoupled semantics have no effect on fault-coverage.* As shown in [32], modifying the semantics of the application with ED support, such that the checks are decoupled from the execution, has a minimal impact on the effectiveness of error detection. This is because in the usual case, the increased delay between the error and its detection is not great enough to let the error propagate to the output. Moreover, it has been shown in [7,13,31] that a significant number of errors such as ISA-defined exceptions can be detected by the operating system. This is a fundamental feature of DRIFT, which guarantees its high fault-coverage despite the modified semantics that allow for better performance.

DRIFT motivating example: In Fig. 2, the example shows the code for 3 cases: *1.* No error detection, *2.* Synchronized ED and *3.* DRIFT which decouples 4 checks. Each sub-figure shows the code before instruction scheduling (left) and the scheduling table (right) of a hypothetical 4-issue machine. All ED, schemes Fig. 2.b–c, contain the same number of checks and replicated instructions (red). This is because all schemes have the same sphere of replication (see Sect. 3). In this work, our baseline is SWIFT [22] which is the state-of-the-art single-core error detection. In SWIFT, checks are added before store instructions. For example the store instruction "[r20]=r3" has its inputs checked. The check "cmp p1,p0 = r3,r3"' makes sure that the instructions "r3=r2+100" and "r3'=r2'+100" produce the same result.

Basic-Block Fragmentation: Checks split the code into numerous basic-blocks. For example the original code of Fig. 2.a is a single basic-block, but the ED code of Fig. 2.b spans over 5 basic-blocks (BB1-BB5). Therefore, checks act as fragmentation points for the Control Flow Graph (CFG).

The difference between the Synchronized scheme (Fig. 2.b) and the DRIFT scheme (Fig. 2.c) is the amount of fragmentation of the basic-blocks. The Synchronized case is the most fragmented one, as checks are regularly injected into the code (see Fig. 2.b left). On the other hand, DRIFT groups together multiple checks. In the example of Fig. 2.c, it groups 4 checks together. We refer to this grouping of checks as "decoupling" and the amount of checks being decoupled as "decouple factor". Increasing the check relaxation decreases the fragmentation of basic-blocks (see Fig. 2.c left).

Performance and Schedule: To understand the impact of decoupling on performance, we have to look into the instruction schedule tables (on the right side of each sub-figure). The schedule is obtained after an inter-block instruction scheduler has scheduled across the basic-blocks of the ED code (left). Inter-block code hoisting is marked with green. The Synchronized scheme is fragmented as checks introduce edges into the control flow. These edges prohibit aggressive code hoisting in several cases. For example, "[r20]=r3" of BB3 cannot be hoisted into BB2 or BB1 as it modifies unknown memory. For the same reason, "r[30]=r5" of BB5 cannot be hoisted as well.

Removing these control flow restrictions improves the schedule considerably, as instructions can be hoisted and parallelized easily. For example in Fig. 2.c, all instructions are within a single basic-block (BB1), which makes it straightforward for any scheduler to parallelize.

3   DRIFT

Sphere of Replication: Similar to other state-of-the-art compiler-based ED techniques [22, 30, 32] DRIFT assumes that the memory is protected by its own mechanisms like Error Correcting Code (ECC), parity checking or other mechanisms. Therefore the data fetched from the memory is considered to be correct. Thus the Sphere of Replication (SoR) in DRIFT is limited to within the processor only.

The instructions that are not replicated are: *1.* Control Flow instructions (e.g., branches, function calls). *2.* Store instructions.

The code of the linked binary libraries is not protected. This can be changed by recompiling them with DRIFT.

The non-replicated instructions are synchronization points since the checks are inserted before them.

Decouple Factor: As explained in Sect. 2, DRIFT decouples the checks off the critical path of the execution by grouping them. Each group of checks contains up to N number of checks. We refer to this as decoupling N checks or setting the *decouple factor* to N. Therefore the decouple factor is a knob that controls the number of checks that are executed later together in a group. For example, if the decouple factor is two, then the checks will execute in pairs. For small values of the decouple factor, the program has similar (though slightly better) behavior to the Synchronized ED and suffers from basic-block fragmentation. As the decouple factor increases, more checks are clustered together giving the scheduler the freedom to schedule the instructions more efficiently.

Increasing the decouple factor has two side-effects: 1. We slightly increase the risk of allowing erroneous data to propagate to memory and corrupt the output of the program. 2. We keep more values in predicate registers which increases the predicate register pressure. This may cause performance degradation if it results in register spilling. Moreover, for big values of decouple-factor, many checks are executed together. This means that there might not be enough units to deal with this workload. Therefore, there is a trade-off between the number of checks that are decoupled, the fault-coverage and the hardware capacity. We explore the effect of the decoupled factor on both performance and reliability in the results Section.

DRIFT algorithm is listed in Algorithm 1 and it operates in four steps:

1. Code Replication: The algorithm checks if an instruction can be replicated (Algorithm 1.a line 11). If this is true, then an exact duplicate of the original instruction (Algorithm 1.a line 13) is emitted just before the original one. The original instruction and its replica are inserted into a table (Algorithm 1.a line 14). This table is used later in the algorithm to recall the replicated instruction that corresponds to any original instruction.

2. Code Isolation: This step isolates the replicated code from the original code (Algorithm 1.a line 17). The isolation makes sure that the replicated code does not write on any of the original code's registers. Register isolation does not let the replicated code affect the original code's execution in any way. This is done by register renaming the replicated instructions. In short, the algorithm iterates over all original instructions in the program (Algorithm 1.a lines 18, 19) and for each of them it retrieves the corresponding replicate instruction from the table (see step 1) (Algorithm 1.a line 21) and renames all registers written by the replicated instructions along with each of their uses (Algorithm 1.a line 22). All renamed registers are filled into a table which is used in step 3.

3. Emit checks: Next, the algorithm finds all the non-replicated instructions. For each non-replicated instruction (Algorithm 1.b line 4), the algorithm finds the registers that the non-replicated instruction reads. For each one of these registers (Algorithm 1.b line 5), it emits one compare instruction right before the non-replicated instruction. The compare instruction compares the original register against the corresponding renamed one (it gets it by accessing the data-structure of step 2). The synchronized ED technique emits a jump instruction immediately after the compare instruction, it updates the control-flow and this is the final step of the algorithm. On the other hand, DRIFT collects all the compare instructions of a basic-block into the vector (CMP_VEC) which is used in step 4 to perform the grouping.

4. Decouple Checks: This function (Algorithm 1.b line 10) emit as many jump instructions as the value of decouple factor. In more details, we push the instructions of CMP_VEC into vector GROUP (line 12), until we either reach the maximum group capacity (= DECOUPLE_FACTOR) (line 13) or we reach the end of the basic-block (line 14). Once one of the above occurs, a jump is emitted for each instruction in the group (line 15). For example, if the decouple factor is two and the length of CMP_VEC is six, then the conditional jumps will be emitted in three pairs: two jump instructions are placed after the second, the forth and the sixth compare instruction.

Algorithmorithm 1.a

```
 1  relaxed_main (DECOUPLE_FACTOR)
 2  {for each BB
 3    replicate_insns (BB)
 4    register_rename (BB)
 5    CMP_VEC = emit_compare_insns (BB)
 6    emit_jump_insns (CMP_VEC,
                 ↪DECOUPLE_FACTOR, BB)
 7  }
 8  /*Emit replicated instructions*/
 9  replicate_insns (BB)
10  {for INSN in BB instructions
11    skip if INSN i) control-flow
12               ii) memory
13    emit an exact duplicate of INSN
                 ↪just before it
14    add the original and the duplicate
           ↪ into the data structure
15  }
16  /*Code isolation.*/
17  register_rename ()
18  {for INSN in BB instructions
19    skip duplicates
20    INSN_ORIG = INSN
21    INSN_DUP = get_duplicate_of (
                 ↪INSN_ORIG)
22    rename_writes_and_uses (INSN_ORIG,
           ↪ INSN_DUP)
23  }
```

Algorithmorithm 1.b

```
 1  /* Inject the CMP instructions. */
 2  emit_compare_insns (BB)
 3  {for INSN in instructions:
 4    skip all but the non-replicated
               ↪instructions.
 5    for each REG read by INSN:
 6    Get REG_RENAMED(the renamed REG
               ↪from the data structure).
 7    Emit CHECK_INSN before INSN
               ↪comparing REG with
               ↪RENAMED_REG.
 8  }
 9  /*Decouple checks.*/
10  emit_jump_insns (CMP_VEC,
               ↪DECOUPLE_FACTOR, BB)
11  {for CMP_INSN in CMP_VEC
12    push CMP_INSN into GROUP
13    if(GROUP has DECOUPLE_FACTOR
               ↪members
14       OR end of BB reached)
15       Emit JMP_INSN.
16       Update Control Flow Graph.
17  }
```

4 Experimental Setup

We implemented our error detection scheme in a compiler pass in GCC-4.5.0 [1]. The DRIFT pass was placed just before the first instruction scheduling pass.

We evaluated our compiler-based error detection scheme using 9 benchmarks from the Mediabench II video [8] and the SPEC CINT2000 [10] benchmarks. These are the benchmarks that we managed to compile with our heavily modified compiler.

All benchmarks were compiled with -O2 optimizations enabled. To prevent optimizations such as Common Sub-expression Elimination (CSE) and Dead Code Elimination (DCE) from removing the replicated code, we disabled them at the *late* back-end stages of compilation, only for the ED schemes (they are enabled in NOED). This is common-practice in compiler-based error detection schemes (e.g., SWIFT [22]). The performance impact of these disabled phases is negligible (1.5 % in the worst case and 0.3 % on average).

The performance evaluation was done on a DELL PowerEdge 3250 server with 2 × 1.4 GHz Intel Itanium 2 processors. For the fault coverage evaluation, we used a modified SKI IA-64 simulator [2] (Table 1). The simulator is a cycle-accurate Itanium 2 simulator, modified to allow fault injection.

5 Results and Analysis

We evaluated our scheme by measuring: *1. NOED* which is the code with no error detection, *2. SWIFT* which is the state-of-the-art synchronized single-core

Table 1. SKI IA64 configuration.

Processor: Itanium2		Cache (same as Itanium [17])				
Issue width	6	Levels	L1	L2	L3	Main
Instruction latencies	Same as Itanium2 [17]	Size	16 KB	256 KB	3 MB	∞
Register file	128GP, 128FL, 64PR	Block size	64B	128B	128B	-
Branch prediction	Perfect	Associativity	4-way	8-way	12-way	-
		Latency(cycles)	1	5	12	150

error detection methodology [22]. For simplicity, SWIFT is usually implemented with branch checking instead of control-flow checking [5,7]. These techniques have the same overhead. The only difference is that control-flow checking verifies the execution of a jump instruction. It should be noticed that data checking is orthogonal to control-flow checking. This means that control-flow checking can be plugged in the proposed technique as well without any performance degradation. 3. *DRIFT* was implemented with various decouple factors (DEC-2, DEC-4, DEC-8, DEC-16, DEC-INF). For example, DEC-4 implies a decouple factor of four. DEC-INF implies an infinite decouple factor which suggests that all checks are placed at the end of the basic-block. A decouple factor of 1 is not measured because it is equivalent to SWIFT.

DRIFT can be applied to multi-threaded applications to protect each of the running threads. In some cases, scalable multi-threaded applications can benefit more from single-core ED than dual-core ED. Because, in the latter case, half of the cores will be used for ED only, hindering the scalability of the application. A detailed comparison against a dual-core scheme is beyond the scope of this paper.

The results are shown in Figs. 3 and 4. Each row shows the results of each benchmark. The first column shows the normalized cycle count of all schemes. The cycles are normalized to NOED. The second column presents the percentage of basic-blocks that have a given number of checks. For example, in cjpeg, over 30 % of the basic-blocks have 2 checks (checks2). This measurement is based on run-time information (we take into account the number of times each basic-block is executed at run-time). The number of checks usually implies the basic-block size. The last column shows the fault-coverage for all the configurations.

5.1 Performance Evaluation

The results of the first column in Figs. 3 and 4 validate our assumption that basic-block fragmentation is a significant slow-down factor of the synchronized single-core ED scheme (SWIFT). Both techniques were scheduled with the same state-of-the-art GCC region-based speculative scheduler. In the case of SWIFT, it is shown that the compiler cannot produce efficient code since the complicated control-flow acts as a barrier to code motion optimizations. On the other hand, DRIFT creates a scheduler-friendly code. As a result, the performance improvement of DRIFT over SWIFT is up to 29.7 % (h263enc, DEC-4) and DRIFT manages to decrease its overhead over NOED down to 1.29×.

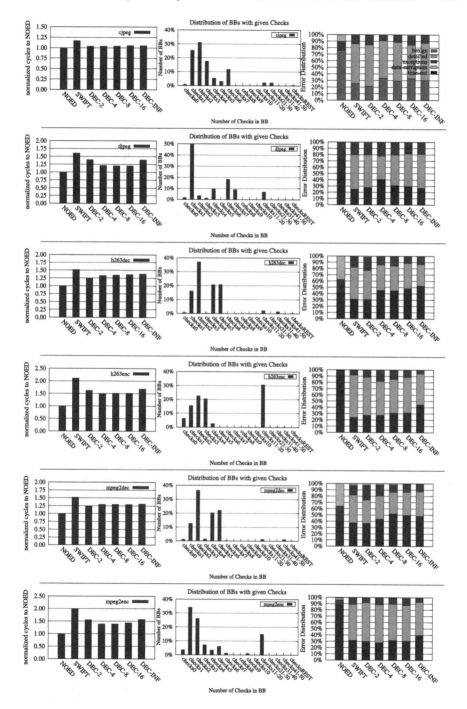

Fig. 3. Results Part 1: The first column shows the performance improvement of DRIFT over SWIFT and NOED, the second one presents the percentage of basic-blocks that have a given number of checks and the third one shows the fault-coverage.

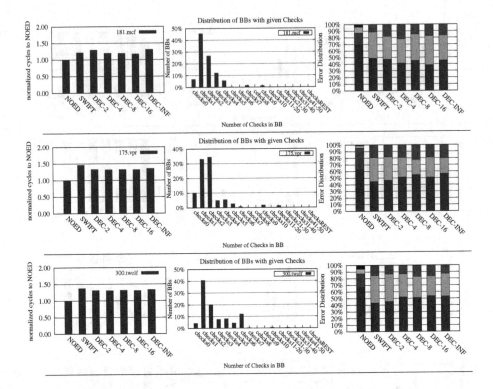

Fig. 4. Results Part 2: Same as Part 1

DRIFT's performance varies across benchmarks and it is largely affected by the check distribution. Benchmarks like cjpeg, h263dec, mpeg2dec, 175.vpr and 300.twolf have small number of checks per basic-block. Therefore, a decouple factor of 2 is enough to improve their performance. On the other hand, a larger decouple factor benefits the applications that contain many checks per basic-block (e.g., djpeg, h263enc and mpeg2enc).

The performance of some benchmarks, however, degrades as the decouple factor reaches very high values (close to DEC-INF). This is the case for djpeg, h263enc and mpeg2enc. These benchmarks have many basic-blocks with a high number of checks (as shown in the second column). A high value of the decouple factor in these cases can lead to high predicate register pressure. In addition, in the end of each basic-block, we have a tree of compare instructions that slows down the code. That's why DEC-4 performs best for h263enc and mpeg2enc (29.7 % and 28 % respectively) and DEC-INF is much worse.

Table 2 shows the decouple factor for which DRIFT achieves the best speedup over SWIFT. From the above discussion, we can see that the best decouple factor is a trade-off between basic-block fragmentation and register pressure. The results show that DEC-4 is a good compromise between the two; DEC-4 is

Table 2. DRIFT's best performance compared to SWIFT and NOED.

Benchmark	Performance gain over SWIFT	Slowdown over NOED	Decouple factor		Benchmark	Performance gain over SWIFT	Slowdown over NOED	Decouple factor
cjpeg	11.1 %	x1.04	2,4		mpeg2enc	28 %	x1.39	4,8
djpeg	25 %	x1.2	8,16		181.mcf	2 %	x1.18	8
h263dec	17.7 %	x1.25	2		175.vpr	10.5 %	x1.31	4
h263enc	29.7 %	x1.48	4		300.twolf	5.1 %	x1.37	4
mpeg2dec	18.2 %	x1.24	2					

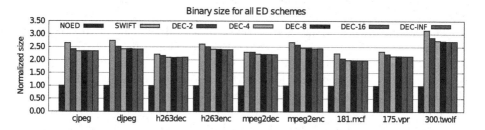

Fig. 5. Binary code size for all benchmarks, normalized to NOED.

big enough to reduce the impact of basic-block fragmentation and small enough to avoid register pressure.

Figure 5 shows that the binary size of SWIFT is about 2.5× greater than NOED. This is expected due to the additional ED code injected into the code stream. DRIFT generates slightly smaller binaries (2.3× greater than NOED), which is further evidence that DRIFT improves the resulting schedule, because the instructions are packed into fewer instruction bundles. As the decouple factor increases the binary size is almost the same. Increasing the decouple factor in benchmarks with small number of checks per basic-block does not change the code any further. In benchmarks (e.g., djpeg, h263enc and mpeg2enc) with large number of checks per basic-block, the ILP might increase as the decouple factor increases, leading to more compact code, but the register spilling adds extra code which counterbalances the code reduction.

5.2 Fault Coverage Evaluation

The fault coverage results presented in this paper are generated using SKI IA-64 simulator [2]. The simulator was modified to inject errors at the output registers of instructions, which is common practice in the literature [5,7,22,30,32].

The fault coverage results are produced with Monte Carlo simulations. The procedure starts with each original binary being profiled in order to count the number of dynamic instructions. The fault injection is done as follows: a dynamic instruction is randomly selected and one of its outputs is randomly picked for injection. Then, a random bit of the register output is flipped. Errors are injected into general purpose and predicate registers. This process is repeated 300 times for each benchmark and each configuration.

For our evaluation, we assume a Single Event Upset (SEU) fault model (double-events are extremely rare [22]). This means that original binaries are injected with one error per run. The binaries that support error detection are much larger ($2.3\times$ larger on average than the original (Fig. 5)). A fair comparison between the original code and the error detection code requires keeping the error rate fixed [22]. Thus, the error detection codes are injected with one error per the number of dynamic instructions of the original binary. It has to be mentioned that, with this methodology, we do inject errors in the system libraries which are out of DRIFT's SoR.

The output of each Monte Carlo trial is classified into one of the following five categories. *1. Benign Errors* (aka masked errors) are the errors that do not affect program's output and they produce the same output and exit code as the good execution. *2.* The errors that DRIFT algorithm successfully detects are classified as *Detected*. *3. Exceptions* are caught by our custom exception handler and are considered as detected (e.g., as in [32]). *4. Data Corrupt Errors*, which are the errors that cause wrong outputs without being detected. *5.* Finally, some errors result in infinite execution. Those errors are detected by our simulator and we name them *Time out Errors*.

The third column of Figs. 3 and 4 shows that DRIFT and SWIFT are almost identical in fault-coverage. In a few cases (h263enc and 181.mcf), some of the detected errors in SWIFT are transformed into exceptions in DRIFT. As we explained in Sect. 3, both SWIFT's and DRIFT's Sphere of Replication does not include store instructions. Therefore, store instructions are not replicated. In SWIFT, a check is inserted before every non-replicated instruction in order to prohibit corrupted data to propagate to memory. DRIFT delays the execution of some of the checks. Thus, some stores might be executed before verification takes place, leading to exceptions raised by the system. These exceptions are detected by our exception handler (as done in DAFT [32]). As in all high fault-coverage techniques, Data-corruption and Time-out errors are very rare. Therefore, DRIFT has practically the same fault-coverage as SWIFT even for high values of the decouple factor.

In the performance evaluation (Sect. 5.1), we showed that a decouple factor of 4 always improves system performance. The fault coverage results show that it has very good fault-coverage as well.

Finally, we observe that the *computational nature of the benchmark* plays an important role on fault coverage. For example, mpeg2enc, cjpeg and h263enc, are encoding benchmarks which means that lots of data get compressed. This may involve the process of sub-sampling, which by definition ignores the value of parts of the input. If an error occurs on data that gets compressed, then it may not propagate at all and it will not appear in the output of the program. For this reason, NOED has almost 90 % benign errors. In this type of applications, decoupling is less risky.

6   Related Work

Code redundancy can take various forms: instruction, thread and process redundancy. EDDI [20] was the first to introduce **compiler-base instruction-level** redundancy. SWIFT [22] significantly improves upon it by reducing the memory overhead. SRMT [30] and DAFT [32] reduce overhead further by allocating the replicated code and the checks to a second core.

Hardware Thread-level redundancy was introduced by AR-SMT [23]. This work proposed the idea of redundant multi-threading (RMT) on SMT cores. The active thread executes the program and puts its results on a delay buffer. The redundant thread executes the same instruction stream and compares the results that it produces with the ones from the delay buffer. The committed state of the redundant thread is also used as a recovery checkpoint.

Several works are based on AR-SMT and extend it. Reference [21] introduces Simultaneous and Redundant Threaded (SRT) processors that take advantage of an SMT processor's extra thread contexts. Similarly, [19] uses the SMT idea on CMPs proposing Chip-level Redundant Threading (CRT). References [12,27] present techniques that exploit the idle cores for redundant thread execution. The main disadvantage of redundant multi-threading is that it reduces the system's total throughput because it occupies more thread contexts and hardware resources. Additionally, compared to compiler-based approaches, it requires custom hardware.

Process level redundancy (PLR) [25] replicates the processes of the application and compares their outputs to ensure correct execution. The processes synchronize to compare their outputs when the value escapes user space to the kernel. RAFT [9] improves this scheme by removing the synchronization barriers. PLR has small overhead since it checks fewer values than other approaches, but this comes at the cost of maintaining multiple memory states.

Wang [31] introduced **symptom-based** error detection. The main idea is that transient errors generate symptoms like memory exceptions, cache misses, branch mis-predictions etc. These symptoms can be used for error detection. In Shoestring [7], the error detection is based on symptoms, requiring less replication. This leads to better performance, but worse fault-coverage.

In **hardware** error detection, correctness is checked on hardware. Hardware-based designs include the watchdog processors in [3,16]. The main idea is that a smaller and simpler in design processor, which is considered safer, follows the execution of the main processor. Commercial processors like IBM's S/390 [26] replicate the entire execution unit.

7   Conclusion

We presented DRIFT, the first work that explores and solves a significant performance limitation in single-core error detection methodologies, namely, basic-block fragmentation. DRIFT is based on the idea of decoupling which breaks the execute-check-confirm-execute synchronization cycle existing in synchronized schemes. DRIFT decouples the execution of the code from the checks, resulting in code that the scheduler can optimize better as it is no longer limited by the complex control flow caused by the frequent checking. Our evaluation on a real machine shows significant performance improvements up to 29.7 % and average performance overhead of 1.29× compared to native, non-fault tolerant, code. The performance gains have no impact on the fault-coverage compared to synchronized schemes.

References

1. GCC: GNU compiler collection. http://gcc.gnu.org
2. SKI, an IA64 instruction set simulator. http://ski.sourceforge.net
3. Austin, T.: DIVA: a reliable substrate for deep submicron microarchitecture design. In: MICRO (1999)
4. Bernick, D., et al.: Nonstop advanced architecture. In: DSN (2005)
5. Chang, J., et al.: Automatic instruction-level software-only recovery. In: DSN (2006)
6. Constantinescu, C.: Trends and challenges in VLSI circuit reliability. IEEE Micro **23**, 14–19 (2003)
7. Feng, S., et al.: Shoestring: probabilistic soft error reliability on the cheap. In: ASPLOS (2010)
8. Fritts, J., et al.: Mediabench II video: expediting the next generation of video systems research. In: SPIE (2005)
9. Ghosh, Y., et al.: Runtime asynchronous fault tolerance via speculation. In: CGO (2012)
10. Henning, J.: SPEC CPU2000: measuring CPU performance in the new millennium. IEEE Comput. **33**, 28–35 (2000)
11. Hwu, W.-M.W., et al.: The superblock: an effective technique for VLIW and super-scalar compilation. J. Supercomput. **7**, 229–248 (1993)
12. LaFrieda, C., et al.: Utilizing dynamically coupled cores to form a resilient chip multiprocessor. In: DSN (2007)
13. Li, M., et al.: Understanding the propagation of hard errors to software and implications for resilient system design. In: ASPLOS (2008)
14. Lowney, P.G., et al.: The multiflow trace scheduling compiler. J. Supercomput. **7**, 51–142 (1993)
15. Mahlke, S., et al.: Sentinel scheduling for vliw and superscalar processors. In: ASPLOS (1992)
16. Mahmood, A., et al.: Concurrent error detection using watchdog processors-a survey. IEEE Trans. Comput. **37**, 160–174 (1988)
17. McNairy, C., et al.: Itanium 2 processor microarchitecture. IEEE Micro **23**, 44–55 (2003)
18. Michalak, S., et al.: Predicting the number of fatal soft errors in Los Alamos national laboratory's ASC Q supercomputer. IEEE Trans. Device Mater. Reliab. **5**, 329–335 (2005)
19. Mukherjee, S., et al.: Detailed design and evaluation of redundant multithreading alternatives. In: ISCA (2002)
20. Oh, N., et al.: Error detection by duplicated instructions in super-scalar processors. IEEE Trans. Reliab. **51**, 63–75 (2002)

21. Reinhardt, S., et al.: Transient fault detection via simultaneous multithreading. In: ISCA (2000)
22. Reis, G., et al.: SWIFT: software implemented fault tolerance. In: CGO (2005)
23. Rotenberg, E.: AR-SMT: a microarchitectural approach to fault tolerance in microprocessors. In: FTCS (1999)
24. Shivakumar, P., et al.: Modeling the effect of technology trends on the soft error rate of combinational logic. In: DSN (2002)
25. Shye, A., et al.: Using process-level redundancy to exploit multiple cores for transient fault tolerance. In: DSN (2007)
26. Slegel, T., et al.: IBM's S/390 G5 microprocessor design. IEEE Micro **19**(2), 12–23 (1999)
27. Smolens, J., et al.: Reunion: complexity-effective multicore redundancy. In: MICRO (2006)
28. Sorin, D.: Fault tolerant computer architecture. Synthesis Lectures on Computer Architecture (2009)
29. Srinivasan, J., et al.: The impact of technology scaling on lifetime reliability. In: DSN (2004)
30. Wang, C., et al.: Compiler-managed software-based redundant multi-threading for transient fault detection. In: CGO (2007)
31. Wang, N., et al.: ReStore: symptom-based soft error detection in microprocessors. IEEE Trans. Dependable Secure Comput. **3**, 188–201 (2006)
32. Zhang, Y., et al.: DAFT: decoupled acyclic fault tolerance. In: PACT (2010)

Algorithms

Optimizing the LU Factorization for Energy Efficiency on a Many-Core Architecture

Elkin Garcia[✉], Jaime Arteaga, Robert Pavel, and Guang R. Gao

Computer Architecture and Parallel Systems Laboratory (CAPSL),
Department of Electrical and Computer Engineering,
University of Delaware, Newark 19716, USA
{egarcia,jaime,rspavel}@udel.edu, ggao@capsl.udel.edu

Abstract. Power consumption and energy efficiency have become a major bottleneck in the design of new systems for high performance computing. The path to exa-scale computing requires new strategies that decrease the energy consumption of modern many-core architectures without sacrificing scalability or performance. The development of these strategies demands the use of scalable models for energy consumption and the reorientation of optimization techniques to focus on energy efficiency, evaluating their trade-offs with respect to performance.

In this paper, we investigate several optimization techniques to reduce the energy consumption on many-core architectures with a software-managed memory hierarchy. We study the impact of these techniques on the Static Energy and the Dynamic Energy of the LU factorization benchmark using a scalable energy consumption model. The main contributions of this paper are: (1) The modeling and analysis of energy consumption and energy efficiency for LU factorization; (2) the study and design of instruction-level and task-level optimizations for the reduction of the Static and Dynamic Energy; (3) the design and implementation of an energy aware tiling that decreases the Dynamic Energy of power hungry instructions in the LU factorization benchmark; and (4) the experimental evaluation of the scalability and improvement in terms of energy consumption and power efficiency of the proposed optimizations using the IBM Cyclops-64 many-core architecture. We study the trade-offs between performance and power efficiency for the proposed optimizations. Our results for the LU factorization benchmark, using 156 hardware thread units, show an improvement in power efficiency between 1.68X and 4.87X for different matrix sizes. In addition, we point out examples of optimizations that scale in performance but not necessarily in power efficiency.

1 Introduction

The many-core revolution brought forward by recent advances in computer architecture has made feasible the integration of hundreds of processing elements on a single chip. With these new architectures, several challenges have arisen. Major efforts and progress have been made in order to achieve high performance

© Springer International Publishing Switzerland 2014
C. Caşcaval and P. Montesinos (Eds.): LCPC 2013, LNCS 8664, pp. 237–251, 2014.
DOI: 10.1007/978-3-319-09967-5_14

on these many-core chips. In particular, optimizations have been developed to improve the number of Floating Point Operations per Second. However, recent developments have shifted the focus to other constraints [1,2]. The design of the new generation of exa-scale supercomputers is restricted by power requirements [3,4]. As a result, Energy efficiency and power consumption have become an imperative.

Energy efficiency is limited by many factors. From the point of view of semiconductor manufacturing processes, the integration of hundreds of independent processors on a single chip within a given area results in an increase in temperature and leakage current. This, in turn, results in more energy and transistors dedicated toward cooling and a deep rethinking of traditional architectures. A feasible alternative is a many-core with a software-managed memory hierarchy where the programmer controls data movement. This can free area previously used for cache controllers and over-sized caches while providing more opportunities to improve performance and energy efficiency at the cost of a higher complexity with respect to programmability.

An interesting case study is the IBM Cyclops-64 many-core architecture [5] with 160 Thread Units able to run independent pieces of code and a software managed memory hierarchy. Extensive studies on performance for the Cyclops-64 have been performed in the past [6–8], energy efficiency has only recently been studied with early efforts resulting in a scalable energy consumption model for Cyclops-64 [9]. A deep understanding of this model can allow for the design of specific optimizations to decrease energy consumption.

In this paper, we study and implement several techniques to target energy efficiency on many-core architectures with software managed memory hierarchies. We study the impact of these techniques on the Static Energy and the Dynamic Energy of LU factorization using a scalable energy consumption model described by Garcia et. al. [9]. The main contributions of this paper are: First, the modeling and analysis of energy consumption and energy efficiency for LU factorization; second, the study and design of instruction-level and task-level optimizations for the reduction of Static and Dynamic energy; third, the design and implementation of an energy aware tiling for the LU factorization benchmark; and fourth, the experimental evaluation of the scalability and improvement in energy consumption and energy efficiency of the proposed optimizations using the IBM Cyclops-64 many-core. The proposed optimizations for energy efficiency increase the power efficiency of the LU factorization benchmark by 1.68X to 4.87X, depending on the problem size, with respect to a highly optimized version designed for performance.

The rest of this paper is organized as follows. In Sect. 2, we discuss the Cyclops-64 architecture, the energy consumption model used and the basics of a parallel LU factorization algorithm. In Sect. 3, we study the impact of several optimizations in the Static and Dynamic Energy. In Sect. 4, we present the experimental evaluation of the proposed optimizations. Section 5 examines related work. Finally, we conclude and present future work in Sect. 6.

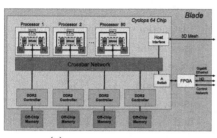

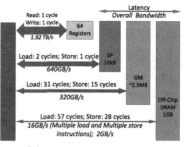

(a) C64 Chip Architecture (b) C64 Memory Hierarchy

Fig. 1. C64 architecture details

2 Background

2.1 A Many-Core Architecture: The IBM Cyclops-64

The IBM Cyclops-64 (C64) is a homogeneous many-core architecture designed by IBM for High Performance Computing. A C64 chip consists of 160 single-issue Thread Units (TUs) running at 500 MHz (see Fig. 1a). A pair of TUs share a single 64-bit Floating-Point Unit (FPU). An FPU can execute a floating-point *Multiply and Add* instruction in one cycle, for a total performance of 80 GFLOPS. C64 features a three-level software-managed memory hierarchy (completely visible to the programmer) instead of a hardware and automatic data cache. This hierarchy consists of an On-Chip Scratch-Pad Memory Level (SP), an On-Chip Global SRAM Memory Level (GM), and an External DRAM Memory Level. Each TU has a 32 KB memory bank, with half of that assigned, by default, as its SP. The SP can be accessed with low latency by the TU that owns it. The remaining halves of all 160 TUs banks form the GM with an approximate size of 2.5 MB that is available to all the TUs. The External DRAM Memory has a size of 1 GB divided into 4 memory banks and connected to the C64 chip through a crossbar network. Figure 1b presents the sizes, latencies, and bandwidth of each level of the Memory Hierarchy.

A C64 processing node needs a 1.2 V regulated power supply for the C64 chip and a 1.8 V regulated power supply for the external DRAM and other glue logic.

2.2 Energy Consumption Model

The model proposed by Garcia et al. is a conceptually simple model that allows scalability with high accuracy for the estimation of energy consumption [9]. This is accomplished by dividing energy consumption into two components: Static Energy and Dynamic Energy. The total energy consumed by a program, Λ, with K different types of instructions, I, can be expressed as:

$$E_T(\Lambda) = E_s(t) + \sum_{j=1}^{K} E_d(I_j)$$ (1)

Table 1. Energy coefficients e

Instruction	e[pJ/Operation]	Instruction	e[pJ/Operation]
load dram	48924.10	store dram	51488.99
load sram	964.65	store sram	548.31
double mult. and add	245.27	double add	178.30
double mult.	210.15	integer mult.	225.43
integer add	127.65	and	126.69
move	105.48	load immediate	86.01

Static Energy, E_s, is the sum total of energy lost due to leakage currents in addition to the energy consumed by hardware units that operate continuously and consume energy even when the system as a whole is idle (e.g. the clock). E_s is proportional to the execution time t, and an architecture dependent coefficient e_0.

Dynamic Energy, E_d, is the energy consumed during the execution of an instruction, minus the leakage component. This is related to the power consumption of all active transistors, registers, and logic. E_d is a function of the number of executed instructions of each type I_j and its energy coefficient associated e_j.

This model has been successfully tested on the Cyclops-64 chip. For this particular architecture, the static coefficient is $e_0 = 63.11\,\mathrm{W}$ and a representative subset of Dynamic Energy coefficients can be found in Table 1. A more detailed explanation of the model can be found in Garcia et al. publication [9].

2.3   LU Factorization

The LU factorization is a matrix factorization which represents the product of two matrices; a lower triangular matrix, L, and an upper triangular matrix, U. This algorithm is often used in linear systems in order to solve linear equations. Assuming A to be a square matrix, it can be represented as $A = L \times U$. This type of LU factorization is called *without pivoting* and is the one presented in this document. An LU factorization with pivoting performs a permutation of the rows or columns of the matrix A using one of several strategies such as Partial Pivoting, Partial Scaled Pivoting, Total Pivoting, or Total Scaled Pivoting. A comprehensive study of different pivoting strategies for LU factorization can be found in [10].

Because the LU factorization is a well studied algorithm, there are many variations such as the Linpack benchmark [11], High Performance Linpack (a parallel version of Linpack) [12], and the SPLASH-2 suite [13].

The classical approach for parallel LU factorization in cache-based systems uses fixed-size blocks that fit into cache to distribute the workload among threads. As shown in Fig. 2, in the first step of the algorithm the matrix A is divided into one *Diagonal* block and several *Column, Row,* and *Inner* blocks. Each block is assigned to one processing element, which further divides the block into tiles in order to improve data reuse and locality. At this point, the *Diagonal* block

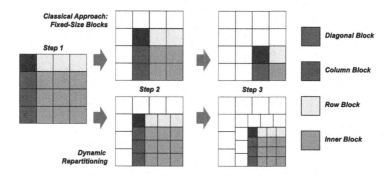

Fig. 2. Progress in each step of LU factorization

is computed individually by one processing element, followed by a concurrent computation of the *Column* and *Row* blocks. Once all the *Column* and *Row* blocks have been computed, the *Inner* blocks are processed. In the second step of the algorithm, the *Inner* blocks of the previous step are grouped again into one *Diagonal* block and several *Column*, *Row*, and *Inner* blocks, which are computed following the rules previously mentioned. This is repeated until there is only one *Inner* block, which is processed as a *Diagonal* block in the last step. The progression of steps following this classical approach is illustrated at the top of Fig. 2. As can be seen, the number of blocks (i.e. the number of tasks assigned to the processing elements) decreases as the algorithm moves forward. This is translated into an increasing number of processing elements becoming idle, which lowers the performance of the application.

The *Dynamic Repartitioning* technique proposed by Venetis and Gao [14] uses varying-size blocks in each step of the algorithm in order to optimize the distribution of work among processing elements. As shown at the bottom of Fig. 2, the size of the blocks is calculated at the beginning of each iteration of the LU factorization. This size is calculated as a function of the number of processing elements, so each processing element has at least one assigned task (i.e. one block to process). This optimization has been proved to increase the overall performance up to $2.8X$ in systems with a software managed memory hierarchy [14].

3   Energy Optimizations

In this section we will study the impact of several optimizations on the energy consumption of the LU factorization algorithm targeting systems with software managed memory hierarchy such as C64. The impact of these optimizations can affect the two sources of energy consumption described in Sect. 2.2: Static Energy E_s and Dynamic Energy E_d. Our baseline implementation is the LU factorization without pivoting by Venetis and Gao [14]. They used the *Dynamic Repartitioning* technique described in Sect. 2.3 and implemented a carefully designed register tiling. All their optimizations were targeting high performance.

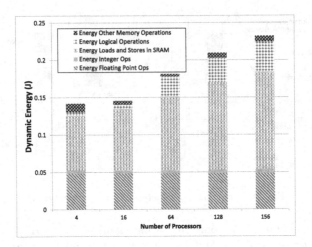

Fig. 3. Dynamic energy distribution for LU factorization of 840 × 840

While the increase in performance obtained by Venetis and Gao is reflected in savings of Static Energy, this high performance LU implementation has some drawbacks from the Energy consumption point of view: First, its register tiling focuses on increasing locality and it is not aware of the energy consumption of each instruction. Second, the static distribution of work does not consider the variance in completion time of processing similar tasks in presence of shared resources such as memory, crossbar interconnections, and FPUs. And finally, the hierarchical division into blocks and further into tiles, produces an increasing amount of smaller tiles in the borders of each block, which can hurt not just the performance but also the energy consumption.

3.1   Energy Aware Tiling Design

To reduce the Dynamic Energy consumption of the LU factorization, we will focus on the instructions that contribute the most to it. Using the Energy consumption model described in Sect. 2.2, we characterized the Dynamic Energy of the LU Factorization implementation optimized for performance by Venetis and Gao [14] using the traces generated during the simulation of the application on a C64 architecture and a matrix of 840 × 840 allocated in on-chip memory.

Figure 3 shows how the Dynamic Energy of the LU factorization increases with the number of processors. As can be seen, Loads and Stores on the on-chip memory (SRAM) are the instructions with the largest contribution to the Dynamic Energy; this contribution also increases with the number of processors. On the other hand, the Energy of Floating point operations remains constant and the contribution of integer, logical, and other memory operations is not significant.

In order to minimize the Dynamic Energy E_d for a particular algorithm Λ, we propose to minimize the energy contribution of the most power hungry operations, in this case Loads LD and Stores ST with energy coefficients e_1 and e_2. The minimization is done on a set of possible tilings T with parameters S and L (e.g. shape and tile size). The optimization problem is shown in Eq. (2).

$$\min_{T(L,S)} E_d\left(\Lambda, T\right) \approx e_1 \left|\text{LD}\right| + e_2 \left|\text{ST}\right|$$
$$\text{subject to} \quad R\left(\Lambda, T\right) \leq R_{\max}, \quad T \text{ is parallel} \tag{2}$$

There are two constraints in the optimization problem: The registers used by the tiling ($R(\Lambda, T)$) need to fit in the available registers R_{max} and the tiling has to allow parallel execution. The former avoids unnecessary energy consumption produced by register spilling and the later prevents solutions with low performance due to increasing execution time produced by inability to exploit task parallelism.

In order to solve this problem for LU factorization, we analyze the energy consumption of each type of block (*Diagonal*, *Row*, *Column* and *Inner*) with sizes $M_0 \times M_0$, $M_0 \times M_1$, $M_2 \times M_0$ and $M_2 \times M_1$ respectively. Each block is assigned to a processor and further divided into tiles. There are 3 cases of sequences to traverse the tiles (e.g. S_0, S_1 and S_2) for each type of block. A detailed explanation of the procedure to find the optimum tiling for the *Inner* block and a summary of the results for the other type of blocks are presented in the next paragraphs.

Inner Blocks: For the computation of an *Inner* block, a *Row* block and a *Column* block are required. *Row*, *Column* and *Inner* blocks are divided into tiles of $L_0 \times L_1$, $L_2 \times L_0$ and $L_2 \times L_1$ respectively. The three possible sequences of traversing tiles reuse tiles on a different operand: The *Row* block (case S_0), the *Column* block (case S_1) and the *Inner* block (case S_2). The problem formulation for the Dynamic Energy is shown in Eq. (3).

$$\min_{\substack{L \in \{L_0, L_1, L_2\}, \\ S \in \{S_0, S_1, S_2\}}} f\left(L, S\right) = \begin{cases} e_1 M_0 M_1 \left(\frac{M_2}{L_0} + \frac{M_2}{L_1} + 1\right) + \frac{e_2 M_0 M_1 M_2}{L_0} & \text{if } S = S_0 \\[2mm] e_1 M_0 M_2 \left(\frac{M_1}{L_0} + \frac{M_1}{L_2} + 1\right) + \frac{e_2 M_0 M_1 M_2}{L_0} & \text{if } S = S_1 \\[2mm] e_1 M_1 M_2 \left(\frac{M_0}{L_1} + \frac{M_0}{L_2} + 1\right) + e_2 M_1 M_2 & \text{if } S = S_2 \end{cases}$$
$$\text{s.t.} \quad L_0 L_1 + L_0 L_2 + L_1 L_2 \leq R_{\max}, \quad L_0, L_1, L_2 \in \mathbb{Z}^+ \tag{3}$$

The non-linear optimization problem was solved using the Karush Kuhn Tucker conditions. We assumed all the variables being positive and M_0, M_1 and M_2 being bigger or equal than L_0, L_1 and L_2. In addition, we used the fact that M_1 and M_2 are equal to M_0 or $M_0 + 1$. We found that the best solution was to reuse the *Inner* tile (case S_2) with parameters $L_0 = 1$, $L_1 = N$ and $L_2 = N$, with $N^2 + 2N \leq R_{\max}$. In this case, an *Inner* block is computed by dividing it into tiles of $N \times N$ elements and loading each *Inner* tile into the registers, which act as accumulators for the partial results. Each partial result is calculated from a pair composed of one tile of $N \times 1$ elements of the corresponding *Column* block and one tile of $1 \times N$ elements of the corresponding *Row* block. The registers

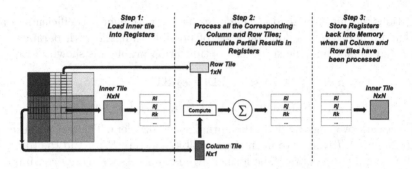

Fig. 4. Optimum energy-aware tiling for an inner block

used as accumulators are stored back into memory only when there are no more pairs of *Column* and *Row* tiles to process. An example of this process is shown in Fig. 4

Row Blocks: To compute a *Row* block, this is divided into tiles of $N \times N$ elements (with N being the same as for the *Inner* block). The process followed to compute each *Row* tile is similar to the one used for an *Inner* tile. The main difference is that the computation of a *Row* tile requires tiles of $N \times 1$ elements of the corresponding *Diagonal* block and tiles of $1 \times N$ elements that have been previously processed in the current *Row* block. Each *Row* tile to be processed is loaded into the registers, which are used as accumulators for the partial results of the computation of each pair of *Diagonal* and *Row* tiles. These registers are stored back into memory when there are no more pairs to process.

Column Blocks: To compute a *Column* block, this is also divided into tiles of $N \times N$ elements. Each *Column* tile is computed using tiles of $1 \times N$ elements of the corresponding *Diagonal* block and tiles of $N \times 1$ elements that have been previously processed in the current *Column* block. In order to minimize the Dynamic Energy of loads and stores, each *Column* tile to be processed is firstly loaded into registers. Then, these registers are used as accumulators for the partial results computed for each pair of *Diagonal* and *Column* tiles. When there are no more pairs to process, the content of the registers used as accumulators is stored back into memory.

Diagonal Block: A *Diagonal* block can be seen as another matrix A' that needs to be LU-factorized. Consequently, the *Diagonal* block can be divided into tiles of $N \times N$ elements, labeled as *Diagonal*, *Column*, *Row*, and *Inner* tiles. They can be latter processed following the same rules used in the computation of the matrix A and the same traversing of tiles previously described for the *Column*, *Row*, and *Inner* blocks.

3.2 Minimizing Static Energy Using Pipelining

The design of specific tilings for energy consumption already targets Dynamic Energy. However, the long latency of memory operations with respect to the latency of arithmetic operations can produce stalls, where each processor is waiting for data required for computation. This scenario becomes worse if hundreds of threads, starvation of shared resources and bandwidth limitations are considered. This behavior can increase the Static Energy consumption due to increasing latency produced by contention.

In order to successfully minimize the impact of Static Energy, further optimizations were done to the implementation of the tilings described in Sect. 3.1. Each *for* loop was software-pipelined and unrolled twice, using different registers for each unrolled iteration if possible and sharing registers when necessary.

Following Fig. 4, a *for* loop iteration computes a partial result for an *Inner* tile of $N \times N$ elements using a *Row* tile of $1 \times N$ elements and a *Column* tile of $N \times 1$ elements; the next iteration uses a different *Row* tile and a different *Column* tile to compute the next cumulative partial result of the same *Inner* tile. Consequently, a *for* loop that has been unrolled twice requires at least $N^2 + 4N$ registers. Since additional registers are required in the loop iterations for loop control and pointers (a pointer for the *Row* tiles and a pointer for the *Column* tiles; no pointer is necessary inside the loop for the *Inner* tile since this tile is the same for all the iterations), some registers were shared between iterations in order to decrease the requirement in the number of registers.

To diminish the impact of this register-sharing, the instructions of the loop were later properly interleaved to ensure that memory-related instructions (i.e. *loads* and *stores*) were already completed at the moment the registers involved in such operations were used in a arithmetic instruction, decreasing the execution time to directly impact the static energy.

3.3   Dynamic Task Scheduling for Energy Reduction

At this point, the fine-grain tasks have been optimized in order to decrease energy consumption while using the performance-oriented Static scheduling proposed by Venetis and Gao [14]. Even though the *Dynamic Repartition* technique is meant to perform an optimized distribution of work among processing elements, it does not take into account the undesirable delays produced by the competition of access to shared resources (e.g. competition for memory bandwidth on shared memory). This results in variations in the completion time between tasks of the same size. As a consequence, the energy consumption per task will not be uniform. This variation will be most significant with fine-grained tasks, such as the tiles described for LU factorization. In the end, a static distribution of limited work, even for cases of very regular tasks, will result in scenarios where the unbalanced distribution of work will have a negative impact on the Static Energy consumption. In addition, division of blocks into tiles produces a set of smaller border tiles per block that are suboptimal in terms of energy consumption.

In order to overcome these problems, a Dynamic Scheduling of tasks was used in the LU factorization, using the tile as a unit of work assigned to each processing element, instead of a block. First, the matrix is divided into tiles of $N \times N$ elements, which are processed following the LU factorization algorithm, that is, first the *Diagonal* tile, then all the *Column* and *Row* tiles, and finally all the *Inner* tiles. However, in this case, the assignment of tiles is not made statically (as in Venetis and Gao [14]) but in a first-come first-served basis: A tile is assigned to a processing element as soon as the processing element becomes available (i.e. as soon as the processing element finishes the computation of the previous assigned tile) and the tile dependencies are satisfied.

Dividing the matrix in tiles of $N \times N$ leads to a significant amount of tasks, which could increase the overhead of the implementation and reduce the data reuse. Nevertheless, the Dynamic Scheduling of tasks has ultimately a positive impact in the Static Energy consumption of the application since it ensures a better workload balance by keeping the number of idle processors low. This is ultimately translated in a reduction of the execution time of the application. In addition to this, the overhead associated with Dynamic Scheduling is diminished thanks to the support of in-memory atomic operations in the C64 [15]. Using an in-memory atomic operation such as L_ADD, a Dynamic Scheduler can be easily implemented with a counter for the number of tasks. Every time a processor is available, it asks for a new task and increments the counter. Since this increment is performed atomically in memory, additional round trips are avoided increasing the throughput of this counter.

To increase the data reuse with Dynamic Scheduling and to avoid that a *Diagonal* tile of $N \times N$ becomes a bottleneck for the whole algorithm (since no tile can be processed until that tile is computed), the size of the *Diagonal* tile can be increased to $bN \times bN$ with $b \in \mathbb{N}$ and $b \geq 2$, while the sizes of other tiles remain as $N \times N$. This reduces by b the number of steps required to compute the LU factorization. The use of a tile as a unit of work for the Dynamic Scheduling, instead of a block, decreases significantly the number of suboptimal border tiles, decreasing the *Dynamic Energy* too.

4   Experimental Evaluation

This section describes the experimental evaluation of the proposed optimizations targeting energy consumption and power efficiency described in Sect. 3. We have used the IBM C64 platform described in Sect. 2.1 and the energy estimations using the model described in Sect. 2.2. All benchmarks were written in C with hand-tuned assembly for the register tiling. Benchmarks were compiled with ET International's C64 C compiler with compilation flags -O3. We ran all of our experiments using FAST [16], a highly accurate C64 simulator.

We implemented several versions of LU factorization using on-chip shared memory. The power-aware tiling proposed in Sect. 3.1 uses $N = 6$ given the 64 registers per Thread Unit (TU) available in Cyclops-64. Also, for the Dynamic Task Scheduling described in Sect. 3.3, we used $b = 2$ so the *Diagonal* tile is 12×12. The Static Energy coefficient e_0 was computed using measurements on a real chip and the number of TUs used, having in mind that 4 additional TUs are reserved: 1 for executing the runtime system and other 3 for managing the communication with other chips using a 3D mesh.

Our first set of experiments uses a matrix of 840×840, the maximum size that fit in on-chip memory. We study the scalability of Dynamic Energy (Fig. 5a)

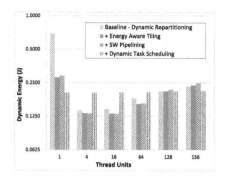 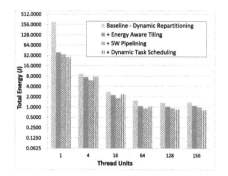

(a) Dynamic Energy vs. Thread Units for a matrix of 840 × 840

(b) Total Energy vs. Thread Units for a matrix of 840 × 840

Fig. 5. Scalability of energy consumption with the number of TUs

and Total Energy (Fig. 5b) using different number of TUs. As expected, our Energy Aware tiling decreases the Total Energy with respect to the baseline version that uses Dynamic Repartitioning. This is also true for the Dynamic Energy up to 128 TUs. The software pipelining do not significantly impact the Dynamic Energy because the instructions executed are practically the same but this technique decreases Total Energy because the total execution time and the Static Energy decreases. In addition, we noticed that the Dynamic Energy consumption of our Dynamic Task Scheduling does not vary with the number of TUs. The reason is that the size of the basic unit of work, the tile, is function of architectural parameters such as the number of registers but it is not function of the number of TUs like the blocks used in Dynamic Repartitioning. Our approach using Dynamic Scheduling seems useful for decreasing dynamic energy and total energy when the number of TUs surpasses 128. In addition, we noticed that total energy and dynamic energy of the baseline implementation using 1 TU are particularly high, compared with higher number of threads. The reason is that the *Diagonal* register tiling used in the *Diagonal* block calculation is highly inefficient compared with the other tilings; a serial execution computes an LU Factorization as a single *Diagonal* block and exposing this fact.

We also study the impact of the optimizations proposed in terms of Power Efficiency (the ratio between performance and power consumption) in order to examine the trade offs between performance and power consumption. Figure 6a shows the scalability of the Power Efficiency with respect to the matrix size using the maximum number of TUs available, while Fig. 6b shows the scalability of the Power Efficiency with respect to the number of TUs for the biggest matrix that fits on SRAM.

For different matrix sizes on Fig. 6a, all the proposed optimizations increase the power efficiency. The increase in power efficiency for the LU factorization varies between 1.68X and 4.87X with respect to a highly optimized version that targets performance (Our baseline that uses Dynamic Repartitioning). The major returns of the techniques proposed are reached with small matrices.

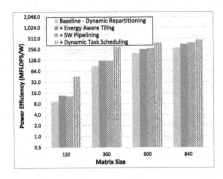

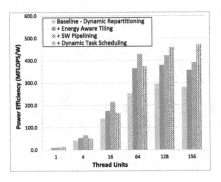

(a) Power Eff. vs. Matrix Size for $TU = 156$ (b) Power Eff. vs. TUs for Matrix Size 840 × 840

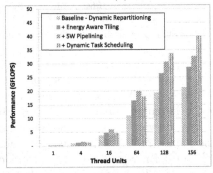

(c) Performance vs. TUs for Matrix Size 840 × 840

Fig. 6. Power Efficiency and Performance for LU factorization

The optimization with the higher impact is the Dynamic Task Scheduling: between 1.2X and 3.5X to the power efficiency.

A careful comparison of the behavior between Power efficiency (Fig. 6b) and Performance (Fig. 6c) shows similarities when few threads are used. For the baseline implementation, as well as for the Energy-aware tiling and the Software Pipelining optimizations, the power efficiency drops after 128 TUs. This is related to the fact that even though the execution time and Static Energy decreases for an increasing number of TUs in all three implementations, the Dynamic Energy increases because these optimizations schedule tasks based on blocks. In contrast, the Power Efficiency of the Dynamic Task Scheduling optimization increases properly with the number of TUs because this type of scheduling does not only scales in terms of performance and Static Energy but also because it keeps the Dynamic Energy constant with the number of TUs.

For the C64 architecture there is a big correlation between the performance and the energy efficiency using few TUs given the high contribution of the static energy to the total energy budget. However, this scenario changes when more TUs are used. While all the techniques proposed improve the performance (as seen in Fig. 6c), the power efficiency decreases after 64 TUs or 128 TUS for the Static scheduling techniques (as seen in Fig. 6b). On the other hand, the Dynamic Task scheduling scales in Performance and Power Efficiency.

5   Related Work

As previously mentioned, the modeling of and optimization for energy consumption is a well researched topic. Many models focus on scheduling and are based on the overall amount of work per unit time [17] or energy [18]. These approaches yield a simplified model that is comparatively easy to use. However, the options and optimizations are limited by the coarse-grained approach.

In contrast, fine-grain approaches [19], like our own, exchange complexity for the potential optimizations that can be applied. Previous works utilized highly accurate, but highly complex, techniques to reduce energy consumption on uniprocessor architectures. These required precise information about the underlying hardware and are based on a sturdy foundation of instruction scheduling techniques [20]. This focus on the individual core worked well for uniprocessor architectures but it is unclear how well it will scale for multi-cores. Additionally, these models do not fit with the comparatively recent worldwide pursuit of energy efficiency on multiprocessors: the development and analysis of hardware features such as energy efficient off-chip memory and dynamic voltage selection [21].

6   Conclusions and Future Work

In this paper, we studied and implemented several optimizations to target energy efficiency on many-core architectures with software managed memory hierarchies using LU factorization. Our starting point was a highly optimized LU factorization designed for high performance [14]. We analyzed the impact of these optimizations on the Static Energy E_s, Dynamic Energy E_d, Total Energy E_T and Power Efficiency. To facilitate this, we used a scalable energy consumption model [9]. We designed and applied further optimizations strategies at the instruction-level and task-level to directly target the reduction of Static and Dynamic Energy and indirectly increase the Power Efficiency. We designed and implemented an energy aware tiling to decrease the Dynamic Energy. The tiling proposed minimizes the energy contribution of the most power hungry instructions. Our experimental evaluation of the scalability and improvement in energy consumption and energy efficiency of the proposed optimizations was made using the FAST simulator for the IBM Cyclops-64 many-core architecture. The proposed optimizations for energy efficiency increase the power efficiency of the LU factorization benchmark by 1.68X to 4.87X, depending on the problem size, with respect to a highly optimized version designed for performance. In addition, we point out examples of optimizations that scale in performance but not necessarily in power efficiency.

Future work includes the implementation and energy analysis of a DRAM-version of the LU factorization algorithm, the extension of the model and methodology to other algorithms (e.g. Linear Algebra and Graphs) and a study of the impact on the energy consumption and power efficiency of the task size with dynamic scheduling techniques. We are also interested in the relation between optimum tiling for increasing performance and optimum tiling for energy efficiency. Additionally, a hybrid approach combining the advantages of static and dynamic scheduling [22] will be investigated.

Acknowledgements. This material is based upon work supported by the Department of Energy [Office of Science] under Award Number DE-SC0008717. This work was partly supported by European FP7 project TERAFLUX, id. 249013. We also thank ET International, Inc. for its support during the course of experiments. Finally, we thank the reviewers for their valuable suggestions.

References

1. Garcia, E., Orozco, D., Khan, R., Venetis, I., Livingston, K., Gao, G.R.: Dynamic percolation: a case of study on the shortcomings of traditional optimization in many-core architectures. In: Proceedings of 2012 ACM International Conference on Computer Frontiers (CF 2012), Cagliari, Italy, May 2012. ACM (2012)
2. Garcia, E., Orozco, D., Khan, R., Venetis, I., Livingston, K., Gao, G.: A dynamic schema to increase performance in many-core architectures through percolation operations. In: Proceedings of the 2013 IEEE International Conference on High Performance Computing (HiPC 2013), Bangalore, India, December 2013. IEEE Computer Society (2013)
3. Bergman, K., Borkar, S., Campbell, D., Carlson, W., Dally, W., Denneau, M., Franzon, P., Harrod, W., Hiller, J., Karp, S., Keckler, S., Klein, D., Lucas, R., Richards, M., Scarpelli, A., Scott, S., Snavely, A., Sterling, T., Williams, R.S., Yelick, K.: Exascale computing study: technology challenges in achieving exascale systems. DARPA Information Processing Techniques Office (IPTO) sponsored study (2008)
4. Torrellas, J.: Architectures for extreme-scale computing. Computer **42**, 28–35 (2009)
5. Denneau, M.: Cyclops. In: Padua, D. (ed.) Encyclopedia of Parallel Computing: SpringerReference, p. 145. Springer, Heidelberg (2011). www.springerreference.com
6. Garcia, E., Venetis, I.E., Khan, R., Gao, G.R.: Optimized dense matrix multiplication on a many-core architecture. In: D'Ambra, P., Guarracino, M., Talia, D. (eds.) Euro-Par 2010, Part II. LNCS, vol. 6272, pp. 316–327. Springer, Heidelberg (2010)
7. Chen, L., Gao, G.R.: Performance analysis of cooley-tukey fft algorithms for a many-core architecture, in Proceedings of the 2010 Spring Simulation Multiconference, SpringSim '10, (San Diego, CA, USA), pp. 81:1–81:8, Society for Computer Simulation International, 2010
8. Orozco, D., Garcia, E., Gao, G.: Locality optimization of stencil applications using data dependency graphs. In: Cooper, K., Mellor-Crummey, J., Sarkar, V. (eds.) LCPC 2010. LNCS, vol. 6548, pp. 77–91. Springer, Heidelberg (2011)
9. Garcia, E., Orozco, D., Gao, G.: Energy efficient tiling on a many-core architecture. In: Proceedings of 4th Workshop on Programmability Issues for Heterogeneous Multicores (MULTIPROG-2011); 6th International Conference on High-Performance and Embedded Architectures and Compilers (HiPEAC), Heraklion, Greece, January 2011, pp. 53–66 (2011)

10. Chen, O.Y.: A comparison of pivoting strategies for the direct lu factorization. In: Electronic Proceedings of the Eighth Annual International Conference on Technology in Collegiate Mathematics Houston, Texas, 16–19 November 1995
11. Dongarra, J.J., Walker, D.W.: Software libraries for linear algebra computations on high performance computers. SIAM Rev. **37**, 151–180 (1995)
12. Dongarra, J., Luszczek, P., Petitet, A.: The linpack benchmark: past, present and future. Concurrency Comput.: Pract. Exper. **15**(9), 803–820 (2003)
13. Woo, S.C., Ohara, M., Torrie, E., Singh, J.P., Gupta, A.: The splash-2 programs: characterization and methodological considerations. SIGARCH Comput. Archit. News **23**, 24–36 (1995)
14. Venetis, I.E., Gao, G.R.: Mapping the LU decomposition on a many-core architecture: challenges and solutions. In: Proceedings of the 6th ACM Conference on Computing Frontiers (CF '09), Ischia, Italy, May 2009, pp. 71–80 (2009)
15. Garcia, E., Orozco, D., Pavel, R., Gao, G.R.: A discussion in favor of dynamic scheduling for regular applications in many-core architectures. In: Proceedings of 2012 Workshop on Multithreaded Architectures and Applications (MTAAP 2012); 26th IEEE International Parallel and Distributed Processing Symposium (IPDPS 2012), Shanghai, China, May 2012. IEEE (2012)
16. del Cuvillo, J., Zhu, W., Hu, Z., Gao, G.R.: FAST: a functionally accurate simulation toolset for the cyclops-64 cellular architecture. In: Workshop on Modeling, Benchmarking, and Simulation (MoBS '05), in Conjunction with the 32nd Annual International Symposium on Computer Architecture (ISCA 05), pp. 11–20 (2005)
17. Yao, F., Demers, A., Shenker, S.: A scheduling model for reduced CPU energy. In: Proceedings of the 36th Annual Symposium on Foundations of Computer Science, October 1995, pp. 374–382 (1995)
18. Weiser, M., Welch, B., Demers, A., Shenker, S.: Scheduling for reduced cpu energy. In: Imielinski, T., Korth, H.F. (eds.) Mobile Computing. The Kluwer International Series in Engineering and Computer Science, vol. 353, pp. 449–471. Springer, Boston (1996)
19. Steinke, S., Knauer, M., Wehmeyer, L., Marwedel, P.: An accurate and fine grain instruction-level energy model supporting software optimizations. In: Proceedings of PATMOS, Citeseer (2001)
20. Lee, S., Ermedahl, A., Min, S.L.: An accurate instruction-level energy consumption model for embedded risc processors. In: LCTES '01: Proceedings of the ACM SIGPLAN Workshop on Languages, Compilers and Tools for Embedded Systems, New York, NY, USA, pp. 1–10. ACM (2001)
21. Andrei, A., Eles, P., Peng, Z., Schmitz, M., Hashimi, B.: Energy optimization of multiprocessor systems on chip by voltage selection. IEEE Trans. Very Large Scale Integr. (VLSI) Syst. **15**, 262–275 (2007)
22. Donfack, S., Grigori, L., Gropp, W., Kale, V.: Hybrid static/dynamic scheduling for already optimized dense matrix factorization. In: 2012 IEEE 26th International Parallel Distributed Processing Symposium (IPDPS), pp. 496–507 (2012)

An Input-Adaptive Algorithm for High Performance Sparse Fast Fourier Transform

Shuo Chen[✉] and Xiaoming Li

University of Delaware, Newark, DE, USA
{schen,xli}@udel.edu

Abstract. Many applications invoke the Fast Fourier Transform (FFT) on sparse inputs, with most of their Fourier coefficients being very small or equal to zero. Compared with the "dense" FFT algorithms, the input sparsity makes it easier to parallelize the sparse counterparts. In general, sparse FFT algorithms filter input into different frequency bins, and then process the bins separately. Clearly, the performance is largely determined by the efficiency and the effectiveness of those filters. However, sparse FFT algorithms are input-oblivious with regard to filter selection, i.e., input characters are not considered in the design and tuning of their sparse filters, which leads to sub-optimal binning and consequently hurts performance. This paper proposes an input-adaptive sparse FFT algorithm that takes advantage of the similarity between input samples to automatically design and customize sparse filters that lead to better parallelism and performance. More specifically, given a sparse signal that has only k non-zero Fourier coefficients similar to another known spectral representation, our algorithm utilizes sparse approximation to estimate the DFT output in the runtime sub-linear to the input size. Moreover, our work automatically adapts to different input characteristics by integrating and tuning several adaptive filters to efficiently package the non-zero Fourier coefficients into a small number of bins which can then be estimated accurately. Therefore, the input-tuned filtering gets rid of recursive coefficient estimation and improves parallelism and performance. We evaluate our input-adaptive sparse FFT implementation in sequential case on Intel i7 CPU and in parallel versions on three NVIDIA GPUs, i.e., NVIDIA GeForce GTX480, Tesla C2070 and Tesla C2075. In particular, our performance is compared to that of the SSE-enabled FFTW and to the results of a highly-influential recently proposed sparse Fourier algorithm. In summary, our algorithm is faster than FFT both in theory and implementation. Furthermore, the range of sparsity k that our approach can outperform dense FFT is larger than that of other sparse Fourier algorithms.

1 Introduction

The Fast Fourier Transform (FFT) calculates the spectrum representation of time-domain input signals. If the input size is N, the FFT operates in $O(Nlog(N))$ steps. The performance of FFT algorithms is known to be determined only by

© Springer International Publishing Switzerland 2014
C. Caşcaval and P. Montesinos (Eds.): LCPC 2013, LNCS 8664, pp. 252–271, 2014.
DOI: 10.1007/978-3-319-09967-5_15

input size, and not affected by the value of input. In real world applications, however, input signals are frequently sparse, i.e., most of the Fourier coefficients of a signal are very small or equal to zero. If we *know* that an input is sparse, the computational complexity of FFT can be reduced. Sublinear sparse Fourier algorithm was first proposed in [16], and since then, has been extensively studied in the literatures when applied to various fields [1,2,6,7,12,15]. A recent highly-influential work [9] presented an improved algorithm in the running time of $O(k\sqrt{NlogN}logN)$ to make it faster than FFT for the sparsity factor k up to $O(\sqrt{N/logN})$.

The input sparsity makes it easier to parallelize FFT calculation. From a very high point of view, the sparse FFT algorithms apply time-domain or spectrum-domain filters to disperse inputs into separate bins, the computational complexity of those filters being lower than $O(Nlog(N))$. The number of bins is usually much smaller than N. After the dispersion, those bins can be further processed separately, for example, even with straightforward DFT algorithms. Combining the two steps, sparse FFT algorithms can achieve complexity lower than $O(Nlog(N))$.

Sparse FFT algorithms are easier to parallelize than normal FFT algorithms. It is because the calculation on the bins are independent. It is also not hard to see that the performance of sparse FFT algorithms, as well as how effectively we can parallelize the following calculation on the bins, are largely determined by the design of input filters. In fact, much of existing work on sparse FFT algorithms focuses on improving the design of sparse filter.

However, the existing filters are really input-oblivious in the sense that their design, unchangeable at runtime, does not consider input characteristics other than input size. The current filters are designed based on the sole assumption that inputs are sparse, but are ignorant to the knowledge of how exactly sparse. The exclusion of input characteristics in filter design appears reasonable at first look, because if we already know how exactly an input is sparse, i.e., its spectrum representation, we don't need to calculate the FFT at all.

Here we make an important observation. What if we don't know the exact spectrum representation of an input, but we know the input has a similar sparsity distribution to another signal whose spectrum representation is known, can the sparsity similarity help improving the sparse FFT on the current input? This paper gives a *Yes* answer. First of all, the sparsity similarity is common in real-world sparse FFT applications. For example, in video compression, two consecutive video frames usually have almost identical spectrum representations, and differ only in the phases of some spectrum coefficients.

This observation motivates this paper. Our basic idea, also our main innovation and contribution, is to use the sparsity similarity as a template to design the customized filters for subsequent similar inputs, so that the filters lead to less waste of calculation on those zero coefficient bins and can better express parallelism in sparse FFT. In particular, our input-adaptive sparse FFT implementation particularly benefits FFT calculation in stream processing.

The remaining of this paper is organized as follows. We first briefly introduce existing sparse FFT algorithms and overview our approach. Then we present how we customize filters based on the sparsity template, and how we use the customized filters to reduce the overhead and the number of iterations in the sparse FFT algorithm presented in [9], which our work is based on. And finally, we compare the performance and accuracy of our input-adaptive sparse FFT algorithm with FFTW and the latest sparse FFT implementation on synthetic and real video inputs.

2   Overview of Sparse FFT Algorithms and Our Approach

In this section we overview prior work on sparse Fourier transform, and then describe our contribution in that context.

A naive discrete Fourier transform of a N-dimensional input series $x(n)$, $n = 0, 1, ..., N-1$ is presented as $Y(d) = \sum_{n=0}^{N-1} x(n) W_N^{nd}$, where $d = 0, 1, ..., N-1$ and twiddle factor $W_N^{nd} = e^{-j2\pi nd/N}$. Fast Fourier transform algorithms recursively decompose a N-dimensional DFT into several smaller DFTs [4], and reduce DFT's operational complexity from $O(N^2)$ into $O(NlogN)$. There are many FFT algorithms, or in other words, different ways to decompose DFT problems. Prime-Factor (Good-Thomas) [8] decomposes a DFT of size $N = N_1 N_2$, where N_1 and N_2 are co-prime numbers. Twiddle factor calculation is not included in this algorithm. In addition, Rader's algorithm [17] and Bluestein's algorithm [3] can factorize a prime-size DFT as convolution. So far, all FFT algorithms cost time at least proportional to the size of input signal. However, if the output of a DFT is k-sparse, i.e., most of the Fourier coefficients of a signal are very small or equal to zero and only k coefficients are large, the transform runtime can be reduced to only sublinear to the signal size N.

Sublinear sparse Fourier algorithm was first proposed in [16], and since then, has been extensively studied in many application fields [1,2,6,7,12,15]. All these algorithms have runtimes faster than original FFT for sparse signals. However, their runtimes have large exponents (larger than 3) in the polynomial of k and $logN$, and their complex algorithmic structures impose restrictions on fast and parallel implementations.

A highly influential recent work [9] presented an improved algorithm with the complexity of $O(k\sqrt{NlogN}logN)$ to make it faster than FFT for k up to $O(\sqrt{N/logN})$. The work in [10] came up with an algorithm with runtime $O(klog Nlog(N/k))$ or even optimal $O(klogN)$. These two approaches, however, only computed a correct sparse Fourier transform in a certain probability and therefore cannot guarantee to generate a completely accurate output. Basically, the new algorithm permutes input with random parameters in time domain to approximate expected permutation in spectral domain for subsequent binning of large coefficients. The probability has to be bounded to prevent large coefficients being binned into the same bucket. In addition, these algorithms iterate over passes of estimating coefficients, updating the signal and recursing on the reminder. Because dependency exists between consecutive iterations, the algorithm can be parallelized only within iterations, but not inter-iteration. Moreover, the selection of the permuting probability, or the filter, is oblivious to input characteristics.

In this paper, we address these limitations by proposing a new sublinear algorithm for sparse fast Fourier transform. Our algorithm has a quite simple structure and leads to a low big-Oh constant in runtime. Our sparse FFT algorithm works in the context that the sparse FFT is invoked on a stream of input signals, and neighboring inputs have very similar spectrum distribution including the sparsity k. The assumption is true for many real-world applications, for example, for many video/audio applications, where neighboring frames have almost identical spectral representations in the locations of large Fourier coefficients, and only differing in the coefficients' values. Our main idea is to use the output of the previous FFT, i.e., the spectral representation of the previous input, as a template to decide, for the current input signal, how to most efficiently bin large Fourier coefficients into a small number of buckets, and each bucket is aimed to have only one large coefficient whose location and magnitude can be then determined. In particular, an n-dimensional filter D that is concentrated both in time and frequency [9,10] is utilized for binning and to ensure the runtime to be sublinear to N. What binning does is essentially to convolute a permuted input signal with the selected filter in spcctral domain. During thc binning, each bucket receives only the frequencies in a narrow range corresponding to the length of pass region of the filter D's spectrum, and pass regions of different buckets are disjoint. The prerequisite of having such a pass region had only one large coefficient is to make all adjacent coefficients have equal distance. The information of likely coefficient locations used in the filter tuning is derived from the sparsity template. We make use of a hash table structure to directly permute coefficients in spectral domain to achieve the expected equal distanced permutation. Figure 1 shows the example of our hash table based permutation in spectral domain, where f_i denotes non-zero Fourier coefficients and the numbers shown above represent locations of the coefficients.

Note that we do not permute input in time domain to approximate the equal distanced permutation with a certain probability bound, but rather directly determine the expected permutation in spectral domain. And in addition each bucket certainly bins only one large coefficient. Therefore our sparse FFT algo-

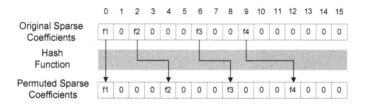

Fig. 1. Hash table based permutation.

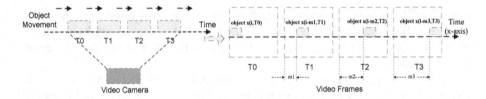

Fig. 2. Application of our input adaptive sparse FFT algorithm.

rithm is always capable of producing a determinatively correct output. Subsequently, once each bucket bins only one large coefficient, we also need to identify its magnitudes and locations. Instead of recovering the isolated coefficients using linear phase estimation [10], we easily look up the hash table reversely to identify binned coefficients. As a result, our algorithm has the runtime at most $O(k^2 log N)$.

Additionally, if all the distances of adjacent frequencies are larger than the minimum length of filter's pass region which is obtained from empirical search, we can reduce the number of permutations and therefore further improve our algorithm to $O(k log N log(k log N))$.

Another notable contribution in our paper is the achievement of parallelization to our sparse FFT algorithm. Since our algorithm is non-iterative with high arithmetic intensity, data parallelism can be exploited from the algorithm. The graphical processing units (GPUs) are used for the well-suited data parallel computations. We parallelize three main sections in our algorithm: permutation to input, subsampled FFT and coefficient estimation.

Our algorithm is evaluated empirically against FFTW, an efficient implementation of FFT with a runtime $O(N log N)$. For $N = 2^{27}$, our optimized sequential and parallel algorithm outperforms FFTW for k up to about 2^{19} and 2^{21}, which is an order of magnitude higher than that in prior algorithms.

Finally, our algorithm are demonstrated to be adaptive to input characteristics. In our evaluation, we use frames from a video camera recording the movement of an object. At the beginning, we capture a video frame of that object at initial time slot T_0 and utilize our sparse FFT algorithm to generate an output. Then we can use the information of that output to help efficiently calculate sparse FFT outputs in subsequent time slots. As a result, our sparse Fourier Transform algorithm saves much time to do the image/video processing and compression. Figure 2 shows the example of application for our adaptive sparse FFT algorithm.

In the following sections, we will describe our methods and their applications in more detail.

3   Input Adaptive Sparse FFT Algorithm

In this section, we use several versions of the sparse FFT algorithm to explain the evolution from a general sparse FFT algorithm to the proposed input-adaptive parallel sparse FFT algorithm. We first describe a general input adaptive sparse FFT algorithm which comprises of input permutation, filtering non-zero coefficients, subsampling FFT and recovery of locations and magnitudes. Subsequently, we discuss how to save the number of permutations and propose an alternatively optimized version for our sparse FFT algorithm to gain runtime improvement. Moreover, general and optimized version are hybridized such that we're able to choose a specific version according to input characteristics. Additionally, we show how the performance of our implementation can be parallelized for GPU and multi-core CPU. Finally, an example of real world application is described for our input adaptive approach.

3.1   General Input-Adaptive Sparse FFT Algorithm

Notations and Assumptions. For a time-domain input signal x with size N (assuming N is an integer power of 2), its DFT is $\hat{x}$. The sparsity parameter of input, k, is defined as the number of non-zero Fourier coefficients in $\hat{x}$. In addition, $[q]$ refers to the set of indices $\{0, ..., q-1\}$. $supp(x)$ refers to the support of vector x, i.e. the set of non-zero coordinates, and $|supp(x)|$ denotes the number of non-zero coordinates of x. Finally, our sparse FFT algorithm works by assuming the locations loc_j of non-zero Fourier coefficients can be estimated from similar prior inputs, where $j \in [k]$. The location template is computed only once for a sequence of signal frames that are similar to each other. The computing of the template by our input-adaptive mechanism which is described in Sect. 3.5. In particular, we invoke existing video processing technology, e.g., [14], to detect the discontinuity in frames' spectral similarities. Therefore, our algorithm is able to compute sparse Fourier transforms for the extracted time-shifting objects within the frames that have homogeneity in the scenes and spectrums, but when we find that homogeneity is broken, our algorithm re-calculates the template and restarts the input-adaptation.

Hashing Permutation of Spectrum. The general sparse FFT algorithm starts with binning large Fourier coefficients into a small number of buckets by convoluting a permuted input signal with a well-selected filter in spectral domain. To guarantee that each bucket is to receive only one large coefficient such that its location and magnitude can be accurately estimated, we need to permute large adjacent coefficients of input spectrum to be equidistant. Knowing the possible Fourier locations loc_j and their order $j \in [k]$ from template, we make use of a hash table to map spectral coefficients into equal distanced positions.

Definition 1. *Define a hash function H: $idx = H(j) = j \times N/k$, where idx is index of permuted Fourier coefficients and $j \in [k]$.*

Next we want to determine the shifting distance s between each original location loc and its permuted position idx to be $s_j = idx_j - loc_j, j \in [k]$. Since shifting one time moves all non-zero Fourier coefficients with a constant factor, so in worst case, it will only make one Fourier coefficient be permuted into the right equidistant location. In addition, since we have total k non-zero coefficients that need to be permuted, therefore, at most k-time shiftings have to be performed to permute all the coefficients into their equal distanced positions.

Moreover, the shifting factors obtained in spectral space should be translated into correspondent operations in time domain so that they are able to take effect with input signal $x_i, i \in [N]$. In effect, shifted spectrum $\hat{x}_{loc-s}$ is equivalently represented as $x_i \omega^{si}$ in time domain, where $\omega = e^{b2\pi/N}$ is a primitive n-th root of unity and $b = \sqrt{-1}$.

Definition 2. *Define the permutation* $P_{s(j)}$ *as* $(P_{s(j)}x)_i = x_i \omega^{is(j)}$ *therefore* $P_{s(j)}x_i = \hat{x}(loc_j - s(j))$, *where* $s(j)$ *is the factor of j-th shifting.*

Therefore, each time when we change the factor $s(j)$, the permutation allows us to correctly bin large coefficient at location loc_j into the bucket. The length of bucket is determined by the flat window function designed in the next section.

Flat Window Functions. In this paper, the method of constructing a flat window function is same as that used in paper [9]. The concept of flat window function is derived from standard window function in digital signal processing. Since window function works as a filter to bin non-zero Fourier coefficients into a small number of buckets, the pass region of filter is expected to be as flat as possible. Therefore, our filter is constructed by having a standard window function convoluted with a box-car filter [9]. Moreover, we want the filter to have a good performance by making it to have fast attenuation in stopband.

Definition 3. *Define* $D(k, \delta, \alpha)$, *where* $k >= 1$, $\delta > 0$, $\alpha > 0$, *to be a flat window function that satisfies:*

1. $|supp(D)| = O(\frac{k}{\alpha} log(\frac{1}{\delta}))$;
2. $\hat{D}_i \in [0, 1]$ *for all* i;
3. $\hat{D}_i \in [1 - \delta, 1 + \delta]$ *for all* $|i| \leq \frac{(1-\alpha)N}{2k}$;
4. $\hat{D}_i < \delta$ *for all* $|i| \geq \frac{N}{2k}$;

In particular, flat window function acts as a filter to extract a certain set of elements of input x. Even if the filter consists of N elements, most of the elements in the filter are negligible and there are only $O(\frac{k}{\alpha} log(\frac{1}{\delta}))$ significant elements when multiplying with x in time domain. In addition, the flat window functions are precomputed in our implementation to save execution time, since their constructions are not dependent on input x but only dependent on N and k. We can lookup each value of the window function in constant time.

Figure 3 shows an example of Gaussian, Kaiser and Dolph-Chebyshev flat window functions. Note that the spectrum of our filters D is nearly flat along the pass region and has an exponential tail outside it. It means that leakage from frequencies in other buckets can be negligible. By comparing the properties of the three window functions, Dolph-Chebyshev window is an optimal one for us to use due to its flat pass region as well as quick and deep attenuation in stopband.

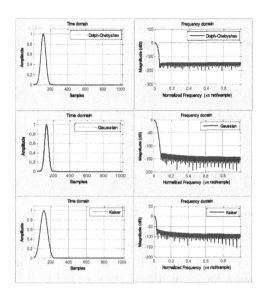

Fig. 3. An example of Dolph-Chebyshev, Gaussian, Kaiser flat window functions for $N = 1024$.

Subsampled FFT. The coefficients binning process is to convolute input spectrum with flat window function. In actual, this convolution is instead performed in time domain by first multiplying input with filter and then computing its subsampled FFT. Suppose we have one N-dimensional complex input series x with sparsity parameter k for its Fourier coefficients, we define a subsampled FFT as $\hat{y}_i = \hat{x}_{iN/k}$ where $i \in [k]$ and N can be divisible by k. The FFT subsampling expects the locations of Fourier coefficients in spectrum domain have been equally spaced. The proof of k-dimensional subsampled FFT has been shown in [9] and the time cost is in $O(|supp(x)| + k\log k)$.

Reverse Hash Function for Location Recovery. After subsampling and FFT to the permuted signal, the binned coefficients have to be reconstructed. This is done by computing the reverse hash function H_r.

Definition 4. *Define a reverse hash function $H_r \colon rec = H_r(idx) = \frac{idx}{(N/k)}$, where idx is index of permuted Fourier coefficients and rec is the order of recovered coefficients.*

Therefore, recovery of Fourier locations can be estimated as loc_{rec} by fetching the locations using the reconstructed order of frequencies.

Algorithm. Combining the aforementioned steps, we can describe our sparse FFT algorithm as following. Note that up to this point, we have not introduced input adaptability, yet. Assuming we have a Fourier location template with k known Fourier locations loc and a precomputed filter D,

1. For $j = 0, 1, 2, ..., k - 1$, where $j \in [k]$, compute hash indices $idx_j = H(j)$ of permuted coefficients, and determine shifting factor $s_j = idx_j - loc_j$.
2. Compute $y = D \cdot P_s(x)$, therefore $|supp(y)| = |s| \times |supp(D)| = O(|s|\frac{k}{\alpha}log(\frac{1}{\delta}))$. We set $\delta = \frac{1}{4N^2V}$, where V is the upperbound value of Fourier coefficients and $V \leq N$.
3. Compute $u_i = \sum_{l=0}^{\frac{|supp(y)|}{k}-1} y_{i+i|y|+lk}$ where $i \in [k]$.
4. Compute k-dimensional subsampled FFT $\hat{u}_i$ and make $\hat{z}_{idx} = \hat{u}_i$, where $i \in [k]$.
5. Location recovery for $\hat{z}_{idx}$ by computing reverse hash function to produce $rec = H_r(idx)$ and finally output $\hat{z}_{loc(rec)}$.

The Computational Complexity. We analyze the runtime of our general sparse FFT algorithm: Step 1 costs $O(k)$; step 2 and 3 cost $O(|s|\frac{k}{\alpha}log(\frac{1}{\delta}))$; step 4 costs $O(klogk)$ for a k-points FFT; step 5 costs $O(k)$. Therefore total running time is determined by $O(|s|\frac{k}{\alpha}log(\frac{1}{\delta}))$. It is very rarely that initial Fourier coefficients have equidistant locations, therefore $|s|$ equals to $|k|$ in general and the runtime becomes $O(\frac{k^2}{\alpha}log(\frac{1}{\delta}))$ which is asymptotic to $O(k^2logN)$.

3.2   Optimized Input-Adaptive Sparse FFT Algorithm

In this section we introduce several transformations of our algorithm that improve performance and facilitate parallelization. The complexity of general adaptive sparse Fourier algorithm is asymptotic to $O(|s|\frac{k}{\alpha}log(\frac{1}{\delta}))$ if initially no adjacent Fourier coefficients are equally distanced. However, if the number of permutations can be reduced, then $|s|$ will be decreased. In fact, it is unnecessary to permute all the Fourier locations to make them equidistant between each other. Since binning the sparse Fourier coefficients is a process of convoluting permuted input spectrum with a well designed filter, so it is guaranteed that if length of filter's pass region ϵ is less than or equal to half of the shortest distance $dist_{min}$ among all the adjacent locations of non-zero coefficients, i.e. $\epsilon <= dist_{min}/2$, then we don't need to permute all coefficients before we do a FFT. Moreover, in this way, we can get rid of aliasing distortions during the binning and each pass region essentially receives only one large coefficient. If we do not do this, aliasing error occurs and we have to permute all spectral samples.

Next we continue to apply the flat window function D to compute filtered vector $y = Dx$ and then we want to compute a FFT for y to produce final output $\hat{y}$. The form of FFT we use here is not a k-dimensional subsampled FFT described previously, since the subsampled FFT requires that locations of non-zero Fourier coefficients are permuted to be equidistant. Instead, we apply a general FFT subroutine into calculation of $\hat{y}$. The size of the FFT is dependent on the length of non-zero elements in y, which is $O(\frac{k}{\alpha}log(\frac{1}{\delta}))$ determined by non-zero region of window function D. We view the size of this FFT as a region with length $O(\frac{k}{\alpha}log(\frac{1}{\delta}))$ (i.e. $O(klogN)$) truncated from size N. Total number of such truncated region is $\frac{N}{klogN}$. In addition, since k sparse Fourier coefficients are distributed in a region consisting of N elements, we have to identify whether output of $O(\frac{k}{\alpha}log(\frac{1}{\delta}))$-dimensional FFT contains all non-zero Fourier coefficients. If not, we would like to shift the unevaluated non-zero coefficient into the truncated region. Our algorithms determines whether to do the shifting before computing FFT. Since the locations of non-zero coefficients and length of truncated region are known from template, we compare the locations with boundary of truncated region to determine the shifting factor sf.

Input-Adaptive Shifting. There are two ways to do shifting:

1. If $k <= \frac{N}{klogN}$, we shift the first unevaluated non-zero coefficient into the truncated region each time;
2. If $\frac{N}{klogN} < k$, we shift the unevaluated non-zero coefficient by a constant factor $klogN$ each time;

In the worst case, the first method performs shifting at most $O(k)$ times, while the second version takes time at most $O(\frac{N}{klogN})$. However, if all large coefficients reside in only one truncated region, we need no shifting and hence we obtain the best case. Meanwhile, the shifting sf_i to spectral coefficients, i.e. $\hat{y}_{i+sf_i}$ corresponds to time domain operation by multiplying input signal y_n with a twiddle factor, i.e. $y_n e^{-b2\pi sf_i n/N}$ where $b = \sqrt{-1}$. Therefore, the cost of shifting for one time is the length of filtered vector y, i.e. $O(klogN)$.

Optimized Algorithm. Adding the optimization heuristics and the input-adaptive shifting, the improved sparse FFT algorithm works as following:

1. Apply filter to input signal x:
   Utilize a flat window function D to compute the filtered vector $y = Dx$. Time cost RT_1 is $O(\frac{k}{\alpha}log(\frac{1}{\delta}))$, i.e. $O(klogN)$.
2. Spectrum shifting: Compare k and $\frac{N}{klogN}$ to select one of the two shifting methods and then do the shifting to filtered vector y. The step-2's runtime RT_2 is $O(klogN) \leq RT_2 < O(min\{k, \frac{N}{klogN}\}\frac{k}{\alpha}log(\frac{1}{\delta}))$, i.e. $O(klogN) \leq RT_2 < O(min\{k, \frac{N}{klogN}\}klogN)$.
3. For $e \in \{1, 2, ..., min\{k, \frac{N}{klogN}\}\}$, each shifting event I_e is to compute $O(\frac{k}{\alpha}log(\frac{1}{\delta}))$-dimensional (i.e. $O(klogN)$-dimensional) FFT $\hat{z}_e$ as $\hat{z}_{e,i} = \hat{y}_i$ in current truncated region, for $i \in [O(\frac{k}{\alpha}log(\frac{1}{\delta})) = O(klogN)]$. Final output is $\hat{z}$. The step-3's runtime RT_3 is $O(klogNlog(klogN)) \leq RT_3 < O(min\{k, \frac{N}{klogN}\}klogNlog(klogN))$.

Therefore, total runtime RT of the improved sparse FFT algorithm is $O(klogNlog(klogN)) \leq RT < O(min\{k, \frac{N}{klogN}\}klogNlog(klogN))$.

3.3   Hybrid Input-Adaptive Sparse FFT Algorithm

Actually, it is clear from the complexity analysis of our general and optimized sparse FFT algorithms that the two algorithm versions are best suit for different input characteristics. That is, the "optimized" version does not perform better than the general version on all cases. We hybridize the two approaches by at runtime selecting the most appropriate version based on input characteristics.

In our optimized version of sparse FFT algorithm, it is worth mentioning that if the required length of pass region is too short, such a filter becomes hard to construct in practice. Therefore, we define a threshold $dist_{TD}$ of minimum distance $dist_{min}$. If $dist_{min} >= dist_{TD}$, then the filter can be constructed to have expected pass region. If $dist_{min} < dist_{TD}$, then our general sparse FFT has to be applied and all the Fourier locations have to be permuted to be equidistant. The threshold can be obtained by empirical search offline.

Therefore, we make the following judgment on an input to decide which algorithm version to apply for the specific input:

1. Determine shortest distance $dist_{min}$ among all adjacent locations of k large coefficients:
   Initialize minimum distance $dist_{min} = 0$; For $j \in 1, 2, ..., k - 1$, compute distances $dist_j = loc_j - loc_{j-1}$ between all k adjacent sparse Fourier locations loc_{j-1} and loc_j; Then if $dist_j <= dist_{min}$, update $dist_{min} = dist_j$. The runtime is $O(k)$.
2. If $dist_{min} >= dist_{TD}$, we choose to use optimized approach to save large number of permutations; If $dist_{min} < dist_{TD}$, then our general sparse FFT has to be applied and all the Fourier locations have to be permuted to be equidistant. The threshold can be obtained by empirical search in our filter design process.

This resolution assists us to create an input-aware algorithm for sparse FFT computation. The cost for the deciding process is only $O(k)$, which can be neglected compared with the runtime of either the general version or the optimized version.

3.4   Parallel Input-Adaptive Sparse FFT Algorithm

Compared with the "dense" FFT algorithms or the existing sparse FFT algorithms, our input-adaptive sparse FFT algorithm can be better parallelized. Specifically, our algorithm is non-iterative with high arithmetic intensity in most portions. The non-iterative nature exposes good coarse-grain parallelism. Moreover, data parallelism of each subsection can be exploited from the algorithm. In this paper, we use Graphic Processing Units (GPUs) for the well-suited data parallel computations. Several architectural-oriented transformations are applied to fine-tune the algorithm for the GPU architecture.

Parallelism Exploitation and Kernel Execution. We first parallelize our general sparse FFT implementation. Since data parallelism is a set of homogeneous tasks executed repeatedly over different data elements, we have such parallelism existing in subsections of hashed index computation, filtering and permuting input, subsampling FFT, and location recovery. Therefore, to achieve high performance we construct GPU computational *kernel* for each subsection. First of all, kernel $HashFunc()$, whose number of threads is k, is responsible to compute hashed indices of permuted coefficients and to determine shift factors. The loop of size k is decomposed and each scalar thread in kernel concurrently works as each index j in the algorithm. In addition, kernel $Perm()$ with total number of threads $k^2 logN$ is used to apply filter and permutation to input. Each thread multiplies filter as well as shifting factor with input for one element. We parallelize subsampling to input in kernel $Subsample()$ with total k threads before we launch our well-tuned FFT kernel $TunedFFT()$. Finally we obtain output from location estimation kernel $Recover()$ with k threads parallelizing the loop of algorithm.

For the parallelization of our optimized version of sparse FFT algorithm, we start to launch kernel $Filtering()$ to parallelize loop size $O(klogN)$ of applying filter to the input. Subsequently, kernel $Shifting()$ with $min\{k, \frac{N}{klogN}\}klogN$ threads is to make each thread shift one input element by a factor. For each shifting event, our tuned FFT kernel $TunedFFT()$ is launched before we gain the output.

Performance Optimizations. Throughout our GPU implementation to two versions algorithms, we take care of several important optimization techniques that enable GPU performance to be improved significantly.

Since GPU global memory accesses are costly, it is crucial to optimize access pattern in order to get maximum memory bandwidth. We organize memory accesses to be coalesced which indicates that threads of a half-warp (16 threads) access 16 consecutive elements at a time so that those individual accesses are grouped into a single memory access. Since in our implementation, most kernels have consecutive access patterns, therefore we enable coalesced accesses by making the size of thread block be 16×2^p where $p \geq 0$, and set grid size to $\frac{\#threads}{blocksize}$.

Moreover, data sharing between kernels can be executed efficiently by increasing data reuse inside local device memory. Host (CPU) and device (GPU) are connected through a PCIe bus that has much larger latency and smaller bandwidth than device memory. Therefore it is of great necessity to increase PCI bandwidth by reducing the number of PCI transfers and keep much more data in local device for reuse. In our implementation, we only have two transfers between CPU and GPU. The first communication is to input all precomputed data including input, Fourier locations and filter information into GPU from CPU. The second transfer is to output final sparse-Fourier results from GPU to CPU. Temporary results are kept into GPU memory and are reused between kernels without transfering back to CPU.

Tuned GPU Based FFT Library. On GPU, our $TunedFFT()$ kernel decomposes a 1D FFT of size $N = N_1 \times N_2$ into multi-dimensions N_1 and N_2, therefore it enables the exploitation of more parallelism for parallel FFT implementation

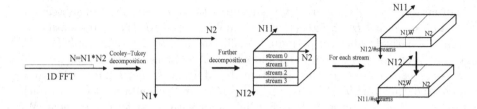

Fig. 4. Working flow of well-tuned GPU based FFT.

on GPU architectures. All N_1 dimensional 1D FFTs are first calculated in parallel across N_2 dimension. If the size of N_1 is still large after decomposition, we would further decompose each $N_1 = N_{11} \times N_{12}$ sized 1D FFT into two dimensional FFTs with smaller sizes N_{11} and N_{12}, respectively. On GPU, device memory has much higher latency and lower bandwidth than on-chip memory. Therefore, shared memory is utilized to increase device memory bandwidth. $N_1 W \times N_{11} \times N_{12}$ sized shared memory needs to be allocated, where $N_1 W$ is chosen to be 16 for half-warp of threads to enable coalesced access to device memory. The number of threads in each block, for both N_{11} and N_{12}-step FFTs, is therefore $N_1 W \times max(N_{11}, N_{12})$ to realize maximum data parallelism on GPU. To calculate each N_1-step 1D FFT, a size N_{11} FFT is executed to load data from global memory into shared memory for each block. Next, all threads in each block are synchronized before data in shared memory is reused by the N_{12}-step FFT and subsequently written back to global memory. Experiment tests show that such shared memory technique effectively hides global memory latency and increases data reuse, both contributing to the performance on GPU. Figure 4 shows the working flow of such GPU based FFT framework.

3.5   Real-World Application

In this section, we demonstrate how our input adaptive algorithm works in real world. Meanwhile, we illustrate how the Fourier location template is generated. We use a sample of video recording in real application shown in Fig. 2. The video sample uses a fix video camera to record the movement of a 2D object along x-coordinate for a duration of time. For each time slot we obtain a 2D video frame containing the object image which can be represented as a 2D matrix $img(g, h)$ whose values stand for color digits, where $g \in [ro]$, $h \in [col]$. The number of rows and columns is ro and col, respectively. Particularly, we substitute the 2D matrix into a row-major 1D array $x_i = x(i = g * col + h) = img(g, h)$. Assuming the interval between the same object in two time-adjacent video frames is m, it can be proved that shifting to $img(g, h)$ is the same to x_i since $img(g, h - m) = x(g * col + h - m) = x_{i-m}$. Therefore, the process of video recording is modeled as a time shifting process to x_i and we want to compute its Fourier transform $\hat{x}_j$ for image/video processing and compression.

At the beginning, we capture input signal $x_{i,T0}$ in a video frame at initial time slot T_0 and calculate its Fourier transform $\hat{x}_{j,T0}$ using a dense FFT.

All locations of large Fourier coefficients and their order can be obtained for $\hat{x}_i$ at T_0. Next we need to compute Fourier transform for x_{i-m_1} at time T_1. Since time-shifted x_{i-m_1} corresponds to $\hat{x}_j e^{-b2\pi m_1 j/N}$ in spectral domain, where $b = \sqrt{-1}$, hence the locations of non-zero frequencies in $\hat{x}_{j,T1}$ is same as those in $\hat{x}_{j,T0}$, but only their values differ. As a consequence, we can make use of Fourier locations gained from $x_{i,T0}$ to compute sparse (not dense) FFT for $x_{i-m_1,T1}$ at T_1 and for $x_{i-m_t,Tt}$ at remaining time slots T_t. Therefore, our sparse algorithm saves much time on dense FFTs since we only compute dense FFT once and then only calculate sparse FFTs according to input characteristics we obtained previously.

Moreover, if time shifting factor m_t is known, we can further directly multiply $\hat{x}_{j,T0}$ at initial time T_0 by $e^{-b2\pi m_t j/N}$ to efficiently attain Fourier transform $\hat{x}_{j,Tt}$ at remaining time T_t without a FFT. However, if shifting factor m_t is unknown, we cannot do this to get spectrums for $x_{i-m_t,Tt}$. This situation is feasible in real application. Suppose we use a video recorder to capture several video frames, but sometimes we don't know the time-shifted distance m_t of the two frames. Hence, we have to know m at first. The worst case is to match $x_{i,T0}$ with $x_{i-m_t,Tt}$ and determine m_t in runtime of $O(N^2)$. Nonetheless, such a process can be efficiently executed in $O(N)$ time when applying the algorithm in [13]. Therefore, if m_t is unknown, we spend time of $O(N)$ on finding m_t and $O(k)$ on multiplying $e^{-b2\pi m_t j/N}$. Total runtime is $O(N + k)$. In the evaluation section, we conduct detailed evaluation to show our sparse FFT outperforms the performance of above two situations including known m_t and unknown m_t.

4   Experimental Evaluation

In this section we evaluate our input-adaptive sparse FFT implementation and its influence on a real-world application. We first discuss the environmental setup that we use for the evaluation and then present performance results.

The double-precision performance evaluation is conducted on three heterogeneous computer configurations. Sequential implementation is executed on Intel i7 920 CPU and the parallel case is run on three different NVIDIA GPUs, i.e. GeForce GTX480, Tesla C2070 and Tesla C2075. For sequential version, we evaluate our general and optimized sparse FFT approaches, and compare them against three highly-influential FFT libraries: (1) FFTW 3.3.3 [5], the latest FFTW which is the most efficient implementation for computing the dense FFTs. In FFTW, Streaming Single Instruction Multiple Data Extensions (SSE) on Intel CPU is enabled for better performance. (2) sFFT 1.0 and 2.0 [9], which is one of the fastest sublinear algorithms of sparse FFT with an open source library. (3) AAFFT 0.9 [11], which is another recent sublinear algorithm with fast empirical runtime. For the parallel version, since there is no parallel sparse-FFT library for us to use, we only compare our GPU based performance to four threads enabled FFTW. The GPU performance reported here includes time of both computation and data transferring between host and device. Furthermore, all FFTW libraries we use are with two flags, i.e. ESTIMATE (a basic version marked as 'FFTW' in the plots) and MEASURE (an optimal version marked as 'FFTW OPT' in the plots). The configurations of GPUs and CPU are summarized in Table 1.

Table 1. Configurations of GPUs and CPU

GPU	Global memory	NVCC	PCI
GeForce GTX480	1.5 GB	3.2	PCIe2.0 × 16
Tesla C2070	6 GB	3.2	PCIe2.0 × 16
Tesla C2075	6 GB	3.2	PCIe2.0 × 16
CPU	Frequency, # of Cores	System memory	Cache
Intel i7 920	2.66 GHz, 4 cores	24 GB	8192 KB

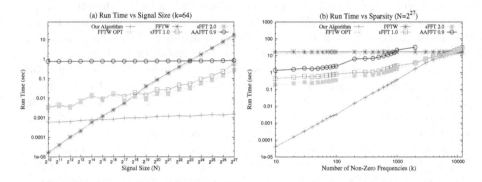

Fig. 5. Performance of our general sparse FFT in sequential case.

4.1   General Input-Adaptive Sparse FFT Algorithm

Both sequential and parallel version of our general sparse FFT are evaluated in two cases: First, we fix the sparsity parameter $k = 64$ and plot the execution time of our algorithm and the compared libraries for 18 different signal sizes from $N = 2^{10}$ to 2^{27}. Second, we fix the signal size to $N = 2^{27}$ and evaluate the running time under different numbers of non-zero frequencies, i.e. k.

Figure 5 shows our sequential sparse FFT on an Intel i7 CPU. In Fig. 5.a, we fix $k = 64$ and change N. The running time of FFTW is linear in the signal size N and sFFT 1.0/2.0 shows approximately linear in N when $N > 2^{20}$. However, our general sparse FFT appears almost constant as the signal size increases, which is a result of our sub-linear property in algorithm. AAFFT 0.9 also shows constantly over different N but its runtime performance is worse than ours and sFFT. Moreover, our approach demonstrates the fastest runtime over sFFT, FFTW and AAFFT. For $N \geq 2^{15}$ our algorithm is faster than FFTW, while sFFT and AAFFT has to reach this goal for $N \geq 2^{19}$ and $N \geq 2^{24}$, respectively. In Fig. 5.b, we fix $N = 2^{27}$ and change k. FFTW shows invariance in performance since its complexity is $O(NlogN)$ which is independent on k. Additionally, our general sparse FFT has a faster runtime than basic and optimal FFTW for k up to 11000 and 10000, respectively. However, sFFT 1.0, sFFT 2.0 and AAFFT 0.9 are faster than basic FFTW only when k is less than 8000, 9000 and 1000. Therefore, our approach extends the range of k where our performance is faster

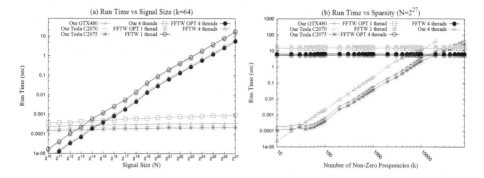

Fig. 6. Performance of our general sparse FFT in parallel case.

than dense FFT. Furthermore, our general algorithm performs better than other compared FFT libraries on average.

Figure 6 shows the parallel versions of our sparse FFT on three high performance GPUs. Since there is no parallel sparse FFT libraries for us to use, we compare our parallel performance to single-thread and 4-thread FFTW. Additionally, to better show our GPU based performance we also add the implementation of our parallel version under 4 CPU threads. In Fig. 6.a, we fix $k = 64$ and change N. Both 1-thread and 4-thread FFTW are linear in the signal size N, however, our parallel approach still appears constant as N increases. Moreover, our three GPU implementations are faster than 1-thread and 4-thread FFTW when $N \geq 2^{14}$ and $N \geq 2^{15}$, while our 4-thread CPU case is exceeds 1-thread and 4-thread FFTW only when $N \geq 2^{15}$ and $N \geq 2^{16}$, respectively. In Fig. 6.b, we fix $N = 2^{27}$ and change k. Specifically, our parallel performance on GTX480, Tesla C2070 and C2075 has a runtime faster than 1-thread FFTW for k up to 40000, 50000, 60000 and than 4-thread FFTW for k reaching to 20000, 30000, 30000, respectively. Meanwhile, our 4-thread CPU based implementation exceeds 1-thread and 4-thread FFTW only when k is less than respective 15000 and 7000.

4.2 Optimized Input-Adaptive Sparse FFT Algorithm

Our optimized sparse FFT algorithm has two situations: the optimal status assumes that all large coefficients reside in only one truncated region of length $O(k log N)$ so that we need no shifting; the average case neglects this assumption but to compute for a random input over 10 runs then takes an average.

Figure 7 shows our optimized sparse FFT in sequential case. In Fig. 7.a, we fix $k = 64$ and change N. Our optimized approach is sub-linear due to its constant curve when N increases. In addition, the optimal and average case of our optimized algorithm is faster than FFTW when $N \geq 2^{14}$ and $N \geq 2^{15}$, respectively. However, sFFT 1.0/2.0 and AAFFT 0.9 has to achieve this purpose for $N \geq 2^{19}$ and $N \geq 2^{24}$, respectively. In Fig. 7.b, we fix $N = 2^{27}$ and change

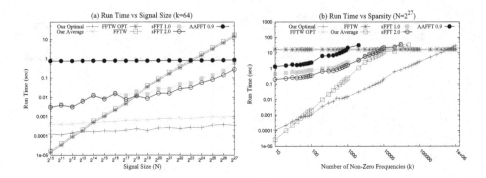

Fig. 7. Performance of our optimized sparse FFT in sequential case.

k. Our optimal and average case has a runtime faster than FFTW for k up to 1000000 and 25000, respectively. However, sFFT 1.0, sFFT 2.0 and AAFFT 0.9 are faster than basic FFTW only when k is less than 8000, 9000 and 1000. On average, our optimized algorithm performs better than other compared FFT libraries.

Figure 8 shows the parallel performance of the optimized algorithm. The experimental configuration is same as that in our general algorithm. In Fig. 8.a, we fix $k = 64$ and change N. Our three GPU implementations are faster than 1-thread and 4-thread FFTW when $N \geq 2^{13}$ and $N \geq 2^{14}$. It is also faster than the dense CUFFT 3.2 when $N \geq 2^{15}$. In Fig. 8.b.c.d, we fix $N = 2^{27}$ and change k. The performance of optimal algorithm on GTX480, Tesla C2070 and C2075 has a runtime faster than 1-thread FFTW for k up to 1500000, 2000000, 3000000 and than 4-thread FFTW for k reaching to 500000, 700000, 900000, respectively. Meanwhile, performance of our optimized method in average case on GTX480, C2070 and C2075 is faster than 1-thread FFTW for k up to 50000, 70000, 80000 and than 4-thread FFTW for k reaching to 30000, 40000, 50000, respectively. In addition, our optimal version on the three GPUs is faster than dense CUFFT when k reaches to 70000, 80000, 90000, while our average case on the GPUs exceeds CUFFT for k up to 6000, 7000, 8000. Particularly, in Fig. 8.c, CUFFT is also added in our Tesla C2070 test as kernel $TunedFFT()$. As a result, our tuned GPU based FFT kernel is 21 % faster than CUFFT counterpart.

4.3   Evaluation of Real-World Application and Accuracy

We show an performance evaluation for better illustrating the real-world application of video recording in Sect. 3.5. Suppose we capture total 10 video frames in 10 time slots. The displacement between the object in adjacent two time slots is set to 2^{10} points. Figure 9.a shows the sequential performance of our hybrid sparse FFT against to the dense FFT performance, i.e. FFTW, and to the performance of two situations including known shifting factor m and unknown m. X-axis represents the time slots T_t. Input signal size is $N = 2^{27}$ points and $k = 64$. The test shows that our hybrid FFT in both sequential and parallel

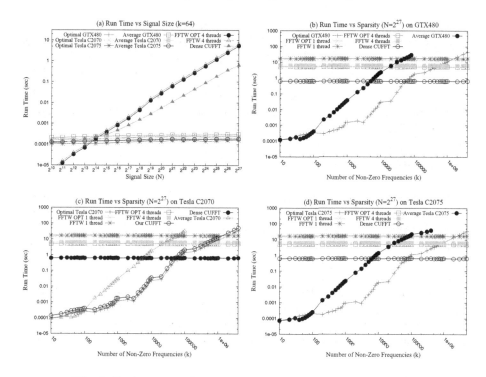

Fig. 8. Performance of our optimized sparse FFT in parallel case.

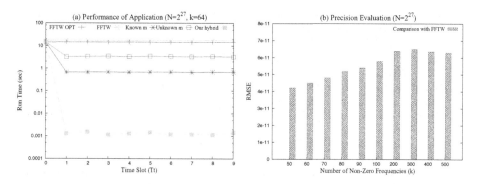

Fig. 9. Performance of a real-world application and accuracy of our algorithm.

version outperform the performance of all other compared situations. It demonstrates that we can spend time to compute a dense FFT once to preprocess the Fourier location template that we need for the FFTs in remaining time. Then we can save much time by using our hybrid sparse FFT for all the subsequent input signals. Furthermore, if the number of frames is large, our sparse FFT outperforms sFFT as well as AAFFT on average in the real application.

The accuracy of our sparse FFT implementation is verified by comparing its complex Fourier transform (F_x, F_y) with FFTW's output (f_x, f_y) for the same double-precision input data. The difference in output is quantized as root mean square error (RMSE) over the whole data set. The RMSE is defined as $\sqrt{\frac{\sum_{i=0}^{N-1}[(F_x - f_x)^2 + (F_y - f_y)^2]}{2N}}$ and is shown in Fig. 9.b for $N = 2^{27}$ and different k. Overall, the RMSE is extremely small and demonstrates a good accuracy of our algorithm.

5   Conclusion

In this paper, we proposed an input-adaptive sparse FFT algorithm that takes advantage of the similarity between sparse input samples to efficiently compute a Fourier transform in the runtime sublinear to signal size N. Specifically, our work integrates and tunes several adaptive filters to package non-zero Fourier coefficients into sparse bins which can be estimated accurately. Moreover, our algorithm is non-iterative with high computation intensity such that parallelism can be exploited for multi-CPUs and GPU to improve performance. Overall, our algorithm is faster than FFT both in theory and implementation, and the range of sparsity parameter k that our approach can outperform dense FFT is larger than that of other sparse Fourier algorithms.

References

1. Akavia, A.: Deterministic sparse fourier approximation via fooling arithmetic progressions. In: The 23rd Conference on Learning Theory, pp. 381–393 (2010)
2. Akavia, A., Goldwasser, S., Safra, S.: Proving hard-core predicates using list decoding. In: The 44th Symposium on Foundations of Computer Science, pp. 146–157. IEEE (2003)
3. Bluestein, L.: A linear filtering approach to the computation of discrete Fourier transform. IEEE Trans. Audio Electroacoust. **18**(4), 451–455 (1970)
4. Duhamel, P., Vetterli, M.: Fast fourier transforms: a tutorial review and a state of the art. Signal Process. **4**(19), 259–299 (1990)
5. Frigo, M., Johnson, S.G.: The design and implementation of fftw3. Proc. IEEE **93**(2), 216–231 (2005)
6. Gilbert, A., Guha, S., Indyk, P., Muthukrishnan, M., Strauss, M.: Near-optimal sparse fourier representations via sampling. In: Proceedings of the 34th Annual ACM Symposium on Theory of Computing, pp. 152–161. ACM (2002)
7. Gilbert, A., Muthukrishnan, M., Strauss, M.: Improved time bounds for near-optimal space fourier representations. In: Proceedings of SPIE Wavelets XI (2005)
8. Good, I.: The interaction algorithm and practical Fourier analysis. J. R. Stat. Soc. Ser. B (Methodological) **20**(2), 361–372 (1958)
9. Hassanieh, H., Indyk, P., Katabi, D., Price, E.: Simple and practical algorithm for sparse fourier transform. In: Proceedings of the 23th Annual ACM-SIAM Symposium on Discrete Algorithms, pp. 1183–1194. ACM (2012)
10. Hassanieh, H., Indyk, P., Katabi, D., Price, E.: Nearly optimal sparse fourier transform. In: Proceedings of the 44th Symposium on Theory of Computing, pp. 563–578. ACM (2012)

11. Iwen, M.: AAFFT (Ann Arbor Fast Fourier Transform) (2008). http://sourceforge. net/projects/aafftannarborfa/
12. Iwen, M.: Combinatorial sublinear-time fourier algorithms. Found. Comput. Math. **10**(3), 303–338 (2010)
13. Knuth, D., Morris, J., Pratt, V.: Fast pattern matching in strings. SIAM J. Comput. **6**(2), 323–350 (1977)
14. Li, L., Huang, W., Gu, I., Tian, Q.: Foreground object detection from videos containing complex background. In: Proceedings of the 11th ACM International Conference on Multimedia, pp. 2–10. ACM (2003)
15. Mansour, Y.: Randomized interpolation and approximation of sparse polynomials. In: Kuich, Werner (ed.) ICALP 1992. LNCS, vol. 623, pp. 261–272. Springer, Heidelberg (1992)
16. Nukada, A., Matsuoka, S.: Learning decision trees using the fourier spectrum. In: Proceedings of the Conference on High Performance Computing Networking, Storage and Analysis, pp. 455–464. ACM (1991)
17. Rader, C.: Discrete Fourier transforms when the number of data samples is prime. Proc. IEEE **56**(6), 1107–1108 (1968)

Caches

Aligned Scheduling: Cache-Efficient Instruction Scheduling for VLIW Processors

Vasileios Porpodas[1][(✉)] and Marcelo Cintra[1,2]

[1] School of Informatics, University of Edinburgh, Edinburgh, UK
v.porpodas@ed.ac.uk
[2] Intel Labs Braunschweig, Braunschweig, Germany
mc@staffmail.ed.ac.uk

Abstract. The performance of statically scheduled VLIW processors is highly sensitive to the instruction scheduling performed by the compiler. In this work we identify a major deficiency in existing instruction scheduling for VLIW processors. Unlike most dynamically scheduled processors, a VLIW processor with no load-use hardware interlocks will completely stall upon a cache-miss of any of the operations that are scheduled to run in parallel. Other operations in the same or subsequent instruction words must stall. However, if coupled with non-blocking caches, the VLIW processor is capable of simultaneously resolving multiple loads from the same word. Existing instruction scheduling algorithms do not optimize for this VLIW-specific problem.

We propose Aligned Scheduling, a novel instruction scheduling algorithm that improves performance of VLIW processors with non-blocking caches by enabling them to better cope with unpredictable cache-memory latencies. Aligned Scheduling exploits the VLIW-specific cache-miss semantics to efficiently align cache misses on the same scheduling cycle, increasing the probability that they get serviced simultaneously. Our evaluation shows that Aligned Scheduling improves the performance of VLIW processors across a range of benchmarks from the Mediabench II and SPEC CINT2000 benchmark suites up to 20%.

1 Introduction

Very Long Instruction Word (VLIW) processors are wide-issue statically scheduled processors. They are used in a wide range of domains: in GPUs (AMD's VLIW-5 architecture on Radeon GPUs and in APUs [4]), in embedded systems as DSPs (Texas Instrument's VelociTI, HP/ST's Lx [8], Analog's TigerSHARC [11], BOPS' ManArray [23]) and as targets of dynamic binary translation (e.g. Transmeta's Crusoe [5,14]). A VLIW-like architecture (with many unique dynamic hardware additions for run-time optimizations) is also used in servers (Intel's Itanium/Itanium2 EPIC architecture [20,27]).

Compared to dynamically scheduled processors, VLIW designs operate at an attractive power/performance point. This is because they are by design both

This work was supported in part by the EC under grant ERA 249059 (FP7).

C. Caşcaval and P. Montesinos (Eds.): LCPC 2013, LNCS 8664, pp. 275–291, 2014.
DOI: 10.1007/978-3-319-09967-5_16

simple (no dynamic scheduling hardware [10]) and wide-issue. They rely on the compiler's instruction scheduling pass to optimally schedule instructions. Instruction scheduling algorithms re-arrange the instructions of the input program to hide pipeline latencies. Schedulers for VLIW processors in particular, explicitly express instruction level parallelism (ILP) in long instruction words.

The simplicity of the VLIW hardware design, however, comes at a cost: VLIW processors are more sensitive to dynamic latencies triggered by microarchitectural events, such as cache misses, than their dynamically scheduled counterparts. This is because a traditional VLIW processor comes to a complete halt upon a cache miss caused by any instruction in the long instruction word, due to the absence of load-use hardware interlocks. Therefore even if there exist instructions that could execute while the miss is being serviced, they do not because the VLIW hardware does not allow it. We refer to these VLIW cache-miss semantics as *Stall-On-Miss* (SOM) (Fig. 1c).

Performance can be improved once we deviate from the VLIW design philosophy and introduce data hazard detection in hardware. This limits the processor stalls to the cases when a VLIW instruction tries to use data that is not available (brought in by the Load-miss). We refer to this model as *Stall-On-Use* (SOU) (Fig. 1d). In this model, the long instruction words remain intact and the dependencies are tracked at the VLIW word level.

If we apply a full-blown register scoreboarding in hardware, we can break down the instruction words into individual instructions and we can allow each instruction to issue and stall independently of the others (Fig. 1e). This allows for optimal pipeline throughput as the execution only stalls when dictated by the data dependencies. This approach, however, requires hardware components that are normally found in dynamically scheduled superscalar processors, thus deviating from the VLIW design concept of keeping the hardware simple. This is the reason why most VLIW processors are designed to be either SOM or SOU. In this work we only consider the SOM and SOU models.

A SOU architecture requires Non-Blocking caches [15] to function. These caches are equipped with a simple hardware mechanism that allows them to resolve multiple misses simultaneously. Their impact on performance on dynamically

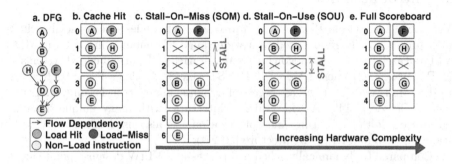

Fig. 1. Dynamic schedules of DFG (a) as we increase hardware complexity.

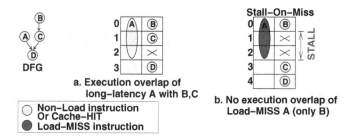

Fig. 2. VLIW semantics of a regular long-latency instruction (a) VS a cache-miss (b).

scheduled processors is significant since they decrease the pipeline stalls. The performance improvement however, on a VLIW processor with SOM semantics is not as impressive under existing instruction schedulers.

Most schedulers can effectively deal with regular long-latency instructions, such as integer division. They try to hide long latencies by executing other low-latency instructions in parallel. Existing instruction schedulers consider Load instructions as regular instructions of some latency: either low-latency (cache-hit), high-latency (cache miss) or something in between. This effectively changes how the scheduler treats the loads: as hits, misses or in between. This approach works fine for dynamically-scheduled processors. The Stall-On-Miss semantics of a VLIW processor however, require special treatment by the instruction scheduler. Figure 2 shows that trying to hide load miss latency by scheduling other instructions in parallel is not suitable for VLIWs. This is because on a VLIW with no load-use interlocks, the semantics of a regular long-latency instruction (Non-Load instruction Fig. 2a) are different from a cache-miss of equal latency (Load instruction Fig. 2b). On one hand the high-latency regular instruction A in Fig. 2a can overlap its execution with B and C. On the other hand, cache-miss A in Fig. 2b cannot overlap with instructions C or D due to Stall-On-Miss semantics. Therefore such VLIW architectures require a radically different scheduling approach for hiding cache-miss latencies.

This paper proposes Aligned Scheduling, a novel instruction scheduling algorithm for statically scheduled VLIW processors with non-blocking caches that treats Load instructions differently than existing schemes. It improves the tolerance of VLIW processors to cache-miss latencies by exploiting four concepts:

1. The VLIW-specific Stall-On-Miss or Stall-On-Use cache-miss semantics.
2. Non-blocking caches [15,28], that can service multiple cache misses simultaneously.
3. The statically provable Memory-Level Parallelism (MLP), that allows multiple memory Load operations to execute on the same VLIW cycle.
4. The explicit instruction parallelism of VLIW instruction words.

These concepts allow the instruction scheduler to hide cache-miss latencies by aligning memory Load instructions together on the same cycle, in a smart way. In this way, during execution, the probability that multiple Load instructions miss simultaneously increases. We refer to this effect of multiple aligned

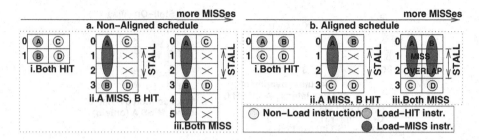

Fig. 3. Two different schedules a and b under increasing miss conditions. Schedule b (Aligned) exhibits miss-overlapping under heavy miss conditions (b.iii).

Load instructions missing simultaneously as *miss overlapping* (Fig. 3). Aligned Scheduling proves particularly effective for VLIWs with no load-use hardware interlocks (SOM), but as shown in the Sect. 5, it could potentially benefit SOU under high miss latency conditions.

2 Motivation

The main concept that Aligned Scheduling is based on is the idea of *miss overlapping* (Fig. 3). If the architecture supports non-blocking caches, then more than a single outstanding cache miss can be serviced simultaneously. Instruction schedulers currently do not exploit this feature of the architecture and tend to generate schedules as in Fig. 3a, which perform well when there are no or few cache misses (Fig. 3a i,ii) but are suboptimal when there are bursts of cache misses (Fig. 3a iii). An optimized scheduler for VLIW should exploit the non-blocking caches to schedule loads in parallel, whenever this is profitable. Aligned Scheduling does so selectively and generates a schedule which still performs well under low cache miss conditions (Fig. 3b i,ii) but manages to outperform the existing approaches under bursts of cache misses (Fig. 3b iii).

The motivating examples (Fig. 4(a) and Fig. 4(b)) describe two different but complementary heuristics that are used in Aligned Scheduling. Each example is based on its own Data Flow Graph (DFG), Fig. 4(a)a and Fig. 4(b)a respectively. Both DFGs contain Load instructions (green) and non-Load instructions (light gray). The examples compare the schedules generated by two schedulers: (i) The baseline scheduler (top sub-figures b,d,f), a state-of-the-art list-scheduler (like the scheduler in GCC [1]) and (ii) Aligned Scheduler (bottom sub-figures c,e,g). The colors on the DFG and schedules are consistent. Red represents a Load that misses in the cache. The leftmost column of each figure (sub-figures b,c) shows the static schedule produced by the scheduler. These schedules also happen to match the dynamic (run-time) schedule when all Load instructions are hits. This is why in both sub-figures b and c the loads are green, suggesting a cache-hit. The other two columns show the case when all Loads miss: The center column (sub-figures d,e) corresponds to a Stall-On-Miss (SOM) architecture and the rightmost column (sub-figures f,g) corresponds to Stall-On-Use (SOU).

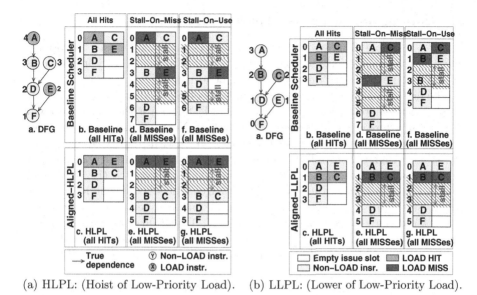

(a) HLPL: (Hoist of Low-Priority Load).   (b) LLPL: (Lower of Low-Priority Load).

Fig. 4. Aligned Scheduling heuristics. The numbers on the DFG are the instr. priorities (Color figure online).

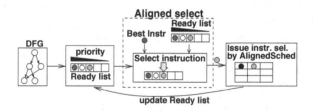

Fig. 5. Aligned Scheduling structure.

The baseline is a list scheduler, like the default scheduler in most industrial-strength compilers (e.g. GCC). It prioritizes the ready instructions based on a priority function (in this case the height of each node in the graph), and emits the highest priority ready instruction into the schedule. Aligned Scheduling is also a list-scheduler based algorithm, but differs from the baseline in the instruction selection process (see Fig. 5 "Aligned-select"). The performance of a scheduler is inversely proportional to the dynamic schedule length. In this example we are interested in comparing the two schedulers in cache-hit (sub-figures b,c) and cache-miss (sub-figures d,e and f,g) scenarios.

Both examples (Fig. 4(a) and Fig. 4(b)) motivate the main concept of Aligned Scheduling, which is that the VLIW stall semantics require that a good schedule, resilient to misses, should have Load instructions scheduled in parallel on the same cycle, so that the cache misses can overlap in time.

2.1   Hoisting of Low-Priority Loads (HLPL)

The first example (Fig. 4(a)) shows that a scheduler that hoists low-priority Loads by giving preference to them instead of other higher priority instructions, can improve performance under a burst of Load misses.

The highest priority instruction of the DFG of Fig. 4(a)a is Load A. At cycle 0, the scheduler's ready list contains A, C and E. Since A is the instruction with the highest priority (4), it gets issued at cycle 0. Next, an unmodified priority-based list scheduler (Fig. 4(a)b,d,f) would select C with priority 3. The HLPL heuristic of Aligned Scheduling, though, will select E with priority 2, since this will allow for both Loads (A and E) to execute on the same cycle (Fig. 4(a)c,e,g).

If at run-time none of the Loads miss, the dynamic schedule will look exactly like the static one (Fig. 4(a)b). If, however, at run-time both Load instructions (A and E) miss, then the execution will look as in Fig. 4(a)d or Fig. 4(a)f, depending on the stall semantics. In this case, the run-time performance of the Baseline scheduler is worse than the Aligned one for both Stall-On-Miss and Stall-On-Use semantics.

The Aligned-HLPL heuristic makes sure that the low-priority Load instructions (like Load E), get hoisted and scheduled on the same cycle as high-priority Load instructions, like Load A on cycle 0 (Fig. 4(a)c). This suggests that unlike the baseline scheduler, in Aligned-HLPL instruction priority does not always drive the scheduling algorithm. Instead low-priority Load instructions may take precedence over high-priority non-Load instructions. For example the high-priority non-Load instruction C gets deferred to a later cycle than the lower-priority E (Fig. 4(a)c). This leads to better performance under bursts of misses, and still a good schedule under the "all HITs" case (Fig. 4(a)c,e,g).

2.2   Lowering of Low-Priority Loads (LLPL)

The previously described HLPL heuristic can only work if a high-priority load is scheduled first on the current scheduling cycle. The LLPL heuristic complements HLPL, by taking action when a high-priority non-Load instruction is scheduled first on the current scheduling cycle.

The LLPL heuristic (Fig. 4(b)) avoids scheduling low priority Load instructions if the highest priority instruction on the current scheduling cycle is not a Load. Even if there are no instructions left to schedule but Loads, LLPL will defer them to some later cycle. This is beneficial for two reasons: **1.** It guarantees that the current cycle remains stall-free, since there are no Load instructions to miss. **2.** It increases the chances that more Load instructions get grouped together and aligned on a future cycle.

LLPL can be better explained through the example of Fig. 4(b). As in Sect. 2.1, the Baseline scheduler is driven purely by instruction priorities and issue slot availability. Therefore Load C gets scheduled on a different cycle than Load B, as shown in Fig. 4(b)b.

Aligned-LLPL however is not guided solely by the instruction priorities. Instead it focuses on deferring low-priority Load instructions of the ready list (e.g., C at cycle 0 which is not the highest priority instruction) to a later cycle as long as the high priority instruction is not a Load (A at cycle 0). The end result is that instruction C gets scheduled later (at cycle 1) along with Load B.

When all instructions are hits ("all HITs" scenario) both the Baseline and Aligned Scheduling-LLPL perform equally well (Fig. 4(b)b and Fig. 4(b)c). When both Loads miss however, Aligned-LLPL is faster (Fig. 4(b)d,f vs Fig. 4(b)e,g). The speedup, is once again due to the overlapping of miss-latencies.

3   Aligned Scheduling

3.1   Overview

Aligned Scheduling is based on the commonly used list-scheduling algorithm. An overview of how the common (baseline) list scheduling algorithm works is shown in Fig. 5, without the "Aligned select" component.

The input to list scheduling is a Data Flow Graph (DFG) with its nodes tagged with priorities. The priority can be calculated based on various heuristics, a common one being the height from the bottom of the DFG. With the term "ready instructions" we mean the instructions that have all their inputs calculated and available to them. The ready instructions of the DFG are placed into a ready list and are sorted based on their priority. The highest-priority instruction is selected and scheduled. Scheduling an instruction causes its DFG successors to become ready and to be added to the ready list. The scheduler steps to the next cycle under two conditions: (1) The ready list is empty, meaning that there are no available instructions to schedule (2) The current cycle is full, so no more instructions can be scheduled in it. This process repeats until all instructions in the DFG are scheduled.

Aligned Scheduling (Fig. 5) adds the "Aligned select" phase to the common list scheduling algorithm. This process is placed in between sorting the ready list and scheduling an instruction. It uses the ready instruction list and the highest priority instruction of the current cycle to make an informed decision on selecting the instruction that should be scheduled at the current scheduling cycle. This is where HLPL and LLPL are used. The instruction that "Aligned select" returns, gets scheduled at the current cycle.

Although Aligned Scheduling is built on top of GCC's EBB-region-based scheduler, in principle the "Aligned select" step can be plugged in to other schedulers as well (e.g., the Selective Scheduler [21], Modulo Scheduling [6,16,18,24] etc.) without major modifications to these algorithms.

The Aligned Scheduling algorithm can be logically split in two parts: **1.** The **main driver** function (Algorithm 1), which performs the high-level actions of a list-scheduler. **2.** The Aligned Scheduling **selection** function (Algorithm 2) which is used for the selection of the instruction that gets scheduled by the main driver function.

Algorithm 1. Aligned Scheduling algorithm.

```
1  aligned ()
2  {
3    /* While there are unscheduled isntr. */
4    while (instructions left to schedule)
5      update READY_LIST with ready + deferred
          ↪instr.
6      sort READY_LIST based on priorities
7      BEST_INSTR = READY_LIST [0]
8      while (READY_LIST not empty)
9        INSN=aligned_select(BEST_INSTR,
            ↪READY_LIST)
10       if (no INSN selected)
11         break
12       if (INSN can be sched. at CYCLE)
13         schedule INSN
14         remove INSN from READY_LIST
15       /* If failed, defer to cycle+1 */
16       if (INSN unscheduled)
17         remove INSN from READY_LIST and re
            ↪-insert it at CYCLE + 1
18     /* READY_LIST is empty */
19     CYCLE ++
20 }
```

Algorithm 2. Aligned Scheduling instruction selection

```
1  /*In1: Highest prio. instr. of curr cycle
2    In2: List of ready instr. of curr cycle
3    Out: Instruction to schedule on cycle*/
4  aligned_select (BEST_INSTR, READY_LIST)
5  {
6    if (BEST_INSTR is LOAD)
7      if (HLPL)
8        for INSTR in sorted READY_LIST
9          if (INSTR is LOAD)
10           return INSTR
11     return READY_LIST [0]
12   else if (BEST_INSTR is not a LOAD)
13     if (LLPL)
14       for INSTR in sorted READY_LIST
15         if (INSTR is not LOAD)
16           return INSTR
17     else
18       return READY_LIST [0]
19   else
20     return READY_LIST [0]
21 }
```

3.2   Aligned Scheduling Driver

The **main driver** function (Algorithm 1) performs the main actions of a list-scheduling algorithm adjusted to work with the Aligned Scheduling heuristics. While there are instructions left to schedule (line 4) it keeps iterating. First, it fills in the ready list with any ready instruction (line 5), then it sorts the ready list (line 6) based on the instruction priorities (which is usually the height of the instruction in the DFG). Next it finds the highest priority instruction for this cycle and stores it into BEST_INSTR (line 7).

The algorithm then schedules the ready instructions one by one (lines 8–17). This part of the algorithm keeps iterating until: (1) the ready list is empty (line 8), or (2) no instruction is selected by the Align-selection function. The ready list empties in two ways: 1. Scheduled instructions are removed from the ready list 2. When no more instructions fit in the current cycle (due to insufficient execution slots) then the ready instructions still get popped out of the ready list without being scheduled and get deferred to the next cycle (line 17).

Instructions get selected from the ready list by the "aligned_select()" function (line 9). The implementation of this function is shown in Algorithm 2. If no instruction is selected by "aligned_select" (i.e. there are no instructions left to schedule in this cycle), then the algorithm breaks out of the innermost while loop (lines 10–11) to abandon scheduling on the current cycle and to step to the next cycle. This enables LLPL to leave a cycle partially scheduled even if there are ready instructions left to schedule. Else, if an instruction has been selected, then it gets scheduled and removed from the ready list (lines 12–14). If, due to resource constraints (e.g., no more issue slots) the instruction cannot be scheduled on the current scheduling cycle, then it is removed from the ready list (lines 16, 17). Finally, if there are no instructions left in the ready list, it is time to move to the next scheduling cycle (lines 18, 19) and restart with a fresh ready list at the top of the outer loop (line 4).

3.3   Aligned Scheduling Selection

At the core of the Aligned Scheduling algorithm lies the **aligned_select ()** function (Algorithm 2). This function decides which instruction, among the ready ones, will be executed on the current scheduling cycle. This function makes use of the HLPL and LLPL heuristics to decide on the instruction selected.

This function exploits the statically (at compile time) analyzable MLP to improve the schedule's performance of VLIW processors with non-blocking caches under high cache-miss rate conditions. The end result of the instruction selection (with the help of the driver function of Algorithm 1) is a hoisting and lowering of Load instructions aiming at **grouping loads** together as much as possible.

Internally, the selection algorithm is composed of two different but complementary heuristics: The "Hoist of Low-Priority Load" (HLPL) heuristic as demonstrated in the motivation Sect. 2.1 and the "Lower of Low-Priority Load" (LLPL) heuristic as discussed in Sect. 2.2. If both are active, either HLPL or LLPL executes **depending on the type of the highest priority instruction** (BEST_INSTR) of the current scheduling cycle (Algorithm 2, lines 6,12). If it is a Load then HLPL performs hoisting of other Loads. Else if it is not a Load, then LLPL forms a Load-free cycle by lowering loads to later cycles. The insight behind it is that the critical path should be honored. Therefore the highest priority instruction (BEST_INSTR) of the cycle should guide the type of instructions that are aligned with it. We can enable each or both of these heuristics by controlling the HLPL and LLPL flags (Algorithm 2 line 7 and line 13, respectively).

The instruction hoisting/lowering of Aligned Scheduling is done in a **balanced** way: **1.** The Load hoisting and lowering is **mild enough** such that the re-arranged instructions do not replace other highly-critical instructions. This guarantees acceptable performance on a low cache-miss rate conditions. **2.** The Load hoisting and lowering is **aggressive enough** that the Load instructions get grouped together so that we get high miss overlapping and performance improvements on high cache-miss scenarios.

The first point is achieved by honoring the critical path and always scheduling the highest priority instruction of the ready list (BEST_INSTR) without any delays (Algorithm 2 lines 9,15 guarantee this). Also the most critical instruction guides the kind of hoisting/lowering that takes place (Algorithm 2 lines 6,12). The second point is achieved by selectively hoisting/lowering all lower priority instructions.

HLPL: If BEST_INSTR is a Load (Algorithm 2, line 6), then the HLPL heuristic can be applied (line 7). It iterates over the list of sorted ready instructions (line 8) and selects the first load instruction encountered (lines 9, 10). If there are no ready load instructions to choose from, HLPL will select a non-Load instruction (line 11) as this can only be beneficial. This is because scheduling non-Load instructions, after all Load instructions have been scheduled on the cycle, cannot cause any further stalls or delays for this cycle, so it can cause no harm. Instead, deferring the execution of non-Load instructions to later cycles can only degrade performance. HLPL will usually not harm performance under low miss-rate conditions.

LLPL: In the opposite case, if BEST_INSTR, the highest priority instruction of the current cycle, is not a Load (line 12), the LLPL heuristic can be applied. In short, LLPL creates a Load-free cycle. It does so by deferring the execution of any Load instruction to future cycles. This is done by iterating across the ready list (line 14) and selecting only non-Load instructions to schedule (lines 15, 16). Unlike HLPL, when LLPL is "on" then even if there are no other non-Load instructions left in the ready list, the algorithm will **not** select a Load, therefore the current scheduling cycle will be partially empty. This is good for two reasons: **1.** It guarantees that the current cycle does not stall (since it contains no Loads) **2.** It enables future co-execution of Load instructions in later cycles. However, LLPL could potentially harm performance as it deliberately leaves resources under-utilized. LLPL proves to be an aggressive heuristic for high miss-rate conditions, but can cause slowdowns on low miss-rate conditions.

Enabling both heuristics is usually the best practice, since the resulting performance is usually better than either them in isolation (see Sect. 5).

4 Experimental Setup

The target **architecture** is a statically scheduled Stall-On-Miss/Stall-On-Use VLIW, that uses the IA64 [27] instruction set due to widespread availability of tools for this ISA. The architecture has a configurable issue width. It is worth noting that the real Itanium processor used in servers is based on the EPIC architecture, which although looking similar to a VLIW one, has many hardware features not found in common VLIW architectures. One of these hardware features is a hardware register scoreboard. Our target is a common VLIW without the full-blown register scoreboard of the Itanium.

We have implemented Aligned Scheduling in the instruction scheduling pass (haifa-sched) of GCC-4.5.0 [1] **compiler** for IA64.

We simulated the architecture on a modified version of SKI [2], IA64 cycle accurate simulator that supports a configurable non-blocking cache hierarchy and both SOM or SOU semantics. The issue width is configurable, ranging from 2 to 4 wide and each issue slot can execute an instruction of any type. The L1 cache is 16K-1way, with a block-size of 64 Bytes and a 1 cycle latency. The L2 cache is 256K-4way with a block size of 128 Bytes and an 8 cycle latency. Both caches are non-blocking. The access to the main memory takes 150 cycles.

We evaluated Aligned Scheduling on 6 of the Mediabench II video [12] and 6 of the SPEC2000 CINT [3] **benchmarks**. All benchmarks were compiled with several optimizations enabled (-O2) and both schedulers running. We ran all benchmarks to completion.

5   Results and Analysis

We first present a detailed case study of Aligned Scheduling on the cjpeg benchmark of the Mediabench II benchmark suite (Sect. 5.1). We then present summarized results for the rest of the benchmarks (Sect. 5.2).

5.1   Case Study: cjpeg

The cjpeg benchmark of the Mediabench II [12] video suite is a representative example for evaluating Aligned Scheduling. This benchmark has a working set of 16KB which is small enough that we can test Aligned Scheduling across a broad range of cache-miss scenarios (ranging from high miss-rates to low miss-rates) by simply changing the L1 size.

Figure 6(a) compares the cycle counts of the Aligned Scheduling-{HLPL, LLPL and BOTH} heuristics against the Baseline scheduling. The comparison is done over various L1 cache sizes, ranging from 4KB to 32KB 1-way, and on three different issue widths of the VLIW processor (issue 2–4). The L2 cache is a 256KB 4-way with 8 cycles latency. Figure 6(b) and (c) complements Fig. 6(a) by providing the L1 and L2 miss rates respectively for each case. Finally, Fig. 6(d) shows the amount of overlapping of cache misses and Fig. 6(e) shows the average load latency. These figures provide some important insights on the strengths and weaknesses of Aligned Scheduling:

a. The first thing to notice in Fig. 6(a) is that for the Stall-On-Miss semantics and small L1 sizes, Aligned Scheduling **outperforms** the baseline by a considerable margin, in fact it performs equally well or better than the baseline with twice as much L1 memory (e.g., Fig. 6(a) 3/4-issue 4K, 8K SOM), improving performance by about 20 %. Therefore, for small cache sizes, Aligned Scheduling bridges half the performance gap between a SOM and a SOU architecture, with **no additional hardware**. Aligned Scheduling performance improvements, however, decrease as the cache size increases. This is because cache misses become less frequent (Fig. 6(b)), therefore the probability of them happening simultaneously (something that Aligned Scheduling could exploit) decreases. The point of diminishing returns for cjpeg is the point when the working set size equals the cache size (16KB). For sizes greater than 32KB, the L1 miss rate drops below 8 % and Aligned Scheduling cannot improve performance, but it does not hurt it either.

b. The two Aligned Scheduling heuristics (HLPL and LLPL) work orthogonally and when both enabled they **act cooperatively**. Enabling both (Aligned-BOTH Fig. 6(a)) outperforms each individual heuristic Aligned-HLPL or Aligned-LLPL, by a significant margin. This is true for both SOM and SOU semantics.

c. Aligned Scheduling performs better as the **issue width** increases. In fact, for cjpeg, and for the degenerate VLIW case of 2-issue and for SOM semantics, Aligned scheduling causes a slowdown. This is an example where the alignment cost outweighs the benefit: Since the issue width is too narrow, the cache misses cannot be effectively overlapped, therefore the scheduling penalty

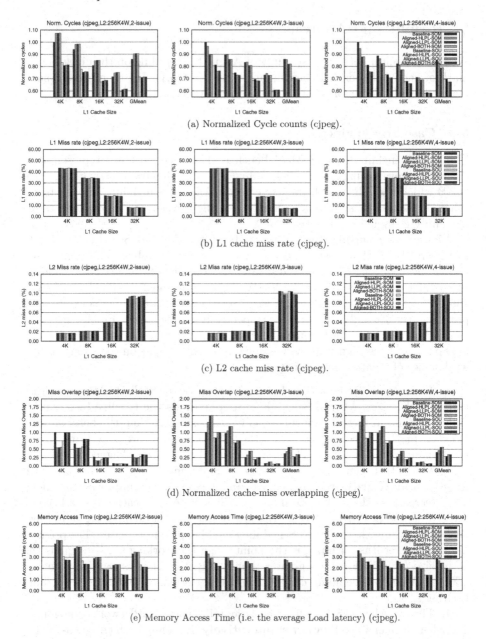

(a) Normalized Cycle counts (cjpeg).

(b) L1 cache miss rate (cjpeg).

(c) L2 cache miss rate (cjpeg).

(d) Normalized cache-miss overlapping (cjpeg).

(e) Memory Access Time (i.e. the average Load latency) (cjpeg).

Fig. 6. Performance of cjpeg for issue widths (2–4 issue) and L1 cache sizes (4K–32K)

of issuing instructions ignoring their priorities outweighs the benefit of doing so. For any issue width higher than 2, Aligned Scheduling improves performance considerably. This is intuitive as the more the issue slots, the more loads can get serviced in parallel, which is exactly what Aligned Scheduling is meant to exploit.

d. An architecture with Stall-On-Use semantics can still benefit from Aligned scheduling, though the performance improvement is less impressive. For small cache sizes, the performance improvement is about 5 %, but as we get close to the working set size, there is little or no improvement. The reason (explained in Sect. 2) is that with SOU semantics there are fewer opportunities to increase the miss overlap, beyond what the hardware provides.

e. A **Miss-Overlap** is the event of multiple cache misses being serviced in parallel. The count of overlapping misses is a measure of the effectiveness of Aligned Scheduling. Figure 6(d) shows that the performance improvements of Fig. 6(a) are indeed caused by the increase in cache overlaps and not some other scheduling side-effect.

f. According to Fig. 6(e), the effective average latency of a Load (**Memory Access Time**) decreases with Aligned scheduling on wide-issue VLIW processors. This proves once more that the performance improvements are due to overcoming the cache bottle-neck.

g. Finally, the L1 and L2 **miss-rate** (Fig. 6(b)) seems to be largely unaffected by the application of Aligned Scheduling. This is because: (i) a miss is still counted as a single miss even if it overlaps with another miss and (ii) Aligned scheduling, does not cause large-scale memory access reordering that could affect the cache behavior. Therefore Aligned Scheduling speedups are not due of fewer misses but rather due to decreasing the total amount of time that the VLIW processor has to wait for the misses to be serviced.

5.2 All Benchmarks

We now consider all benchmarks (Fig. 7). We measured the cycle count, the miss rate on both L1 and L2 caches, the overlapping of cache misses, and the average memory access time. We ran the benchmarks on a 4-issue VLIW processor with 16KB-1way L1 and 256KB-4way L2 cache (see Sect. 4). We focus on the performance of Aligned Scheduling compared to the Baseline Scheduler, all on SOM. We compare them against the Baseline on SOU, which is hardware supported and is therefore an estimate of the best we could expect from Aligned Scheduling, a software-only approach. Aligned-SOM in Fig. 7, is equivalent to Aligned-BOTH-SOM (both HLPL and LLPL enabled).

The results in Fig. 7 show that Aligned Scheduling works for a variety of benchmarks and achieves significant speedups on this architecture configuration. In memory-bound benchmarks (e.g. 181.mcf) it even manages to reach the performance levels of the hardware-based SOU. Aligned Scheduling is successful at increasing the count of misses that overlap, as shown in the Miss-overlap graph of Fig. 7. In some cases (e.g. h263enc), the performance improvement can also be attributed to a lower miss-rate, a side-effect of the instruction re-ordering. Only few benchmarks (197.parser and 300.twolf) have fewer miss overlaps compared to the baseline, but even in these cases the performance achieved is either close to the baseline or better, due to overlapping fewer misses but ones of greater latency, leading to better average memory access time.

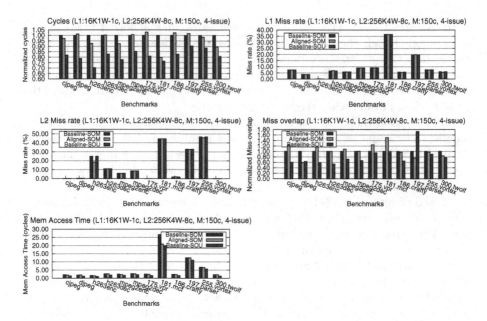

Fig. 7. Cycle count, Miss Rates, Miss overlaps and average Memory Access Time for 6 of the Mediabench II and the SPEC CINT2000 benchmarks.

Some of the benchmarks however are marginally worse than the baseline with 175.vpr on this processor setup, reaching a slowdown of 2.5 %. These slowdowns can be attributed to one of the following: **1.** The small working set of most benchmarks(e.g. it is 16KB for the majority of the Mediabench II [12]). Therefore with the current cache setup Aligned Scheduling has a small headroom to improve the cache behavior. As shown in Sect. 5.1 in Fig. 6(a), Aligned Scheduling can indeed improve performance on such benchmarks as long as the cache sizes are smaller than their working sets. **2.** High sensitivity to the priority of the critical path instructions. In such cases any instruction re-ordering done by Aligned Scheduling can lead to a slowdown (this is true for 186.crafty, 255.vortex and h263dec). In 175.vpr this effect is so strong, that even with substantially increased miss-overlap (more than 20 %), it takes a performance hit. **3.** Inability of Aligned Scheduling to form more effective groups of Load instructions than those formed by the baseline. This happens rarely (see "Miss overlap" in Fig. 7 djpeg,197.parser).

Benchmarks with high miss rates (L1 or L2) usually perform well under Aligned Scheduling. As long as a benchmark has adequate amounts of statically analyzable MLP, and is not very sensitive on its critical path instructions then a high miss rate should provide opportunities for Aligned Scheduling to improve the execution cycles. This is evident in 181.mcf and h263enc. In particular h263enc, has a low L1 miss rate but a high L2 miss rate and gets a performance improvement of about 7%. This suggests that Aligned Scheduling effectively overlaps some of the performance-critical high latency L2 misses, leading to significant performance improvements.

6   Related Work

Non-blocking (also known as lockup-free caches) were introduced by [15] and have been studied in detail since (e.g. [26,28]). Non-blocking caches are a cost-effective optimization and are common in all processors, including VLIW ones. Aligned Scheduling exploits the non-blocking feature to improve performance on VLIW processors.

Instruction scheduling optimized for cache memories has been studied in the past. The majority of the work [7,13,17,19] focuses on improving instruction scheduling for processors with non-blocking caches and stall-on-use execution semantics. Balanced Scheduling [13] proposes a scheduling algorithm for pipelined architectures that makes sure that the processors stalls less upon a cache miss. The main goal of the instruction scheduler is to schedule the right number of instructions after a load, such that, in case of a miss, there are enough independent instructions to execute until the loaded value (that missed) is used by an instruction. Lo et al. [19] improves Balanced Scheduling by applying ILP enhancing optimizations. An extension to Balanced Scheduling is introduced in [17], which proposes using profiling information to drive instruction scheduling so that it makes more informed decisions. Ding et al. [7] proposes a static cache-reuse model that helps the instruction scheduler make informed decisions on the latency of a memory instruction. The paper shows that this produces better schedules than considering all memory instructions as either all-hits or all-misses.

Aligned Scheduling is very different from these approaches. It mainly targets VLIW processors that have Stall-On-Miss execution semantics, enabling them to improve their performance close to that of Stall-On-Use. Therefore the optimization that Aligned Scheduling introduces exploits a completely different architectural feature. There is no indication that any of the schemes that target stall-on-use semantics will consistently outperform our baseline on a stall-on-miss VLIW target, which is why we do not compare against them.

The only work we are aware of that focuses on VLIW processors is Cache Sensitive Modulo Scheduling [25]. It proposes a software-pipeline cyclic scheduling algorithm that improves performance in one of two ways: it either schedules memory instructions early or issues pre-fetch instructions. Both ways lead to fewer cache misses, with the former one proving to be the most effective one. This work is orthogonal to Aligned Scheduling as it focuses on the pre-fetching problem rather than on grouping loads together.

Code optimizations that exploit the non-blocking caches have been proposed in the past. Pai et al. [22] proposes an analysis and transformation framework for optimizations that cluster misses together, leading to significant performance improvements. The scheme involves high-level transformations, usually at loop level. Aligned Scheduling on the other hand, is a scheduling algorithm, performing fine-grain optimization in the compiler back-end.

7   Conclusion

This work proposes Aligned Scheduling, a new scheduling algorithm for VLIW processors that generates schedules that are more resilient to cache misses than the existing schemes. It does so by incorporating the micro-architectural knowledge of non-blocking caches and the absence of load-use interlocks into the scheduling algorithm. Aligned Scheduling exploits the statically known MLP to group together Load instructions on the same cycle. This increases the probability that cache misses overlap and get serviced simultaneously by the non-blocking cache, therefore decreasing the amount of time the processor spends on cache stalls. Our simulation results show that significant speed-ups can be achieved across a wide range of benchmarks and VLIW architecture configurations.

References

1. Gcc: Gnu compiler collection. http://gcc.gnu.org
2. ski IA64 simulator. http://ski.sourceforge.net
3. SPEC benchmark. http://www.spec.org
4. Branover, A., et al.: AMD Fusion APU: Llano. IEEE Micro **32**(2), 28–37 (2012)
5. Dehnert, J., et al.: The Transmeta code morphing software: using speculation, recovery, and adaptive retranslation to address real-life challenges. In: CGO (2003)
6. Dehnert, J., et al.: Compiling for the Cydra. J. Supercomput. **7**, 181–227 (1993)
7. Ding, C., Carr, S., Sweany, P.: Modulo scheduling with cache reuse information. In: Lengauer, C., Griebl, M., Gorlatch, S. (eds.) Euro-Par 1997. LNCS, vol. 1300, pp. 1079–1083. Springer, Heidelberg (1997)
8. Faraboschi, P., et al.: Lx: a technology platform for customizable VLIW embedded processing. In: ISCA (2000)
9. Fisher, J.: Trace scheduling: a technique for global microcode compaction. IEEE Trans. Comput. **30**(7), 478–490 (1981)
10. Fisher, J.A., Faraboschi, P., Young, C.: VLIW processors. In: Padua, D. (ed.) Encyclopedia of Parallel Computing, pp. 2135–2142. Springer, Heidelberg (2011)
11. Fridman, J., Greenfield, Z.: The TigerSHARC DSP architecture. IEEE Micro **20**(1), 66–176 (2000)
12. Fritts, J., et al.: Mediabench II video: expediting the next generation of video systems research. In: SPIE (2005)
13. Kerns, D., Eggers, S.: Balanced scheduling: instruction scheduling when memory latency is uncertain. In: PLDI (1993)
14. Klaiber, A., et al.: The technology behind Crusoe processors. Transmeta Corporation White Paper (2000)
15. Kroft, D.: Lockup-free instruction fetch/prefetch cache organization. In: ISCA (1981)
16. Lam, M.: Software pipelining: an effective scheduling technique for VLIW machines. In: PLDI (1988)
17. Lindenmaier, G., McKinley, K.S., Temam, O.: Load scheduling with profile information. In: Bode, A., Ludwig, T., Karl, W.C., Wismüller, R. (eds.) Euro-Par 2000. LNCS, vol. 1900, pp. 223–233. Springer, Heidelberg (2000)
18. Llosa, J.: Swing modulo scheduling: a lifetime-sensitive approach. In: PACT (1996)
19. Lo, J., et al.: Improving balanced scheduling with compiler optimizations that increase instruction-level parallelism. In: PLDI (1995)

20. McNairy, C., et al.: Itanium 2 processor microarchitecture. IEEE Micro **23**(2), 44–55 (2003)
21. Moon, S., et al.: An efficient resource-constrained global scheduling technique for superscalar and VLIW processors. In: MICRO (1992)
22. Pai, V., et al.: Code transformations to improve memory parallelism. In: MICRO (1999)
23. Pechanek, G., Vassiliadis, S.: The ManArrayTM embedded processor architecture. In: Euromicro (2000)
24. Rau, B., Glaeser, C.: Some scheduling techniques and an easily schedulable horizontal architecture for high performance scientific computing. In: Workshop on Microprogramming (1981)
25. Sánchez, F., González, A.: Cache sensitive modulo scheduling. In: MICRO (1997)
26. Scheurich, C., et al.: Lockup-free caches in high-performance multiprocessors. J. Parallel Distrib. Syst. **11**(1), 25–36 (1991)
27. Sharangpanim, H., et al.: Itanium processor microarchitecture. IEEE Micro **20**(5), 24–43 (2000)
28. Sohi, G., Franklin, M.: High-bandwidth data memory systems for superscalar processors. In: ASPLOS (1991)

Compile Time Modeling of Off-Chip Memory Bandwidth for Parallel Loops

Munara Tolubaeva[✉], Yonghong Yan, and Barbara Chapman

Computer Science Department, University of Houston, Houston, Texas, USA
durriyekta@live.com
http://www2.cs.uh.edu/~hpctools

Abstract. In this paper, we present a statistical model to predict the off-chip memory bandwidth required by a parallel loop during its execution. It is a compile-time modeling technique that derives the correlations between memory bandwidth requirement and data access patterns of multithreaded applications. This model could be used by the compiler and performance tools to predict when the sustainable memory bandwidth of the system will be reached by the application during execution, and to determine an optimal number of threads that should be configured to execute a specific parallel loop according to its memory reference patterns. Awareness of the performance impact of oversubscribed memory bandwidth can also help programmers to take into account the additional latency caused by the contention, and to minimize the overhead by tuning the memory access behavior of applications. We evaluated this model in terms of both technical accuracy and prediction accuracy by comparing the modeling results with the measured results. The evaluation demonstrates its accuracy in both system bandwidth modeling and application bandwidth modeling.

Keywords: Off-chip memory bandwidth · Performance modeling · Parallel loops · Contentions

1 Introduction

Multicore and multiprocessor systems are designed to allow clusters of cores to share various hardware resources such as caches, memory bandwidth and interconnects. Efficient use of these resources requires both to maximize the sharing of these resources among concurrent threads, and also to minimize the contentions and conflicts of using them. Software tools including compiler and runtime systems play a very important role in optimizing and scheduling an application with regards to the resource sharing and usage conflicts.

There has been a large amount of previous work that focus on increasing the sharing of resources by runtime co-scheduling with the help of compiler optimizations [6–8,15]. However, with the increase of the number of cores in a system, and the increasing depth of memory hierarchy that comes with higher

© Springer International Publishing Switzerland 2014
C. Cașcaval and P. Montesinos (Eds.): LCPC 2013, LNCS 8664, pp. 292–306, 2014.
DOI: 10.1007/978-3-319-09967-5_17

non-uniformity of memory access, the inter-core resource conflict and contention increase as well. Reducing the conflict use of shared resources becomes critical when dealing with parallel applications on multicore and parallel systems. It is very important that an application does not demand resources more than the architecture can supply. If this is the case, the application may unnecessarily stall due to unavailability (contention) of some resources.

Off-chip memory bus is a shared resource that is commonly used among different cores on the same processor. Increasing the number of cores for a parallel application may not necessarily increase the performance of the application if the application requires more data than the memory bus can transfer at a time. High contention for memory bandwidth may even cause a significant performance degradation in parallel applications [12,21]. This situation is often referred to as memory bandwidth bottleneck [7].

In this paper we present an off-chip memory bandwidth model developed to estimate the bandwidth requirement of a parallel loop at runtime. This mechanism uses statistical polynomial curve fitting technique on a set of bandwidth measuring data to derive the model that can be applied to other applications. The main support for our model is provided by a compiler analysis to estimate the number of memory accesses that would result in a cache miss. This paper makes the following contributions:

- We introduce a modified STREAM kernel that is used with the curve fitting technique to derive the statistical memory bandwidth model for a particular system with regards to the parallelism and concurrent cache misses.
- We propose a compile-time statistical model that can be used to predict the memory bandwidth requirement of parallel loops when being executed with specific number of threads.

The model can serve as a cost model to determine an optimal configuration of concurrent memory accesses and the number of threads to run a memory-intensive loop with in order to prevent the memory bandwidth bottleneck. Knowing maximum number of concurrent memory accesses per thread would help programmers, compilers as well as performance tuning tools to evaluate the benefits of certain level of compiler optimizations. Knowing the memory bandwidth performance with respect to the number of threads would also help in deciding the best configuration of threads to run the application with.

The rest of the paper is organized as follows: Sect. 2 describes our experiments performed for memory bandwidth analysis. Section 3 presents our statistical model derived from the bandwidth analysis step. Section 4 details the evaluation setup for our model and presents the experimental results. Related work is described in Sect. 5. Finally, Sect. 6 concludes the paper and suggests directions for future research.

2   Memory Bandwidth Analysis

Computer vendors often provide a theoretical (peak) bandwidth of the memory system of a machine, and practically, the sustainable bandwidth is used to

```
double a[N]; double b[N]; double c[N];
T1 = tick()
#pragma omp parallel for
for (i=0; i<N; i++) {
    a[i] = b[i] + q*c[i];
}
T2 = tock()
```

Fig. 1. Original STREAM Triad kernel

```
double a[N][100]; double b[N][100]; double c[N][100];
T1 = tick()
#pragma omp parallel for
for (i=0;i<N;i++) {
  a[i][0] = b[i][0] + q*c[i][0];
}
T2 = tock()
```

Fig. 2. Our Version of STREAM Triad kernel

represent performance of a memory system. The sustainable bandwidth could be determined by performing benchmarking experiments with varied number of threads and number of memory accesses, for example, the Triad kernel from STREAM benchmark [14] shown in Fig. 1. The sustainable memory bandwidth is computed using the Eq. 1 where $T_2 - T_1$ is the time it takes to run the kernel.

$$Bandwidth = \frac{Data_{transferred}}{T_2 - T_1} \tag{1}$$

The sustainable memory bandwidth represents the maximum bandwidth of the memory system that is available to applications. However, an application often exhibits different memory bandwidths during its execution within the sustainable bandwidth. To create a model for measuring the application memory bandwidth, we slightly modified the STREAM Triad kernel to allow us to control the number of memory accesses, as shown in Fig. 2. Let us assume that the default cache line size is 64 bytes. Figure 2 shows that three array references of each iteration of the parallel loop will result in three cache misses, referred to as *concurrent cache misses* of each thread. Then in the Eq. 1, the total amount of data transferred would be equal to $N * \#ofconcurrentmisses * cachelinesize$. Unlike the original Triad kernel, using the *concurrent cache misses* approach, we are able to co-relate the required memory bandwidth to the number of cache misses happened in one iteration of the loop by each thread. This is an important parameter that reflects the data access pattern of arrays in the loop. Programmers can change the access pattern of the loop body, thus to exhibit different memory bandwidth requested. In our example, in order to increase the number of concurrent cache misses per iteration, one needs to duplicate the statement in the block and change the array indices as in Fig. 3.

Using the modified Triad kernel in Fig. 3, we measured the memory bandwidth with regards to the number of threads and the number of concurrent cache

```
double a[N][100]; double b[N][100]; double c[N][100];
#pragma omp parallel for
for (i=0;i<N;i++) {
  a[i][0] = b[i][0] + q*c[i][0];
  a[i][16] = b[i][16] + q*c[i][16];
  a[i][32] = b[i][32] + q*c[i][32];
  ...
}
```

Fig. 3. The STREAM Triad kernel with increased number of concurrent cache misses

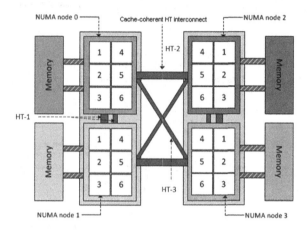

Fig. 4. Crill system architecture

misses, and also studied the effect of data and thread placement on the overall bandwidth performance. All experiments were performed on a Non-Uniform Memory Access (NUMA) system, named Crill, whose architecture is shown in Fig. 4. The Crill system has two 2.2 GHz 12-core AMD Opteron processors, where each processor has two 6-core CPU chips. The four CPU chips are interconnected through cache-coherent HyperTransport (HT) links, HT_1, HT_2 and HT_3. The three HT links differ in size: $HT_3 = \frac{HT_2}{2} = \frac{HT_1}{3}$ where HT_3, HT_2 and HT_1 links connect $node0$ to $node3$, $node0$ to $node2$ and $node0$ to $node1$, respectively.

Figure 5a shows the memory bandwidth achieved via local memory channel when threads access the data located on the same NUMA node. Figures 5b, 6a and b show the bandwidth performance achieved via each of the three HT links, i.e. when threads access the data located on another node of the NUMA system. The bandwidth performance results are represented with respect to the number of threads executed the loop and the number of concurrent cache misses occurred per iteration of the loop.

These experimental results showed that, in general, the maximum memory bandwidth can be reached quite easily with a small number of threads and a small number of concurrent cache misses. When this happens, increasing the number of threads and/or the number of concurrent cache misses won't necessarily increase the memory performance, but perhaps degrade the performance due

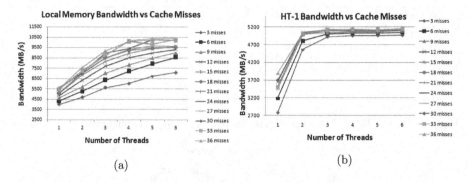

(a)   (b)

Fig. 5. Bandwidth achieved, on Crill architecture, through (a) local memory and (b) HT-1 links for different number of threads and cache misses.

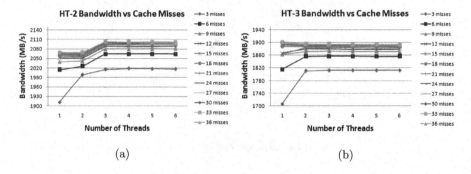

(a)   (b)

Fig. 6. Bandwidth achieved, on Crill architecture, through (a) HT-2 and (b) HT-3 links for different number of threads and cache misses.

to the resource contention. Therefore, knowing when the sustainable memory bandwidth is reached when executing a parallel loop under specific configurations (number of threads and memory accesses in our example) would be helpful for programmers, compilers, performance tuning tools to determine an optimal configuration of execution, thus improving the resource utilizations.

3   Memory Bandwidth Model

The experimental data obtained from benchmarking our modified Triad kernel allows us to correlate the parallelism (number of threads) and the data access patterns (concurrent cache misses) to the memory bandwidth required at a particular point of execution of an application. Using those data, we are able to derive a memory bandwidth model that accurately represents such correlation. Our proposed bandwidth model is based on a *polynomial curve fitting technique* [5]. In this approach, the results of our bandwidth experiments are considered as a collection of data that can be represented as a function or a curve of interest.

Using the curve fitting technique, we generate the best fit function of bandwidth to the input experimental data. Let τ represent the number of threads executing the loop and μ represent the number of concurrent cache misses occurring per iteration of the loop. Using the curve fitting technique, we determine the polynomial coefficients P of the curve.

$$f_\tau(\mu) = p_1\mu^n + p_2\mu^{n-1} + \ldots + p_n\mu + p_{n+1} \tag{2}$$

Given $P = \{p_1, p_2 \ldots p_{n+1}\}$ where n refers to the polynomial degree, in our case $n = 5$, our model can predict the required memory bandwidth f_τ for given number of threads and the number of concurrent cache misses using Eq. 2.

For a given computer system, by performing the experimental analysis using kernels in Fig. 3 and then applying the curve fitting technique, we can obtain a separate function that becomes a bandwidth model of the system. Using the generated model in a compiler, we can predict the maximum sustainable bandwidth that an OpenMP loop can achieve for the given system.

The techniques we used made the following assumptions:

- Memory access dominates the execution time of the loop body, thus the time spent to perform other instructions are neglected in this model. Since memory access latencies are normally in hundreds of CPU cycles, this assumption is valid for scientific kernels that exhibit up to moderate computation intensity.
- When relying on compiler analysis to obtain the concurrent cache misses for a given loop, we assume the cache line size is 64 bytes and array variables used inside the loop are declared cache aligned.
- The cache is fully associative. Set associative caches are complicated due to the reason that knowing the corresponding line in a set an array reference will be placed at compile time is very challenging. Moreover, assuming the fully associative caches is mostly valid for high level associative caches [17].

We have also observed that the memory bandwidth does not depend on the number of iterations of the loop due to the Equation in 3.

$$BW = \frac{data}{time} = \frac{total_{iterations} \times bytes_{periteration}}{time_{periteration} \times \frac{total_{iterations}}{\#threads}} = \frac{\#threads \times bytes_{periteration}}{time_{periteration}}$$
$$\tag{3}$$

The Eq. (3) in fact shows that the bandwidth depends solely on the number of threads, and the amount of data being transferred in one iteration as well as the time spent to execute one iteration of the loop. According to the equation, the sustainable bandwidth is not related to the number of iterations of a loop. We conducted a set of experiments to validate whether this assumption is satisfied in practice i.e. whether the memory bandwidth performance is really dependent on the number of iterations or not. The experimental results given in Table 1 show that our theoretical assumption is correct. Therefore the loop boundaries are not used as an input to our model, however they are used in determining the number of concurrent cache misses that happen per iteration.

The model predicts the bandwidth performance for one loop iteration i.e. the results are obtained for a specific iteration at a time. Accurately predicting an

Table 1. Bandwidth versus I * J number of iterations

I (M = 10^6, K = 10^3)	J	Bandwidth (GB/s)
1.4 M	100	12.7
1.4 M	200	12.9
1.2 M	100	12.7
1.2 M	200	12.9
1 M	100	12.5
1M	200	12.9
800 K	100	12.9
800 K	200	12.9
600 K	100	12.6
600 K	200	12.7
400 K	100	12.9
400 K	200	12.7

average bandwidth performance for all iterations combined is very challenging if there is large divergence of the behaviors of the loop body. Instead by evaluating iterations one-by-one, our model identifies the specific iterations where the bandwidth performance may change drastically, and outputs the predictions for these identified iterations only.

For a given OpenMP parallel loop, the concurrent cache misses are obtained through compiler analysis. A separate compiler pass was implemented in Open64 compiler's LNO phase [1] that is applied to the intermediate representation of the source code to collect information about the loop and its memory references. The loop itself supplies information such as loop boundaries, step sizes, index variables and array references with regards to the index variables. The OpenMP parallel and for directives have clauses (by default or user specified) such as scheduling policy and chunk sizes to guide a compiler analysis and transformation when parallelizing the loop among a given number of threads. The *chunk size* is the number of iterations of the loop distributed to each thread. In cases when the loop boundaries are not known at compile time, our model evaluates iterations in one full scheduling step only. One full scheduling step contains a set of iterations distributed to each thread in one scheduling cycle.

After the compiler collects all the necessary information about the loop, the # of concurrent cache misses happening per iteration is determined using an analysis that was implemented in [19]. The method of determining the # of concurrent cache misses at each iteration is performed as follows:

1. Compiler gathers details about each array reference such as array base name, index variables, access type (read/write), and stores them in an *array reference list*.
2. Using the array reference list and each new value of loop indices, the compiler then generates a list of cache lines separate for each thread that will be

accessed by the corresponding thread at specific iteration. This list, referred
to *cache line ownership list*, contains details about which cache line is being
read or written by a thread at that specific iteration. We can generate the
list by assuming that all array variables used inside the loop are aligned with
the cache line boundary. Compiler analysis in our model supports only static
scheduling policy allowing us to generate the cache line ownership list at
compile time. In static scheduling policy, the number of iterations are evenly
distributed to each thread and the scheduling order is determined by the
policy.

3. The compiler then generates a *cache state* for each thread separately. The
cache states store the current state of each thread's private cache. The cache
states are updated everytime when a new cache line ownership list is generated
(from the previous step). At the last step, the compiler applies a stack distance
analysis [18] on the cache states, and determines which recently accessed cache
lines are a cache miss or a hit.

4   Evaluation of Memory Bandwidth Model

Our model is evaluated in terms of both technical accuracy and prediction accuracy. To demonstrate the technical accuracy, we compared the measured and
the modeled bandwidth results obtained from the Triad kernel experiments.
Figures 7 and 8 show the comparison of both the measured and the modeled
bandwidths for different # of concurrent cache misses. The number of threads
used in this experiment is 4. One can see that the curve fitting technique used
in the model is very accurate, thus making the technical accuracy of the model
very high.

To demonstrate the prediction accuracy, we evaluated our model using
OpenMP parallel loops from several widely known applications including Jacobi
method [4], Scalar Penta-diagonal solver (SP) and Multigrid kernel (MG) from

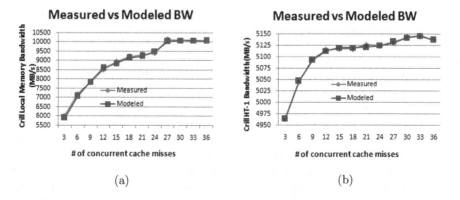

(a)   (b)

Fig. 7. Comparison of measured and modeled bandwidths for STREAM Triad kernel
via (a) local memory and (b) HT-1 links on Crill architecture.

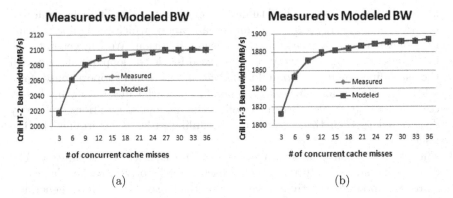

Fig. 8. Comparison of measured and modeled bandwidths for STREAM Triad kernel via (a) HT-2 and (b) HT-3 links on Crill architecture.

NAS benchmarks [3]. We compared the measured bandwidth results obtained by running the applications against the estimated bandwidth by our model. Our model predicts bandwidth only for certain iterations of the loop. It is very challenging to accurately predict the bandwidth utilization for the whole execution time period of the loop at compile time. This is because the bandwidth utilization can change throughout the execution of the loop. Therefore, the model does not estimate the average bandwidth utilization, instead it estimates the bandwidth for specific iterations at a time.

The Jacobi kernel is a doubly nested OpenMP loop, hence the number of cache misses per iteration varies based on the iteration being executed. Let (i,j) be a notation to represent an iteration where the outer and inner loops' indices are i and j, respectively. For the Jacobi loop, at the very first iteration (1,1),considered that a cache line size is 64 bytes and array elements are of size 8 bytes, four concurrent cache misses will occur. For period of (1,2)–(1,7) iterations, there will not be any cache misses. At (1,8) or any (1,m) iteration, where m is a multiple of 8, there will be four cache misses again. This pattern is continued till the loop reaches (2,1) or any (*,1) iteration. At each iteration our model re-analyzes the number of concurrent cache misses based on the current cache states of each thread. As one can see, in Jacobi kernel, not all iterations cause cache misses to happen, thus not all of the iterations require back and forth memory accesses. Therefore, it would be technically incorrect to estimate the memory bandwidth performance for all the iterations as a whole. Instead, our model estimates the bandwidth performance for specific iterations such as (1,1), (1,2), (1,8) etc. where the # of concurrent cache misses change, hence the bandwidth performance changes. Moreover, since (1,1) and (1,8) incur the same # of concurrent cache misses, we consider only one of them and eliminate the other. Iteration (1,2) does not incur any cache misses, thus the model does not perform any bandwidth predictions. In this way, our model estimates the bandwidth performance for (1,1) iteration only which is depicted in Figs. 9 and 10.

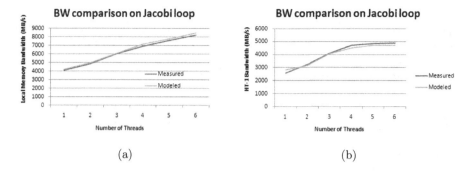

Fig. 9. Comparison of measured and modeled bandwidths for Jacobi kernel via (a) local memory and (b) HT-1 links on Crill architecture.

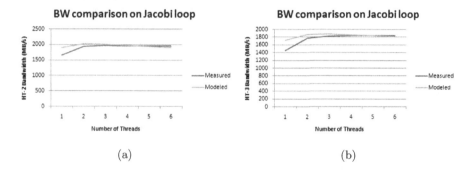

Fig. 10. Comparison of measured and modeled bandwidths for Jacobi kernel via (a) HT-2 and (b) HT-3 links on Crill architecture.

Figures 9, 10, 11, 12, 13, and 14 show the comparison between the modeled bandwidth estimations and the measured bandwidth values obtained from using different memory links for the Jacobi, MG and SP kernels respectively. The Jacobi kernel exhibits 4 cache misses at iterations (1,1), (1,8), (1,16), ..., (2,1), (2,8) and so on (as discussed earlier), so the modeled bandwidth performance results in Figs. 9 and 10 are obtained for 4 concurrent cache misses. Figures 11, 12, 13, and 14 show the modeled bandwidth performance results obtained for 7 and 2 concurrent cache misses, respectively.

Using our bandwidth prediction model, programmers, compilers, performance analyzing or tuning tools will be able to know the loop's bandwidth utilization levels at various iterations at compile time. This information would be useful in preventing the memory bandwidth bottleneck by decreasing the number of memory references performed in the loop block, or by executing the loop with fewer number of threads.

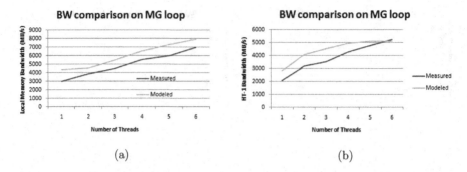

(a)   (b)

Fig. 11. Comparison of measured and modeled bandwidths for a kernel from MG benchmark via (a) local memory and (b) HT-1 links on Crill architecture.

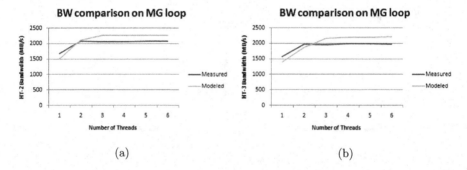

(a)   (b)

Fig. 12. Comparison of measured and modeled bandwidths for a kernel from MG benchmark via (a) HT-2 and (b) HT-3 links on Crill architecture.

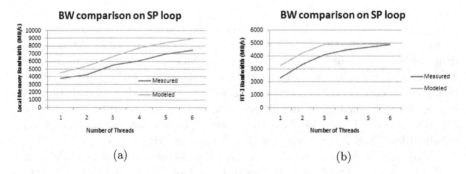

(a)   (b)

Fig. 13. Comparison of measured and modeled bandwidths for a kernel from SP benchmark via (a) local memory and (b) HT-1 links on Crill architecture.

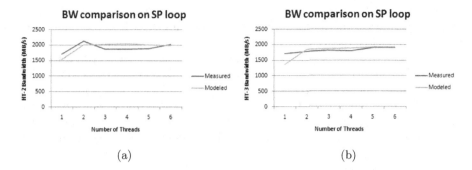

Fig. 14. Comparison of measured and modeled bandwidths for a kernel from SP benchmark via (a) HT-2 and (b) HT-3 links on Crill architecture.

5 Related Work

The topic of improving the efficiency of memory bandwidth has been studied quite extensively in the literature. Reducing the memory bandwidth of applications has been studied in [2,7,13]. Compiler optimizations/techniques such as loop fusion, store elimination, storage reduction are one of the methods that are referred in those works for reducing the memory bandwidth pressure to the system. Techniques to improve overall system performance, such as optimal memory bandwidth partitioning techniques, have also been studied in [10,16,20].

Closely related work on modeling the off-chip memory bandwidth analytically or statistically has been performed in [9,11,12,21]. Authors of [12] have used pChase benchmark to perform experimental multi-socket, multicore memory bandwidth study, using which they developed an analytical memory bandwidth model. The model characterizes memory bandwidth performance at three levels which are bandwidth per core, socket and node levels. The authors compared the experimental results obtained from the pChase benchmark against the modeled results for several multi-socket, multicore architectures. Their goal was to model bandwidth performance for various architectures by generating a model using the pChase benchmark and comparing the model against the pChase benchmarking results for different architectures. In our paper we aim at modeling bandwidth performance for various loop kernels by generating a model based on the STREAM benchmark and predicting the bandwidth performance based on a loop signature (# of threads and # of concurrent cache misses).

Authors of [11] analyzed the effect of memory controllers on a local and remote memory bandwidth performance, and developed a model to evaluate the performance of on-chip and cross-chip interconnect of a multicore processor. Their model predicts the memory bandwidth performance based on the number of processes running on local and remote nodes. Authors showed that in some cases, accessing data via the cross-chip interconnect may be more advantageous than accessing it from the local node in terms of the bandwidth usage. Our paper at this time does not consider cases when the data is accessed both locally and remotely. Nevertheless, we are planning to work on the idea in the near future.

Authors of [21] proposed a performance model for OpenMP, MPI and hybrid applications based on the memory bandwidth contention and communication time. The model predicts the execution time of an application. Authors first measured the memory bandwidth for one and two cores using the STREAM benchmark. Using the performance data obtained from one and two cores, referred as baseline values, the model predicts the execution time of an application on higher number of cores. Their model, essentially, relies on the memory bandwidth ratio of higher cores to baseline values. However, we believe that the memory bandwidth ratio does not increase linearly as the number of active cores increases. Therefore, our model does not rely on initial baseline values when predicting for higher number of cores.

In [9] an analytic model to estimate the optimal cache size and the memory bandwidth for many-core based systems is proposed. The model is used to estimate the lower-level memory bandwidth given the upper-level cache size and the statistical behavior of a program. The model uses central limit theorem and the stochastic behavior of cache misses that is generated using traces during simulation.

6   Conclusions and Future Work

In this paper, we presented our compile time off-chip memory bandwidth model and discussed how the defined model can be used to estimate the bandwidth performance of OpenMP parallel loops. We used the statistical polynomial curve fitting technique on a set of bandwidth measuring data obtained through experiments by the modified STREAM benchmark. This model could be used by the compiler and performance tools to predict when the sustainable memory bandwidth of the system will be reached by the application during execution, and to determine an optimal number of threads that should be configured to execute a specific parallel loop according to its memory reference pattern. To evaluate our memory bandwidth model, we compared the measured and the modeled bandwidth performance results for several common-used OpenMP kernels such as Jacobi, MG and SP from NAS benchmarks. Our experimental results show that this model can be used for accurately estimating the memory bandwidth performance at compile time. Our ongoing and future work include the enhancement of this model to consider more factors that impact the memory performance, such as hardware data prefetching. We also plan to develop a performance model focusing on the impact of resource sharing and contention for parallel applications.

Acknowledgement. This work was supported in part by the National Science Foundations Computer Systems Research program under Award No. CCF-0833201 and Department of Energy under Award Agreement No. DE-FC02-12ER26099. The evaluation platform used for this work was supported by the National Science Foundation's Computer Systems Research program under Award No. CNS-0833201 and CRI-0958464.

References

1. The Open64 compiler. http://open64.sourceforge.net
2. Agarwal, D., Liu, W., Yeung, D.: Exploiting application-level information to reduce memory bandwidth consumption. In: Proceedings of 4th Workshop on Complexity-Effective Design (2003)
3. Bailey, D.H., Barszcz, E., Barton, J.T., Browning, D.S., Carter, R.L., Dagum, D., Fatoohi, R.A., Frederickson, P.O., Lasinski, T.A., Schreiber, R.S., Simon, H.D., Venkatakrishnan, V., Weeratunga, S.K.: The NAS parallel benchmarks. Int. J. Supercomput. Appl. 5(3), 63–73 (1991)
4. Black, N., Moore, S., Weisstein, E.W.: Jacobi method. http://mathworld.wolfram.com/JacobiMethod.html
5. Coope, I.D.: Circle fitting by linear and nonlinear least squares. J. Optim. Theor. Appl. 76(2), 381–388 (1993)
6. Ding, C., Kennedy, K.: Improving cache performance in dynamic applications through data and computation reorganization at run time. In: Proceedings of the ACM SIGPLAN Conference on Programming Language Design and Implementation, pp. 229–241 (1999)
7. Ding, C. Kennedy, K.: The memory bandwidth bottleneck and its amelioration by a compiler. In: Proceedings of the 14th International Symposium on Parallel and Distributed Processing (2000)
8. Jeremiassen, T., Eggers, S.J.: Reducing false sharing on shared memory multiprocessors through compile time data transformations. In: Proceedings of the Fifth ACM SIGPLAN Symposium on Principles and Practice of Parallel Programming, pp. 179–188 (1994)
9. Lee, H.-J., Cho, W.-C., Chung, E.-Y.: Analytical memory bandwidth model for many-core processor based systems. IEICE Electron. Express 9(18), 1461–1466 (2012)
10. Liu, F., Jiang, X., Solihin, Y.: Understanding how off-chip memory bandwidth partitioning in chip multiprocessors affects system performance. In: Proceedings of High Performance Computer Architecture (HPCA), pp. 1–12 (2010)
11. Majo, Z., Gross, T.R.: Memory system performance in a numa multicore multiprocessor. In Proceedings of the 4th Annual International Conference on Systems and Storage (SYSTOR), pp. 12:1–12:10 (2011)
12. Mandal, A., Fowler, R., Porterfield. Modeling memory concurrency for multi-socket multi-core systems. In: ISPASS, pp. 66–75 (2010)
13. Marchal, P., Gómez, J.I., Catthoor, F.: Optimizing the memory bandwidth with loop fusion. In: Proceedings of the 2nd IEEE/ACM/IFIP International Conference on Hardware/Software Codesign and System Synthesis, pp. 188–193 (2004)
14. McCalpin, J.D.: Memory bandwidth and machine balance in current high performance computers. In: IEEE Computer Society Technical Committee on Computer Architecture (TCCA) Newsletter, pp. 19–25 (1995)
15. McKinley, K.S., Carr, S., Tseng, C.-W.: Improving data locality with loop transformations. ACM Trans. Program. Lang. Syst. 18(4), 424–453 (1996)
16. Mohideen, R.M., Sankaranarayanan, V.: An analytical model for optimum off-chip memory bandwidth partitioning in multicore architectures. In: Proceedings of the 2nd International Conference on Computer Science and Information Technology (ICCSIT) (2012)

17. Sandberg, A., Eklov, D., Hagersten, E.: Reducing cache pollution through detection and elimination of non-temporal memory accesses. In: Proceedings of the International Conference for High Performance Computing, Networking, Storage and Analysis, pp. 1–11 (2010)
18. Schuff, D., Parsons, B., Pai, V.: Multicore-aware reuse distance analysis. In: IPDPS Workshop on Performance Modeling, Evaluation, and Optimization of Ubiquitous Computing and Networked Systems (2010)
19. Tolubaeva, M., Yan, Y., Chapman, B.: Compile-time detection of false sharing via loop cost modeling. In: Parallel and Distributed Processing Symposium Workshops (IPDPSW), pp. 557–566 (2012)
20. Wang, R., Chen, L., Pinkston, T.M.: An analytical performance model for partitioning off-chip memory bandwidth. In: Proceedings of the IPDPS (2013)
21. Wu, X., Taylor, V.E.: Performance modeling of hybrid mpi/openmp scientific applications on large-scale multicore cluster systems. In: CSE, pp. 181–190 (2011)

Compiler Optimizations for Non-contiguous Remote Data Movement

Timo Schneider[1], Robert Gerstenberger[2], and Torsten Hoefler[1]($\boxtimes$)

[1] Department of Computer Science, ETH Zurich, Zurich, Switzerland
{timos,htor}@inf.ethz.ch
[2] Technische Universität Chemnitz, Chemnitz, Germany
gerro@hrz.tu-chemnitz.de

Abstract. Remote Memory Access (RMA) programming is one of the core concepts behind modern parallel programming languages such as UPC and Fortran 2008 or high-performance libraries such as MPI-3 One Sided or SHMEM. Many applications have to communicate non-contiguous data due to their data layout in main memory. Previous studies showed that such non-contiguous transfers can reduce communication performance by up to an order of magnitude. In this work, we demonstrate a simple scheme for statically optimizing non-contiguous RMA transfers by combining partial packing, communication overlap, and remote access pipelining. We determine accurate performance models for the various operations to find near-optimal pipeline parameters. The proposed approach is applicable to all RMA languages and does not depend on the availability of special hardware features such as scatter-gather lists or strided copies. We show that our proposed superpipelining leads to significant improvements compared to either full packing or sending each contiguous segment individually. We outline how our approach can be used to optimize non-contiguous data transfers in PGAS programs automatically. We observed a 37 % performance gain over the fastest of either packing or individual sending for a realistic application.

1 Introduction

Communication of non-contiguous data is of utmost importance for real application performance. The traditional approach, called "packing" is to copy non-contiguous data into a single contiguous buffer that is then communicated over the network. This practice originated in times where the network was orders of magnitude slower than local processing and copying. However, today, local copies (read and write from/to main memory on one machine) are only slightly faster than remote copies using remote direct memory access (RDMA) over high-performance interconnects (that offer read from main memory at the source machine and write to main memory at the target machine).

The significance of RDMA networking goes beyond the higher bandwidth. It also motivates new Remote Memory Access (RMA) programming models (e.g., UPC [21], Fortran 2008 Coarrays [14], or MPI-3 One Sided [13]) that allow full

© Springer International Publishing Switzerland 2014
C. Cașcaval and P. Montesinos (Eds.): LCPC 2013, LNCS 8664, pp. 307–321, 2014.
DOI: 10.1007/978-3-319-09967-5_18

exploitation of the new hardware. RMA programming exposes the direct memory access to the user who can issue remote memory writes and reads directly. In addition, such RMA programs are easier to analyze by compilers than message passing programs because the complex message matching problem [4] does not apply (each remote access specifies the target buffer explicitly). This motivates us to explore automatic optimizations, such as pipelining and partial packing, for remote memory accesses.

We now demonstrate a typical parallel application using a simple two-dimensional Laplacian stencil example. The serial version iterates over a two-dimensional array and computes the value of each point from the old value at that point and the old value at the neighboring points (aka. "five-point stencil"). A two-dimensional decomposition for distributed memory parallelism requires communication at the boundaries of each process. Depending on the array layout in memory, one or more directions of communication will access non-contiguous data.

For example, if matrices are stored in row-major order, then data exchanged in the north-south direction is *contiguous* in local memory, while data exchanged in east-west direction is *non-contiguous*. More formally, we can describe any transfer of k Bytes (in total) as a set of k pairs (s_i, d_i) where $1 \leq i \leq k$. Each pair describes a single Byte of the transfer, which is copied from the address s_i at the sender to d_i at the receiver. Without changing the semantics of the transfer, we can sort the pairs, using s_i as a key in ascending order. A transfer is contiguous if $(\forall i \in \{1, \ldots, k\} : s_i = d_i + s_1 - d_1) \land (\forall i \in \{1, \ldots, k-1\} : s_i = s_{i+1} - 1)$, otherwise, it is non-contiguous.

Programmers often pack data for all communication directions in order to retain easy maintainability and portability of their code. The following listing shows pseudo-code for the communication part of the Laplacian stencil application:

```
 1  for(int iters=0; iters<niters; iters++) {
       compute_2d_stencil(array, ...);
 3     // swap arrays (omitted for brevity)
       for(int i=0; i<bsize; ++i) sbufnorth[i] = array[i+1,1];
 5     // ... omitted south, east, and west pack loops
       RMA_Put(sbufnorth, rbufnorth, bsize, north);
 7     // ... omitted south, east, and west communications
       RMA_Fence();
 9     for(int i=0; i<bsize; ++i) array[i+1,0] = rbufnorth[i];
       // ... omitted south, east, and west unpack loops
11  }
```

The loop at line 4 exemplifies the packing of data from the array (potentially non-contiguous) into sbufnorth, a contiguous buffer. The contiguous buffer is then communicated at line 6 (RMA_Put represents the language-specific remote write, e.g., assignment to a shared pointer in UPC). The call to RMA_Fence represents the language-specific synchronization method (e.g., upc_fence).

As mentioned before, similar packing loops can be found in most parallel distributed memory applications, for example WRF [20], MILC [3], NAS LU, MG, SP and BT [22], and SPECFEM3D_GLOBE [6]. In the following we will not differentiate between packing and unpacking as they are symmetric—with "packing" we refer to both packing and unpacking.

If copy overheads (in time and energy) have to be avoided, then one could simply issue all the contiguous pieces using a separate transfer for each. This is exemplified in the following pseudo-code for the same Laplacian application:

```
1  for(int iter=0; iter<niters; ++iter) {
     compute_2d_stencil(array, ...);
3    // swap arrays (omitted for brevity)
     for (int i=0; i<bsize; i++) {
5      RMA_Put(array[i+1, 1], array[i+1, 0], size, north);
       // ... omitted south, east, and west communications
7    }
     RMA_Fence();
9  }
```

Instead of packing the array using a pack loop, all consecutive blocks are sent separately in the loops around lines 4 and following. We call this approach *maximal block* communication. However, sending many small pieces (e.g., a single floating point number in our example) can be very inefficient due to fixed overheads for each transfer.

In this work, we demonstrate how *partial packing* combined with (super) pipelining can improve the communication performance of many scientific codes significantly. Figure 1 provides a high-level overview.

Explicit Datatype Specification. Some programming environments offer high-level abstractions for specifying non-contiguous data accesses. MPI, for example, allows the specification of datatypes that simplify and optimize non-contiguous communications. We have shown in a previous study that runtime compilation techniques can speed up the packing of MPI DDTs by a factor of seven [19], and therefore make it competitive with manual packing. The proposed techniques in this work automatically overlap packing and communication to enable further

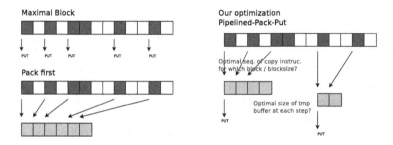

Fig. 1. Methods for sending non-contiguous data in one-sided programming models.

optimization. In addition, most RMA programming models do not support explicit datatype specifications making our technique necessary for optimizations.

Even if explicit datatype specification is offered, users tend to utilize pack loops [18]. One can go as far and argue that explicit data-access declarations are not necessary because copy loops and other communication constructs can be easily identified using static analysis and transformed into more efficient representations. For example, Kjolstad et al. demonstrated a simple static analysis that detects and optimizes common pack loops [12].

Our work applies to both, library implementations and compiled code. However, we argue that (super)pipelining techniques are most efficient when the communication and partial packing can be integrated into the application computation. In this work, we step into this direction by modeling the optimization of non-contiguous transfers by pipelining and overlapping packing and sending.

The detailed contributions of this paper are the following:

- We show how a compiler can generate an instruction sequence for near-optimal copying of data into a temporary buffer. Our tuned copy code is up to two times faster than copy functions such as bcopy and memcpy. The resulting code shall be inlined as partial pack-code.
- We show how modeling communication and copy performance can be utilized to transform a sequence of communication and pack statements into an efficient pipelined schedule for a near-optimal combination of packing and communicating.

2   Pipelining for Non-contiguous Put Operations

In the rest of this paper we assume that we have a set S whose elements are tuples of the form (s, r, l). Each element of this set describes one block of data which is l Bytes in size and resides on the sender at s and has to be transferred to the receiver at address r. Furthermore we assume that S is *minimal*, that means there exists no set S' that describes the same data-movement pattern with a smaller number of elements in the set.

A minimal set S can be constructed by simulating a program execution. Each put operation would be recorded as one tuple of the set K. The set K can be minimized to S using the following procedure: The tuples in K are sorted according to their s elements and elements are checked pair-wise in the sorted list. If $(s_i + l_i = s_{i+1}) \wedge (r_i + l_i = r_{i+1})$ then we can combine the tuples i and $i+1$ into a new tuple $(s_i, r_i, l_i + l_{i+1})$. This procedure is repeated until a fixpoint is reached. This can be extended to symbolic analysis, for example, by using abstract interpretation [7].

Maximal block communication would now put every block (as identified by a tuple) separately. Let the cost to issue a single put operation of length l be $T_{put}(l)$, and let $x.l$ identify the l element in tuple x. The overall cost of maximal block communication is:

$$T = \sum_{a \in S} T_{put}(a.l)$$

Another option would be to search for certain features in the set S and exploit them. One such feature is that, while the data is non-contiguous at the sender, it is actually placed in a consecutive buffer at the receiver. A very common example for this is the transposition of a matrix which is distributed across multiple processes. Such a communication pattern is required in multi-dimensional FFT codes and seismic wave propagation codes, such as SPECFEM3D_GLOBE [18]. In such a case, instead of sending each element of S individually, we could also copy all elements into a single temporary buffer on the sender side, and transfer this buffer to the receiver using a single RMA put operation. In that case the cost for the entire transfer would not only depend on the performance of the put, but also of the copy operation, which we denote as $T_{copy}(l)$. The overall cost of this scheme can therefore be expressed as:

$$T = \sum_{a \in S} T_{copy}(a.l) + T_{put}\left(\sum_{b \in S} b.l\right)$$

When compared to the first scheme, it is clear that the second one can only be faster if the difference between many small put operations and one big put operation is big enough to offset the time required for the copy operations. This has been exploited before [9], especially by systems which perform message vectorization. Small transfers attain a smaller bandwidth than bigger ones, due to a constant latency and send overhead. In Fig. 2 we plot the time it takes to send 800 KB of data, with a different number of put operations, so that the size of each put varies between 8 and 1000 Bytes.

We can see that if the transfer is realized with small puts, i.e., one double precision floating point value per put, it takes 110 times longer to transfer the data then using puts of size 1 KB. The reason is that each put operation has some constant overhead on the host CPU and also on the Network Interface Card (NIC). It seems like minimizing the number of put operations can lead to higher performance. However, the benchmark above only considered communication (on the NIC and CPU) and no parallel packing (on the CPU).

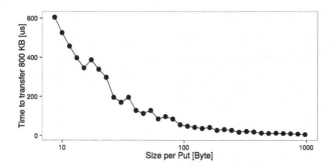

Fig. 2. Varying the number (and therefore the size) of put operations to transfer 800 KB of data shows that bigger puts are more efficient than small ones.

The LogGP network model [1] models CPU and NIC overheads separately as o and g. Those two terms may overlap and a put operation can be performed in $\max(o,g)$. Therefore to minimize the total transfer time T it is beneficial to overlap some of the packing with put operations. This can be done by partitioning the data movement operation expressed by the set S into a series of (non-empty) partitions P_i ($1 \leq i \leq n$, we assume that elements in S can be split into multiple pieces that belong to different partitions P_i). Copying the first partition P_1 into the temporary buffer cannot be overlapped, similarly the sending of the last partition P_n cannot be overlapped. Therefore the total time can be expressed as:

$$T = \sum_{a \in P_1} T_{copy}(a.l) + \sum_{i=2}^{n} \max\left(T_{put}\left(\sum_{b \in P_{i-1}} b.l \right), \sum_{c \in P_i} T_{copy}(c.l) \right) + T_{put}\left(\sum_{d \in P_n} d.l \right)$$

Fixed pipeline. To minimize the total transfer time we would need to minimize this function over all possible partitionings of S. This optimization problem can be solved with traditional optimization methods or heuristics. A simple heuristic would be to fix the size of the put operations we want to perform, and partition S in such a way that all puts (except the last) are of this size. We call this method the *fixed pipeline* method.

Superpipelining. The simple fixed-size-put scheme can be improved by increasing the size of each partition P_i as we progress. The rationale for this is that we should keep the size of the first put operation low, as the copy operations before it cannot be overlapped with anything. On the other hand we want to minimize the total number of puts. If we assume that $\forall s : T_{copy}(s) < T_{put}(s)$ we can increase the size of each put. The goal is to keep the network (which is then the bottleneck of the transfer) saturated. This will be the case if we ensure that the time to pack the data for the i-th put operation is smaller than the time taken to perform the $i-1$st put operation with which the copying is overlapped. To compute the optimal pipeline, we need to know the functions $T_{put}(s)$ and the inverse of the function $T_{copy}(s)$, since we want to know how many Bytes we can copy for the next put. This approach of gradually increasing the size of pipeline stages to achieve optimal overlap and throughput is called superpipelining.

In the following we show a semi-analytic performance model for the performance of RDMA put operations to get an approximation for $T_{put}(s)$. Unfortunately the performance of copy operations cannot be modeled that nicely due to the vast number of influencing factors (cache state, cache sizes, cache associativity, instruction choice for the copy operation, unrolling of copy operations, etc.). Therefore we propose a method to generate a fast copy code, which at the same time gathers performance measurements which can be used to approximate the inverse of $T_{copy}(s)$.

3   Data Movement Operations

Modern CISC architectures offer a plethora of instructions capable of copying data in main memory. For this study we focus on x86-64, since it is the most prevalent architecture in parallel computing today. On modern x86-64 architectures copying data between memory locations can be done in two different ways. Most data-movement instructions only copy between registers and memory, therefore a copy between memory locations consists of two parts: Copying the data from memory into a register and copying it back from the register into a different memory location. In addition, the movs instruction family is able to copy directly from memory to memory. There are many different ways how to copy data in and out of a register. Perhaps the most well known one is the mov instruction family (this includes all variants of the mov instruction for different widths, i.e., movb to copies a single Byte, movw copies two Bytes, movl copies four Bytes and movq copies eight Bytes). Being a CISC design, the x86 instruction set also includes specialized instructions to copy strings: the load-string lods and store-string instruction family stos. They essentially behave like the mov instruction, however, the programmer is free to choose where he places operands for the mov instructions, those use the registers %rsi, %rdi for the source and destination address and use %rax as temporary buffer. All those instruction can only operate on up to eight Byte at a time. With the SIMD extensions (i.e., SSE2 and AVX) load/store instructions became available that are able to load/store 16 (SSE2) or 32 (AVX) Byte from/to a register in one instruction.

SIMD instructions offer another interesting set of features to the programmer: Not only can loads and stores be performed using much wider registers, but also special loads and stores are offered for aligned data. Another novelty is the introduction of non-temporal stores, which bypass the cache and write directly into memory. Of course, writing directly into memory is much slower than writing into the cache. However, when copying large blocks of data (larger than the last level cache) it is useless to write any (but the last chunk) of data to the cache, since this data will be evicted from the cache anyway by later writes. Knowingly bringing useless data into the cache is of course suboptimal, since it inflicts additional overhead because of the cache coherency protocol. Therefore temporal store instructions also have to be considered carefully.

Another important choice the programmer (or compiler) has to make when writing a copy-loop is the choice of the loop instructions he uses. When data is copied using a movs instruction, a loop can be formed by simply prefixing this instruction with the rep prefix. This prefix repeats the prefixed instruction until the %rcx register is zero and decrements the %rcx register after each iteration. The direction of operation (decrementing or incrementing %rsi and %rdi) is set with the direction flag. Of course the rep prefix is only an option when the movs instruction is used, as all other alternatives require more than one instruction to perform a memory to memory copy operation. For those cases we again have multiple options: We can use the loop instruction, which jumps to a label if %rcx is not zero and decrements this register before each jump. However, with this variant we have to adjust the value of the source and destination pointers manually in the loop. The third option is to manually do a comparison at the end of the loop body and then use an instruction of the jmp family to jump to the start of the loop, depending on the result of the comparison.

Figure 3 gives an overview over the possibilities of combinations of data-movement and loop forming instructions offered by the x86-64 instruction set. Another variable the programmer has to consider is the unrolling factor of the copy loop: the overhead of the branching instruction can be alleviated by performing several copy operations inside of the loop body. However, since copy operations are memory bandwidth bound, too much unrolling can also be detrimental to the performance since loading of the instruction stream also creates memory pressure.

The x86-64 instruction set offers even more data-movement instructions (i.e., push/pop, compare-and-swap) which are not considered here since they are specialized instructions with more functionality than data movement and should therefore always be slower than the simpler instructions.

We optimize the code used for copying automatically, using algorithm outlined in Fig. 4 select the optimal combination of data-movement instruction and unroll factor combination for selected block sizes.

For each block size all possible combinations of instruction(-swidth) and unroll factor is computed, since not every combination supports all sizes. The measurement of the performance of each combination is repeated several times (1,000 times in our case) and for each combination the median of those times is computed. The optimal combination of instruction and unroll factor for a given block size is then chosen.

This algorithm is performed for a number of sizes and assuming the source data is in cache or not in cache. We tuned only sizes up to one Megabyte because our superpipelining does not require larger blocks. The gathered information is then used to construct a near-optimal sequence of CPU instructions to perform the copy for packing.

The performance of our copy code, which we call *fcopy* is shown in Fig. 5. We compare it to the memcpy() and bcopy() function. We optimize for two cases: (1) the source data resides in cache ("Cache Hot") and (2) the source data needs to be loaded from main memory ("Cache Cold"). We assume that a compiler analysis could determine the reuse distance of the to-be-copied data and decide on the best instruction sequence.

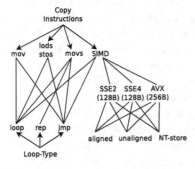

Fig. 3. Data-movement and loop-forming instructions on x86-64.

for all $s \in \{2^0, 2^1, ..., 2^{20}\}$ do
    for all $i \in \{\text{copy inst.} \times \text{loop type}\}$ do
        for all $f \in \{2^0, 2^1, ..., 2^{10}\}$ do
            $t_i^f \leftarrow$ time to copy s Byte with
                instruction i, unrolled f times
                (median of 1000 runs)
        end for
    end for
    copyroutine$(s) \leftarrow \min(t_i^f)$
end for

Fig. 4. Algorithm used to generate optimized copy code.

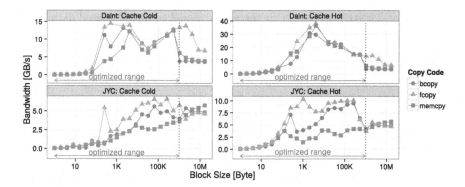

Fig. 5. Performance of our copy code *fcopy* compared to the performance of memcpy and bcopy on JYC and Daint. Our optimized code is up to seven times faster than memcpy and up to 2.6 times faster than bcopy. Note that we optimized the code for block sizes up to 1 MB (left of the dotted line).

For the performance data presented in this paper, we use two different machines: JYC, the Blue Waters test system at the National Center for Supercomputing Applications, which consists of a single cabinet Cray XE6 (approx. 50 nodes with 1,600 Interlagos 2.3–2.6 GHz cores) and Piz Daint, a Cray XC30 at CSCS with dual-socket 8-core 64-bit Intel SandyBridge CPUs clocked at 2.6 GHz.

4   Modeling Communication

To be able to model the performance of one-sided non-contiguous data transfers, we need to model not only the performance of the local copying of data, but also the performance of the remote memory copies.

One-sided data transfers follow the same general scheme, independent of the actual API in which they are implemented: A synchronization epoch is started, then a number of remote memory operations is started, after which the synchronization epoch is again closed. Those operations are combined into a single statement if synchronization is not relaxed. In our case however, the goal is to overlap packing with RMA operations. Thus, we utilize a relaxed synchronization model for our communication. In this model the time to execute n put operations, with sizes s_i can be modeled as $t = L + n \times o_{put} + G \sum_{i=1}^{n} s_i$. This model is similar to the LogGP model [1]. The constant overhead (latency, synchronization overhead) is denoted as L, where o_{put} is the overheads for the put operation, which is independent of the size of the data buffer being transferred. In LogGP we would differentiate between the overhead on the NIC, g and the overhead on the host CPU o, however, in practice these values are hard to measure independently. Therefore we model $\max(o, g)$ as o_{put}. The inverse bandwidth of the transfer is expressed by G.

We parametrize this model by performing between 1 and 50 puts in a loop, each with the same data buffer size. The data buffer size is varied between a single Byte and 800 KB. Then we fit the above model to the measured data. Each measurement is repeated 50 times, and we use the median value to minimize the effects of outliers due to noise.

The results of these measurements on JYC are plotted in Fig. 6 for out-of-cache inter-node communication. We focus on inter-node communication in this work, because on our test system intra-node communication is handled by copying the data directly from the target to the destination buffer, using the XPMEM [23] kernel module to access another processes address space. Since this copy operation is not performed in an extra progression thread, overlapping intra-node communication is therefore not possible.

If we use the data collected on JYC to parametrize our model we get $L = 1$ μs, $o = 0.68$ μs (0.44 μs for in-cache data), $G = 0.17$ ns/B. This model fits the measured data quite well, the R^2 value is 0.999. This means 99.9 % of the variance observed in the data is explained by the model. For Daint the values are $L = 1$ μs, $o = 0.66$ μs (same for in-cache data), $G = 0.6$ ns/B and an R^2 of 0.979.

We can now use the performance model for communication and the data collected during the construction of the copy method to determine optimal sizes for the partitions of S which are transferred with a single put operation, and by which factor we can increase this size for consecutive puts. To do this we look at the quotient $r = \frac{T_{put}(s)}{T_{copy}(s)}$ for different sizes s. This ratio is plotted in Fig. 7.

If $r < 1$ it means that we should never copy this much data into a temporary buffer, the put will be faster than copying this data was, therefore we will not enlarge the partitions of S beyond this point. If we plot that ratio for our test system, we can see that for 500 KB and larger, collecting more data (for a larger put operation) takes longer than sending it immediately, therefore we stop to increase the size of the partitions, once we copied a block of size 500 KB. Note that $T_{copy}(s)$ is an upper bound for the performance of filling the temporary buffer for a put of size s. The real performance of this operation

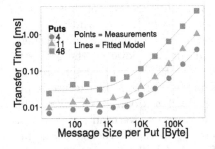

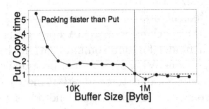

Fig. 6. Inter-node communication performance on JYC. If we parametrize the model with this data we get: $L = 1$ μs, $o = 0.686$ μs, $G = 0.17$ ns/B.

Fig. 7. Relationship between put and copy performance for different block sizes. Below 10 KB puts are much more expensive than additional copies, while above 500 KB it is slower to pack more data than to send it over the network directly.

is $\sum_{a \in P_i} T_{copy}(a.l)$ which can be much lower in case of very small consecutive blocks in the data layout on the sender side, therefore the start value and the rate at which to increase partition sizes have to be computed for each data layout. Furthermore we can see that below 10 KB puts are much more expensive than additional copies (the ratio is above 2), therefore it would be inefficient to perform smaller puts. Because of that we start our superpipeline protocol with an initial partition size of at least 10 KB.

5   Results

In this section we will demonstrate the performance of our optimization with two examples. The first example is the matrix transpose part of an FFT code. The consecutive blocks on the sender side are (depending on the total size) between 128 and 1792 Byte in size. On the receiver the data is stored in one contiguous buffer. The stride between the blocks on the sender side (for a given total size) is constant.

We show the performance of the three strategies to transfer non-contiguous data with RMA put operations explained in this paper in Fig. 8. When each consecutive block is transferred individually, the achieved bandwidth is very low, and grows for bigger problem instances due to the growth of the size of the consecutive blocks. This method is labeled as *Maximal Block* (cf. Fig. 1). The performance of this approach can be improved considerably by packing data on the sender, prior to sending it. We can either pack all data and send it with one put operation (labeled as *Packed*), or overlap packing and put operations. If all (except the last) chunks have the same size, 20 KB in our example, labeled as *FP(20K)* for fixed-pipeline we can improve the total bandwidth by 1.3 GB/s (42 %, compared to Maximal Block). Our superpipeline protocol can achieve an additional performance increase for the larger problem instances of about 652 MB/s (13 %, compared to FP) when the size of each put is increased by a

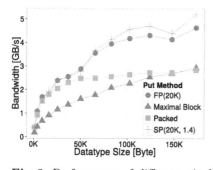

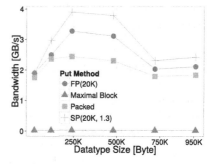

Fig. 8. Performance of different pipelining approaches on JYC for an FFT code. Consecutive blocks at the sender grow with the problem size from 128 Byte blocks to 1792 Byte.

Fig. 9. Performance of different pipelining approaches on JYC for a data transfer in SPECFEM3D_GLOBE. For this transfer, each block is 12 Byte in size.

factor of 1.3, while the first put is again 20 KB in size. This variant is labeled as *SP(20K, 1.3)* where SP stands for superpipeline protocol.

In Fig. 9 we conduct the same experiment with a send data layout from the SPECFEM3D_GLOBE seismic wave propagation simulation code [6]. Here the individual consecutive blocks are much smaller, only 12 Bytes in size, and their size remains constant when the problem size is increased. The sender stride between blocks is 24 Byte while the data is put into a contiguous buffer at the receiver. Since the blocks are so small, *Maximal Block* performs much worse than in the FFT example. In this plot, one can clearly see that the performance gain attainable by superpipelining depends heavily on the speed of the copy operations. As long as the extent of the data layout fits (together with the pack buffer) in the 2 MB L2 cache, the performance of superpipelining is much better than that of fixed size pipelining. After that point their performance becomes similar again. Superpipelined packing is 148 times faster than sending each block individually, up to 37 % faster than packing everything into one block before sending and 17 % faster than fixed-pipeline packing. To show the portability of our method we conduct the same experiments on Daint, a Cray XC30 with Intel SandyBridge CPUs. The results are plotted in Figs. 11 and 12. In Fig. 10 we perform the same comparison with another data layout present in the SPECFEM3D_GLOBE code, where the data blocks on the sender are not stored with a regular stride, but in a irregular fashion (indexed type in MPI). Each block is four Byte in size and the data is stored consecutively on the receiver. Because of the small block size and the resulting high copy overhead, the difference between the packing methods is small. Superpipelining is 118 times faster than *Maximal Block*, 18 % faster than *Packed* and up to 8 % faster than fixed size pipelining.

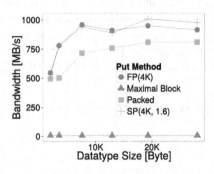

Fig. 10. Performance comparison of an irregular data transfer on JYC in SPECFEM3D_GLOBE. The blocks at the sender are 4 Byte in size.

6   Related Work

Many compiler optimizations are based on peephole optimization techniques: Matching rules are applied to an intermediate compilation result and if a match is found, the code is replaced with a functionally equivalent, but faster, alternative. Those transformations are often created manually by domain experts. However, approaches where the optimization opportunities are automatically generated, similar to our approach of optimizing copy code, also have been suggested. Superoptimization [2] tries to optimize an instruction sequence by generating *all* possible instruction sequences up to a certain length and checking if they are functionally equivalent to the target instruction sequence. The problem with superoptimization is the exponential growth of the search space with the length of the considered instruction sequence and the number of available instructions. The interest in superoptimization also seems to have become smaller since this technique has been initially proposed — to the best of our knowledge, there is no publicly available superoptimizer which includes the whole instruction set (incl. AVX, SSE4, etc.) of a modern x86 CPU. Recent applications of superoptimization techniques [17], use heuristics to keep the search space manageable.

Superpipelining [8] was first proposed to overlap memory registration with RDMA operations. We extended this technique for copying non-contiguous data. Santhanaraman et al. [16] suggested to use gather/scatter support offered by modern network stacks [5,15] to implement MPI datatypes for two-sided point to point transfers and collectives. Since MPI allows that sender and receiver specify different datatypes in the respective send or receive call, this information (the datatype layout) has to be communicated first. After that the non-contiguous data is sent using an InfiniBand gather operation [15]. At the receiver, the data is stored (possibly in a different layout) using an InfiniBand scatter operation. In this work we are focusing on the one-sided programming model, where the sender has complete knowledge over the data layout at the receiver. Furthermore we do not rely on special hardware features for the transfer. The problem of transferring data does not only occur in message passing and RDMA programming, but also when programming for accelerators, which have a private memory, such as GPUs. Jablin et al. [10] for example strive to optimize CPU to GPU communication by using compiler passes and a run time layer which optimize the scheduling of the communication, i.e., achieve communication-computation overlap by early binding. Jenkins et al. [11] propose GPU kernels to pack MPI datatypes, which gives large improvements over packing them with the host CPU.

Schneider et al. [19] also optimized the packing of MPI derived datatypes. MPI DDTs are traditionally interpreted at runtime, which is often slower than manual pack loops written for a specific case and optimized by the compiler

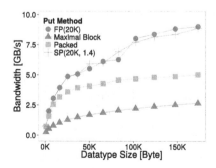

Fig. 11. Performance of different pipelining approaches on Daint for an FFT code. Consecutive blocks at the sender grow with the problem size from 128 Byte blocks to 1792 Byte.

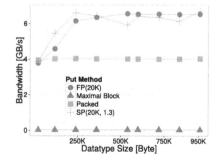

Fig. 12. Performance of different pipelining approaches on Daint for a data transfer in SPECFEM3D_GLOBE. For this transfer, each block is 12 Byte in size.

at compile time. We mitigate that by generating machine code to pack MPI DDTs at runtime. This increased packing performance by up to a factor of seven. However, none of the pipelining techniques described in this work have been used, the generated pack function pack the complete message into a buffer before sending.

7   Conclusions

In this work we showed which optimizations a compiler for partitioned global address space languages can perform, in order to accelerate non-contiguous data transfers, without the requirement of special purpose hardware. We showed two main targets for optimization: the scheduling of RMA put operations and the instruction sequence used to copy small chunks of data into a temporary buffer for sending them. We show an algorithm to optimize the copy code and show that the resulting code outperforms readily available compiler builtins such as memcpy and system functions such as bcopy. We show how pipelining copying data and transferring it can improve performance and how we can leverage performance models of the network operations, as well as performance data of the copy code to choose suitable parameters for the suggested pipelining protocols. All optimizations can be implemented in compilers for PGAS languages or RMA libraries using well-known techniques.

Acknowledgments. We thanks the Swiss National Supercomputing Center (CSCS) and the Blue Waters project at NCSA/UIUC for access to the test systems. We also thank the anonymous reviewers for comments that greatly improved our work.

References

1. Alexandrov, A., Ionescu, M.F., Schauser, K.E., Scheiman, C.: LogGP: incorporating long messages into the logP model - one step closer towards a realistic model for parallel computation. In: Proceedings of the 7th Annual ACM Symposium on Parallel Algorithms and Architectures (SPAA'95), pp. 95–105 (1995)
2. Bansal, S., Aiken, A.: Automatic generation of peephole superoptimizers. ACM SIGPLAN Not. **41**(11), 394–403 (2006)
3. Bernard, C., Ogilvie, M., et al.: Studying quarks and gluons on MIMD parallel computers. Int. J. High Perform. Comput. Appl. **54**, 61–70 (1991)
4. Bronevetsky, G.: Communication-sensitive static dataflow for parallel message passing applications. In: Proceedings of the 7th Annual IEEE/ACM International Symposium on Code Generation and Optimization (CGO'09) (2009)
5. ten Bruggencate, M., Roweth, D.: DMAPP - an API for one-sided program models on Baker systems. In: Cray User Group Conference (CUG'10) (2010)
6. Carrington, L., Komatitsch, D., et al.: High-frequency simulations of global seismic wave propagation using SPECFEM3D_GLOBE on 62 K processors. In: Proceedings of the 22nd International Conference on Supercomputing (SC'08) (2008)

7. Cousot, P., Cousot, R.: Abstract interpretation: a unified lattice model for static analysis of programs by construction or approximation of fixpoints. In: Proceedings of the 4th ACM SIGACT-SIGPLAN Symposium on Principles of Programming Languages (POPL'77), pp. 238–252 (1977)

8. Denis, A.: A high performance superpipeline protocol for InfiniBand. In: Proceedings of the European Conference on Parallel Processing, pp. 276–287 (2011)

9. Hiranandani, S., Kennedy, K., Tseng, C.W.: Evaluating compiler optimizations for Fortran D. J. Parallel Distrib. Comput. **21**(1), 27–45 (1994)

10. Jablin, T.B., Prabhu, P., Jablin, J.A., Johnson, N.P., Beard, S.R., August, D.I.: Automatic CPU-GPU communication management and optimization. ACM SIGPLAN Not. **46**(6), 142–151 (2011)

11. Jenkins, J., Dinan, J., et al.: Enabling fast, noncontiguous GPU data movement in hybrid MPI + GPU environments. In: Proceedings of the IEEE International Conference on Cluster Computing (CLUSTER'12) (2012)

12. Kjolstad, F., Hoefler, T., Snir, M.: Automatic datatype generation and optimization. In: Proceedings of the 17th ACM SIGPLAN Symposium on Principles and Practice of Parallel Programming (PPoPP'12), pp. 327–328 (2012)

13. MPI Forum: MPI: A Message-Passing Interface Standard. Version 3

14. Numrich, R.W., Reid, J.: Co-array Fortran for parallel programming. SIGPLAN Fortran Forum **17**(2), 1–31 (1998)

15. Pfister, G.F.: An introduction to the infiniband architecture. In: Hai, J., Toni, C., Buyya, R. (eds.) High Performance Mass Storage and Parallel I/O, pp. 617–632. Wiley, New York (2001)

16. Santhanaraman, G., Wu, J., Panda, D.K.: Zero-copy MPI derived datatype communication over infiniband. In: Kranzlmüller, D., Kacsuk, P., Dongarra, J. (eds.) EuroPVM/MPI 2004. LNCS, vol. 3241, pp. 47–56. Springer, Heidelberg (2004)

17. Schkufza, E., Sharma, R., Aiken, A.: Stochastic superoptimization. In: Proceedings of the International Conference on Architectural Support for Programming Languages and Operating Systems (ASPLOS'13), pp. 305–316 (2013)

18. Schneider, T., Gerstenberger, R., Hoefler, T.: Application-oriented ping-pong benchmarking: how to assess the real communication overheads. J. Comput. **964**, 279–292 (2013)

19. Schneider, T., Kjolstad, F., Hoefler, T.: MPI datatype processing using runtime compilation. In: Proceedings of EuroMPI'13, September 2013

20. Skamarock, W.C., Klemp, J.B.: A time-split nonhydrostatic atmospheric model for weather research and forecasting applications. J. Comput. Phys. **227**(7), 3465–3485 (2008)

21. UPC Consortium: UPC language specifications. Version 1. 2 (2005)

22. der Wijngaart, R.F.V., Wong, P.: NAS parallel benchmarks version 2.4. Technical report, NAS Technical Report NAS-02-007 (2002)

23. Woodacre, M., Robb, D., Roe, D., Feind, K.: The SGI AltixTM 3000 global shared memory architecture (2005)

Transactional Memory

Combining Lock Inference with Lock-Based Software Transactional Memory

Stefan Kempf$^{(\boxtimes)}$, Ronald Veldema, and Michael Philippsen

Computer Science Department, Programming Systems Group,
University of Erlangen-Nuremberg, Martensstr. 3, 91058 Erlangen, Germany
{stefan.kempf,veldema,philippsen}@cs.fau.de

Abstract. An atomic block is a language construct that simplifies the programming of critical sections. In the past, software transactional memory (STM) and lock inference have been used to implement atomic blocks. Both approaches have strengths and weaknesses. STM provides fine-grained locking but has high overheads due to logging and potential rollbacks. Lock inference is a static analysis that computes which locks an atomic block must acquire in order to guarantee atomicity. Lock inference avoids both logging overhead and rollbacks, but with a growing number of variables accessed in an atomic block, locking becomes coarse-grained and hence reduces parallelism.

The first contribution of this paper is an approach that combines these advantages without the drawbacks. A compiler analysis determines if lock inference can achieve a fine-grained synchronization or if STM is better for an atomic block. The generated code then either uses lock inference, STM, or a combination of both that allows the atomic block to switch from STM to lock inference during its execution. The second contribution are two optimizations that remove some of the limits of state-of-the-art static lock inference analysis and therefore extend its applicability. These optimizations make more atomic blocks amenable to fine-grained lock inference.

We use the STAMP benchmark suite to prove the practicability of our work. The reduced contention due to fine-grained locking and less transactional overhead lead to execution times that are between 1.1 and 6.0 times faster than a pure STM or lock inference implementation.

1 Introduction

The ubiquitous availability of multicore processors has spurred research activity on new language paradigms that simplify concurrent programming. Atomic blocks allow programmers to mark critical sections in the code, but the implementation of the atomicity is left to the compiler or runtime system. Two such implementation approaches are software transactional memory (STM) and lock inference, both of which have advantages and disadvantages. STM provides fine-grained locking but its overheads due to logging of read/write accesses and due to potential rollbacks negatively impact performance, especially if transactions

© Springer International Publishing Switzerland 2014
C. Caşcaval and P. Montesinos (Eds.): LCPC 2013, LNCS 8664, pp. 325–341, 2014.
DOI: 10.1007/978-3-319-09967-5_19

access many variables or if contention is high. Lock inference is a compiler analysis that statically computes which locks an atomic block must acquire/release on entry/exit in order to guarantee atomicity. This eliminates the logging overhead and tends to produce faster code for small atomic blocks. But current lock inference approaches lead to coarse-grained locking (and thus reduced parallelism) if an atomic block uses a larger or statically unknown number of shared variables. For example, for an atomic block traversing the nodes of a linked list, lock inference cannot acquire one lock per node, but instead it must map all the nodes to one global lock.

For a fast *and* fine-grained implementation of atomic blocks, we suggest a combination of both techniques, where an atomic block either uses lock inference (we say it runs in *lock mode*) or STM (it runs in *TM mode*), but it can also start in TM mode and switch to lock mode during its execution. To our knowledge, this paper is the first work to present such a combination.

Our first contribution is a compiler analysis that implements atomic blocks with lock inference as long as a fine-grained locking suffices, and that uses transactional memory for the remaining parts of the atomic block. Our second contribution are two optimizations of state-of-the-art lock inference algorithms, namely runtime loop inspection and specialized collection data structures. They let us implement fine-grained lock inference even if the memory locations accessed by an atomic block cannot be statically precomputed. Our evaluation using the STAMP benchmarks proves that our technique is practical, since the reduced contention due to fine-grained locking and less transactional overhead lead to execution times that are between 1.1 and 6.0 times faster than a pure STM or lock inference implementation.

The remainder of this paper first covers the building blocks of software transactional memory and lock inference in Sec. 2. Section 3 then discusses how we combine lock inference and STM to implement atomic blocks. Section 4 shows how the use of runtime loop inspection and specialized container data structures makes our combined technique more aggressive. Section 5 evaluates our approach, Sec. 6 discusses related work, and Sec. 7 concludes and gives directions for future research.

```
atomic {
  p = list;
  while (p != NULL) {
    p.value = 0;
    p = p.next;
  }
  ─────────────────
  y = r.v;
  if (R> 1) { x = 1; }
  else { y.g = 2; }
}
```

Fig. 1. An atomic block.

2   Building Blocks

To understand when a combination of lock inference and STM is useful and how it works technically, we need to briefly cover the foundations of both approaches. We use the running example in Fig. 1 to illustrate the basic ideas. In its atomic block, x, y.g, and the value fields (p.value) of the list elements are shared variables.

2.1   Software Transactional Memory

Let us first describe the workings of a lock-based STM that protects accesses to shared variables by means of mutexes. There are also lock-free STMs, but as our approach combines STM and lock inference, we of course need a lock-based STM. It is sufficient to only sketch the high-level ideas of lock-based STMs, as the combinability of lock inference and lock-based STMs is not affected by implementation details. (Some STMs acquire locks during a transaction while others acquire locks at the end of the commit. Some STMs use in-place updates of shared variables and perform undo-logging upon rollback while other STMs update shared variables in the commit. Such implementation details are orthogonal to our approach.)

To implement atomic blocks, the compiler of a lock-based STM instruments the code of Fig. 1 and adds primitives of the STM runtime library, as shown in Fig. 2. Upon entering an atomic block, it creates a transaction that manages all accesses to the shared variables used in the block. Every read/write access to a shared variable is rewritten to call a transactional read/write routine. A transactional write to a shared variable v does not change v directly. Instead the new value for v is stored in a write-log. A transactional read

```
L1:
  Txn  t  =  new  Txn(L1);
  p  =  list;
  while  (p  !=  NULL)  {
    t.write(p.value,   0);
    p  =  p.next;
  }
  y  =  r.v;
  if  (R> 1)  {  t.write(x,   1);  }
  else  {  t.write(y.g,   2);  }
  t.commit();
```

Fig. 2. ... implemented with STM.

of v first checks whether the write-log already holds a value for v. Otherwise, it reads the value from main memory and creates an entry in a read-log to indicate that v was read. Since the effects of atomic blocks appear to take effect instantly, the values of shared variables that are read must have the same values during the whole execution of the atomic block. A transactional read makes sure this is the case before it returns the value read from memory. If the value has changed in the meantime, the transaction aborts and restarts from the beginning.

At the end of the atomic block, the transaction commits. A commit (see pseudo code in Fig. 3) acquires a lock for every variable that is to be updated (stm_acquire_locks). We assume that there is some mapping from variables to locks, for example by hashing a variable into an entry of a table of locks. This prevents concurrent transactions from accessing the corresponding variables. To prevent deadlocks, a transaction does not spin infinitely on a lock that is held by another transaction. Instead, it releases all currently held locks and restarts if it cannot acquire the lock in a finite number of spins. The transaction then checks that all variables that were read from main memory still have their original values, i.e., that no concurrent transaction has modified them (stm_verify_reads). In case of modifications, the transaction releases all locks and restarts. Otherwise the transaction writes back all variables into main memory (stm_writeback) and finally releases all locks (stm_unlock_all).

```
LockSet locks;

void stm_lock(Variable v) {
  Lock l = map_var_to_lock(v);

  // lock with timeout to
  // prevent deadlocks
  if (try_lock(l) == false) {
    // release locks and
    // restart transaction.
    restart();
  }
  locks.add(l);
}

void stm_acquire_locks() {
  locks = {};
  foreach (entry in write_log) {
    stm_lock(entry.variable);
  } }
```

```
void stm_verify_reads() {
  foreach (entry in read_log) {
    if (var_value_has_changed(entry)) {
      restart();
  } } }

void stm_writeback() {
  foreach (entry in write_log) {
    entry.variable = entry.value;
  } }

void stm_unlock_all() {
  foreach (l in locks) { unlock(l); }
}

void commit() {
  stm_acquire_locks();
  stm_verify_reads();
  stm_writeback();
  stm_unlock_all();
}
```

Fig. 3. Pseudo code for the commit operation of an STM.

2.2   Lock Inference

While STM is a runtime approach, lock inference is a static interprocedural compiler analysis. We cover the ideas of the basic lock inference analysis by Gudka et al. [7] here. In Sec. 4, we will extend it with our optimizations.

A lock inference algorithm takes an atomic block as input and computes the set of locks that the atomic block needs to acquire in order to ensure atomicity. Upon entering the atomic block, all locks in the set are acquired in some order, and at the block's end, these locks are released. In contrast to an STM, the body of the atomic block executes without any further instrumentation. Shared variables are written directly to memory, since all accesses to them are protected by the locks that were acquired initially. The strategies to prevent deadlocks when acquiring multiple locks are similar to what STMs use, i.e., if the locks cannot be acquired within a finite number of spins, all locks acquired so far are released, and the acquiring starts over. Figure 4 shows how lock inference transforms the atomic block of Fig. 1. (Ignore the comments in the code for now.)

The computation of the locks that must be acquired uses a backwards analysis that walks backwards through the code and visits every statement s of the atomic block. When the analysis processes s, it computes the set of shared variables that are potentially accessed on any path from s to the exit of the atomic block. Once the analysis has terminated, the set computed for the first statement of the atomic block holds all variables that the block potentially reads or writes. The comments in Fig. 4 show the sets for every statement. We will show below how this computation works in detail. At the first statement of the atomic block, there is a path to the exit that uses x, which is therefore included in the set of the first statement. Likewise, there is a path that uses y.g, but since y is set to r.v in the middle of the block, the first set holds r.v.g in order to be able to lock the memory location addressed by y.g. The value fields of the list nodes are potentially accessed as well, but since their number is statically unknown, the third item in the first set uses a finite representation to statically refer to all nodes of the list. The compiler then maps every shared variable to a lock and generates the appropriate lock and unlock statements. Although the atomic block may access an unbounded number of variables, the original lock inference approach always acquires a finite number of locks. In the example, all nodes of the list are mapped to one global lock. The approach of Gudka et al. works on Java and uses type locks, i.e., if p has the type Node, every p.value gets mapped to a static lock field in the class Node. Of course, reader-writes locks allow more parallelism when acquired in read mode for read-only variables. But for simplicity we assume ordinary locks throughout the remainder of this paper.

Let us now follow the lock inference algorithm in detail. It starts with the last statement of Fig. 1, i.e., it processes the branches individually and first analyzes y.g=2. Since y.g is a shared variable, it adds it to the assignment's set. The same happens for x=1. Since there are

```
lock(x, r.v.g, Node.lock);
p = list;    // x, r.v.g, list((.next)*).value
while (p != NULL) {
    p.value = 0; // x, r.v.g, [p((.next)*).value]
    p = p.next;  // x, r.v.g [p((.next)*).value]
}
y = r.v;     // x, r.v.g
             // x, y.g
if (R>1) { x = 1; }  // x
else { y.g = 2; }    // y.g
unlock_all();
```

Fig. 4. ... implemented with lock inference.

two paths from the if-statement to the end of the atomic block and the analysis cannot determine which branch will be taken at runtime, it must conservatively assume that the if-statement accesses both variables. It therefore merges the sets of both branches, i.e., the atomic block will later have to acquire locks for x and y.g. Further up, y is set to r.v. The algorithm propagates the set of the if-statement to that assignment and replaces all appearances of the LHS (y) with the RHS of the assignment (r.v). Since the algorithm then needs to capture the effects of the entire loop, it performs a fix-point iteration on the loop statements in order to compute the sets of shared variables. The comments at the statements in the loop show the sets after the fix-point is reached. Elements that were added in repeated iterations are shown in brackets. Since the above rewriting transformation for assignments would lead to infinitely many rewritings for p=p.next, we use a finite representation that specifies that p could be rewritten to p.next infinitely often. After the algorithm has processed the loop, it reaches the first assignment and rewrites all occurrences of p as shown.

3   Combining Lock Inference with STM

Now that the basics of STM and lock inference have been covered, we can investigate how to combine STM and lock inference. Our goal is to implement every atomic block with fine-grained synchronization and with as little overhead as possible. If an atomic block uses a small statically known number of variables, then the whole atomic block should run in lock mode since it provides fine-grained synchronization with little overhead. If the number of shared variables cannot be bounded at all, for example if the atomic block traverses the nodes of a list, the whole atomic block better runs in TM mode, as we assume that the benefits of fine-grained synchronization outweigh the transactional overhead. The atomic block in Fig. 1 has a mixed flavor. It uses a statically unknown number of **value** fields of the list nodes, but also some of the variables are statically known (x and r.v.g or y.g). For best performance, that parts of an atomic block that access an unbounded number of variables do better in TM mode. The other parts that access a statically bounded number of variables should run in lock mode. Our technique therefore needs to address three challenges. First, it must determine which parts of the atomic block should run in TM mode (if any) and which parts should run in lock mode (if any). Second, it must also be correct for concurrently running atomic blocks that access the same subset of shared variables, regardless of the mode used for them. Third, for mixed flavor of atomic blocks, we need a mechanism to switch from TM mode to lock mode.

Switching from lock mode to TM mode is impossible, as in lock mode changes to shared variables directly affect their main memory locations. After a switch from lock mode to TM mode, a subsequent abort would require undoing these effects. Hence, undo information would need to be kept which negates the benefits of lock inference and contradicts the performance goals.

To determine which parts of an atomic block should run in TM mode or lock mode, and where to switch (if at all), a compiler performs a lock inference analysis. In contrast to Sec. 2.2, the algorithm does not necessarily analyze the entire atomic block. The backwards analysis prematurely stops at a statement that accesses an unbounded number of variables (such as p.value=0 in Fig. 1). The

```
L2:
    Txn *t = new Txn(L2);
    p = list;
    while (p != NULL) {
        t.write(p.value, 0);
        p = p.next;
    }
```

```
    stm_lock(x);
    stm_lock(r.v.g);
    stm_acquire_locks();
    stm_verify_reads();
    stm_writeback();
    y = r.v;
    if (R>1) { x = 1; }
    else { y.g = 2; }
    stm_unlock_all();
```

Fig. 5. ...implemented with a switch from TM mode to lock mode after the loop.

upper part of the atomic block, including this statement, therefore has to run in TM mode. The remaining statements (already analyzed) can run in lock mode. Note that the switch between modes cannot be inside a loop, or at a statement that is executed more than once. Hence we hoist the switching out of loop nests and up the method-call-graph. In Fig. 1, p.value=0 prematurely stops the lock inference analysis. Hence this assignment and the surrounding loop has to run in TM mode before we switch (at the line in Fig. 1). If the analysis does not stop prematurely because an atomic block accesses a bounded number of variables it can fully run in lock mode.

To allow an atomic block in TM mode to run concurrently to another atomic block in lock mode, we let both modes protect an access to a shared variable with the same mutex, i.e., the lock mode uses the TM mode's stm_lock routine (see Fig. 3) to acquire locks. Then all atomic blocks will use the same locks for shared variables, independent of their modes. This guarantees proper synchronization, since an atomic block in TM mode cannot commit until an atomic block in lock mode has released its locks. Vice versa, an atomic block in lock mode cannot enter the critical section as long as a concurrently running block in TM mode commits. Note that since our technique only uses lock inference for code fragments that access a bounded number of variables, we never need to map multiple variables to global locks as in Fig. 4. Every variable is mapped to an individual lock, as in STM.

Figure 5 illustrates the switch from TM mode to lock mode. Above the line there is a transaction that uses transactional operations to access p.value. For the switch from TM mode to lock mode at the line in Fig. 1, the following conditions must be met: since x and y.g will be used, locks for x and y.g must be acquired. But before the code that runs in lock mode can access x and y.g, the variables must have their most recent values in memory. Although it is not the case in the example, it is possible that the code that ran in TM mode transactionally wrote x or y.g. Therefore, all variables that were transactionally written must be committed to memory, i.e., the switch from TM mode to lock mode needs to acquire the respective locks, verify all variables that were transactionally read and, finally write transactionally written variables back to memory. Note that acquiring locks and verifying reads could abort and rollback the transaction. But besides wasted execution time, the rollback is harmless since the atomic block only has executed transactionally so far. After that point, the switch from TM mode to lock mode was successful and the code can now directly access x and y.g. The atomic block finishes by releasing all locks, i.e., the locks that were acquired for lock mode *and* the locks that were acquired for the commit.

4 Optimizations

Although we can now often combine STM and lock inference to always guarantee fine-grained synchronization with little overhead, it is a show-stopper for some atomic blocks that the lock inference analysis sometimes has to give up because the number of variables accessed is unbounded. In this section, we present two optimizations (runtime loop inspection and specialized container data structures) that make more atomic blocks amenable to lock mode. These optimizations are enhancements of current lock inference algorithms and are not limited to our mode-combining technique.

4.1 Runtime Loop Inspection

In the code on the left of Fig. 6 x, *p, z, A[i], and B[i] are shared variables. With a standard lock inference algorithm, only the assignment z=2 can execute in lock mode since the loop accesses an unbounded number of variables.

```
atomic {                                        lock(x, z);
  p = &x;  // x, z, for(A,B)                     for (i = 0;  i < N;  i++) {
  for (i = 0;  i < N;  i++) {  // *p, z, for(A,B)  lock(B[i]);
    int t = B[i];  // z, *p, for(A,B)              int t = B[i];
    if (t < 5) { A[t] = *p; }  // z, *p, for(A)    if (t < 5) { lock(A[t]);
  }                                               } }
  ─────────────────────────────────────          p = &x;
  z = 2;  // z                                    for (i = 0;  i < N;  i++) {
}                                                   int t = B[i];
                                                    if (t < 5) { A[t] = *p;
                                                } }
                                                z = 2;
                                                unlock_all();
```

Fig. 6. Example for runtime loop inspection.

Although standard lock inference cannot determine statically which locks the code must acquire, an added runtime mechanism can make more atomic blocks amenable to lock inference. Remember that code that runs in lock mode consists of three phases: lock acquisition, execution of the body of the atomic block, and lock release. The idea is to clone a loop that accesses an unbounded number of variables. The cloned loop only records which shared variables are accessed but also acquires the corresponding locks. It is similar to an inspector [14]. Afterwards, the unchanged original loop (= executor loop) reads/writes those variables. The compiler hoists the inspector into the lock acquisition phase to acquire all the necessary locks up front so that the executor can run without races. That way, an atomic block runs in lock mode and uses fine-grained synchronization even though it uses an unbounded number of variables.

The code on the right of Fig. 6 shows the application of this technique. The regular analysis has figured out that x (pointed to by p) and z need to be locked initially. The clone of the original loop is hoisted up front into the lock acquisition phase. The clone is stripped of all expressions that do not contribute to the computation of addresses of shared variables. Instead of accessing those variables, it acquires the corresponding locks. After that, the original body of the atomic block is executed.

The transformation is applied to loops that we call *inspectable*. In an inspectable loop, (a) the inspector only reads shared variables that were locked before (a dependence analysis finds that we must first lock and read B[i] to acquire the lock for A[t]) and (b) the only side effects may be lock acquisitions. To implement this optimization, an additional step before the backwards analysis described in Sec. 2.2. Determines for every loop in an atomic block whether it is inspectable. For inspectable loops, the lock inference analysis only needs some straightforward propagation rules to compute the set of shared variables. See the comments on the left of Fig. 6.

In the example, the whole atomic block can run in lock mode. The generated code initially locks every variable that is not part of an inspectable loop. For the other variables, the compiler generates an inspector that locks shared variables before it reads them, that replaces writes with lock acquisitions, and that removes all other operations that do not contribute to the computation of variable addresses or loop termination conditions. Other than that, the code of the atomic block (including the executor loop) remains unchanged. At the end of the atomic block all locks are released.

This technique is orthogonal to the switching from TM mode to lock mode, i.e., it also works if only a part of the atomic block can run in lock mode. If the atomic block of Fig. 6 held a non-inspectable loop that modifies all B[i], the switch from TM mode to lock mode would happen after that loop, and the analysis would generate the same lock acquisitions and (almost) the same inspector as before. The switch from TM mode to lock mode then first acquires locks before it writes transactionally written variables back into memory. The inspector runs before the write-back operation and it now reads B[i] that were transactionally written by the non-inspectable loop. For atomic blocks that run in both TM mode and lock mode, our optimization therefore transforms ordinary reads in an inspector into transactional reads if the compiler must assume that the B[i] were changed in TM mode.

While an inspector acquires locks and may access the write-log, the original loop accesses the write-log for writes and both the read-log and write-log for reads. In some STMs, it also acquires locks during the transaction. Rewriting this loop trades costly log accesses for small executor loop overhead and makes larger parts of the atomic block amenable to lock inference, which reduces transactional overhead.

4.2   Specialized Container Data Structures

The atomic block on the left of Fig. 7 performs the usual operations find, add, and del on a container c. As container operations typically access a statically unbounded number of elements, up to now, TM mode must be used.

Although TM mode provides fine-grained synchronization, turning sequential container data structures into concurrent ones using transactions is sub-optimal [2,8]. Since containers are typically implemented as linked data structures, two atomic blocks that add different elements to the container (a conflict-free operation at the semantic level) may still lead to conflicting pointer updates and hence aborting transactions.

The above runtime loop inspection does not help either, even if it made the code amenable to lock inference. To add an element e to a container c, an inspector still traverses and locks the data structure pointers of c until it reaches the location where to insert e. Locking of all the traversed pointers increases the probability that two atomic blocks adding different elements mutually exclude each other.

Transactional predication [2] is known to solve the problem for TM mode by using highly concurrent data structures. The idea is to only access the key/value fields of elements transactionally, while the concurrent implementation performs the addition/deletion of elements. This prevents low-level conflicts; only semantic conflicts cause mutual exclusion of atomic blocks.

```
atomic {                                           n1 = cont_lock(c,  5);
  tmp = 0; // add(c,7),  del(c,6),  find(c,5)      n2 = cont_lock(c,  6);
  if (find(c,  5)) {// add(c,7),  del(c,6),  find(c,5)  n3 = cont_lock(c,  7);
    tmp = 1; // add(c,7),  del(c,6)                 if (find(c, n1)) {
  }                                                   tmp = 1;
  del(c,  6); // add(c,7),  del(c,6)               }
  add(c,  7); // add(c,7)                           del(c, n2);
}                                                   add(c, n3);
                                                    unlock_all();
```

Fig. 7. Example for specialized container data structures.

We now present an analogous technique for lock inference. We build container data structures into the language and provide implementations that compose with both lock inference and transactional predication. The idea is that for every add, del, or find operation on a key k, there is a corresponding cont_lock operation in the lock acquisition phase that only locks the container element e corresponding to k instead of link pointers. The lock operation also returns a pointer to e for the actual container functions to work with when executing the atomic block.

Figure 7 shows the transformation. As the body of the given atomic block operates on elements with the keys 5, 6, and 7, there is one cont_lock call per container operation. The resulting code afterwards performs its container operations on the elements returned by the lock calls.

Let us first look at how we extend the lock inference algorithm. When the backwards analysis now processes a statement, it checks whether the statement is a built-in container operation. In that case, it adds the operation along with its arguments to the set of shared variables, as shown in the comments on the left of Fig. 7. The set at the first statement of the atomic block holds all the shared variables that the atomic block will access plus the container operations that it will perform. The generated code locks all shared variables and invokes cont_lock per container operation (with the container and the key as arguments). The operations in the body of the atomic block are rewritten to use the element returned by the corresponding call of cont_lock.

There are two problems left open. First, cont_lock always has to return a reference to a container element, even if the element with the given key is not present in the container. Second, since the atomic blocks now lock container elements at the beginning, a del must be delayed until the atomic block is left. Suppose that an atomic block performs a del(k) followed by an add(k). At the start of the atomic block, the two added invocations of cont_lock lock the same element e. If the atomic block deleted e immediately, then (a) the mapping of the *second* cont_lock call from k to e would be destroyed and (b) a cont_lock for k in a concurrently running atomic block that happens *between* the del(k) and the add(k) would lock some other element e', i.e., the two blocks would run concurrently despite the semantic conflict.

To simplify the discussion of the solutions for both problems, we use the implementation details of a singly linked list as shown in Fig. 8. A similar

```
class Node {
    int key, rm;
    bool dummy;
    Node next;
};

Node cont_lock(List l, int k) {
again:
    Node p = l.head, prev = NULL;
    for (; p != NULL; p = p.next) {
        if (p.rm != -1 && done(p.rm)) {
            prev.next = p.next;
            free(p);
        }
        prev = p;
        if (p.key == k) {
            lock(p.key);
            if (p.rm != -1 && done(p.rm)) {
                unlock(p.key); goto again;
            } else return p;
        } }
    p = new Node(k);
    lock(p.key);
    prev.next = p;
    return p;
}
```

```
bool del(List l, Node p) {
    p.rm = TS;
    if (p.dummy == false) {
        return false;
    }
    p.dummy = true;
    return true;
}

bool add(List l, Node p) {
    p.rm = -1;
    if (p.dummy == false) {
        return false;
    }
    p.dummy = false;
    return true;
}

bool find(List l, Node p) {
    if (p.dummy == true) {
        p.rm = TS;
        return false;
    }
    p.rm = -1;
    return true;
}
```

Fig. 8. Improved container operations for use in lock inference.

reasoning applies to other types of containers. Another simplification to ease understanding is that the code in Fig. 8 is not thread-safe.

To solve the first problem, cont_lock searches for the desired key (ignore the removability/p.rm checks for now). If successful, it locks the key field and returns a reference to the element. If the element is not present in the container, cont_lock creates a new dummy with the given key, locks it, and returns a reference to it. The other container operations have to deal with these dummies. For instance, add detects that an element was not already present if cont_lock returns a dummy.

To solve the second problem, an atomic block could keep a log of the elements that need to be removed upon exit. Instead, we leave deleted elements in the container, flag them as removed, and let the next atomic block actually purge them when its cont_locks traverse the container. Thus a deletion of an element e has its rm set to the start timestamp (TS) of the deleting an atomic block. In addition, the element is also turned into a dummy so that add can work correctly. If later another atomic block's cont_lock sees an element with an coderm field set to the TS of a terminated atomic block, the element is purged. This check is needed twice, as there is a small window of time between a successful key comparison and a lock operation, during which another atomic block may have marked the element as removed. We use hazard pointers [13] to safely reclaim memory of removed elements.

Our technique also works with container operations in atomic blocks that concurrently executed in TM mode or that switch between modes. The reason is that container operations in TM mode use transactional predication. Since this technique accesses the `key` field of an element transactionally and `cont_lock` locks the `key` field, atomic blocks that run in different modes correctly mutually exclude each other.

Although we presented our technique for a simplified singly linked list, our prototype also provides the lock-free singly linked lists of Fomitchev et al. [5], hash tables with the singly linked list as their foundation, the concurrent self-balancing binary search tree from Bronson et al. [1], and a priority queue using the concurrent heap implementation from Hunt et al. [5]. The overhead for container operations and memory reclamation compared to a straightforward implementation of a transactional container is comparable to the overhead of containers that use transactional predication [2], since roughly the same amount of instrumentation is needed.

5   Evaluation

We evaluate our approach on 6 of 8 programs of the STAMP benchmark suite [3] (*Genome, Intruder, Kmeans, Labyrinth, SSCA2*, and *Yada*). We omitted the other two codes since our prototype cannot handle them yet. As as most of their atomic blocks cannot run in lock mode, we would see the run times of a pure TM implementation anyways. We changed the codes to use lists, sets, etc. by calling macros and adjusted the macro definitions to use either the original STAMP containers or our specialized containers. All measurements were performed on a 2.66 GHz, 8 core Xeon (X5550) with 8 MB cache and 24 GB main memory, with Linux 2.6, using 1, 2, 4, or 8 cores.

We time three versions of our runs: (a) Pure STM uses SwissTM [4] as STM. We made its lock operations callable from lock mode and changed the commit code to have the structure of the code in Fig. 2. (b) Pure lock inference. (c) Our combined approach which is implemented as a whole-program analysis within LLVM [12].

Figure 9 shows all execution times as speedups relative to the normalized measurements of the single core STM (set to 1). The absolute execution times are given above the bars. We omit single core measurements since the runtime differences between the three configurations are irrelevant. We also omit single core non-STM runs since we are interested in relative execution time differences between pure STM/lock inference and our work. These differences are independent of the chosen baseline.

The general results demonstrate that our combined technique and optimizations work well. For *SSCA2* and *Yada*, our combined technique has about the same performance as STM, but it outperforms STM in the other benchmarks, since it provides the same fine-grained locking with less overhead. With the exception of *Kmeans*, the combined approach is always better than lock inference, since the latter generates a coarse-grained locking in most benchmarks, which reduces parallelism.

Let us now take a closer look at the results of the individual benchmarks. *SSCA2* is a benchmark with little contention. As the 10 small atomic blocks

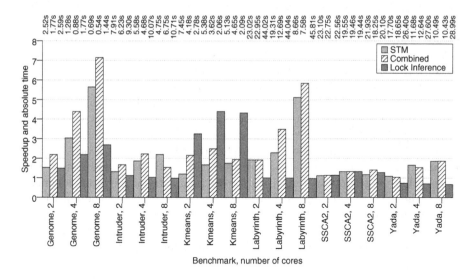

Fig. 9. Speedups (higher is better) and absolute execution times.

access only up to 5 shared variables each, our technique cannot reduce the already negligible STM overheads much. Turning 9 atomic blocks into lock mode and having the last block switch from TM mode (access to 4 variables) to lock mode (access to 1 variable) does hence not alter the runtimes - we see almost the same results with pure lock inference.

From *Yada's* 6 atomic blocks we can turn 5 into lock mode. Three of them only use a bounded number of variables. One atomic block benefits from a specialized heap container class. The fifth block benefits from runtime inspection and from a loop of hoisted cont_lock calls. It traverses a thread-private vector and adds some of its elements to the heap. Unfortunately, *Yada's* largest and longest-running atomic block must stay in TM mode as it is recursive and its variable accesses cannot be statically precomputed. In total, our technique can hence only improve performance by a factor of 1.4 to 2.8. Pure lock inference is worst as it generates a coarse-grained locking for both the recursive atomic block and the blocks that operate on the heap.

Kmeans has 3 atomic blocks. Two of them we can easily turn into lock mode. The third block updates one element of an array A and several elements of an array B. As the element of A is known at the entry of the atomic block and the loop that changes B is inspectable, this block can also run in lock mode. In total, our technique makes *Kmeans* run 1.1 to 1.9 times faster than pure STM. The reason is that compared to STM, the loop that updates B runs without any overhead. Pure lock inference needs to acquire a single global lock for the loop. Although this is more coarse-grained than what our technique can achieve, it is faster because *Kmeans* only has little contention.

Intruder also has 3 atomic blocks. There is one atomic block that removes items from some queue, and another block that adds items to its queue.

The queueing codes are simple enough that both pure lock inference and our technique can generate fine-grained synchronization for them. The third atomic block assembles fragments of network packets. By means of an ID that is used as a key into a map, each of the fragments refers to the packet it belongs to. The map entry is a list of all fragments that belong to the same packet. The atomic block keeps adding packets to their list until it sees the last fragment of a packet. At that point it assembles the packet by traversing the list and by adding the assembled packet to a queue. With our specialized maps and lists, we can turn this atomic block into lock mode and outperform STM by a factor of 1.2 to 1.9 for small thread counts. Only for 8 threads STM is still 1.4 times faster. The reason is that we generate a cont_lock for the map entry of the input fragment and lock the *entire* list to protect the traversal against concurrent modifications. At higher thread counts, STM wastes less time compared to the sequential bottleneck of locking the entire list. Compared to pure lock inference, we are 1.5 to 2.2 times faster because we generate a finer-grained locking for the third atomic block.

Labyrinth also has 3 atomic blocks. One block removes an item from a queue and both pure lock inference and our technique generate fine-grained synchronization for it. Another block adds an element to a list, which we can turn into lock mode by using a specialized container. The third block holds an inspectable loop that traverses and updates shared elements stored in a thread-private vector. Pure lock inference generates a coarse-grained locking for the second and third block, whereas all atomic blocks run in lock mode in our approach. For these reasons, we are 1.1 to 1.4 times faster than STM and even 1.9 to 6.0 times faster than pure lock inference.

Genome has 5 atomic blocks. The first block contains a loop that adds elements to a hash table, which runs in TM mode and uses transactional predication for the hash table. In principle, this block could be made to run in lock mode by generating an inspector with cont_lock calls that store the references in an array for later use by the executor. But with the exception of the heap in *Yada*, our prototype currently does not support specialized container operations within inspectable loops. We can run the remaining atomic blocks in lock mode though. Two of them only insert into a specialized hash table. One of them holds an inspectable loop that searches for the first element with a NULL field, which is overwritten at the end of the loop. Turning 4 of 5 blocks into lock mode outperforms STM by a factor of 1.3 and 1.4. It is also 1.4 to 2.7 times faster than pure lock inference, because the latter has to use coarse-grained synchronization for since 4 of the 5 atomic blocks due to their statically unbounded number of variables.

6 Related Work

Usui et al. [15] combine TM and locks for their adaptive locks. We determine the lock set automatically, but in their system, a programmer has to specify which locks an atomic blocks needs. At runtime, an atomic block either acquires the locks or it uses TM. A profiling mechanism determines which mode is more efficient. However, their atomic blocks cannot switch from TM to locks during execution. Moreover, *all* their atomic blocks use the same mode, while we allow the modes to coexist concurrently.

FastLane [16] is an STM implementation that lowers transactional overheads for low thread counts. An atomic block is either executed speculatively inside a transaction or with little logging overhead by holding a global mutex. If the thread count is low, using a single mutex has less overhead than the transactional overhead. As in our work, transactions may run concurrently to the atomic block that holds the global mutex. However, our approach is not limited to low thread counts and our lock mode uses fine-grained locking instead of a single global mutex.

As the building blocks of our work are transactional memory (TM) [9] and lock inference [7], some optimizations from these fields are related to our optimizations.

Transactional boosting [8] and transactional predication [2] provide efficient container data structures to be used in transactions in order to avoid low-level conflicts. We extend these ideas from their restricted applicability to TM only, and ensure a fine-grained locking with lock inference in coexistence with TM.

The work of Golan-Gueta et al. [6] automatically determines a fine-grained locking for container data structures. Like our specialized containers, it renders atomic blocks that use containers amenable to lock inference. Unlike our work, it is not designed for arbitrary code, e.g., for container operations embedded in some larger atomic block. We could however use their work to derive fine-grained synchronized containers from sequential code instead of building-in specialized containers by hand.

It is important to reduce the number of locks that atomic blocks must acquire. Zhang et al. [17] show how to compute a minimal lock assignment (MLA). Since MLA is NP-hard, lock dominance [10] is an approximation algorithm. If one atomic block needs locks a and b, and another atomic block needs locks b and c, it is sufficient if both blocks only acquire b. Since lock dominance is performed after lock inference, atomic blocks that access an unbounded number of variables do not benefit from it, whereas our optimizations achieve fine-grained synchronization. It is open research how to use lock assignment optimizations when there is a coexistence of lock mode and TM mode.

Galois [11] is an optimistic parallelization system where programmers write classes and a specification which methods can or cannot run concurrently to each other. However, it is not a general technique to implement atomic blocks.

7   Conclusions

This paper has shown how the advantages of lock inference and transactional memory can be combined in order to implement atomic blocks with fine-grained synchronization and little overhead. We have also presented two optimizations that remove some of the limits of state-of-the-art static lock inference. With those optimizations, we (a) achieve fine-grained synchronization even if the number of variables accessed is statically unbounded and (b) we see improved performance on standard container types. The evaluation with a widely used benchmark suite shows speedups between 1.1 and 6.0 compared to pure STM or pure lock inference. Future studies will examine how to combine our technique with upcoming hardware transactional memory systems. Another line of future work will integrate automatic fine-grained synchronization of containers and lock assignment optimizations and extend them towards mode-combining.

References

1. Bronson, N.G., Casper, J., Chafi, H., Olukotun, K.: A practical concurrent binary search tree. In: PPoPP'10: Proceedings of the Symposium on Principles and Practice Parallel Programming, Bangalore, India, pp. 257–268, Jan 2010
2. Bronson, N.G., Casper, J., Chafi, H., Olukotun, K.: Transactional predication: high-performance concurrent sets and maps for STM. In: PODC'10: Proceedings of the Symposium on Principles of Distributed Computing, Zurich, Switzerland, pp. 6–15, Jul 2010
3. Cao Minh, C., Chung, J., Kozyrakis, C., Olukotun, K.: STAMP: stanford transactional applications for multi-processing. In: Proceedings of the Symposium on Workload Characterization (IISWC'08), Seattle, WA, pp. 35–46, Sep 2008
4. Dragojević, A., Guerraoui, R., Kapalka, M.: Stretching transactional memory. In: PLDI '09: Proceedings of the Conference on Programming Language Design and Implementation, Dublin, Ireland, pp. 155–165, June 2009
5. Fomitchev, M., Ruppert, E.: Lock-free linked lists and skip lists. In: PODC'04: Proceedings of the Symposium on Principles of Distributed Computing, St. John's, Newfoundland, Canada, pp. 50–59, Jul 2004
6. Golan-Gueta, G., Bronson, N., Aiken, A., Ramalingam, G., Sagiv, M., Yahav, E.: Automatic fine-grain locking using shape properties. In: OOPSLA'11: Proceedings of the International Conference on Object Oriented Programming Systems Languages and Applications, Portland, OR, pp. 225–242, Oct 2011
7. Gudka, K., Harris, T., Eisenbach, S.: Lock inference in the presence of large libraries. In: Noble, J. (ed.) ECOOP 2012. LNCS, vol. 7313, pp. 308–332. Springer, Heidelberg (2012)
8. Herlihy, M., Koskinen, E.: Transactional boosting: a methodology for highly-concurrent transactional objects. In: PPoPP'08: Proceedings of the Symposium on Principles and Practice Parallel Programming, Salt Lake City, UT, pp. 207–216, Feb 2008
9. Herlihy, M., Moss, J.E.B.: Transactional memory: architectural support for lock-free data structures. ACM SIGARCH Comput. Archit. News 21(2), 289–300 (1993)
10. Hicks, M., Foster, J.S., Prattikakis, P.: Lock inference for atomic sections. In: Proceedings of the Workshop on Languages, Compilers, and Hardware Support for Transactional Computing (TRANSACT'06), Ottawa, Canada, pp. 304–315, June 2006
11. Kulkarni, M., Pingali, K., Walter, B., Ramanarayanan, G., Bala, K., Chew, L.P.: Optimistic parallelism requires abstractions. In: PLDI '07: Proceedings of the Conference on Programming Language Design and Implementation, PLDI '07, San Diego, CA, pp. 211–222, June 2007

12. Lattner, C., Adve, V.: LLVM: a compilation framework for lifelong program analysis and transformation. In: CGO'04: Proceedings of the International Symposium on Code Generation and Optimization, Palo Alto, CA, pp. 75–85, March 2004
13. Michael, M.M.: Hazard pointers: safe memory reclamation for lock-free objects. IEEE Trans. Parallel Distrib. Syst. **15**(6), 491–504 (2004)
14. Saltz, J.H., Mirchandaney, R., Crowley, K.: Run-time parallelization and scheduling of loops. IEEE Trans. Comput. **40**(5), 603–612 (1991)
15. Usui, T., Behrends, R., Evans, J., Smaragdakis, Y.: Adaptive locks: Combining transactions and locks for efficient concurrency. In: PACT'09: Proceedings of the International Conference on Parallel Architectures and Compilation Techniques, Raleigh, NC, pp. 3–14, Sep 2009
16. Wamhoff, J.T., Fetzer, C., Felber, P., Rivière, E., Muller, G.: FastLane: improving performance of software transactional memory for low thread counts. In: PPoPP'13: Proceedings of the Symposium on Principles and Practice Parallel Programming, Shenzhen, China, pp. 113–122, Feb 2013
17. Zhang, Y., Sreedhar, V.C., Zhu, W., Sarkar, V., Gao, G.R.: Minimum lock assignment: a method for exploiting concurrency among critical sections. In: Amaral, J.N. (ed.) LCPC 2008. LNCS, vol. 5335, pp. 141–155. Springer, Heidelberg (2008)

Speculative Execution of Parallel Programs with Precise Exception Semantics on GPUs

Akihiro Hayashi[✉], Max Grossman, Jisheng Zhao, Jun Shirako, and Vivek Sarkar

Department of Computer Science, Rice University, Houston, TX, USA
{ahayashi,jmg3,jisheng.zhao,shirako,vsarkar}@rice.edu

Abstract. General purpose computing on GPUs (GPGPU) can enable significant performance and energy improvements for certain classes of applications. However, current GPGPU programming models, such as CUDA and OpenCL, are only accessible by systems experts through low-level C/C++ APIs. In contrast, large numbers of programmers use high-level languages, such as Java, due to their productivity advantages of type safety, managed runtimes and precise exception semantics. Current approaches to enabling GPGPU computing in Java and other managed languages involve low-level interfaces to native code that compromise the semantic guarantees of managed languages, and are not readily accessible to mainstream programmers.

In this paper, we propose compile-time and runtime technique for accelerating Java programs with automatic generation of OpenCL while preserving precise exception semantics. Our approach includes (1) automatic generation of OpenCL kernels and JNI glue code from a Java-based parallel-loop construct (**forall**), (2) speculative execution of OpenCL kernels on GPUs, and (3) automatic generation of optimized and parallel exception-checking code for execution on the CPU. A key insight in supporting our speculative execution is that the GPU's device memory is separate from the CPU's main memory, so that, in the case of a misspeculation (exception), any side effects in a GPU kernel can be ignored by simply not communicating results back to the CPU.

We demonstrate the efficiency of our approach using eight Java benchmarks on two GPU-equipped platforms. Experimental results show that our approach can significantly accelerate certain classes of Java programs on GPUs while maintaining precise exception semantics.

1 Introduction

Programming models for general-purpose computing on GPUs (GPGPU), such as CUDA and OpenCL, can enable significant performance and energy improvements for certain classes of applications. However, these programming models provide system experts with low-level C/C++ APIs and require programmers to write, maintain, and optimize a non-trivial amount of application code.

In contrast, large numbers of programmers use high-level languages, such as Java, because these languages provide high-productivity features including

© Springer International Publishing Switzerland 2014
C. Caşcaval and P. Montesinos (Eds.): LCPC 2013, LNCS 8664, pp. 342–356, 2014.
DOI: 10.1007/978-3-319-09967-5_20

type safety, a managed runtime, and precise exception semantics. However, the performance of an application can often suffer due to runtime overheads caused by the additional logic required to enforce these guarantees. In addition, using heterogeneous systems to accelerate applications in these high-level languages is a difficult and error-prone task. Accessing OpenCL or CUDA's C/C++ API from Java requires the use of the Java Native Interface (JNI) API, immediately removing many of the programmability benefits of Java software development.

In our recent work [6], we introduced Habanero-Java [3] with OpenCL generation (HJ-OpenCL), an extension to the parallel HJ programming language. HJ-OpenCL enables execution of parallel `forall` loops on any heterogeneous processor in an OpenCL platform without any code change to the original HJ source. However, this approach requires programmers to use a `safe` language construct to explicitly specify conditions which are required to preserve Java exception semantics. With the `safe` construct, the programmer provides a boolean condition that ensures a parallel loop is not expected to throw an exception and can be safely executed outside of the JVM. However, the use of `safe` construct requires additional development effort. The runtime overhead of manual exception checking is not negligible when running applications which have indirect array access and non-affine array access.

In this work, we propose extensions to the compile-time and runtime techniques introduced in HJ-OpenCL which preserve precise exception semantics when executing a parallel `forall` loop outside the JVM. Unlike our previous work, the compiler automatically translates a `forall` loop into two parallel routines. The first routine contains an equivalent OpenCL implementation of the original `forall` loop, including all initialization, communication, and computation code required to transfer execution to an OpenCL device. The second routine is a transformation and subset of the instructions in the original forall loop which guarantees any runtime exception thrown by the original loop will also be thrown by the transformed version. If an exception occurs during execution of this specialized exception-checking code, execution transfers to a JVM-only implementation of the parallel loop. The runtime speculatively executes the specialized-checking code and the full OpenCL implementation in parallel to reduce the overhead of exception checking.

This paper makes the following contributions:

1. Automatic generation of OpenCL code from Habanero-Java for speculative execution on GPUs.
2. Automatic generation of optimized and parallel exception-checking code for execution on the multiple CPU cores.
3. Performance evaluation of the proposed scheme on multiple heterogeneous platforms with CPU and GPU cores.

2   Motivation

While past evaluation of GPUs on extremely parallel and computationally heavy applications have demonstrated clear performance benefits for appropriate applications [18,22], there still remain application domains which could make use of

GPUs but do not. This missed opportunity is primarily caused by the sub-par programmability offered by existing GPU programming models: CUDA and OpenCL. In addition, these programming models are still only accessible from low-level programming languages, out of the scope of most high-level program-mers' experience. To make the performance benefits of GPUs available to a wide range of developers it is necessary to build interfaces which are similar to and compatible with the managed languages in widespread use today. Arguably, the most pervasive example of this category of programming languages is Java.

Today, Java programmers can manually utilize GPUs using CUDA and OpenCL through JNI. However, native, OpenCL, or CUDA execution through JNI eliminates one of the primary safety benefits of the Java development envi-ronment: exceptions. Java's precise exception semantics provide a Java pro-grammer with safety guarantees in regards to the correct execution of their application code. For example, these guarantees include checks for null pointer references, out-of-bounds array accesses, and division-by-zero. On the other hand, many natively compiled language provide no guarantees that a reference does not jump into a completely separate array, or object. As a result, incorrect appli-cation behavior can be difficult to diagnose in the absence of precise exception semantics.

As an illustrative example we consider the case of sparse matrix-matrix mul-tiplication. Executing this computation the JVM would ensure that the row and column indices stored to represent a sparse matrix are within the bounds of a full output matrix. However, if the Java programmer took advantage of JNI to achieve improved performance through native execution all exception semantics would be forfeit. To maintain the same guarantees, the programmer would have to manually insert exception checking code in their Java or native code which checked the stored row and column indices against the bounds of the output matrix before submitting the kernel to the GPU. Doing so would increase code complexity and future maintainability.

This work addresses the problem of melding the performance characteristics of native GPU execution with the safety guarantees of JVM execution. It does so by enabling execution of a parallel Java application on any OpenCL hard-ware platform without any hand-written native code. This approach removes the pain points of JVM-OpenCL applications while providing the benefits of both managed and native execution.

3   Habanero Java Language

This section describes features of the Habanero-Java (HJ) parallel programming language and compilation flow for supporting OpenCL code generation.

3.1   Overview of HJ Language

The Habanero Java (HJ) parallel programming language under development at Rice University [3] provides an execution model for multicore processors that

builds on four orthogonal constructs, and was derived from early experiences
with the X10 [5] language:

1. Lightweight *dynamic task creation and termination* using *async* and *finish*,
   future and *forall* constructs [19].
2. *Locality control* with task and data distributions using the *place* construct
   [15].
3. Mutual exclusion and isolation among tasks using the *isolated* construct [21].
4. Collective and point-to-point synchronization using the *phasers* construct [10]
   along with their accompanying *phaser accumulators* [11].

In HJ-OpenCL, programmers use the `forall` language feature to identify
parallel loops as candidates for OpenCL execution. The statement "`forall`(`point`
`p` : *region*) ⟨*stmt*⟩" indicates a parallel loop whose iteration space is defined by
a *region*. The region can be one- or multi-dimensional space, e.g., `[0:M-1,0:N-1]`
for a 2-D iteration space. Each iteration instance executes the loop body ⟨*stmt*⟩
for a distinct *point* in the iteration space. All `forall` loops end with an implicit
barrier. In addition, HJ-OpenCL supports all-to-all synchronization points in
those parallel loops [6] through the *next* statement. The HJ-OpenCL compiler
and runtime trust these annotations when generating and executing code on
GPUs.

3.2   Compilation Flow

Figure 1 illustrates the HJ compilation and runtime flow for HJ-OpenCL. The
HJ-OpenCL compiler leverages APARAPI [1], a comprehensive, open-source
framework for executing computational kernels from Java applications on
OpenCL devices. For this work we extended the APARAPI component that
generates OpenCL code from Java bytecode. In addition to OpenCL kernels,
glue code must be automatically generated to transfer execution and data from
the JVM to the OpenCL device and back. This functionality is provided internally by the HJ-OpenCL compiler, and includes the generation of JNI functions,
OpenCL API calls, and transformed bytecode.

In summary, the HJ-OpenCL compiler takes an HJ program as input, and
produces:

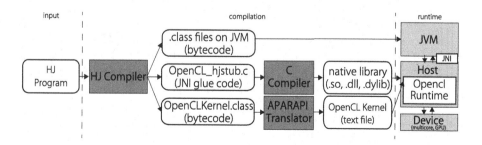

Fig. 1. Compilation and runtime flow

1. Java CLASS files for execution on the JVM;
2. JNI glue code to mediate between the JVM and OpenCL kernels;
3. A Java CLASS file which contains the bytecode to be translated to OpenCL kernels by the APARAPI bytecode translator.

4   Speculative Exception Checking Scheme

In the approach introduced in this paper, the HJ-OpenCL compiler from [6] is extended to automatically generate exception checking code and OpenCL kernel code for the `forall` loops in an HJ program. The exception checking code is a specialized version of the original `forall` loop which replaces all stores with loads. By enclosing this specialized loop with a Java *try-catch* block, HJ-OpenCL can detect all runtime exceptions generated by the original `forall` loop. The details of the code transformation algorithm for generating this exception loop is shown in Sect. 4.2. The exception checking loop is run in parallel on CPU cores in parallel with a speculatively and optimistically launched OpenCL kernel running on the GPU. Optimizing the exception checking code is important for cases where it is on the critical path of the application, i.e. where the exception checking code in the JVM finishes later than the OpenCL kernel.

The rest of this Section is organized as follows: Sect. 4.1 introduces the HJ-OpenCL runtime design. Section 4.2 describes optimizations applied to the exception checking loop by the HJ-OpenCL compiler.

4.1   Speculative Exception Checking Runtime

Figure 2 illustrates the runtime interactions between the HJ runtime, the JVM, the OpenCL runtime on the host, and the OpenCL kernel on the device. The following steps (illustrated by the example generated code in Fig. 3) explain the basic workflow of speculatively executing a `forall` loop on the GPU while running exception checking code in the JVM.

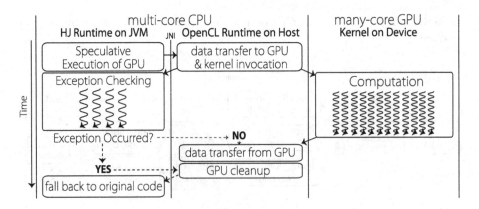

Fig. 2. The execution model of speculative exception checking

```
 1 public class Example {
 2   static { System.loadLibrary(''libCalc''); }
 3   public static native void openCL_Kernel0_first (...) ;
 4   public static native void openCL_Kernel0_second (...) ;
 5   public static void main(String [] args) {
 6     ...
 7   boolean excpFlag = false ;
 8   /* (1) Speculative GPU execution through JNI */
 9   openCL_Kernel0_first (...) ;
10   /* (2) Exception Checking Code on JVM */
11   try {
12     forall (point [i]:[0:N-1]) {
13       int dummy1 = A[i];
14       int dummy2 = B[i];
15       int dummy3 = C[i];
16     }
17   } catch (Exception e) {
18     excpFlag = true ;
19   }
20   /* (1) Second JNI Call */
21   openCL_Kernel0_second (excpFlag , ...) ;
22   if (excpFlag) {
23     /* (3) Original Implementaion */
24     forall (point [i]:[0:N-1]) {
25       A[i] = B[i] + C[i];
26     }
27   }
28 }
```

Fig. 3. Generated code for Vector Addition by the HJ-OpenCL compiler

Step 1: The HJ runtime invokes the first JNI function. In the callee, the OpenCL API is called to perform host-to-device data transfer and asynchronously launch the corresponding OpenCL kernel on a device. The host application immediately returns to JVM execution. Blocking data transfers are necessary so that Java objects can be released before returning to the JVM. This step is done in the native method call to *openCL_Kernel0_first()* on line 9 of Fig. 3.

Step 2: The exception checking loop is run in the JVM, as seen on lines, seen on lines 12–16 of Fig. 3. This loop is a transformation of the original `forall` loop which:
1. Reduces computational load.
2. Reduces I/O load and eliminates any externally visible state change caused by the loop.
3. Guarantees the same exceptions thrown by the original loop would also be thrown by the transformed version.

Step 3: The HJ runtime invokes a second JNI call (line 21 of Fig. 3) which waits for the completion of computation on the OpenCL device[1], transfers data from the device, and performs OpenCL cleanup. If an exception occurs during execution of the exception checking loop, the OpenCL runtime does not transfer any state back to the host and the HJ runtime executes the original `forall` loop in the JVM, thus maintaining Java exception semantics.

---

[1] The OpenCL runtime has to wait for the completion of the kernel execution even in the event of an exception because there is no OpenCL API to terminate kernel on device currently.

4.2   Generation and Optimization of Exception Checking Code

This section describes how to generate and optimize the exception checking code. The generated exception checking code must meet two requirements. It must be side-effect free, i.e. have no memory store operations and no invocation of system APIs. It must also preserve all exceptions which would be triggered from the original `forall` loop. If either of these requirements cannot be met, the HJ-OpenCL compiler aborts code generation and reverts to parallel execution within the JVM.

The basic workflow of the generation and optimization of exception checking code is described in Algorithm 1. It takes the original `forall` loop (L) as input and generates the optimized exception checking code (OCC) as output. Before applying Algorithm 1, some analysis and transformations are performed to verify the correctness of running the `forall` loop with speculative exception checking:

1. Side-effect analysis to identify procedures which potentially have side-effects.
2. Function inlining applied for all non-recursive functions invoked within the `forall` loop.
3. Alias analysis which works out may or must equality between any two object references.
4. Data dependence analysis which calculates def-use chains.

After pre-analysis and transformation, if the `forall` loop still contains unanalyzable array or procedures which may have side-effects, then it is not suitable for speculative OpenCL execution and the HJ-OpenCL compiler aborts exception code generation (Line 1).

Algorithm 1 begins by inspecting all array access statements in the `forall` loop to retain any statements which may throw an `ArrayIndexOutOfBounds Exception`. For each array store statement *aStore*, the HJ-OpenCL compiler replaces the statement by an array read statement *aLoad* (lines 6–20) and traverses the def/use chain (built by pre-analysis) to check its users. In the case that the stored value is loaded by successors within the same loop iteration, the compiler applies scalar replacement on the load statement with the stored value and marks it as keep (lines 13–15). For the case that the store value is loaded in the successors which cross loop iterations, the HJ-OpenCL the compiler sets *excpFlag* with *true* (line 10–12) and aborts code generation. For the array load statement, the HJ-OpenCL compiler marks it as *keep* (line 24–27). The last step is to mark statements which derive denominator of division statement to keep statement, as they may trigger an `ArithmeticException`.

After applying Algorithm 1 to generate conservative exception checking code, HJ-OpenCL compiler performs two optimization on the generated code to eliminate redundancy: loop invariant code motion (LICM) and redundant load elimination.

Figure 4 provides an example of HJ-OpenCL code generation and optimization. Figure 4(a) contains the `forall` loop of a sparse matrix multiply application in 3-address code. Figure 4(b) shows the same 3-address code, but optimized by the HJ-OpenCL compiler for exception checking. Because there are indirect

Algorithm 1. Exception Checking Code Generation and Optimization

---

    input : L: One Forall Loop
    output: OCC: Optimized Checking Code

1 **if** *loop has unanalyzable array references or method calls* **then**
2 | abort
3 **end**
4 // For Array Bounds Check;
5 $A \leftarrow getAllArrayAccessStatement(loop)$;
6 **foreach** *aStmt in A* **do**
7 | // Get All Loop Index at Current Loop Nest;
8 | $I \leftarrow getOuterLoopIndices()$;
9 | **if** *aStmt is ArrayStore($A[i_1, i_2, ..., i_n] \leftarrow x$)* **then**
10 | | **transform** *aStmt to dummy* $\leftarrow A[i_1, i_2, ..., i_n]$;
11 | | $markedList \leftarrow aStmt$;
12 | | **if** $A[i_1, i_2, ..., i_n]$ *is used in followed statements* **then**
13 | | | **if** $A[i_1, i_2, ..., i_n]$ *drives array subscript in the future iteration* **then**
14 | | | | **abort**
15 | | **end**
16 | | **else**
17 | | | **rename** $A[i_1, i_2, ..., i_n]$ to x in each statement (as in scalar replacement);
18 | | **end**
19 | **end**
20 | **foreach** i_p *such that* $1 \leq p \leq n \wedge i_p \notin I$ **do**
21 | | $S \leftarrow$ statements which derive i_p (considering control flow);
22 | | $markedList \leftarrow S$;
23 | **end**
24   **end**
25   **else if** *aStmt is ArrayLoad ($x \leftarrow A[i_1, i_2, ..., i_n]$)* **then**
26 | $markedList \leftarrow aStmt$;
27 | **foreach** i_p *such that* $1 \leq p \leq n \wedge i_p \notin I$ **do**
28 | | $S \leftarrow$ statements which derive i_p (considering control flow);
29 | | $markedList \leftarrow S$;
30 | **end**
31   **end**
32 **end**
33 // For ArithmeticException;
34 $markedList \leftarrow \forall stmt$ such that $stmt$ derives denominator;
35 // Delete not marked statement;
36 $OCC \leftarrow \forall stmt$ in L such that $stmt \in markedList$;

```
1  forall (point [id]:[0:M]){
2      i1 = row[id];
3      row_begin = i1
4      i2 = id + 1;
5      i3 = row[i2];
6      row_end = i3;
7      i4 = row_end - row_begin;
8      for (i = 0; i < i4; i++) {
9          for (j = 0; j < inter; j++)
                {
10             i5 = row_begin + i;
11             d1 = Av[i5];
12             i6 = row_begin + i;
13             i7 = Aj[i6];
14             d2 = x[i7];
15             d3 = d1 * d2;
16             d4 = sum + d3;
17             sum = d4;
18         }
19     }
20     y[id] = sum;
21 }
```

(a) Original 3-address Code

```
1  forall (point [id]:[0:M]){
2      i1 = row[id];
3      row_begin = i1
4      i2 = id + 1;
5      i3 = row[i2];
6      row_end = i3;
7      i4 = row_end - row_begin;
8      for (i = 0; i < i4; i++) {
9          i5 = row_begin + i;
10         d1 = Av[i5];
11         i6 = row_begin + i;
12         i7 = Aj[i6];
13         d2 = x[i7];
14     }
15     dummy = y[id];
16 }
```

(b) Optimized 3-address Code

Fig. 4. Optimization example for sparse matrix multiply

accesses of arrays *row*, *Av*, *Aj* and *x*, the HJ-OpenCL compiler does not remove statements which derive array subscripts of these arrays.

5   Performance Evaluation

This section presents experimental results for HJ-OpenCL on two platforms.

The first platform is an AMD *A10-5800K* APU. This APU includes an AMD Radeon HD 7660D GPU with 6 Streaming Multiprocessors (SMs). The CPU of the *A10-5800K* includes 4 cores, 16 KB of L1 cache per core, and 32 MB of L2 cache. Each SM in the GPU has exclusive access to 32 KB of local scratchpad memory. The CPU and GPU can each access the same system memory, but share bandwidth when doing so. While physical memory is shared, it is partitioned between devices such that the CPU has 6 GB and the GPU has 2 GB. We conducted all experiments on this system using the Java SE Runtime Environment (build 1.6.0_21-b06) with Java HotSpot 64-Bit Server VM (build 17.0-b16, mixed mode).

The second platform has two hexacore Intel X5660 CPUs and two NVIDIA Tesla M2050 discrete GPUs connected over PCIe. There is a total of 48 GB within a single node that is shared by all 12 cores. Each GPU also has approximately 2.5 GB of global memory. Only 1 of the 2 available GPUs was used at a time to evaluate this work. In this platform, we used the Java SE Runtime Environment (build 1.6.0_25-b06) with Java HotSpot 64-Bit Server VM (build 20.0-b11, mixed mode).

The eight benchmarks shown in Table 1 were used in our experiments. Note that SparseMatMult, SAXPY and GEMVER have indirect array access.

Table 1. Information on the benchmarks used to evaluate HJ-OpenCL

Benckmark	Summary	Data size
SparseMatmult	Sparse matrix multiplication from the Java Grande Benchmarks [20]	Size C with $N = 500,000$
Doitgen	Multi-resolution analysis kernel from PolyBench [24], ported to Java	$128 \times 128 \times 128$
Crypt	Cryptographic application from the Java Grande Benchmarks [20]	Size C with $N= 50,000,000$
Blackscholes	Data-parallel financial application which calculates the price of European put and call options	16,777,216 virtual options
MRIQ	Three-dimensional medical benchmark from Parboil [23], ported to Java	Large size ($64 \times 64 \times 64$)
MatMult	A standard dense matrix multiplication: $C = A.B$	1024×1024
SAXPY	Sparse version of SAXPY from [12], ported to Java	$25,000 \times 25,000$
GEMVER	Sparse BLAS function from [12], ported to Java	10,000,000

The baseline for this evaluation was sequential Java. We tested execution on Open-CL GPUs using HJ-OpenCL's code generation and runtime in the following modes:

- **No checking:** execute the full computation on the GPU without any exception checking, removing precise Java exception semantics.
- **Non-speculative execution:** run the unoptimized or optimized exception checking code in the JVM, followed by the full computation on the GPU. This mode retains precise Java exception semantics but serializes exception checking and computation, leading to higher overhead.
- **Speculative execution:** run the unoptimized or optimized exception checking code in the JVM in parallel with the full computation on the GPU. This mode retains precise Java exception semantics while minimizing overhead.

In the following sections, these five variants are referred to as HJ OpenCL GPU(No checking), HJ OpenCL GPU(Non-speculative, unoptimized), HJ OpenCL GPU(Non-speculative, optimized), HJ OpenCL GPU(Speculative, unoptimized) and HJ OpenCL GPU(Speculative, optimized) respectively. We

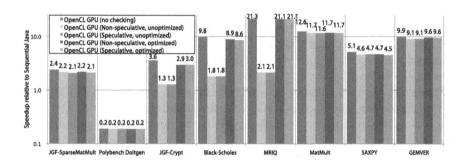

Fig. 5. Performance improvements relative to sequential Java on the *A10-5800K*

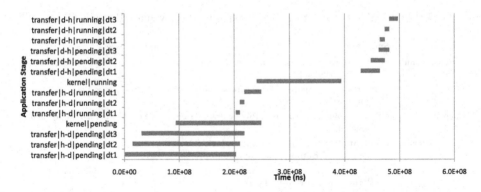

Fig. 6. Sample timeline of the Black-Scholes application on the *A10-5800K*

run each benchmark 10 times and report the median value as the result. Note that we exclude the overhead of the OpenCL context and command queue creation from these measurements for precise measurements because we see timing in variation.

5.1 Performance on AMD A10-5800K

Figure 5 shows the speedup numbers on the AMD *A10-5800K* APU relative to the sequential Java version. On the AMD APU system, exception checking is done in parallel on 4 cores. OpenCL(Speculative, optimized) approach shows speedups of up to 21.1× relative to sequential Java, while maintaining Java exception semantics. Only one benchmark (Polybench DoitGen) showed a slowdown due to OpenCL execution on this platform, though (as we will see later) it showed a speedup on the Westmere+Tesla platform. Performance differences between OpenCL(No Checking) and OpenCL(Speculative, optimized) range from 0.5 %(Polybench Doitgen) to 18.6 %(JGF-Crypt). JGF-Crypt, BlackScholes, MRIQ and GEMVER each show significant improvement from exception checking code optimization. For these applications, exception checking takes longer than OpenCL execution. Additionally, deleting java.lang.Math method calls which does not derive array index dramatically accelerates exception checking code for BlackScholes and MRIQ.

Polybench Doitgen, MatMult, and SAXPY exception checking code, these benchmarks do not show speedup from optimization because the checking code is not on the critical path.

Figure 6 shows a timeline of OpenCL execution on the AMD APU. Figure 6 was gathered using the OpenCL *cl*GetEventProfilingInfo function to get information on when commands are submitted to the device for execution, when commands actually begin execution, and when commands complete execution. Each row in the figure is categorized as either a pending operation, which shows the time between a command being submitted and starting, or a running operation, which shows the time between a command starting and finishing. Each

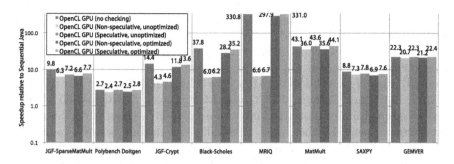

Fig. 7. Performance improvements relative to sequential Java on *Westmere*

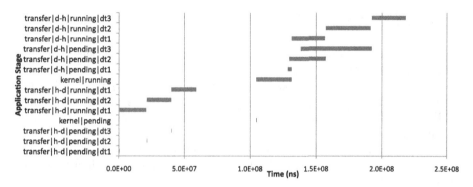

Fig. 8. Sample timeline of the Black-Scholes application on *Westmere*

operation is also categorized as either a kernel or transfer operation, and transfer operations are broken down by the variable being transferred the direction of transfer. *h-d* indicates a copy from the host system to the GPU, and *d-h* indicates a copy from the GPU to the host. On the AMD APU, pending time accounts for a significant amount of execution time for both transfers and kernels. That is why no application shows speedup with speculative execution unlike NVIDIA GPU. For example, the AMD OpenCL runtime does not start three data transfers for the first 2.0E+08 (ns). This seems to be an issue with the AMD OpenCL libraries. Despite this, we see a gap between the completion of the *k*ernel—running operation and the start of *t*ransfer—d-h—pending—dt1 operation. This indicates that the critical path on the AMD APU for Black-Scholes is the exception checking code, which explains the significant improvements from optimized exception checking in Fig. 5.

5.2   Performance on Westmere

Figure 7 shows the speedups on the *Westmere* platform with two NVIDIA Tesla GPUs (of which we currently only use one) and two hexacore Intel CPUs.

On this platform, exception checking is done by 12 cores. The proposed OpenCL(Speculative, optimized) mode shows speedups of up to 331.0× relative to sequential Java while maintaining Java's exception semantics. Performance differences between OpenCL(No Checking) and OpenCL(Speculative, optimized) vary from -2.4%(MatMult)[2] to 27.9%(JGF-Crypt). JGF-Sparse-MatMult, Polybench Doitgen, JGF-Crypt, BlackScholes, MRIQ and GEMVER shows speedups from optimization because exception checking is on the application's critical path. Further, there is no difference in time between command submission and actually starting work on it (See Fig. 8). Additionally, more cores enable a shorter exception checking time. As a result speculative execution enables performance improvement in the range of 2.0% to 24.7%.

6 Related Work

The GPU code generation has been widely supported in high level language compilation systems.

Lime [7] is a JVM compatible language which generates OpenCL code automatically. Lime provides language extensions that express coarse grain tasks, SIMD parallelism. Its compiler generates Java bytecode, JNI glue code, and OpenCL kernels.

RootBeer [13] compiles Java to CUDA by specifying the code region within *gpuMethod*. The RootBeer compiler translates *gpuMethod()* method in *Kernel* interface into CUDA kernel.

JCUDA [17] provides programming interface which can be used by Java programmers to invoke CUDA kernels. Programmers can write Java codes that call CUDA kernels with special interface and JCUDA compiler generates the JNI glue code between the JVM and CUDA runtime by using this interface.

Android RenderScript [4] provides C-like programming model for GPUs. Programmer manually write a kernel and invoke it by using provided Java APIs.

To the best of our knowledge, none of these three systems (Lime, RootBeer, JCUDA, RenderScript) preserve Java's precise exception semantics with speculative execution, as in our work.

There also been related work on eliminating redundant checks for null pointer and array bound exceptions by generating dual version code. In Artigas et al. [2] and Moreira et al. [9], Their work generates dual-version code which consists of exception-safe regions and -unsafe regions. In exception-safe regions the compiler can perform aggressive loop optimization such as loop tiling. In contrast, the automatically generated exception-checking code in our approach that sets excpFlag can express more general conditions than in this past work e.g., see Fig. 3.

There has also been related past work on array bounds check elimination. Würthinger et al. [16] proposed an algorithm for Static Single Assignment (SSA) form for the JIT compiler which eliminates unnecessary bounds checking. ABCD [14] provides powerful array bounds checking elimination algorithm by creating an SSA-based inequality graph. Von Ronne et al. [8] proposed an static

---

[2] Theoretically this is unlikely, This is due to variation in timing.

annotation framework to reduce the overhead of dynamic checking in the JIT compiler. These past results complement our work since the exception checking code generated by our compilation system can be further optimized by these techniques.

In the context of speculative execution for parallel processing GPGPU, Paragon [12] runs the C/C++ loop speculatively, while monitoring the dependencies. The runtime transfers the execution to the CPU in case a conflict is detected. In contrast, we generate exception checking code that is executed on the CPU.

7   Conclusions

In this paper, we introduce a new compile-time and runtime approach for accelerating Java programs through automatic generation of OpenCL while maintaining precise exception semantics. To maintain precise exception semantics, the HJ-OpenCL compiler automatically generates code for the speculative execution of OpenCL kernels on GPUs alongside optimized and parallel exception checking code for execution on the CPUs.

On an AMD APU, our results show speedups of up to $21.1\times$ relative to sequential on the integrated GPU, only 0.8% slower than unsafe execution on the GPU. For a system with an Intel Xeon CPU and a discrete NVIDIA Fermi GPU, the speedups relative to sequential Java are up to $331.0\times$ on the GPU, equivalent performance to unsafe execution. These experiments show that our approach can automatically and effectively accelerate the execution of Java programs on GPUs while maintaining precise exception semantics.

References

1. APARAPI. API for Data Parallel Java. http://code.google.com/p/aparapi/
2. Artigas, P.V., et al.: Automatic loop transformations and parallelization for Java. In: Proceedings of the 14th International Conference on Supercomputing, ICS '00, pp. 1–10. ACM, New York (2000)
3. Cavé, V., et al.: Habanero-Java: the new adventures of old X10. In: PPPJ'11: Proceedings of 9th International Conference on the Principles and Practice of Programming in Java (2011)
4. Android Developers. Renderscript. http://developer.android.com/guide/topics/renderscript/index.html
5. Ebcioğlu, K., Saraswat, V., Sarkar, V.: X10: programming for hierarchical parallelism and nonuniform data access (extended abstract). In: Language Runtimes '04 Workshop: Impact of Next Generation Processor Architectures On Virtual Machines (Colocated with OOPSLA 2004), October 2004. www.aurorasoft.net/workshops/lar04/lar04home.htm
6. Hayashi, A., et al.: Accelerating Habanero-Java program with OpenCL generation. In: PPPJ'13: Proceedings of 10th International Conference on the Principles and Practice of Programming in Java (2013, under submission)

7. Dubach, C., et al.: Compiling a high-level language for GPUs: (via language support for architectures and compilers). In: Proceedings of the 33rd ACM SIGPLAN Conference on Programming Language Design and Implementation, PLDI '12, pp. 1–12. ACM, New York (2012)
8. Von Ronne, J., et al.: Safe bounds check annotations. Concurrency Computat. Pract. Exper. **21**(1), 41–57 (2009)
9. Moreira, J.E., et al.: From flop to megaflops: Java for technical computing. ACM Trans. Program. Lang. Syst. **22**(2), 265–295 (2000)
10. Shirako, J., et al.: Phasers: a unified deadlock-free construct for collective and point-to-point synchronization. In: Proceedings of the 22nd Annual International Conference on Supercomputing, ICS '08, pp. 277–288. ACM, New York (2008)
11. Shirako, J., et al.: Phaser accumulators: a new reduction construct for dynamic parallelism. In: IPDPS 2009 (2009)
12. Samadi, M., et al.: Paragon: collaborative speculative loop execution on GPU and CPU. In: Proceedings of the 5th Annual Workshop on General Purpose Processing with Graphics Processing Units, GPGPU-5, pp. 64–73. ACM, New York (2012)
13. Pratt-Szeliga, P.C., et al.: Rootbeer: seamlessly using GPUs from Java. In: 2012 IEEE 14th International Conference on High Performance Computing and Communication 2012 IEEE 9th International Conference on Embedded Software and Systems (HPCC-ICESS), June 2012, pp. 375–380 (2012)
14. Bodík, R., et al.: ABCD: eliminating array bounds checks on demand. SIGPLAN Not. **35**(5), 321–333 (2000)
15. Chandra, S., et al.: Type inference for locality analysis of distributed data structures. In: PPoPP '08: Proceedings of the 13th ACM SIGPLAN Symposium on Principles and Practice of Parallel Programming, pp. 11–22. ACM, New York (2008)
16. Würthinger, T., et al.: Array bounds check elimination for the Java HotSpot client compiler. In: Proceedings of the 5th International Symposium on Principles and Practice of Programming in Java, PPPJ '07, pp. 125–133. ACM, New York (2007)
17. Yan, Y., Grossman, M., Sarkar, V.: JCUDA: a programmer-friendly interface for accelerating Java programs with CUDA. In: Sips, H., Epema, D., Lin, H.-X. (eds.) Euro-Par 2009. LNCS, vol. 5704, pp. 887–899. Springer, Heidelberg (2009)
18. Fan, Z., et al.: GPU cluster for high performance computing. In: Proceedings of the 2004 ACM/IEEE Conference on Supercomputing, SC '04, p. 47. IEEE Computer Society, Washington, DC (2004)
19. Guo, Y., et al.: Work-first and help-first scheduling policies for async-finish task parallelism. In: IPDPS '09: International Parallel and Distributed Processing Symposium (2009)
20. JGF. The Java Grande Forum benchmark suite. http://www.epcc.ed.ac.uk/javagrande/javag.html
21. Lublinerman, R., et al.: Delegated isolation. In: OOPSLA '11: Proceeding of the 26th ACM SIGPLAN Conference on Object Oriented Programming Systems Languages and Applications (2011)
22. Manavski, S.A., Valle, G.: CUDA compatible GPU cards as efficient hardware accelerators for Smith-Waterman sequence alignment. BMC Bioinform. **9**(Suppl 2), S10 (2008)
23. Parboil. Parboil benchmarks. http://impact.crhc.illinois.edu/parboil.aspx
24. PolyBench. The polyhedral benchmark suite. http://www.cse.ohio-state.edu/pouchet/software/polybench

Author Index

Angerer, Christoph M.   39
Arteaga, Jaime   237

Bharambe, Girish   121

Chandrasekaran, Sunita   105
Chapman, Barbara   20, 105, 292
Chen, Shuo   252
Cintra, Marcelo   217, 275
Curtis, Tony   20

Ding, Wei   20

Gao, Guang R.   237
Garcia, Elkin   237
Gerstenberger, Robert   307
Goto, Takashi   155
Grewe, Dominik   87
Grossman, Max   342
Grover, Vinod   121

Hayashi, Akihiro   342
Hernandez, Oscar   20
Hillenbrand, Dominic   155
Hirano, Tomohiro   155
Hoefler, Torsten   307

Kamil, Amir   3
Kasahara, Hironori   155
Kelly, Paul H.J.   136
Kempf, Stefan   325
Kimura, Keiji   155
Konstantinidis, Athanasios   136

Lee, Jae-Woo   202
Lee, Sean   121
Li, Xiaoming   252

Marathe, Jaydeep   121
Midkiff, Samuel P.   202
Mikami, Hiroki   155

Mitropoulou, Konstantina   217
Murphy, Mike   121
Muto, Kohei   155

O'Boyle, Michael F.P.   87
Odersky, Martin   55

Pavel, Robert   237
Philippsen, Michael   325
Porpodas, Vasileios   217, 275
Prokopec, Aleksandar   55

Rajopadhye, Sanjay   169
Ramanujam, J.   136

Sadayappan, P.   136
Sarkar, Vivek   342
Schneider, Timo   307
Shirako, Jun   342

Takamura, Moriyuki   155
Tian, Xiaonan   105
Tolubaeva, Munara   292

Veldema, Ronald   325

Wang, Zheng   87

Xu, Rengan   105

Yamamoto, Hideo   155
Yan, Yonghong   105, 292
Yelick, Katherine   3
Yin, Le   187
Yuki, Tomofumi   169
Yun, Zhifeng   105

Zhao, Jisheng   342